Only recently have books and films appeared that allow the fullest possible range of expression. Among these are many which are discussed here, such as *The Story of "O"*, De Sade's *Justine*, the works of Henry Miller, and *Candy* by Terry Southern and Mason Hoffenberg.

There are still many books of literary merit, or of considerable social and psychological value, which are not available to the American public. By providing clear and consistent standards for the distinction of erotic realism from hard-core pornography, PORNOGRAPHY AND THE LAW has played a signficant part in the defense of literature and the clarification of the law.

The final section refines the definition of publications that should be legally permissible, and examines a number of books that will be in the legal and literary spotlight as the erotica of the future.

Other Titles by Eberhard and Phyllis Kronhausen

SEX HISTORIES OF AMERICAN COLLEGE MEN

WALTER THE ENGLISH CASANOVA AUTHOR
OF MY SECRET LIFE

THE SEXUALLY RESPONSIVE WOMAN

Available from Ballantine Books

PORNOGRAPHY AND THE LAW

The Psychology of Erotic Realism and Pornography

EBERHARD AND PHYLLIS KRONHAUSEN

BALLANTINE BOOKS • NEW YORK
An Intext Publisher

SBN 345-02004-9-125

Grateful acknowledgment is made to the following for
permission to quote:

The Saturday Evening Post, October, 1903
Esquire Magazine, October, 1958
The New York Times Book Review, March 22, 1959
W. B. Saunders Co., Harrisburg, Pa.
Random House, New York, N.Y.
W. W. Norton & Co., New York, N.Y.
Rinehart & Co., New York, N.Y.
Research Center, New York University, New York
The Psychiatric Quarterly, Utica, New York
Grune and Stratton, New York, N.Y.
Olympia Press, Paris, France
Grove Press, New York, N.Y.
Minnesota Law Review, Minn.

First Printing: October, 1959
Second Printing: February, 1960
Third Printing: January, 1961
Fourth Printing: November, 1961

Export Edition: October, 1964

Revised Edition First Printing: October, 1964
Second Printing: January, 1965
Third Printing: August, 1970

Printed in the United States of America

BALLANTINE BOOKS, INC.
101 Fifth Avenue, New York, N.Y. 10003

PORNOGRAPHY and the Law

(REVISED EDITION)

TABLE OF CONTENTS

FOREWORD TO THE FIRST EDITION

There are books that have the power to change men's minds, and this is one of them. The question of what is or is not "obscene" in books is of small importance in a world which is faced with the problem of physical survival, but the problem of what is legally permissible in the description of sexual acts and feelings in art and literature is of the greatest importance in a free society. It raises not only the question of the limits of freedom granted to an artist or writer, but the freedom which is permitted to any of us in our access to an enjoyment of ideas.

The recent decision of the United States Southern District Court, denying the right of the Postmaster General of the United States to ban the unexpurgated edition of *Lady Chatterley's Lover* from the mails, is in conformity with the trend of legal opinion over the last thirty years.

It is generally established that the intention of a book as a whole, rather than the language of any particular passage, is the criterion of judging obscenity. Nevertheless, it is true that *there is no legally workable definition of obscenity*. It is the contribution of PORNOGRAPHY AND THE LAW to show why the usual attempts to define obscenity have failed, and to substitute in their place clear criteria for distinguishing between "hard core" pornography and erotic realism, the honest portrayal of man's sexual nature which no sane society can afford to suppress.

Neither Phyllis nor Eberhard Kronhausen are lawyers, and they have not approached their support by a comparison of judicial decisions. Instead, as psychologists, they have concentrated on the effects of erotic realism and pornography on the reader, and the way in which the creators of such material have brought these effects about.

It is a polite fiction that nice people do not react physiologically to erotic realism or pornography. In fact they do. Both erotic realism and pornography stimulate sexual feeling in perfectly normal, healthy people. Nor is the degree of excitation in any particular passage any clue to the discrimination between what is sexually realistic and what is obviously pornographic. Readers will react to such material according to their own sexual tastes.

To wander through a library of such books applying the yardstick of "prurient" or "obscene" is like trying to judge the color of a horse by how fast he can run. What is "prurient"? And to whom? The layman usually tries to answer these questions in generalities. "Prurient" is "lewd," "lascivious" or some other synonym that defies precise definition. And the material so described is dangerous to some unspecified "young person" or "susceptible reader." It is interesting that the person applying such standards in censorship never feels that his own psychic or moral health is in jeopardy. The desire to censor, however, is not limited to crackpots and bigots. There is in most of us a strong desire to make the world conform to our own ideas, and it takes all the force of our reason and our legal institutions to defy so human an urge. Similarly, the standards of judgment so often invoked are not the result of deliberate obtuseness. The courts themselves have long wandered in the same maze, and in their efforts to apply the concept of "contemporary community standards" have often appeared to be deciding matters of law by reference to the barometer of public opinion.

But obscenity need not be determined on the basis of a straw vote. There are, as you will see, standards that apply. Between erotic realism and "hard core" por-

nography there are differences not only in purpose but
also in technique. The authors cite extensively from the
literature of both categories, analyzing structure and content, and the underlying intention of the writer. Erotic
realism, they find, aims to show the sexual side of man's
nature in terms that are psychologically based in reality,
and on a scale that allows room to explore the anti-
erotic impulses and circumstances in even the most
erotic situations. "Hard core" pornography, on the other
hand, is invariably concerned with presenting a wish-
fulfillment fantasy. The treatment deliberately omits real
life considerations to present a steadily mounting excitation through the exclusive depiction of sexual acts arranged in a series according to the strength of the social
taboo—or psychological repression—which would deter
the reader from performing those same acts himself.

Without proven research on the effects, no one wishes
to give free license for the publication of "obscene"
works. Yet the difficulties in deciding what is or is not
"obscene" have forced many of us into extreme positions. The liberal sees the threat of censorship and would
let everything pass to give freedom to what is good.
Another man would risk the suppression of an occasional book like *Lady Chatterley's Lover* to guard the
community from what he considers the danger of "obscene" literature. The authors contend that there is no
clinical evidence that anyone has ever been harmed
psychologically by reading even the most "obscene"
publications provided that the approach to such reading
is healthy. It is an interesting point, and I am inclined
to agree with them. The psychological effect of reading
is a subject that falls within their special field of knowledge. But for the moment, that is beside the point. The
great value of this book is that it shows clearly the difference between so-called obscene material and works of
erotic realism entitled to the full protection of the law.
These differences are not matters of dirty words or
erotic situations. They are differences that derive from
the entire method and purpose of the work. Erotic real-

ism and obscenity are two separate and distinguishable things, and no reader of this book can ever be confused on that point again.

The battle of censorship is not finally settled by the *Lady Chatterley* case. Indeed, the liberal position of the courts is already under attack in many states—and the fight is getting hotter. In the discussions that will be taking place all over the country, PORNOGRAPHY AND THE LAW is certain to play an important part.

I wish that every judge considering an obscenity case, and every citizen concerned with the problem of censorship in his own community, could read this book. As a lawyer I have had occasion to appear in court as defense attorney in censorship cases. I have seen the efforts of the prosecution to build up a case by counting four-letter words. I have seen the honest confusion of jurors trying to determine what is obscene with no real background of information to help them. I have seen judges struggling with the semantic nonsense that is written into the law books as definitions of obscenity. It is darkness compounded on darkness. This book brings light.

J. W. EHRLICH

San Francisco, 1959

INTRODUCTION

There are strange coincidences that seem not to be accidental. Take, for instance, the following case: there were three occasions during a single day which led my thoughts to the bawdy or ribald language of Shakespeare and his contemporaries. Only the last of these occasions was directly connected with the Bard. The first: a patient, who is a nurse, about thirty-six years old, and single, told me, during her psychoanalytic session, the following dream. *There is a race going on among the girls. They are mounting their horses. I cannot find my pants and I will miss the race.* The patient had no thought-associations that could help me in the interpretation of the dream. Before reporting the dream the patient had mentioned that a nurse, serving the same hospital, had become engaged to be married. Here was, it seemed, the only likely connection with the thought of a race among the girls. While the patient was silent, a line from Shakespeare's *Antony and Cleopatra* (Act I, Scene 5) crossed my mind. The Egyptian queen, thinking of her lover who is so far away in war, says:

"O happy horse, to bear the weight of Antony!"
There is no doubt that Shakespeare intended to make a sexual allusion.

The next association in my thoughts made the concealed content of the patient's dream clear. The thought was a memory: a few years after the first World War, I once took a walk in the surroundings of London and came to a wide place on which soldiers took riding exercises. Since I had served as a cavalry officer in the Austrian army, I was interested in the exercises, which were supervised by a sergeant. The soldiers were, it seemed, reservists, because they were not young men.

The sergeant often sharply criticized their way of riding. He shouted to one of the men: "God have mercy on your wife, if you cannot ride her better than this mare!"

The dream of the patient can easily be understood when its interpretation is attempted as a reversal of the main latent thought: the man does the riding, the woman is identified with the horse. As in that statement of the sergeant, riding is compared with sexual intercourse. The race is, of course, to be understood as the visual image of the competition of the girls who are in search of a husband. The patient cannot find a spouse ("I cannot find my pants") and is afraid she will miss the race.

The second occasion on which my thoughts led to Shakespeare's licentious language occurred a few hours later: I read in a magazine that a judge in Ohio was endeavoring to tighten the state law against sex-offenders. It was mentioned that a fine of not more than $200 would be imposed on persons convicted of using obscene or licentious language in the presence or hearing of a female. I imagined this to mean that a man would be fined because he made a sexual allusion in a public place when women are present, for instance during a performance in the theater. In the newspaper of the same day, the plan had been discussed to present Shakespeare performances in a New York park before a wide audience.

The scene from *Hamlet* (Act III, Scene 2) occurred to me in which the prince during the spectacle explains the plot of the play to Ophelia, and with it the next lines of the dialogue:

Ophelia: You are as good as a chorus, my lord.

Hamlet: I could interpret between you and your love, if I could see the puppets dallying.

Ophelia: You are keen, my lord, you are keen.

Hamlet: It would cost you a groaning to take off my edge.

Ophelia: Still better, and worse.

The inconsistency between Shakespeare's ribald lines

and the proposed state law in Ohio came vividly to mind.

The third occasion: shortly afterwards, the mailman brought me a big manila envelope. The voluminous, registered letter came from San Francisco and brought the manuscript here presented. I read the analysis of Mark Twain's essay "1601," in which the Queen, Shakespeare and some of his contemporaries are introduced at an imagined fireside conversation. Mark Twain's essay had been unknown to me and so were many of the samples of erotic poetry of the Elizabethan period as well as some of the newer and almost totally inaccessible erotica quoted in this book.

The interesting discussion of Mark Twain's "1601" is, of course, not the only startling literary discovery in this unusual book. Between its covers the reader will find revealing, amusing and instructive examples of erotic realism, reaching from Poggio and Aretino to Harris, Miller and other writers of our own time.

The second part of the book concerns itself with the definition and discussion of "hard core obscenity," and the authors demonstrate the folly of confusing high-quality works of erotic realism like D. H. Lawrence's *Lady Chatterley's Lover* or Edmund Wilson's *Memoirs of Hecate County* with pornography (as defined). *I am convinced that the reader will follow this stimulating and sagacious discussion with great interest. Here is, for the first time, a psychological analysis of "hard core obscenity" and its criteria.*

The authors, Drs. Eberhard and Phyllis Kronhausen had long been students of mine in New York. One need not agree with them on all points, but I will gladly acknowledge, as will most readers, that this book presents a most important contribution in this field. It is the more welcome, coming at a time when feelings run high about such matters as the unexpurgated American edition of Lawrence's *Lady Chatterley's Lover* and the planned publication of some of Henry Miller's works.

The valuable defense of erotically realistic writings and the courageous fight against narrow-minded, puritanical and hypocritical laws will, I am sure, be appreciated by all persons of good will who are seriously interested in the freedom of the press and of communication in general. Reading some of these pages, reporting the attempts of censorship to block the road of erotically realistic writings, one is again and again reminded of Mephisto's words:

"Man darf das nicht vor keuschen Ohren nennen
Was keusche Herzen nicht entbehren Können."

"To chaste ears you must not say aloud
The things chaste hearts can't do without."

We welcome the psychologist couple who acquired deep insights into human nature in their psychoanalytic practice as brave fighters for freedom of thought. They justly point out how necessary this freedom is for mental hygiene.

The cause for which they fight certainly has other merits also. To my way of thinking, one of the special merits lies in the enlargement of our knowledge and the illumination of unknown aspects of human nature which are revealed by this frank and fearless discussion of erotic literature.

From its earliest days, America has stood for freedom of thought and expression. We speak of America as "the home of the brave." This includes that courage of the mind which seeks truth and strives for enlightenment, regardless of consequences. The material and approach presented in this book, follow in this tradition.

Men and women arriving in the United States of America are greeted by the Statue of Liberty: its highest point is the hand that carries the torch!

THEODOR REIK

New York, June 1959

PREFACE

A Book Grows in the Courtroom

Books, like trees, may grow in very unlikely places. The material for this volume was gathered over a period of several years. But the first ideas for this book came to us during the hearings of a California State Legislative committee on pornography in the fall of 1958 which the authors attended as interested observers.

At one of the committee hearings a young police officer testified to the effect that a certain picture on the cover of a brochure was "obscene," because it showed the female genitalia. One of the authors, herself a female, resented the idea that any part of a woman's body should be considered "obscene." Indeed, if any part of the human body is indecent, lewd, or obscene, then the whole body is obscene. If the human body is obscene, then life is obscene and the whole creation in a sorry mess.

Recently, the sort of "ill-logic" presented at the California pornography hearings was invalidated in connection with a nudist case. The judge ruled that the human body was *not* obscene. The same kind of sensible juristic thinking apparently prevailed in the equally recent *Maya* case, involving the famous royal nude by the Spanish 18th century painter, Francisco Goya. We had just had the opportunity of seeing the original of this beautiful picture in the Prado Museum in Madrid, where among others, thousands of devout Catholics, including whole classes of school children, admire the painting every day. We were therefore shocked when, shortly after our return to the United States, we found that in our own country, where state and religion are clearly separated by the Constitution, reproductions of the picture had been declared unmailable, while in Spain, a Catholic country, the government had felt no hesitation in using it on an official postage stamp!

The second impetus for the writing of this book came when one of the authors was asked to testify in the same year (1958) as expert witness in a United States District Court case involving the alleged obscenity of several paperback books (*United States* v. *Aday*).

At the trial it quickly became apparent that there was confusion as to the meanings in usage, and even under the law, of certain words crucial to a clear resolution of the case. Therefore, before we go any further and in order to make this book, at least, as clear as possible from the onset, it becomes necessary for us to state what we mean by *"hard core obscenity or pornography,"* and what we shall call *erotic realism*.

Both the technique and the aim of pornography (hard core obscenity) are diametrically opposed to those of erotic realism, and even when, by the accident of context, the effects are at times identical, it is well to keep in mind that the overall intent is very different.

In pornography (hard core obscenity) *the main purpose is to stimulate erotic response* in the reader. And that is all. *In erotic realism, truthful description of the basic realities of life, as the individual experiences it, is of the essence,* even if such portrayals (whether by reason of humor, or revulsion, or any other cause) have a decidedly anti-erotic effect. But by the same token, if, while writing realistically on the subject of sex, the author succeeds in moving his reader, this too, is erotic realism, *and it is axiomatic that the reader should respond erotically to such writing,* just as the sensitive reader will respond, perhaps by actually crying, to a sad scene, or by laughing when laughter is evoked.

Armed with this information, we can now return to a report of the trial. In preparing her testimony, Dr. Phyllis Kronhausen focused first—in accordance with the argument of the defense—on the comparison of the indicted books with other literature on the market. She soon came to see that the allegedly obscene books did not substantially exceed "contemporary community standards" in candor and description of erotic matters any more than accepted books such as *Peyton Place, Ten North Frederick,* and scores of others.

In her testimony, Dr. Phyllis Kronhausen also pointed out the change in community attitudes during the past twenty or so years, reflecting a general trend toward liberalization of the sex mores. This, she told the court, was a healthy trend.

As far as the allegedly obscene books were concerned, she testified that the language, action, and attitudes reflected in them were realistic for certain sub-groups in our culture and that these books had, therefore, a legitimate right to exist.

But even the test of whether a book went substantially beyond contemporary community standards seemed to the authors no genuine standard to settle the question of obscenity. Granted that one could prove, as in the case at hand, that the supposedly obscene books were no worse than many others which circulated freely in the community, this was not necessarily an indication that any of them were or were not obscene. By the same argument one could, for instance, make a plea for a common thief in pointing out that thievery was very widespread in the community, and that a thief was therefore not going substantially beyond contemporary community standards in robbing his neighbors.

We were also appalled by the fact, which had already transpired during the preceding pornography hearings of the legislative committee, that neither the assemblymen on the committee nor the law-enforcement officers who testified, nor yet the judge, the lawyers, the prosecuting attorney or the jurors who figured in the trial, had read any appreciable amount of genuine pornography with which to compare the allegedly obscene books.

True, the assemblymen had been studying a number of pamphlets, photographs, and "stag" movies which were purely pornographic ("obscene"), but along with them they had picked up dozens of "girlie" magazines and booklets from the newsstands, throwing them all into the same hopper with the pornographic material, obviously unable to distinguish the one from the other.

To us, who in the course of our sexological research had read hundreds of pornographic texts and had seen a still greater number of "obscene" pictures, the difference between "hard core pornography," as opposed to the "girlie-or-cheesecake-type" of publication and books or pictures of erotic realism, seemed unmistakable. However, when in discussions with lawyers, colleagues, and friends we tried to explain what we meant by this difference, we generally found ourselves at a loss to clearly communicate to them what to us was so obvious.

The difficulty in communication both exasperated and intrigued us. During the weeks of the trial we re-read a number of pornographic books and tried to formulate more precisely in what respects these books differed from those which the government had held to be "obscene." At first the task of conceptualizing that which we felt to be the true difference between pornographic or, in legal terms, "obscene" books and others with erotic subject matter which are not pornographic or obscene, appeared completely unmanageable.

It was then that we decided to publish our findings by contrasting examples of erotic realism with those of hard core obscenity, thereby enabling the reader to duplicate the same experience which we have had and— if not to arrive at the same conclusions—at least to follow us on the way in which we had arrived at ours.

It is crucial to an understanding of the problem at hand that the difference between pornography and erotic realism be made clear from three aspects, namely, intent, content and effect, and it has been our experience that *this can only be done by an examination of both kinds of writing*. This understanding achieved, it then becomes possible to apply one's thinking to the much larger sociological and moral problems of "community standards," and to see how a measurable yardstick can be applied from the legal point of view.

We felt it best not to limit ourselves to only one period of time, as is done when one considers contemporary community standards, but to try to see erotic literature in a wider perspective. If one has seen erotic realism in writings of the Renaissance, the Elizabethan period, and the present, one begins to have a clearer understanding of this kind of literature.

The same holds true for hard core obscenity. An obscene book may consist of only a few pages, or several hundred pages. It may originally have been written in French, Spanish, German, Russian, or any other language. It may emphasize flagellation or any other fetish or deviation. It can even be of the "true confession" type, or it can be written as straight fiction. It may have been written yesterday, or three hundred years ago. Regardless of all these considerations, the basic psychological principles which govern its style, format, structure, content, and presentation are essentially the same.

We have, therefore, organized this book so that the reader gains first an impression of erotic realism which occurs in all types of literature, including satire, poetry, fiction and autobiography. We have deliberately selected pieces from different Western cultures and periods of time, ranging all the way from Italian Renaissance writers like Poggio and Aretino, to the Elizabethan period in England, to continental Europe, and from there to examples of modern erotic realism from Frank Harris, D. H. Lawrence, Edmund Wilson, and Henry Miller.

In Part II of the book the reader becomes acquainted with a cross-sectional view of pornographic writings (hard core obscenity), both classical and contemporary, and of European as well as American origin.

Finally, two famous mistaken "borderline" cases— Edmund Wilson's *Memoirs of Hecate County,* and D. H. Lawrence's *Lady Chatterley's Lover*—are examined in the light of the previous discussion. At that point it will be apparent that neither of these two books, nor a great number of other erotically realistic writings, could ever have been confused with "hard core obscenity" or genuine pornography if definite criteria of pornography had been available.

The criticism against our position will be made that

the difficulty of the courts has been precisely with the so-called "borderline" cases and not with "hard core obscenity" on which everybody could easily enough agree. Our answer to this objection is:

The Supreme Court of the United States has made it clear that the intention of the law is to leave the door of censorship only "the slightest bit ajar" so as to protect the fundamental freedoms of speech and press as guaranteed by the United States Constitution (particularly amendments one and fourteen, which are here most applicable). Only those books which have clearly and unmistakably no other "redeeming social value," that is, those writings which are only "dirt for dirt's sake" (as one popular definition puts it), in other words, "hard core obscenity" or genuine pornography alone, and no other writings, are to be considered outside of the protective arm of the first and fourteenth amendments.

The first objective was therefore to define more clearly what "hard core obscenity" or pornography actually consists of in order to make it possible for the courts to apply the standards upheld by the United States Supreme Court. One need not agree with that position, but as the first step in the clarification of that thorny question we thought it to be imperative to establish testable criteria of pornography before entering into any meaningful discussion of the pros and cons of erotic literature in general and of "hard core obscenity" in particular.

The last chapter of this book deals with what we know concerning the possible effects of erotic reading matter on adults as well as on adolescents and younger children. The lack of dependable research data in this area of human behavior is contrasted with the bitterness of uninformed partisan prejudice which insists on putting erotic ("salacious") reading matter and similar material into a causal relationship with juvenile delinquency and crime.

It behooves the authors to inform the reader of the fact that their clinical experience and research have led them to certain impressions concerning the role of erotica in the lives of individuals and in civilized society. Their feeling is that both erotic realism and pornography, each in their own way, fulfill certain functions and answer basic needs in the human psyche which have been recognized by many societies and periods; for instance, in ancient Greece and Rome, in the Near East, as well as in China, Japan, and India, where erotic art and literature have always been integral parts of the total culture.

In regard to *erotic realism,* the authors hope to demonstrate by the material presented that it reflects a basically healthy and therapeutic attitude toward life. The denial of man's basic corporeality can only lead to distortions of the body image, which have been shown to be responsible for the mental states of depersonalization and irreality which mark the more severe emotional disturbances. On the other hand, familiarity with one's body and a relaxed attitude with regard to its natural functions are prerequisites of mental hygiene. Literature which emphasizes these qualities is therefore especially welcome at a time when automation, push-button housekeeping, mass production, and progressive eradication of individual differences make everybody's search for identity a matter of spiritual survival.

The authors favor a realistic education for life which does not stop short of acknowledging and providing for the individual's physical and emotional needs. This they consider to be a more reliable prophylactic against delinquency, crime, and mental illness than denial, suppression, and authoritarian rule.

The problem of the psychological effect of pornographic writings (hard core obscenity) is, on the other hand, a matter which demands further exploration and thorough research of its own. Indeed, at least one of our objectives in writing this book is to point to the urgent necessity for enlightened and scientific information in this area. We will discuss in the concluding chapter of this book the pattern of effect that is presently indicated by any reliable research material that is available on this important phase of human motivation, and will outline some of the possible research approaches which would help to clarify this controversial subject.

In the meantime, it is our aim to provide a more objective basis for the evaluation of erotic literature and to stake out the whole scope of this large problem. At the present time we shall be content to introduce some of the psychological principles which will help to bring at least a measure of order and system into the current confusion concerning the nature and effects of erotic literature in general.

PART I

THE PSYCHOLOGY OF EROTIC REALISM

The reaction against hypocrisy in art and literature which we came to call *erotic realism* is not a fad, nor a sign of our time, nor yet a vanguard idea of Bohemians, "beatniks," and "hipsters." Erotic realism is nothing modern or futuristic. It has a long tradition in the arts and literature. Wherever and whenever society saddled the poet and artist with artificiality, sham, and pretense, there were those disciples of the Muse who refused to go along with the trend. If they were painters and sculptors, they did the human figure without fig leaves, showing pubic hair and genitals with the same taken-for-grantedness as they painted faces with mouths, noses, and head hair. If they were writers and poets, they described, treated, and discussed the sex lives of men and women with the same naturalness with which they spoke of their other, non-sexual affairs.

Erotic realism is not an isolated phenomenon. It represents a realistic orientation in art and literature and is part of a greater whole, just as one cannot be a Zen Buddhist without being a Buddhist, or a Lutheran without embracing Christianity.

Getting down to cases, Samuel Pepys was a realist in politics and finance, as well as in whoring. Casanova was accurate to the point of boring compulsiveness in keeping score about his endless card games. He was equally meticulous about his sex life, which, besides cards, was his other main obsession.

Henry Miller, whom we have called the "apostle of the gory detail," is as realistic about bedbugs and lice in cheap Paris hotel rooms as he is about the underwear of the girls with whom he slept.

Brantôme, Poggio, Aretino, and the other realistic writers mentioned, covered tedious pages with the genealogies of their heroes, their dress, their jewelry, their castles, and so forth. Less tedious examples of their attention to realistic detail are, for example, Poggio's story about the naïve bride who thought her husband's member inadequate because even the dumb donkey in the field had more to show for himself. Here, detail is used to achieve not only the realistic illusion, but also the desired humorous effect.

Frequently, erotic realism in art and literature is part of a basic rebellion against the social suppression of elemental drives and needs common to all mankind. This was true even in times like the Renaissance or the Elizabethan period, when man's corporeality was acknowledged to a much larger extent than at other times —including our own epoch. The reason for this is that there has never been any period in the Western world of the past two thousand years or so when there has been a complete absence of sexual suppression.

In its attempt to suppress the sexual needs of the individual, society has always exercised a certain amount of literary and artistic censorship. In defiance of this limitation, erotic realism insists on giving the sexual interests—and other basic human needs—their proportionate share in the particular medium of the artist. If this amounts to a high percentage of the total artist's output (in some cases), one need not be too surprised. The erotic element plays a predominant role, if not in the lives of all people, then at least in the total experience of many, and perhaps the majority, of individuals.

In brief, erotic realism is a historical movement in art and literature, representing in part the artist's or writer's rebellion against social pressures to deny and falsify life by forcing him to exclude, minimize, and distort the sexual element in his artistic creation. Erotic realism is the counterforce against this social pressure and expresses the artist's and writer's healthy assertion to include, and in some instances to emphasize, the erotic aspects of life and to portray and describe them to the extent and in as much detail as he sees fit.

If one were to include the pre-Christian era of Western civilization and the oriental cultures in a psychological definition of erotic realism, the element of rebellion or reaction against outward pressures would, of course, be considerably reduced. The Venus of Milo, the intercourse scenes on the walls of Pompeian villas, the writings of Greek and Roman poets, the beautiful, extremely realistic erotic paintings on the walls of the Ajanta cave-temple in India, or classic Hindu erotica like the Ananga Ranga and the better-known Kamasutra, can hardly have been inspired by the same sense of rebellion which undoubtedly motivated the later Western artists and poets. For the pagan and oriental artist there was little erotic censorship in the culture to rebel against. Their erotic realism represents, therefore, mainly an expression of their acceptance of life in its totality, of which the sexual drive is an important part, rather than the retort of the repressed (which accounts for some of the overemphasis on the erotic) in the realistic artists of our time.

Yet, even in some of the pre-Christian Western literature, as in the erotic realism of Ovid, one can find definite traces of a reaction against anti-erotic cultural trends. In fact, Ovid paid dearly for his frankness in the discussion of the sexual part of life by being exiled from his beloved Rome. But by and large there was so much less social suppression of the erotic in Western antiquity and in the Orient (until the present time) that the erotic realism which these civilizations produced must be regarded as basically the expression of a more positive and accepting attitude toward the body, its functions and appetites, than anything later Western society has been able to tolerate.

Erotic realism (and, as we shall see, pornography as well, to a certain extent) represents a breakthrough of this essentially pagan attitude toward life. Erotic realism, however, limits itself strictly to the description of the realistic aspects of life. It does not aim at exciting sexual passion, nor does it act as a psychological aphrodisiac, except by the coincidence of context. Its only goal is to depict life as it is, including man's basic biological needs.

In the examples from literature which follow, we shall find erotic realism in satirical, humorous, anecdotal, autobiographical, and fictional writing. The common denominator of erotic realism in all these forms will be found to be the author's desire to communicate about the realities of life and their specific meaning to him as he, subjectively, experienced them. His main intent is always to penetrate reality and to express its meaning as it appears to him. He may have other, subsidiary motives, such as to entertain, educate, be humorous, convey certain political, philosophical, or religious ideas. But the dominant theme of erotic realism will be seen to be life itself in all its manifestations, with the focus on that which in our culture is most repressed, denied, and emasculated; namely, the sexual life in the wider meaning, including its simplest and most complicated manifestations.

EROTIC REALISM IN HISTORICAL PERSPECTIVE

Freud once said that a person who has no regard for history is a "Nichtsnutz" (good-for-nothing). He apparently meant that an individual who lives only in the present, without awareness and relation to the past, leads mentally an isolated, atomized existence, much like the lower mammalian species, though without the benefit of animal instinct which, for the latter, takes the place of the historical dimension.

In psychoanalysis, the individual attempts, with the help of the therapist, to relate the experience of the present moment to events in the personal history. Psychoanalysis rejects the idea that the present can be sufficiently understood and appreciated by considering only that which takes place at a given moment. It wants to see the present in the light of the past, and with reference to the future, thus giving the moment a three-dimensional perspective in time.

We have tried to accomplish the same with regard to erotic literature: for example, instead of being satisfied with interpreting Mark Twain's "1601" as an isolated example of erotic realism, we wish to relate it to the past by reference to its classical forerunners. By seeing the story in such a larger context, we believe that we are adding to its present meaning and projecting its significance beyond the present into the future.

Recently, the authors were present at a "freewheeling" poetry session among the "beat generation" of San Francisco's North Beach section. During the evening, one of the poets improvised some facetious, erotic poetry which we thought was uproariously funny. The whole scene and the impromptu poetry reminded us of some of the writings of Poggio, Aretino, Rabelais and Mark Twain. These associations rendered the modern poet's satirical improvisations doubly meaningful to us. We hope that our readers will have a similar experience in connection with Mark Twain's "1601" by discussing it in the framework of its precursors in erotic realism in general, and in the context of erotic wit and humor in particular. We are therefore presenting both prose and poetry from other centuries which, we think, will set off Mark Twain's relatively modern and yet historically oriented erotic satire, "1601." We believe this technique will also open up different avenues of approach to other types of literature from various periods, such as the writings of Brantôme and the erotically realistic work of such dissimilar authors as Casanova, Frank Harris, and Henry Miller.

The poetry and art of a period are its most faithful mirrors. Both are close to the unconscious and therefore reflect a less censored and more immediate, or more naïve, picture of life than one is apt to receive from any other source.

Pictures and poems are spontaneous creations of the deeper unconscious, or subconscious, aspects of the mind. They are not subject to the same degree of conscious premeditation and deliberate attempt at a certain effect as other historical documents of an era, such as political speeches, conference records, accounts of battle, or exchanges of property, all of which are tendentious, whether intentionally so or merely because of the greater interference of considerations of conscience, conviction, and purpose.

Pictures and poems are in fact at once an expression of a general emotional climate and (necessarily) an expression of the emotions of the individual artist, whether in rebellion against the prevailing social mores of his time or in fulfillment of them. The *popular* Elizabethan poems and ballads which follow are a clear expression of the social climate of the times. The poems have been chosen more for their readability than for their subject matter, because, as to the latter, the greater part of Elizabethan poetry deals with identical themes.

The reader will, therefore, expect examples of cuckoldry, of women's easy virtue, of hypocrisy, of the pleasures of sexual intercourse, of the importance and the uselessness of virginity; and he will find that the poems meet these expectations. And the artistically sensitive person will find Elizabethan poetry also rich in erotic symbolism, which lifts these verses out of their temporal and geographic setting and gives them the same timeless, universal, and we maintain, therapeutic, appeal which "1601" exemplifies to such an outstanding degree.

We will then present our discussion of Mark Twain's work in the context of this selection of poetry which corroborates the realism of his *A Fireside Conversation* by the most unbiased documents of the Elizabethan period.

PROFFERED LOVE REJECTED

By Sir John Suckling. *Poems,* 1638

It is not four years ago,
   I offered forty crowns
To lie with her a night or so:
   She answer'd me in frowns.

Not two years since, she meeting me
   Did whisper in my ear,
That she would at my service be,
   If I contented were.

I told her I was cold as snow,
   And had no great desire;
But should be well content to go
   To twenty, but no higher.

Some three months since or thereabout,
   She that so coy had been,
Bethought herself and found me out,
   And was content to sin.

I smiled at that, and told her I
   Did think it something late,
And that I'd not repentance buy
   At above half the rate.

This present morning early she
   Forsooth came to my bed,
And gratis there she offered me
   Her high-prized maidenhead.

I told her that I thought it then
　　Far dearer than I did,
When I at first the forty crowns
　　For one night's lodging bid.

I DREAMED MY LOVE

From the Percy Folio Manuscript, 1620-50

I dreamed my love lay in her bed:
　　It was my Chance to take her:
Her legs and arms abroad were spread;
　　She slept; I durst not wake her.
O pity it were, that one so fair
　　Should Crown her love with willow;
The tresses of her golden hair
　　Did kiss he[r] lovely pillow.

Methought her belly was a hill
　　Much like a mount of pleasure,
Under whose height there grows a well:
　　The depth no man can measure.
About the plea[s]ant mountain's top
　　There grows a lovely thicket,
Wherein two beagles trampled,
　　And raised a lively pricket.

They hunted there with pleasant noise
　　About the pleasant mountain,
Till he by heat was forced to fly,
　　And skip into the fountain.
The beagles followed to the brink,
　　And there at him they barked;
He plunged about, but would not shrink;
　　His Coming forth they waited.

Then forth he Came as one half lame,
　　Were weary, faint, and tired;
And laid him down betwixt her legs,
　　As help he had required.

The beagles being refresht again,
  My Love from sleep bereaved;
She dreamed she had me in her arms,
  And she was not deceived.

ROOM FOR A JOVIAL TINKER: OLD BRASS TO MEND

Anonymous. *Roxburghe Ballads,* ca. 1616

It was a lady of the North she loved a Gentleman,
And knew not well what course to take, to use him now
            and then.
Wherefore she writ a Letter, and sealed it with her hand,
And bid him be a Tinker, to mend both pot and pan,
    With a hey ho, hey, derry derry down; with hey trey,
            down down, derry.

And when the merry Gentleman the Letter he did read,
He got a budget on his back, and Apron with all speed,
His pretty shears and pincers, so well they did agree,
With a long pike staff upon his back, came tripping o'er
            the Lee.
    With a hey ho, hey, derry derry down; with hey trey,
            down down, derry.

When he came to the Lady's house, he knocked at the
            gate,
Then answered this Lady gay, "Who knocketh there
            so late?"
" 'Tis I, Madam," the Tinker said, "I work for gold
            and fee:
If you have any broken pots or pans, come bring them
            all to me."
    With a hey ho, hey, derry derry down; with hey trey,
            down down, derry.

"I am the bravest Tinker that lives beneath the Sun,
If you have any work to do, you shall have it well done;

I have brass within my budget, and punching under
my Apron,
I'm come unto your Ladyship, and mean to mend your
Coldron."
With a hey ho, hey, derry derry down; with hey trey,
down down, derry.

"I prithee," said the Lady gay, "bring now thy budget in,
I have store of work for thee to do, if thou wilt once
begin."
Now when the Tinker came in, that did the budget bear,
"God bless," quoth he, "your Ladyship! God save you,
Madam fair."
With a hey ho, hey, derry derry down; with hey trey,
down down, derry.

But when the Lady knew his face, she then began to
wink,
"Haste, lusty Butler!" then quoth she, "to fetch the man
some drink.
Give him such meat as we do eat, and drink as we
do use,
It is not for a Tinker's Trade good liquor to refuse."
With a hey ho, hey, derry derry down; with hey trey,
down down, derry.

But when that he had eat and drunk, the truth of all
is so,
The Lady took him by the sleeve, her work to him
to show,
"Let up thy Tools, Tinker," quoth she, "and see there
be none lost,
And mend my Kettle handsomely, what ere it doth
me cost."
With a hey ho, hey, derry derry down; with hey trey,
down down, derry.

"Your work, Madam, shall be well done, if you will pay
me for't'
For every nail that I do drive, you shall give me a mark.

If I do not drive the nail to th' head, I'll have nothing
for my pain,
And what I do receive of you shall be return'd again."
With a hey ho, hey, derry derry down; with hey trey,
down down, derry.

At last being come into the Room, where he the work
should do,
The Lady lay down on the bed, so did the Tinker too:
Although the Tinker knocked amain, the Lady was not
offended,
But before that she rose from the bed, her Coldron was
well mended,
With a hey ho, hey, derry derry down; with hey trey,
down down, derry.

But when his work was at an end, which he did in the
dark,
She put her hand into her purse and gave him twenty
mark,
"Here's money for thy work," said she, "and I thank
thee for thy pain,
And when my Coldron mending lacks I'll send for thee
again."
With a hey ho, hey, derry derry down; with hey trey,
down down, derry.

The Tinker he was well content for that which he had
done,
So took his budget on his back, and quickly he was gone.
Then the Lady to her husband went, "O my dear Lord,"
quoth she,
"I have set the bravest Tinker at work that ever you did
see."
With a hey ho, hey, derry derry down; with hey trey,
down down, derry.

"No fault at all this Tinker hath, but he takes dear for
his work,

That little time that he wrought here it cost me twenty
mark."
"If you had been so wise," quoth he, "for to have held
your own,
Before you set him to his work the price you might
have known."
With a hey ho, hey, derry derry down; with hey trey,
down down, derry.

"Pray hold your peace, my Lord," quoth she, "and
think it not too dear.
If you could do't so well 'twould save you forty pound a
year."
With that the Lord most lovingly, to make all things
amends,
He kindly kist his Lady gay, and so they both were
friends.
With a hey ho, hey, derry derry down; with hey trey,
down down, derry.

You merry Tinkers, every one, that hear this new-made
Sonnet,
When as you do a lady's work be sure you think upon it;
Drive home your nails to the very head, and do your
work profoundly,
And then no doubt your Mistresses will pay you for it
soundly.
With a hey ho, hey, derry derry down; with hey trey,
down down, derry.

A MAIDEN'S DENIAL

From Sportive Wit; The Muses' Merriment, 1656

Nay, pish; nay, phew! nay, faith and will you? fie!
A gentleman and use me thus! I'll cry.
Nay, God's body, what means this? Nay, fie for shame,
Nay, faith, away! Nay, fie, you are to blame.
Hark! somebody comes! hands off, I pray!
I'll pinch, I'll scratch, I'll spurn, I'll run away.

Nay, faith, you strive in vain, you shall not speed
You mar my ruff, you hurt my back, I bleed.
Look how the door stands ope, somebody sees!
Your buttons scratch, in faith you hurt my knees.
What will men say? Lord, what a coil is here!
You make me sweat; i' faith, here's goodly gear.
Nay, faith, let me entreat you, if you list,
You mar my clothes, you tear my smock, but, had I wist
So much before, I would have shut you out.
Is it a proper thing you go about?
I did not think you would have used me this,
But now I see I took my aim amiss.
A little thing would make me not be friends:
You've used me well! I hope you'll make amends.
Hold still, I'll wipe your face, you sweat amain:
You have got a goodly thing with all your pain.
Alas! How hot am I! what will you drink?
If you go sweating down what will men think?
Remember, sir, how you have used me now;
Doubtless ere long I will be meet with you.
If any man but you had used me so,
Would I have put it up? in faith, sir, no!
Nay, go not yet; stay here and sup with me,
And then at cards we better shall agree.

TOTTINGHAM FROLIC

Anonymous. From *Choyce Drollery*

As I came from Tottingham
      Upon a market-day,
There I met with a bonny Lass
      Cloathed all in Grey,
Her Journey was to London,
      With Butter-milk and Whey.
To come Down a down,
To come Down, down a down a.

Sweet-heart, quoth he,
      You're well over took,

With that she cast her Head aside,
    And lent him a Look;
Then presently these two
    Both Hands together shook:
To come, *etc.*

And as they rode together,
    Along side by side,
The Maiden it so chanced,
    Her Garter was unty'd;
For fear that she should lose it,
    Look here, Sweet-heart, he cry'd,
Your Garter is down a down, *etc.*

Good Sir, quoth she,
    I pray you take the Pain,
To do so much for me,
    As to take it up again,
With a good will, quoth he,
    When I come to yonder Plain,
I will take you down, *etc.*

And when they came unto the place,
    Upon the Grass so green,
The Maid she held her Legs so wide,
    The young man slipt between,
Such tying of a Garter,
    You have but seldom seen.
To come down, *etc.*

Then she rose up again.
    And thanked him for his pain:
He took her by the middle small,
    And Kiss'd her once again:
Her journey to London,
    And he from Highgate came,
To come down, *etc.*

Thus Tibb of Tottingham,
    She lost her Maiden-Head,

But yet it is no matter,
    It stood her in small stead,
For it did often trouble her,
    As she lay in her Bed.
To come down, *etc.*

But when all her Butter-milk
    And her Whey was sold,
The loss of her Maiden-head,
    It waxed very cold:
But that which will away, quoth she,
    Is very hard to hold,
To come, *etc.*

You Maids, you Wives, and Widows,
    That now do hear my Song,
If any young man proffer Kindness,
    Pray take it short, or long;
For there is no such Comfort
    As lying with a Man.
To come Down a down,
To come Down, down a down, a.

NARCISSUS, COME KISS US!

Rawlinson Ms. Poet; ca. 1610-50;
Also *Ane Pleasant Garden*

As I was a walking, I cannot tell where,
Nor whither, in verse or in prose;
Nor know I the meaning, altho' they all sate,
Even, as it were, under my nose.
But ever and ever the ladies all cried,
"Narcissus, come kiss us, and love us beside."

There came in a lad from I cannot tell where,
With I cannot tell what in his hand;
It was a fine thing, tho' it had little sense,
But yet it would lustily stand.

Thus ever and ever the ladies all cried,
"Narcissus, come kiss us, and love us beside."

Some shaked it, some stroked it, some kiss'd it, 'tis said,
For it looked so lovely indeed,
Then ever and ever the ladies all cried,
"Narcissus, come kiss us, and love us beside."

At length he did put his pretty fine toy
(I cannot tell where 'twas) below,
Into one of these ladies, I cannot tell why,
Nor wherefore, that he should do so.
Thus ever and ever the ladies all cried,
"Narcissus, come kiss us, and love us beside."

But when these fair ladies had sported all night,
And rifled Dame Nature's scant store;
And pleasured themselves with Venus' delight,
Till the youth could hardly do more.
Then ever and ever the ladies all cried,
"Narcissus, come kiss us, and love us beside."

The lad being tired, began to retreat,
And hang down his head like a flower;
The ladies the more did desire a new heat,
But alas! it was out of his power.
But ever and ever the ladies all cried,
"Narcissus, come kiss us, and love us beside."

When full forty weeks were expired,
A pitiful story to tell,
These ladies did get what they little desired,
For their bellies began for to swell.
Still ever and ever the ladies all cried,
"Narcissus, come kiss us, and love us beside."

Lucina in pity then sent them her aid,
To cease them of all their sorrow;
But when these fair ladies were once brought to Bed,

They still had the same mind tomorrow.
And dandling their babies they rantingly-cried,
"Narcissus, shan't miss us, and be by our side!"

EROTIC WIT AND HUMOR

Erotic wit and humor represent a special, and in some respects a paradoxical, type of erotic realism. The paradox lies in the fact that humor has, by necessity, a dimension of fantasy which is absent, or less pronounced, in other types of erotically realistic literature. It is, for instance, most noticeable in the facetious writings of men like Poggio, Aretino, or Rabelais, of which we give examples later on; or as the reader may have encountered it in the better-known works of Boccaccio. Traces of it are present, perhaps, in all types of writing, including autobiographies, though these are the most realistic form of literature and the least given to flights of fancy.

But erotic wit and humor are basically reality-oriented, or refer to reality situations in which the humorous aspects have been selected and exaggerated to achieve a specifically comic or satiric effect, much as a political cartoon points the paradox in a realistic situation. We hope to demonstrate this by discussing and quoting excerpts from at least one example of erotic wit and humor from the pen of Mark Twain. One of these, his famous—and yet generally unknown—short essay, "1601," represents erotic satire. As such, it is tendentious, has a hidden political and philosophical message, seeks to convey certain ideas unrelated to love and sex, and implies a sweeping social criticism. This in itself relates the piece to reality—to things as they are and to things as they, perhaps, ought to be.

Furthermore, "1601" was written in a style which makes it possible to regard it as a bit of Elizabethan England in the time of the Tudors, humorously come to life in the 19th century. This historical perspective also relates the story to reality. It makes the events it describes and the language it uses credible, at least as far as the past is concerned, even though it cannot lay claim to such reality-relatedness with regard to the present. Another example from Mark Twain is his speech delivered at the Stomach Club in Paris, *Some Thoughts on the Science of Onanism.*

One does occasionally find islands of erotic wit and humor in otherwise pornographic books, as, for instance, in *Fay and Her Boy Friend,* or as in some of the more or less witty puns of *The Oxford Professor*; a technique which already is apparent in the full title of the latter and recurs here and there throughout the text. Such examples of erotic humor in obscene books are extremely rare, and, if they do occur at all, are either rather trite or they are the most realistic portions of the whole book.

On the other hand, erotic wit and humor are frequent and integral elements in erotic realism. There are quite a few hilariously funny episodes in Casanova's *Mémoires,* in the autobiography of Frank Harris, and in Henry Miller's books. The humorous element is still more pronounced in other works of erotic realism, as even the titles of Aretino's *Caprices,* or Poggio's *Facetiae,* indicate. The same is true for Brantôme's *Lives of Fair and Gallant Ladies,* where we find a marked humorous undertone; not to mention the writings of Rabelais, Montaigne, and many others.

Again, the humorous element is not only present, but dominant in most of the erotic poetry of the Elizabethan period of which we have given representative examples. It is also obvious in the broadly erotic and scatologic art of that period; nor is humor absent in the writings and utterances of such seriously dedicated men as Martin Luther.

In view of this, one is tempted to say that humor is not only generally absent in obscene writings, and that erotic wit and humor is a special art form of erotic realism, but that it is a characteristic element of erotic realism, both in literature and in the fine arts (for example, Rembrandt's drawings of a urinating cow, the rape of a peasant girl by a monk [*The Monk in the Corn-Field*], an intercourse scene [*The French Bed*]; Jan Steen's painting *Odor*, and many others).

Finally, a word about the reason why we have chosen Mark Twain's "1601" as our main specimen of erotic wit and humor instead of any of the other possible choices from the vast treasure house of satirical erotic writings.

In the first place, the piece is the purest example of erotic satire and plain, undiluted erotic wit. Secondly, Mark Twain ranks among the greatest humorists of all times. Examples of erotic wit and humor from his pen are therefore doubly valuable, both from a literary point of view and from that of the psychologist who wishes to identify and describe the dynamics of erotic humor which Mark Twain so masterfully employed.

And finally, it seems to us highly regrettable that any part of the works of this American writer should be denied to readers in his own country except through the dubious and implicitly degrading channels of "under-the-counter" sales. We shall therefore attempt to give the background of the writing of "1601" together with excerpts and our analysis of its contents, followed by a short discussion of *Some Thoughts on the Science of Onanism*.

THE UNKNOWN MARK TWAIN

"1601" is an imaginary conversation as it might have taken place in the time, and at the fireside of, Queen Elizabeth I. Its secret author, Samuel Langhorne Clemens (Mark Twain), wrote it between finishing *Tom Sawyer* and starting *The Adventures of Huckleberry Finn*. That summer Mark Twain had spent more time in reading and re-reading one of his favorite books, *The Diary of Samuel Pepys*. Its frank, down-to-earth language, which did not leave out the erotic or the excrementitious, has, because of the writer's naïveté, a certain humorous effect which must have been very much to Mark Twain's liking. Anyway, it is certain that, delighted with Samuel Pepy's *Diary* and the language and customs of the Elizabethan period which it reflects, the idea struck him to write a story in the same genre and of the same period.

Mark Twain addressed his essay to the Rev. Jos. Twichell, "that robust divine . . . who had no special scruples concerning Shakespearian parlance and customs," and who had not only solemnized Mark Twain's wedding, but had also presided at the baptisms of all his children.

However, the first person ever to see the manuscript, even before it was mailed to Twichell, was David Gray. He was spending a Sunday with Mark Twain in Elmira, and after reading "1601" he exclaimed, "Print it and put your name on it, Mark. You have never done a greater piece of work than that."

John Hay, who later became Secretary of State, read the essay in 1880 and pronounced it "a classic—a most exquisite bit of old English morality." A. B. Paine, Mark Twain's friend, biographer, and literary executor, claims that Hay, in his enthusiasm, committed the indiscretion of surreptitiously having some copies made of it. A notice which appeared in *The Saturday Evening Post* of October 1903 seems to corroborate Mr. Paine's assertion. The article said:

"An early instance of that fine diplomacy which has made the name of John Hay famous throughout the world has just come to light in Cleveland.

"He was on terms of intimate friendship with the late Alexander Gunn—and had sent him for perusal the manuscript of a little sketch by Mark Twain, unknown to collectors—A CONVERSATION AS IT WAS AT THE SOCIAL FIRESIDE IN THE TIME OF THE TUDORS. This Mr. Hay described as *a serious effort to bring back our literature and philosophy to the chaste and Elizabethan standard.*

"*Mr. Gunn was pleased with the effort and wrote to*

*Hay, proposing to print a few copies for private circu-
lation, to which he replied:*

"MY DEAR GUNN:—I have your letter, and the proposition which you make to pull a few proofs of the master-
piece is highly attractive, and, of course, highly immoral.
I cannot properly consent to it, and I am afraid the
great man would think I was taking an unfair advantage
of his confidence. Please send back the document as
soon as you can, and if, in spite of my prohibition, you
take these proofs, save me one.

*"It is needless to say that with this hint the proofs
were pulled—one for Hay and one for Gunn."*

Two years later (1882) a special font of antique type
was cast and the first hard-cover edition of "1601" was
printed in 100 copies on handmade linen paper at the
most unlikely-likely place of all, the United States Mili-
tary Academy at West Point.

At that time, still another friend of Mark Twain's,
Lt. C. E. S. Wood, was in charge of the Academy's
printing press, and thought he could put it to no better
possible use than to run through a deluxe edition of
"1601."

Most of the copies from this printing found places in
the libraries of high political and ecclesiastical dignitaries, from Berlin to Rome to Tokyo. ("1601" has
always been better known and therefore better appreciated abroad than in its native land.)

Still, "1601" has seen 44 editions here in the United
States and many more in foreign languages overseas,
ample proof of its constant popularity wherever it becomes available.

The best and one of the most recent editions of *Ye
Fireside Conversation* was prepared by The Mark Twain
Society in Chicago in 1939. The title page reads, "Embellished with an illuminating introduction, facetious
footnotes and a bibliography by Franklin J. Meine."
The work was illustrated by A. H. Winkler. However,
that edition also was limited, and, we are told, the few

copies occasionally available are already much in demand by collectors and literary students.

In our analysis of Mark Twain's "1601," we shall not limit ourselves merely to the techniques which the author used to produce the humorous effects of the story, but we shall also consider its psychological symbolism and "latent" content. In that respect, we shall treat it *as if* it were a non-literary product of the imagination, such as a dream, or a fantasy, which a talented patient might bring into the analytic hour. In so doing we cannot detract from the high artistic merits of the story, but only add to our understanding through the advantage of seeing it from unexpected angles which would have escaped us otherwise.

The setting is the fireside of Queen Elizabeth I, and the story is related by Her Majesty's cup-bearer, who is, perforce, present to serve the guests gathered about the Queen. These include, ". . . Lord Bacon, his worship Sir Walter Raleigh, Mr. Ben Jonson, and ye child Francis Beaumonte. . . . Also came with these ye famous Shaxpur. . . . Ye Duchess of Bilgewater, twenty-two yeres of age; ye Countesse of Granby, twenty-six; her doter, ye Lady Helen, fifteen . . . as also these two maides of honor, to wit, ye Lady Margery Boothy, sixty-five, and ye Lady Alice Dilberry, turned seventy, she being two yeres ye queens graces elder."

The cup-bearer reports that "in ye heat of ye talk it befel yt one did breake wind," whereupon the Queen, far from being embarrassed, starts with lively curiosity an enquiry as to the authorship of the flatulence, remarking in obvious admiration, "Verily in mine eight and sixty yeres have I not heard the fellow to this fart."

Each of the ladies in turn modestly disavows any responsibility in the matter, the elderly Lady Margery exclaiming, ". . . an' I had contained this wonder, foresoothe, [I would not have] launched it sudden in its matchless might, taking mine own life with violence. . . ."

The Queen then turns her attention to the male dignitaries present. Mark Twain skillfully couches their replies according to the personage involved: thus, Lord Bacon, "Not from my leane entrails hath this prodigy burst forth. . . . Naught doth so befit ye grete as grete performance; and haply shall ye finde yt 'tis not from mediocrity this miracle hath issued."

Here the cup-bearer makes an acid aside, "(Tho' ye subject be but a fart, yet will this tedious sink of learning pondrously phillosophize . . .)." Next "ye worshipful Master Shaxpur" begins his speech of disavowal with the bombastic line, "In the great hand of God I stand and so proclaim mine innocence. Though ye sinless hosts of heaven had foretold ye coming of this most desolating breath, proclaiming it a work of uninspired man, its quaking thunders . . . his own achievement in due course of nature, yet had I not believed it; but had said the pit itself hath furnished [it], and heaven's artillery hath shook the globe in admiration of it."

In this declamatory protest, Mark Twain achieves a double-barbed comment, first on Shakespeare himself and his uncritical admirers, and second on the insincerity of the professedly devout.

When Sir Walter Raleigh finally admits to having produced the noise under discussion, he does so again by way of a lengthy apology, not for the faux pas itself, but for having "fathered" such a "weakling . . . in so august a presence. It was nothing—less than nothing, madam—," and he tries to make amends with something more "worthy." In an aside from the cup-bearer we then learn that Raleigh "(. . . delivered he himself of such a godless and rock-shivering blast that all were fain to stop their ears. . . . By God, an I were ye Queene, I would e'en tip this swaggering braggart out o' the court, and let him air his grandeurs and break his intolerable wind before ye deaf and such as suffocation pleaseth.)"

Throughout, the cup-bearer plays the down-to-earth counterpoint to the ridiculous conversation of these elevated ladies and gentlemen. One has to read the story very carefully to get the full benefit of Mark Twain's sarcasm, which remains focused throughout on the hollowness of social conventions, the folly of attributing superhuman qualities to personages of high rank, the pretense which is unable to hide the vulgarities of human nature, and the mockery implicit in the supposed delicacy of the fair sex against whom Mark Twain uses his wit with especially "sharp-toothed unkindness."

For instance, at this point in the chronicle, the conversation takes a turn from the anal-erotic to genital sexuality, when Shakespeare tells of a book by Montaigne in which the author mentions a custom of the widows of Périgord (France) who supposedly wear a wilted phallus-emblem in their headdress. The Queen laughs heartily at this, remarking that there is nothing extraordinary in the custom, as English widows also wear phalli, though not on the hat, but between their legs, "and not wilted neither!"

The incident is of special interest psychologically, because Mark Twain's choice of topic cannot have been totally accidental. There were certainly other equally fascinating possibilities for erotically toned discourse, outside of customs relating to widowhood.

It is perfectly correct that widows have always been one of the focal points of sexual humor and that the "merry widow" occupies a central place in literature. Still, we cannot help but feel that Mark Twain had a more than casual interest in widows and their problems, for one recalls that his own mother became a widow when he was a pre-adolescent boy, and that his mother's widowhood influenced his life profoundly.

We know from clinical experience that a young boy whose father is deceased will guard his mother with especially jealous eyes and suspect every man with whom she has contact of usurping his father's rightful place. The boy's own possessiveness, an idealized image of his father, and projected sexual guilt feelings of his own, combine to make such children the acknowledged dread and horror of any widow's prospective suitor.

But to go on with our analysis of "1601" and how Mark Twain used it for the purpose of puncturing with his sharp wit such an astounding number of "sacred cows" in so few pages: we hear in Mark Twain's story that Montaigne has supposedly spoken of a certain emperor of such enormous vigor and potency that he managed to take ten maidenheads in a single night. There would be nothing humorous about this were it not for the added information that during the same time, his empress outdid him by entertaining "two and twenty lusty knights between her sheetes, yet was not satisfied."

We notice in this detail the tendency throughout "1601" to expose the women as at least as lecherous, lascivious, and passionate as the men, notwithstanding all outward appearances to the contrary. This corresponds in part to a man's wishful thinking that it were really so, and it is also indicative of Mark Twain's sex hostility and his desire to unmask the predatory female animal beneath the crinoline and petticoats. Lady Granby's remark only confirms this, for she unblushingly and matter-of-factly declares that "a ram is yet ye emperor's superior, sith he will tup a hundred ewes 'twixt sun and sun; and after, if he can have none more to shag, will masturbate until he hath enrich'd whole acres with his seed."

Even while introducing his characters, Mark Twain begins to throw barbs at the women. Very casually he mentions that Countess Granby is twenty-six years old. In the next sentence we learn that her daughter is fifteen years old, and later the cup-bearer comments that "little Lady Helen [was] born on *her* mother's wedding-day." The other women in the story do not fare any better. The Queen is shown to be as salacious and suggestive in her remarks as any of the others present. Of Shakespeare's wife we learn that she was "four months gone with child when she stood uppe before ye alter," and Lady Alice and Lady Margery are said to be "mouthing religion" while they had been "whores from ye cradle."

Following Lady Granby's comment about the ram, the cup-bearer, still carrying on his private feud with Raleigh, remarks, "Then spake ye damned windmill, Sr. Walter, of a people in ye utermost parts of America, yt copulate not until they be five and thirty yeres of age, ye women being eight and twenty, and do it then but once in seven years."

At that, the Queen teasingly turns to young Lady Helen, asking her how she would like to go there "and preserve thy belly." The girl replies that her old nurse told her that "there are more ways of serving God than by locking the thighs together," adding that she would nevertheless be willing to serve Him that way too, ". . . sith you highnesses grace hath set ye ensample."

Lady Helen's remark constitutes not only a typically feminine "dig" at another woman, but as it is directed against the Queen, who represents an authority-and-mother-figure for the girl, it is also highly disrespectful. Yet, completely in keeping with the tenor of "1601," the Queen commends her for her witty answer, rather than rebuking her. She also praises young Master Beaumonte for his insinuative reference comparing Lady Helen's genitals to the "downy nests of birdes of Paradise" by saying that with such a "neat-turned compliment" he is sure to "spread the ivory thighs of many a willing maid."

Throughout, Twain succeeds in producing a humorous effect by what we call the "reversal of affect," a common psychological mechanism, especially in the more severe emotional disturbances. The psychology of the humorist here consists in accepting, indeed embracing, that which is normally unacceptable or even rejected.

The Queen then mentions having met Rabelais when she was a girl, and of how "he did tell her of a man his father knew that had a double pair of bollocks." The weary cup-bearer reports, ". . . whereon a controversy followed as concerning the most just way to spell the word, ye contention running high betwixt ye learned Bacon and ye ingenious Jonson, until at last ye old Lady Margery, wearying of it all, saith, Gentles, what mattereth it how ye spell the word? . . . Before I had gained my fourteenth year I had learned that them that would . . . stop'd not to consider the spelling o't."

Raleigh agrees that "when a shift's turned up, delay is meet for aught but dalliance," and relates a story by Boccaccio in which he tells of a monk who was thanking God in prayer for having sent a pretty girl to his cell, unaware that the abbot was making good use of the time meanwhile, so that the monk, his prayers done, discovers the little maid "already occupied to her content." Again the "reversal affect" is used, for despite the sacrilegious nature of this story, Twain makes it appear as if the real trouble lay not in the moral issue but in the fact that the girl could accommodate only one man at a time!

There follows some general conversation on topics which at last appear more suitable for ladies and gentlemen. "Master Shaxpur" reads from *Henry IV,* and from *Venus and Adonis,* on which the cup-bearer comments, ". . . I, being sleepy and fatigued withal, did deme it but paltry stuff, and was the more discomforted in that ye bloody bucanier had got his wind again . . . with such villain zeal that presently I was like to choke once more. God damn this windy ruffian and all his breed."

But presently a social gaffe is committed when the talk turns to a former scandal in which Raleigh was involved, at which "ye queene did give the damned Sr Walter a look yt made hym wince—for she hath not forgot he was her own lover in yt olde day." After an uncomfortable silence which the cup-bearer uses to reflect to himself that the Queen's attitude to "a little harmless debauching" is extravagant in view of the questionable morals of all the ladies present, the conversation turns to Cervantes and "the new painter, Rubens." "Fine words and dainty-wrought phrases from the ladies now," is the cup-bearer's caustic remark. But once again, Twain punctures the artificiality and pretense, for the Queen, who considers herself an authority on this subject, grows jealous. "Wherefore 'twas observable yt ye queene waxed uncontent; and in time a labor'd grandiose speeche out of ye mouthe of Lady Alice, who manifestly did mightily pride herself thereon, did quite exhauste ye queene's endurance, who listened till ye gaudy speech was done, then lifted up her brows, and with vaste irony, mincing saith, *O Shitte!* Whereat they alle did laffe, but not ye Lady Alice, yt olde foolish bitche."

In all these examples, it is perfectly amazing how Mark Twain succeeds in condensing into so few words so much psychological subject matter and such an abundance of humor. "1601" brings everything and everybody down to a common denominator: the human animal "as is," and not as we pretend that it is. The political authority figures which we have set up, the intellectual wizards to whom we turn for counsel, the religious creeds to which we give lip service, and the social finesse on which we pride ourselves—all come under the same pitiless scrutiny of Mark Twain's relentless humor.

Only through painstaking analysis of unconscious patterns have Freud and other analysts been able to demonstrate the dynamics of the processes involved in the creation of wit and humor which Mark Twain has intuitively understood and been able to employ with such singular effectiveness. Freud would have been the first to recognize this, for he used to have the highest regard for the genius of artistic creation, and often remarked, upon the discovery of some new aspect of the human psyche by psychoanalytic investigations "Yes, but the poets have been there long before. . . !"

"1601" illustrates many of Freud's statements about the psychology of wit and humor, the role of pre-genital (infantile) aspects of sexuality in the sex life of the adult, and man's uneradicable interest in the sexual organs and his own waste products.

Freud once said that it is one of the fundamental desires of mankind to see the sexual exposed. He felt that this itself was already a sign of development along the way of civilization, the more primitive pleasure being that of direct touch.

In his *Wit and Its Relation to the Unconscious,* he called attention to the fact that "the smutty joke is like the denudation of a person of the opposite sex, toward whom the joke is directed. Through the utterances of obscene words the person attacked is forced to picture the parts of the body in question, or the sexual act, and is shown that the aggressor himself pictures the same thing. There is no doubt that the original motive of the smutty joke was the pleasure of seeing the sexual displayed."

What Freud here says about "smutty jokes" is, of course, just as applicable to erotic satire and, we suggest, to other forms of erotic literature and art as well.

Freud was also the first one to show how, for the child, sex and elimination are inextricably linked together, and that these elements still play a role in the sex life of the adult. This is due mainly to the anatomical proximity or identity of the organs serving these functions.

In this respect again, "1601" is the example "par excellence," for in this little story anal and genital-erotic elements are presented almost in the same breath, and the transition from one to the other is so well handled that it is almost imperceptible.

Having analyzed Mark Twain's erotic essay "1601" from all these aspects, we can only arrive at the conclusion that, in spite of its fictional character and intentional distortions, it is both socially and psychologically a work of erotic realism.

We have already shown how faithfully the story follows Freud's psychoanalytic principles of erotic wit and humor, but it is also psychologically accurate with respect to the sexual customs of the period in which it is set.

These are some of the things one has to keep in mind in appraising works like "1601." Seen and judged in isolation from other writings of the time to which it refers, one might be misled into thinking it to be utterly unrealistic. But, if we put "1601" into its proper contemporary frame, we will have to agree with its author, who, in a notebook of a later period, said: "I built a

conversation which *could have happened*—I used words
such as were used at that time—1601."

As a result of having written "1601" Mark Twain
was not only invited by the German Emperor to browse
at will through his vast private collection of erotica, he
was also asked to be the guest of honor at the famous
Stomach Club in Paris. On that occasion he addressed
the group with a speech which is modestly titled, *Some
Thoughts on the Science of Onanism.*

The speech is short, pungent and extremely clever,
but it is neither a particularly great work of art and
oratory, nor can it lay claim to historical or psychological realism. Nor yet does it seem to have any "other
redeeming value of social importance," except—and in
this one exception lies its whole justification, legal and
otherwise—that its main purpose was obviously *not* to
stimulate its listeners erotically, but *to appeal to their
sense of humor.* As such, it is the purest example of
erotic wit and humor we have ever seen. In terms of
reality-orientation, however, it certainly also had a value,
in its time, which is less applicable now; namely, that
masturbation was wrongly regarded as highly dangerous,
capable even of leading to insanity if indulged in too
much, and in any event certainly a reprehensible and
shameful occupation. By making this universal practice
the subject of a humorous speech, Twain contributed to
exploding the medical and social myth which surrounded it. Moreover, the speech does not pretend to
be anything else but a farce. In other words, it does not
confuse the real with the imaginary, as is the case with
pornography.

Put differently, Mark Twain as a human being was
simply interested, as is the rest of humanity, in that
which is taboo, and he resented the restrictions which
a hypocritical morality imposes on every member of
society. This inner rebellion against superficial conventions caused him to write "1601" and led ultimately to
his facetious speech at the Stomach Club.

The fact that in Mark Twain's "1601" and in his
speech at the Stomach Club "obscenity" is presented in

the context of wit and humor, robs the taboo words and erotic allusions of their potentially aphrodisiacal effect. One might compare this situation with, let us say, the delivery of a mock sermon in which the would-be "preacher" facetiously admonishes his "parishioners" under threat of hell-fire and damnation to repent of their sins "as it were" and turn from their wicked ways "as soon as may be convenient." Here we have several highly emotionally toned words like "hell-fire," "damnation," "sin," "repentance," etc., which might evoke guilt and fear in many people under proper conditions, e. g., if the sermon were delivered minus the facetious references by an ordained minister in a regular church and with all indications that he really meant what he was saying.

The two examples from entirely different areas of life show how certain emotionally toned words, whether of an erotic or other nature, depend for their effect on the total situation in which they are presented. In the case of Mark Twain's *A Fireside Conversation,* the taboo words and erotic references are neutralized, first by the historical setting which removes them from ourselves and the present scene, secondly by the realization that what we are reading is realistic in the sense that such a conversation *might* have happened at that time, and finally by the humorous twists which the author gives to everything said.

As to Mark Twain's speech at the Stomach Club, the humor alone removes it from any suspicion of salaciousness, for if laughter can kill anything, it certainly can make short shrift of sexual excitement. We all know from our own experiences how, at one time or another, an otherwise highly seductive situation has been turned into its opposite by humor. One of the authors witnessed a scene once in a night club where an extremely sensuous burlesque queen was producing a highly erotic audience-response with her exotic dance number. The atmosphere was saturated with sex as the very capable strip-tease artist went, to the accompaniment of jungle rhythms, into her climactic finale, her hair disheveled, hips violently jerking in coital movements, and every male eye tensely fixed on the scene. Suddenly, all this erotic effect was dispelled in one moment when the girl, clad only in her spike-heeled shoes, slipped and landed with a hard thump on the freshly waxed floor of the stage! There was no use trying to get the audience back into the right erotic mood. The whole house just shook with hilarity and laughter, produced by the unscheduled comical interlude.

This is exactly what Mark Twain managed to achieve in the two examples here discussed. He first leads the reader or listener on into believing that he is going to entertain him with a "sexy" story, but then he begins to poke fun at the erotic, while ridiculing the hypo-critical denial of sexuality, which remains the dominant theme of "1601." In that sense, "1601" and Mark Twain's speech, taken together, constitute a fairly complete exposé of human weakness or that which the philosopher Nietzsche called the "all too human" part of humanity.

EROTIC REALISM FROM POGGIO TO MARTIN LUTHER

We shall see from certain references in Pepys' *Diary* as we have seen from the quoted samples of Elizabethan poetry that the moral code of the 17th century made it permissible for men and women alike to discuss openly, and unambiguously, the most intimate details of their own and other people's love lives. This was not only so for the lower, uneducated classes, but also and even more so among the princes, nobles, and ecclesiastics.

This trend had originated in the Renaissance of the two preceding centuries, during which time unbridled sexual license and violence had followed the fanatic attempt of the medieval church to suppress the natural instincts of man. When this large-scale experiment in "sublimation" failed, there resulted an explosion of the instinctual forces which came to dominate every aspect of life, often at the expense of other values and interests.

The freedom of expression which the writers and poets of the Renaissance enjoyed, and which lasted well into the English Restoration period, has been unequalled ever since.

A typical example of such freedom of expression is, for instance, the collection of over 300 satires of *Facetiae* by Poggio, the Italian humanist, Apostolic Secretary, and subsequent chancellor of Florence during the Renaissance. Similar to Boccaccio's *Decameron,* and even more so to his compatriot Aretino's *Dialogues,* Poggio's stories deal with the most risqué subject matter with a frankness which leaves little to the imagination.

One has to keep in mind that under Pope Martin V these stories formed the main topic of conversation for the bishops and cardinals who used to congregate every day at a certain place in the Vatican for this purpose. The popes themselves sometimes took part in these discussions, despite the fact that they were frequently the butt of the witty and salacious stories.

To give the reader at least a flavor of these earlier erotic writings, we shall begin with a story of Poggio's, "About a Young Wife Who Accused Her Husband of Being Insufficiently Furnished." The reader will keep in mind that the chief characteristic of all these stories (and of the material which has preceded it) is the quality of humor, either satirical, witty, or broadly farcical. In their time, they were intended primarily to amuse. To us, they serve the additional purpose of being historically instructive as to the social atmosphere of the times and in revealing the primitiveness of what was regarded as humorous.

A noble and beautiful young man was married to the daughter of Nereo de' Pazzi, a distinguished Florentine aristocrat. A few days after the nuptials, the young woman came to visit her parental home, according to the custom, but not happy and gay as is the case with most brides, but looking pale and letting her head hang sadly. Secretly questioned by her mother, the young thing cried and said, "Wretched am I, for you have not married me to a real man, but to somebody who is no man, having nothing or too little of that for which one does get married."

Much distressed about her daughter's misfortune, the mother revealed the situation to her husband, and soon, as it happens with such matters, all of the friends and relatives who had assembled for the banquet knew and talked about the poor girl's predicament and lamented her fate of having been sacrificed instead of being given into marriage. Finally the bridegroom arrived in whose honor the banquet was being held, and seeing the guests full of grief and with downcast and tearful eyes, he inquired about the cause of their unexpected mourning. At first nobody dared to confess to him the true nature of their grief, but in the end one who was more forward than the others, told him that the bride had intimated that his masculinity left much to be desired. The bridegroom only replied, "Don't let thoughts of this kind disturb your meal, for I shall quickly disprove this accusation."

With that, the company sat down to eat, and when the meal was almost finished, the young man arose and said, "I hear that I have been accused of a certain matter, and am now calling upon you to judge for yourselves." With these words, he presented to them an exceedingly beautiful member (in those days men were wearing short garments), put it on the table, and asked all present whether they would complain about it, or reject it.

The majority of the women wished that their husbands were as well supplied as the bridegroom, and many of the men felt themselves vanquished by this impressive tool. Now they all turned to the bride and reproached her for having criticized her husband. But she said, "Why do you blame me! Our donkey who I just recently saw in the field is only an animal, and yet he has a member that long (whereby she held out her arm), and my husband, who is human, has only half as much." The naïve child thought that humans ought to be more richly endowed in that respect than animals.

The question of potency was one of Poggio's favorite themes. His stories convey the impression, and correctly so, that neither religious and moral considerations nor tender sentiments and affection were the strongest bonds of marriage in the society of which he writes, but only physical considerations of beauty and prowess. His 242nd satire is typical of this attitude and reads as follows:

A friend of mine told me of a Florentine gentleman whom he knew who had a beautiful wife who was much sought after by other admirers. Some of them used to serenade her at night by the light of torches, as was the custom. One evening, as the Florentine, who was a very witty fellow, was once again awakened by the familiar sound of trumpets outside, he got up and had his wife appear with him in the window. Then he called to the group below, asking them to look up at them for a moment, and when everybody's glance was directed at the pair, he pulled out a tremendous member, stuck it out of the window, and told them their efforts were obviously in vain, for as they could see for themselves, he was better able to satisfy his wife than any of them, and therefore advised his competitors to no longer inconvenience him uselessly. This clever speech had the result that he was henceforth left alone and no longer molested by his wife's inamoratos. [Compare Lord Sedley's exhibition on the balcony, referred to in Pepys' *Diary*.]

Like Poggio, the "divine" Aretino as he was surnamed, also was a favorite of the Pope, but in this particular case, he lost the Pope's patronage when he composed sixteen sonnets to Guilio Romano's famous series of paintings showing a large variety of intercourse posi-

tions. He moved to Venice and lived there in grand
style, being able to afford a whole harem of mistresses,
who were called "Aretines" and whom he housed in the
various floors of his palatial home. He had numerous
children born to him by these courtesans, who also cuckolded him thoroughly and finally robbed him of most
of his possessions.

Aretino's death is said to have corresponded to his
way of life. Legend has it that on hearing a report about
the promiscuous life of his sister, he went into such a fit
of laughter that he lost his balance on the chair, and
falling, broke his neck.

Aretino had already shown his mettle as a major
writer of erotica in his sixteen sonnets, the first edition
of which dates probably as early as 1524, though there
exist no known copies of that printing. Examples from
another edition of the *Sonetti,* done in Venice in 1556,
also count among the greatest rarities of bibliophiles.
There have been later editions of this work in Italian
and French, but most important and most lascivious of
his writings are the *Dialogues,* or *Caprices,* as he called
them, which were later assembled in three parts as the
well-known *Ragionamenti* and of which many editions
have come down through the centuries, including several
excellent printings in English.

Almost contemporary with Aretino was the French
writer Pierre Brantôme, who was born about 1540 in
Périgord, the same region which is mentioned in "1601"
in connection with the alleged custom of widows from
that part of central France to wear phallic emblems in
their headdress.

Brantôme, who died in 1614, seems to have spent the
earlier part of his life at the court of Queen Marguerite
of Navarre, who is likewise referred to in "1601" and
who was the author of another collection of racy and
witty stories called *One Hundred Merry and Delightful
Stories* (*Les Cent Nouvelles Novelles*).

After having accompanied Mary Stuart to Scotland,
Brantôme served in the Spanish army in Africa, joined

the expedition of St. John against the Sultan, and engaged in other errantry, until he fell from a horse and was confined to bed for a period of four years. During that time, when he was also in more straitened circumstances and poor health, he wrote the collection of stories known as *Lives of Fair and Gallant Ladies*.

The abiding popularity of these anecdotes is demonstrated by the many editions of this work in several of the Western languages. However, some of his best and psychologically most interesting stories, which we shall here discuss, are absent in the edited English translations of his works.

His stories, which in style and content bear a strong resemblance to "1601" as well as to Pepy's *Diary,* are not only a faithful mirror of the culture of his period, but also an unusually rich source for the historian, the student of literature, and last but not least, for the sexologist and psychologist interested in the dynamics of sexual behavior.

In many of his stories, Brantôme proves himself to be quite an expert in sex differences and female psychology (such as we shall later encounter in Frank Harris), as in his comments on *The Rape of Women,* which also show the same undertone of subtle mockery that we found in Mark Twain's *Fireside Conversation.* Brantôme says:

I have heard speak of a Frenchwoman, town-bred, a lady of birth and of handsome looks, who was violated in our civil wars in a town taken by assault, by a multitude of men-at-arms. On escaping away from these, she did consult a worthy father as to whether she had sinned greatly, first telling him her story. He said, "no!"—inasmuch as she had been had by force and deflowered without her consent, but entirely misliking the thing. Whereon she did make answer: "Now God be praised, for that once in my life I had my fill, without sinning or doing offence to God!" . . .

To this, Brantôme adds the following insightful remarks:

> I once knew well a lady who . . . was used to say: Never did she feel so great a pleasure in these doings as when she was half forced and all but violated as it were, and then was there much pleasure therein. The more a woman showeth herself rebellious and recalcitrant, so much the more doth the man wax ardent and push home the attack; and so having forced the breach, he doth use his victory more fiercely and savagely, and thereby giveth more appetite to the woman. . . . Indeed, the same lady did actually further say, that oftentimes she would make these ados and show resistance to her husband, and play the prudish, capricious and scornful wife, and so put him the more on his mettle. Whereby when he did come to it, both he and she did find an hundredfold more gratification.

Other Brantôme anecdotes are reminiscent of Poggio's bride-and-groom stories; as, for instance:

> I have heard speak of another husband who did hold his new-made wife in his arms the first night; and she was so ravished with delight and pleasure that quite forgetting herself she could not refrain from a slight turning and twisting and mobile action of the body, such as new-wed wives are scarce wont to make. At this he said naught else, but only, "Ha, ha! I now know!" and went on his way to the end. These be cuckolds "in embrio". . . . And the worst thing I see in them is when they wed cow and calf at once, as the saying is, and take them when already with child. [Compare the narrator's remark in "1601," "and was not our little Lady Helen born on her mother's wedding day?" in which Mark Twain expresses the same kind of sentiment as this writer; or as we find in Pepys' *Diary*: "He that do get a wench with child and marry her afterwards is as if a man should shit in his hat and then clap it on his head."]

Another story, called *Quaint Distinctions Drawn by Some Women,* reads as follows:

Other ladies there be which are complaisant herein up to a certain point of conscience and charity. Of this sort was one which would never suffer her lover sleep with her as oft as he might, to kiss her the least in the world on the lips, giving as her reason that 'twas her mouth had made the oath of faith and fealty to her husband, and she would fain not foul the same by way of the very mouth that had made and taken it. But as for that of the belly, the which had said never a word and promised naught, this she did let him do with at his good pleasure, and made no scruple to yield it up to her lover, seeing it is not in the competence of the upper mouth to pledge itself for the lower, and more than for the lower for the upper. For that the custom of Law doth say that none can bind himself for another without the consent and word of either party, nor one only for the whole.

Another most conscientious and scrupulous dame, when granting her friend enjoyment of her body, would always take the upper station and bring her man under her, never abating one jot of this rule. For, by observing the same straitly and regularly, she would say, if her husband or other did ask whether such an one had done it to her, that she could deny even on oath, and assuredly protest, without sinning against God, that never had he done so nor mounted upon her.

The writers of this period were particularly preoccupied with problems of virginity and cuckoldry, as we have already seen reflected in the poetry of that time. Brantôme tells, for example, the story of a bride who, no longer virgin, took good care of her reputation by seeing to it that her bed linen would be stained with chicken blood by the next morning. Unfortunately for her, the husband proved himself impotent on the wedding night and did not consummate their union until a much later time. The girl found herself therefore in the awkward position of having to explain the bloodstains on the sheets.

Other anecdotes deal with voluntary forms of cuckoldry, either for financial gains, political protection, or for reasons of sexual deviation. About the latter, Brantôme says the following:

Next there is yet another sort of cuckolds, one that of a surety is utterly abominable and hateful before God and man alike, they who, enamoured of some handsome Adonis, do abandon their wives to men of this kind in order to enjoy their favour in return.

The first time ever I was in Italy, I did hear of an example of this at Ferrara, the tale being told me of one who, captivated by a certain handsome youth, did persuade his wife to accord her favours to the said young man, who was in love with her, and to appoint a day and consent to do all he should bid her. The lady was willing enow, for truly she did desire no better venison to regale herself withal than this. At length was the day fixed, and the hour being come when the young lover and the lady were at their pleasant game and entertainment, lo! the husband, who was hid near at hand, according to the compact betwixt him and his wife, did rush in. So catching them in the very act, he did put his dagger to the lover's throat, deeming him worthy of death for such an offence, in accordance with the laws of Italy, which herein be something more rigorous than in France. So was he constrained to grant the husband what he did desire, and they made exchange one with the other. The young man did prostitute himself to the husband, and the husband did abandon his wife to the young man. Thus was the husband cuckold after an exceeding foul fashion.

In the next anecdote on the same topic, we hear even of simultaneous bisexual intercourse, practiced by a husband who finds his wife in bed with another man. We know of no companion to this unusual account, except a Japanese picture story about a husband who finds his wife in the same compromising situation with a female impersonator, whereupon he has regular vaginal intercourse with his wife while at the same time masturbating the other man.

Brantôme's version of this theme runs as follows:

> I have heard tell how in a certain spot in the world (I had rather not name it) there was an husband, and of high quality to boot, which was desperately enamoured of a young man, who himself was deep in love with the former's wife, and she likewise with him. Now whether it was that the husband had won over the wife, or that it was a pure surprise quite unexpected, at any rate he did catch the pair a-bed and coupled up together. Whereon threatening the young man, if he would not consent to his will, he did enter him lying just as he was, and coupled up and glued to his wife, and he did take his will of him. And thus was the problem solved, how three lovers could enjoy and be contented all at the same time together.

Brantôme adds another story to this, namely, of a wife who reassures her lover that he need not fear from her husband, if he dared to make a scandal of their affair, since she would blackmail him, "of having wished to practice the back-door Venus, which might well bring about his death. . . ." Thus we see that Western sex morality has always lent itself to sexual blackmail, even in the time of the Tudors, with perhaps the only exception of the all-powerful ruling class during the height of the Renaissance in Italy.

Brantôme even has a few anecdotes about Lesbian love, as in the following:

> I have heard a tale told by the late M. de Clermont-Tallard, . . . how that as a boy he had the

honour to be comrade with M. d'Anjou, since King
Henry III of France, in his study; and to study
regularly with him, under the tutorship of M. de
Gournay. Well, one day at Toulouse, studying with
his master as aforesaid in his private closet, and
being seated in a corner apart, he saw by a little
crevice (for the closets and chambers were of
wood, and had been made suddenly and in haste
by the pains of the Cardinal d'Argmaignac, Arch-
bishop of that See, the better to receive and accommodate the King and all his Court) in another
adjoining closet, two very great ladies, with petticoats all tucked up and drawers down, lying one
atop of the other, and kissing like doves, rubbing
and frigging one another, in a word making great
ado, wantoning and imitating men. And this their
pastime did last well nigh a whole hour, so that at
the end they were exceeding hot and tired out, and
were left so red and wet with exertion that they
could not move, and were constrained to rest them
somewhat. And he said he did see this same game
played several other days, so long as the Court
tarried there, in the same fashion. But never after
did he get opportunity to see the like pastime,
seeing that particular spot did favour him, but nowhere else could he manage it.

Naïvely, Brantôme thinks:

Weasels are touched with this sort of love, and
delight female with female to unite and dwell together. And so in hieroglyphic signs, women loving one another with this kind of affection were
represented of yore by weasels. I have heard tell
of a lady which was used always to keep some of
these animals, for that she had dealings with this
mode of love and so did take pleasure in watching
her little pets in their intercourse together.

This is the only story of homosexual animal intercourse for exhibitionistic purposes related in a work of

erotic realism which has ever come to our attention. There are, of course, numerous accounts of exhibitions of copulating animals, particularly between a stallion and a mare, which were quite customary at feasts of the nobility in that day. Even exhibitions of human intercourse for the entertainment of special guests were not at all rare occurrences from the time of the Renaissance through part of the 18th century in France, and it is well to remember that these exhibitions took place before mixed audiences of men and women, who seemed to take equal delight in these performances. In England, however, we know only of animal exhibitions, which were given to serve the same purpose, though in a somewhat more conservative fashion.

Brantôme then tells how a great prince once came upon two ladies of the court as they were making love to each other with the use of an artificial dildo or godemiché, and how he used the opportunity to learn all he could of Lesbian practices. Brantôme relates:

> This did so well succeed that one of them was surprised in the act and found to be fitted with a great big one between her legs, fastened so prettily with little straps around her body that it seemed like a natural member. She was caught so suddenly she had no time to take it off, so that the Prince did actually constrain her to show him how the pair of them did the thing betwixt them.

We shall quote one more example of Brantôme's erotically realistic humor, dealing with the delicate subject of a lady and her dildo:

> I have heard a story related, myself being at the Court at that time, how that the Queen Mother having given order to visit one day the chambers and chests of all such as were lodged in the Louvre, without sparing either dame or damsel, to see there were no arms or perhaps mayhap pistols concealed therein, at the time of the civil troubles, one lady

was surprised by the Captain of the Guard and
found to have in her chest, no pistols indeed, but
four great godemichés cunningly made. This did
give folk much cause for laughter and great confusion to the lady. I know the dame in question, and
I think she is yet alive; but she was never well to
look upon [!].

Brantôme, like most men, could not imagine that any
woman would not prefer a real man instead of a substitute or another woman, if truly given the opportunity.
Nor was he in any degree an exception with regard to
either the subject matter with which he dealt, or the
manner of his presentation. We only need to refer to
Montaigne or Rabelais for confirmation of this statement, but we do feel that Brantôme's anecdotes are more
readily understandable and seem less dated than those of
other writers of that period.

In contrast to Brantôme, Rabelais' stories seem much
more coarse, and yet he was a favorite of Marguerite,
Queen of Navarre, as well as of her brother, the King
of France. The King commended Rabelais especially
for the fourth volume of his series *Gargantua* and
Pantagruel, which he dedicated to the edification of
syphilitics.

In one of his stories Rabelais suggests, for instance,
that in order to better fortify the city walls of Paris,
they should be constructed of female organs (callibristis
or contrapunctums of women, which, he says, are
cheaper than stones). Here we shall have to keep in
mind that Rabelais liked to use quaint and unusual expressions and was not averse to making up words which
had more personal meaning to him than to the reader;
one will not find many of his self-coined words in the
dictionary, nor even in the usage of his own time:

. . . Of them should the walls be built, ranging
them in good symmetry, by the rules of architecture
and placing the largest in the first ranks, then slop-
ing downwards ridgewise, like the back of an ass.

The middle-sized ones must be ranked next, and last of all the least and smallest. This done, there must be a fine little interlacing of them, like points of diamonds, as is to be seen in the great tower of Bourges, with a like number of nudinnudos, nilnisistandos, and stiff bracmards, that dwell in amongst the claustral cod-pieces. What devil were able to overthrow such walls? There is no metal like to resist blows, in so far that, if culverin-shot should come to graze upon it, you would incontinently see distil from thence the blessed fruit of the great pox as small as rain. Beware, in the name of the devils, and hold off. Furthermore, no thunderbolt or lightening would fall upon it. For why? They are all either blest or consecrated. I see but one inconveniency in it. Ho, ho, ha, ha, ha! said Pantagruel, and what is that? It is, that the flies would be so liquorish of them that you would wonder, and would quickly gather there together, and there leave their ordure and excretions, and so all the work would be spoiled. But see how that might be remedied: they must be wiped and made rid of the flies with fair foxtails, or great good viedazes, which are ass-pizzles, of Provence.

In another story, Rabelais tells of a miracle-working codpiece which has the effect of sexually arousing anybody who comes near it. Its owner accidentally enters a theater in which a passion play is just in progress, with the results that both spectators and performers, angels and devils, men and animals, are so affected by its magnetism that they leave their posts and begin to copulate with one another.

Lest the reader come to think that such imagery and language were only used by certain anticlerical writers like Rabelais, we hasten to emphasize again that even the clergy, not only of the Renaissance, but also of the following two centuries, expressed themselves often in very similar terms.

Martin Luther is an outstanding example in that respect. His writings and table talk abound in anal references which would be unimaginable as coming from the mouth of a modern religious authority. And even though Luther represents perhaps a pathological case, he is in this respect not out of line with the general spirit of the era.

The psychologist Erikson says, in his fascinating study of Martin Luther's personality, "Luther could be so vulgar that he became easy game for the priest and the psychiatrist, both of whom quote with relish: 'Thou shalt not write a book unless you have listened to the fart of an old sow, to which you should open your mouth wide and say "Thanks to you, pretty nightingale; do I hear a text which is for me?" ' But what writer, disgusted with himself, has not shared these sentiments—without finding the right wrong words?" (Erik H. Erikson, *Young Man Luther, A Study in Psychoanalysis and History.*)

In another place Luther says, "A Christian should and could be gay, but then the devil shits on him." He felt that the devil likes to express his scorn by exposing his rear parts, but that man can beat him to it by using anal weapons in turn and by taunting him with graphic insults. So strongly was this kind of anal imagery established in Luther's mind that at one time he claimed to have been visited by the devil, who departed, leaving a foul stench behind; and even a few days before his death he saw the devil sitting on a rain-pipe outside his window, exposing his naked posteriors to him.

Luther's enemies were not at all above replying in the same vein as the great reformer, as becomes immediately clear by a look at the many anti-Reformation tracts which used equally unequivocal and anal language in defamation of Luther, just as he liked to use it against the Pope and the Roman clergy. However, Luther's language was not all pre-genital, but contains genital references as well; for instance in a letter to his friend Spalatin, for whom he had made a match with an ex-nun. In very broad language he wishes Spalatin luck for the wedding night, and promises to think of him during a parallel performance to be arranged in his own marital bed.

It seems to our way of thinking preferable for Luther to have abreacted much of his hostility against the Pope (who represented for him very likely the "bad" father, as Erikson has pointed out) by abusing him verbally in the vilest anal terms than to have murdered him, as another father-hater, John Wilkes Booth, acted out with his gun by killing President Lincoln, instead of merely attacking him with the less dangerous phallic symbol of the pen.

This is precisely the aim of all realistic psychotherapy in those cases of severe emotional disturbance in which hostile or aggressive sexual impulses are close to the surface and where the patient's control mechanisms are sufficiently weakened to conjure up the specter of violent acting out. The therapist tries in these instances to open channels of communication for the patient by providing a permissive atmosphere for him in which he dares to express even the most dangerous thoughts and the most violent fantasies which trouble him. In so doing, we are trying to neutralize these antisocial impulses, to syphon off some of the emotional energy which nourishes them and gives them impetus, so that the patient is better able to deal with what is left of them in their reduced strength. We have often found that the patient's ego-controls are quite adequate to cope with such fantasies and action-tendencies after he has been able to drain off some of their potential threat by talking out, airing his griefs, and indulging in his vengeful fantasies in the protecting presence of a therapist who is not afraid of, or shocked by, what is fearful and shocking to the patient.

If we apply this same principle of individual psychotherapy to a whole society, we shall have to conclude that it is potentially more therapeutic for a group to be allowed expression of its socially objectionable ideas and feelings than to be forced into various forms of denial, such as all overt or covert moral censorship implies. For sheer self-preservation, we would, for instance, much prefer a verbal mud-slinging contest between Russians and Americans to the unleashing of atomic weapons which can be accomplished quite silently and in all good taste by quiet men pushing noiseless buttons to set off the deadly reaction.

Of course, catharsis, or verbal abreaction of feelings, is not the whole answer either in individual therapy, nor could it be the cure-all for our social ills. Matters concerning the human psyche and the social organism are never as simple as that. However, and we cannot stress this strongly enough, the guilt-free expression of otherwise unacceptable ideas is by far preferable to suppression, both in the case of the individual and the group.

We advisedly say the "guilt-free" ventilation of the socially unacceptable, because without this qualification much, if not all, of its potential therapeutic value is lost. If we encourage a patient who does not dare to pronounce a taboo word to use it, without removing, simultaneously, from his conscience the gnawing sense of wrong-doing, we are doing him more harm than good. Such attempts would be just as ill-advised as telling a sexually inhibited person to go ahead and indulge himself, while he is still plagued by feelings of remorse and shame, which are merely increased by our suggestion. All such naïve therapeutic attempts, which fortunately are by now no longer as popular as during the 1920's, are necessarily doomed to complete failure.

EROTIC REALISM IN AUTOBIOGRAPHY

Much of Brantôme's material presented in the previous chapter can be considered autobiographical. Not a few of the anecdotes which he tells are his own experiences, though he disguises them, very much like a modern case history, in the form of stories told about others than himself.

As we are about to introduce the reader to the erotic aspects of other autobiographies, a few general statements about the role of the sexual element in these personal histories seem to be in place.

After having read the life stories of famous personalities in political, and at times even in literary texts, one is often left with the impression that these individuals must have been asexual, or that their sexuality was irrelevant as far as their work was concerned, because nothing is said about that phase of their lives.

Yet, serious political scientists, art critics, and literary historians have long realized that the life works of those who make history in one form or another remain incomplete, at best a matter of conjecture, unless one does know a good deal about their sexual behavior.

To take an example from the world of literature: without realizing that Walt Whitman was apparently capable of both heterosexual and homosexual relations, one might completely misunderstand some of his references to the love of one man for another.

Or, to take another example from the more recent past: how much more would we know about the rise and nature of the Nazi movement if Hitler had not concealed his early (and later) sexual experiences in his autobiography, *Mein Kampf*! Hardly anyone would deny that Hitler's sex life must have been anything but "normal." But what did it consist of? Its psychological homo-eroticism is unmistakable, but did he actually engage in homosexual acts? Did he have sexual relations with women—for instance, with Eva Braun, with whom he had a long-standing relationship and whom he officially married in his bunker before their joint suicide? Was he a sadist, whose sexual excitement was dependent on torturing or contemplating the torture of others? If so, it would explain much that remains otherwise unexplainable.

As a more benign example of how a sexual event influenced a prominent person's life and determined its future course, we can cite the case of Gandhi. This revered seeker of the truth, political hero, and religious leader mentions in his autobiography that at the time his father was dying he was having intercourse with his wife. He credits the massive guilt aroused by his enjoying himself sexually at the time of his father's death as a determining factor in the choice of his future way of life—asceticism. Without this interesting information, it would be far more difficult to understand why Gandhi chose to live with his wife as a brother instead of as a husband. Without this *fact,* mere speculation could create many other reasons. Nor does it seem too farfetched to assume that the principle of sexual abstinence must have had its motivating effects with regard to his pacifist philosophy and the policy of passive resistance which he inaugurated and practiced.

It is highly regrettable from our point of view that so many clinicians, analysts, anthropologists, and other professional workers have lacked the moral courage of Mahatma Gandhi and have therefore failed to put the painstaking attention to detail and acuteness of observation, for which they have been trained, into the writing of their own autobiographies.

One might have expected greater impetus in that direction from the psychoanalytic movement, for every individual analysis (which does not stop short of an investigation of the patient's sexual history and present sex life) constitutes an erotic autobiography. Not that a person's entire analysis, nor even the major part of it, necessarily concerns itself directly with the sexual side of his life. But, as psychoanalytic experience has shown, the sexual has a pattern-forming tendency for the individual's general behavior. It provides, so to speak, the undertones to whatever may be in the foreground of the analytic process at any given time.

We know of only two or three published autobiographical accounts of the writer's own psychoanalysis.

Nor can we report better success by checking the huge mass of psychoanalytic literature itself for autobiographical material of professional therapists. Freud himself, of course, did analyze some of his own dreams and made many self-revealing comments. But he never went beyond a certain point in these disclosures, protesting that one owed it to oneself to keep certain things strictly private.

Theodor Reik was the first, and thus far remains the only one, of the great psychoanalytic writers who went considerably beyond Freud in his public self-analysis. In books like *The Secret Self, Listening With the Third Ear,* and *Fragments of a Great Confession,* he boldly speaks about some of the most intimate details of his personal life, including its erotic aspects.

Unable to find similar references elsewhere in psychoanalytic writings, we turned to the great sexologists. Here again, there is little if anything about themselves in the thousands of pages by Hirschfeld, Forel, Krafft-Ebing, Stekel, or any of the others who contributed so much toward the sexual liberation of mankind.

Even Havelock Ellis apparently omitted to include much material about his own sexual life in his autobiography although, we know that this aspect of human expression was of concern to him personally as it was of importance professionally.

The following quotation has been said to be autobiographical. Actually there is considerable doubt as to its authenticity and we are indebted to Havelock Ellis's executrix for first questioning its origin. We quote the material merely as a piece of *curiosa* which does, however, bear the stamp of complete realism:

Our first night consisted in simply sharing the same room. We had discovered the French kiss, but it did not have the same effect on her clitoris as it did later on, whereas it caused me to have an emission. We spent several nights together, I sleeping outside the bedclothes. Then very naïvely she finally asked me to get under them. I had taken good care to undress in the dark. From time to time our bodies touched; and then, it being full summer, we threw off the sheets. Some inborn instinct inspired me to caress and kiss her breasts and this made her quiver. I had learned from books the meaning of the symptom and I touched her "love flesh" as Walt Whitman so beautifully expresses it. Little by little I went on, exploring without hindrance from her; I found the way, instinctively my fingers took the required position, my lips touched hers, our tongues met, her whole body was shaken by tremors, she held me tight for a moment and then sighed deeply.

I concealed my emission as best I could; neither of us dared speak, and I could not say how long we remained thus. When I again had an erection I drew her to me, lifted her thighs and explored the vestibule, into which I introduced my glans; I then began a rhythmic movement and found I could penetrate just deep enough for the foreskin to be pushed back between her compressed labiae. We kissed again and our orgasms came simultaneously.

Others have added revealing facts about Havelock Ellis' sex life. Mr. Quennell writes in *The New York Times Book Review* (March 22, 1959) as follows:

Now Havelock Ellis, although his "Psychology of Sex" runs to seven massive volumes, was neither an experienced amorist nor a happily married man; and the student who first consults his treatise and then turns the pages of his autobiography must reflect that here was yet another physician who,

despite a passionate longing to explain and en-
lighten, found it almost impossible to cure himself.

He suffered, for example, from some degree of
sexual impotence which he did not completely
overcome until he had passed his sixtieth birthday;
while a rather unpleasant form of deviation—
known to specialists as urolagnia—colored his
amatory feelings throughout his adolescence and
his later life. His marriage lasted three decades;
but it could scarcely be described as happy, since
Edith Ellis—a small, bustling, possessive energetic
woman—soon developed a passionate interest in
members of her own sex, and her husband fell back
on the companionship of a docile, affectionate girl
named Amy.

Amy was not his mistress, however, according to
the ordinary sense of the word—that, at least, is the
inference he seems to intend that we should draw—
just as his love-affair, before he married, with the
well-known South African novelist, Olive Schrei-
ner, appears to have ended in a partial fiasco. Only
when he was an aging man did he at length meet
a woman, a young French-woman, Francoise De-
lisle, who both stimulated his emotions and
thoroughly aroused his sexual instincts.

From the above accounts it is obvious that the sex
life of all of these men was a determining factor in their
personalities, their social life, and in their creative work.
Havelock Ellis' attraction to urolagnia could well have
been one of the factors in his ability to be more tolerant
and objective than most other writers in describing the
behavior of sex deviants.

In the autobiographical studies which follow, the
erotic aspects are represented in varying ratios to the
total volume of these works. The five-volume autobiography of Frank Harris probably does not contain
more references to his sexual experiences than *The
Diary of Samuel Pepys,* though he goes into greater
detail than Pepys. In either case, the *bulk of the text
consists of nonsexual material.*

Even in the *Mémoires* of Casanova, stark realism is relatively rare. The twelve volumes of the most complete privately printed Casanova Society edition of his works are replete with political and philosophical discussions, character studies of various personalities, general descriptive passages of all kinds, and adventurous reminiscences such as his escape from the lead-chambers of Venice. However, since the erotic element played such a prominent role in Casanova's life, his affairs with a large number of women occupy a corresponding percentage of his total literary output.

Nevertheless, there are those who say of Casanova that he wasted the best part of his life on erotic adventures and is wasting our time by their description in his *Mémoires*. As to Casanova himself, he realized that much of his life had been taken up with erotic concerns, and—to a point—he regretted that fact, admitting that his accomplishments might have been more in accordance with his high intelligence had he put it into the pursuit of other interests. However, we are not at all sure whether his possibly devoting more time and energy to achieving political power, amassing great wealth, or increasing his intellectual knowledge, would have made him a happier man and his world a better place to live in.

In Henry Miller's case all his writings, which, as their author declares, are autobiographical, include a great deal of erotic realism. Yet Miller claims that his sexual experiences have not been extraordinary, nor especially plentiful, as compared to those of others. If they, perhaps, take up more space than they might deserve on the basis of his own statements and in relation to the total life experience of the author, we would explain this as owing to his deliberate selection and arrangement of the material along these lines in order to stress those aspects of reality which other writers have been neglecting or misrepresenting.

By the same token, we do not agree with the criticism that has been voiced against Miller by some who contend that his writings reflect a morbid preoccupation, or obsession, with sex. Every writer selects and arranges his material according to certain principles which seem to serve his literary aims best. For Henry Miller, the emphasis on erotic realism serves to express his rebellion against the cultural and literary artificialities from which he struggled to free himself.

In our opinion, sex is not only suitable for autobiography, it is a condition of it. For most of us, sex is a large part of life; if not in actuality, then at least in fantasy. The autobiographies of those few who had the courage and honesty to include both in their personal histories are therefore all the more significant for the student of human nature and all those who, like our three dissimilar authors, are striving toward self-fulfillment in their own individual ways.

There are, of course, other autobiographies besides those which we have been discussing which go into the sex lives of their authors. Among these, some are classics, such as the two famous *Confessions* of St. Augustine and Rousseau. If they are not here included, this is mostly due to the fact that those writings are well known and readily accessible, whereas the autobiographies here represented are not nearly as well known, are almost unavailable, and are much richer in erotic realism than the more popular autobiographical works.

SAMUEL PEPYS—THE "SQUARE" WITH MORAL COURAGE

We felt that Samuel Pepys' *Diary*, which was the immediate stimulus for the production of "1601," certainly deserved to be included in any serious discussion of erotic realism. Since the entire *Diary* is somewhat more than 2,500 pages, it was, of course, necessary to limit our study, even with regard to those passages which have a direct and obvious bearing on the question of erotic realism in general and on Mark Twain's "1601" in particular.

The Diary of Samuel Pepys is in itself a study in the folly of literary censorship. As honest as Samuel Pepys was with himself, his literary executors did not share in his moral courage, but proceeded to excise this passage and that phrase which to their limited minds seemed to be either too "corrupt," as one of them (Lord Braybrooke) put it, or "which cannot possibly be printed," as another (H. B. Wheatley) submitted, asking the reader not to think that his omissions "are due to an unnecessary squeamishness." Unfortunately, we are not told what other considerations might have led to this self-imposed censorship.

Consequently, there exists today no complete, unexpurgated version of *The Diary of Samuel Pepys,* nor was it possible for Mark Twain to have been in possession of such an edition. However, the editors were not too vigilant, for at times we find four-letter words or identical incidents published in a later portion of the *Diary* which had been omitted earlier.

Samuel Pepys was born in 1633 and died in 1703. He started his career first as the secretary of a wealthier relative. He then became a clerk in the British naval office, from which humble position he worked up to Secretary of Navy Affairs, amassing a sizeable estate.

He kept an intimate record of his daily life, most of it in a shorthand type of code, which came to be known as *The Diary of Samuel Pepys.*

Of the *Diary,* it has been said by Mr. Russell Lowell, American Minister to England, at the unveiling of a monument to Samuel Pepys in 1844 (substituting on this occasion for the Earl of Northbrook, First Lord of the Admiralty), that Pepys "left . . . some of the most delightful pictures of the time in which he lived. . . . There was hardly any book which was analogous to it. . . . If one were asked what were the reasons for liking Pepys, it would be found that they were as numerous as the days upon which he made an entry in his *Diary,* and surely that was sufficient argument in his favour." There was no book, Mr. Lowell said, that he knew of, or that occurred to his memory, "with which Pepys' *Diary* could fairly be compared, except the journal of L'Estoile, who had the same anxious curiosity and the same commonness, not to say vulgarity of interest, and the book was certainly unique in one respect, and that was the absolute sincerity of the author with himself. Montaigne is conscious that we are looking over his shoulder, and Rousseau secretive in comparison with him. . . ."

It is no wonder that a man like Mark Twain, who hated sham and pious pretense, should have found such delight in Pepys' *Diary*. He must have felt an intuitive affinity toward the author who in so many respects seemed so much like himself.

Both men were "square" in the sense that they conformed outwardly to the conventions and customs of their times and social groups. To that extent, Pepys was a bourgeois. But both of them remained rebels at heart who delighted in poking fun at their less intelligent fellow "squares": Pepys, mostly in private, on the pages of his secret *Diary;* Mark Twain, publicly, by his caustic humor, the implication of which, fortunately for him, escaped the crowds whom he thus entertained at their own expense.

As far as erotic realism in autobiography is concerned, Pepys' *Diary* differs from the other examples of art form by the fact that it was not written for public consumption. It represents a naïve attempt at self-analysis; an attempt at private honesty on the part of a high official of the British navy who in public life had to maintain a certain amount of official decorum.

Undoubtedly, his secret diary meant a great deal to Samuel Pepys. On its silent pages he at least could let down his hair, or rather take off his official wig, and give himself a true account of his feelings. It was not so much the language he used, nor yet the erotic subject matter, nor other intimate personal detail which he could not have shared with his more robust contemporaries, but rather that he could not confide extra-marital intimacies to his pathologically jealous wife: nor could he have burdened his family and friends with his conflicts of conscience about his peccadilloes, his attachments to some of his extra-marital loves, and his domestic humiliations on account of them.

All of these matters he could confide to his trusty *Diary,* to which he unburdened himself much as modern men and women are apt to do behind the sound-proofed doors of their psychoanalysts' consultation rooms. The *Diary* was Samuel Pepys' substitute for personal analysis, just as it has been for thousands of others before and after him. Finally, he was forced to yield even this last private retreat when, in later years, his eyesight began to fail him and he had to call upon the help of others to make the necessary entries. But without his *Diary,* Samuel Pepys would have been a lonelier man, and we would have been deprived of the gems of erotic realism from which we here present the following selection.

Excerpts from *The Diary of Samuel Pepys*

. . . I to Mrs. Ann, and Mrs. Jem, being gone out of the chamber, she and I had a very high bout, I rattled her up, she being in her bed, but she becoming more cool, we parted pretty good friends.

. . . Among other discourse held here, he told me how the pretty woman that I always loved at the beginning of Cheapside that sells child's coats was served by the Lady Bennett (a famous strumpet), who by counterfeiting to fall into a swoon upon the sight of her in her shop, became acquainted with her, and at last got her ends of her to lie with a gentleman that had hired her to procure this poor soul for him. To Westminster to My Lord's, and there in the house of office vomited up all my breakfast, my stomach being ill all this day by reason of the last night's debauch.

. . . To my Lord's . . . and telling me the story how the Duke of York hath got my Lord Chancellor's daughter with child, and that she do lay it to him, and that for certain he did promise her marriage, and she signed it with his blood, but that he by stealth had got the paper out of her cabinet. And that the King would have him to marry her, but that he will not. So that the thing is very bad for the Duke, and them all; but my Lord do make light of it, as a thing that he believes is not a new thing for the Duke to do abroad. Discoursing concerning what if the Duke should marry her, my Lord told me that among his father's many old sayings that he had wrote in a book of his, this is one—that he that do get a wench with child and marry her afterwards is as if a man should shit in his hat and then clap it on his head.

. . . thence to the Theatre, where I saw again "The Lost Lady," which do now please me better than before; and here I sitting behind in a dark place, a lady spit backward upon me by a mistake, not seeing me, but after seeing her to be a very pretty lady, I was not troubled at it at all.

. . . I took him to the Mitre and there did drink with him, and did get of him the song that pleased me so well there the other day, "Of Shitten comes Shites the beginning of love."

. . . After supper my father told me of an odd passage the other night in bed between my mother and him, and she would not let him come to bed to her out of jealousy of him and an ugly wench that lived there lately, the most ill-favored slut that ever I saw in my life, which I was ashamed to hear that my mother should become such a fool, and my father bid me to take notice of it to my mother, and to make peace between him and her.

. . . God forgive me, I was sorry to hear that Sir W. Pen's maid Betty was gone away yesterday, for I was in hopes to have had a bout with her before she had gone, she being very pretty. I had also a mind to my own wench, but I dare not for fear she should prove honest and refuse and then tell my wife.

. . . Coming home I brought Mr. Pickering as far as the Temple, who tells me the story is a very true of a child being dropped at the ball at Court; and that the King had it in his closett a week after, and did dissect it; and making great sport of it, said that in his opinion it must have been a month and three hours old; and that, whatever others think, he hath the greatest loss (it being a boy, as he says), that hath lost a subject by the business.

. . . being come to some angry words with my wife about neglecting the keeping of the house clean, I calling her beggar, and she me pricklouse, which vexted me.

. . . and in my way did take two turns forwards and backwards through the Fleet Ally to see a couple of pretty (strumpets) that stood off the doors there, and God forgive me I could scarce stay myself from going into their houses with them, so apt is my nature to evil after once, as I have these two days, set upon pleasure again.

. . . Mr. Batten telling us of a late Trial of Sir Charles Sydly the other day, before my Lord Chief Justice Foster and the whole bench, for his debauchery a little while since at Oxford Kate's,[1]

---

[1] The details in the original are very gross. Dr. Johnson relates the story in the *Lives of the Poets*, in his life of Sackville, Lord Dorset: "Sackville, who was then Lord Buckhurst, with Sir Charles Sedley and Sir Thomas Ogle, got drunk at the Cock, in Bow Street, by Covent Garden, and going into the balcony exposed themselves to the populace in very indecent postures. At last, as they grew warmer, Sedley stood forth naked, and harangued the populace in such profane language, that the publick indignation was awakened; the crowd attempted to force open the door, and being repulsed, drove in the performers with stones, and broke the windows of the house. For this misdemeanour they were indicted, and Sedley was fined five hundred pounds; what was the sentence of the others is not known. Sedley employed (Henry) Killigrew and another to procure a remis-

coming in open day into the balcone and showed his nakedness, . . . and abusing of scripture and as it were from thence preaching a mountebank sermon from the pulpit, saying that there he had to sell such a powder as should make all the (women) in town run after him, 1,000 people standing underneath to see and hear him, and that being done he took a glass of wine, . . . (urinated) in it and then drank it off, and then took another and drank the King's health. . . .

. . . Up and to the Wells (Epsom medicinal wells), where great store of citizens, which was the greatest part of the company, though there were some others of better quality. I met many that I knew, and we drank each us two pots and so walked away, it being very pleasant to see how everybody turns up his tail, here one and there another in a bush, and the women in their quarters the like.

. . . So homeward, and called at my little milliner's where I chatted with her, her husband out of the way, and a mad merry slut she is. So home to the office, and by and by comes my wife home from the burial of Captain Grove's wife at Wapping (she telling me a story how her mayd Jane going into the boat did fall down and show her arse in the boat).

. . . Up, and going out saw Mrs. Buggin's dog, which proves as I thought last night so pretty that I took him and the bitch into my closet below, and by holding down the bitch helped him to line her, which he did very stoutly, so as I hope it will take, for it is the prettiest dog that I ever saw.

. . . My Uncle Wight came to me to my office this afternoon to speak with me about Mr. Mae's business again, and from (there) went to my

sion from the King, but (mark the friendship of the dissolute!) they begged the fine for themselves, and exacted it to the last groat." The woman known as Oxford Kate appears to have kept the notorious Cock Tavern in Bow Street at this date.

house to see my wife, and strange to think that
my wife should by and by send for me after he
was gone to tell me that he should begin discourse
of her want of children and his also, and how he
thought it would be best for him and her to have
one between them, and he would give her 500 lb.
either in money or jewells beforehand, and make
the child his heir. He commended her body, and
discoursed that for all he knew the thing was law-
ful. She says she did give him a very warm answer,
such as he did not excuse himself by saying that
he said this in jest, but told her that since he saw
what her mind was he would say no more to her
of it, and desired her to make no words of it. It
seemed he did say all this in a kind of counterfeit
laugh, but by all words that passed, which I cannot
now so well set down, it is plain to me that he was
in good earnest, and that I fear all his kindness is
but only his lust to her. What to think of it of a
sudden I know not, but I think not to take notice
yet of it to him till I have thought better of it.

. . . But from thence walked toward Westminster, and being in an idle and wanton humour,
walked through Fleet Ally, and there stood a most
pretty wench at one of the doors, so I took a turn
or two, but what by sense of honour and conscience I would not go in, but much against my
will took coach and got away, and away to Westminster Hall, and there 'light of Mrs. Lane, and
plotted with her to go over the water. So met at
White's stairs in Chanel Row, and over to the
old house at Lambeth Marsh, and there eat and
drank, and had my pleasure of her twice, she being
the strangest woman in talk of love of her husband
sometimes, and sometimes again she do not care
for him, and yet willing enough to allow me a liberty of doing what I would with her. So spending
5s or 6s upon her, I could do what I would, and
after an hour's stay and more back again and set
her ashore there again, and I forward to Fleet
Street, . . .

. . . and so home, where I found my wife not

well, and she tells me she thinks she is with child,
but I neither believe nor desire it.

. . . So home, where my wife having (after all
her merry discourse of being with child) her
months upon her is gone to bed.

. . . I waked in the morning about 6 o'clock
and my wife not come to bed; I lacked a pot, but
there was none, and bitter cold, so was forced to
rise and piss in the chimney, and to bed again.
Slept a little longer, and then hear my people
coming up, and so I rose, and my wife to bed at
8 o'clock in the morning, which vexed me a little,
but I believe there was no hurt in it all, but only
mirthe, therefore took no notice.

. . . Here come in, in the middle of our discourse Captain Cocke, as drunk as a dogg, but
could stand, and talk and laugh. He did so joy himself in a brave woman that he had been with all
the afternoon, and who should it be but my Lady
Robinson, but very troublesome he is with his
noise and talke, and laughing, though very pleasant. With him in his coach to Mr. Glanville's where
he sat with Mrs. Penington and myself a good
while talking of this fine woman again and then
went away. Then the lady and I to very serious
discourse and, among other things, of what a bonny
lasse my Lady Robinson is, who is reported to be
kind to the prisoners, and she said to Sir G. Smith,
who is her great crony, "Look! there is a pretty
man, I would be content to break a commandment with him," and such loose expressions she
will have often. After an hour's talke we to bed,
the lady mightily troubled about a pretty little bitch
she hath, which is very sicke, and will eat nothing,
and the worst was, I could hear her in her chamber
bemoaning the bitch, and by and by taking her into
bed with her. The bitch pissed and shit abed, and
she was fain to rise and had coals out of my chamber to dry the bed again.

. . . and so took my wife and Betty Mitchell
and her husband, and away into the fields, to take
the ayre, as far as beyond Hackny, and so back

again, in our way drinking a great deale of milke, which I drank to take away my heartburne, where with I have of late been mightily troubled, but all the way home I did break abundance of wind behind, which did presage no good but a great deal of cold gotten. . . . I was mighty in pain all night long of the winde griping of my belly and making of me shit often and vomit too, which is a thing not usual with me, ...

. . . I will remember that Mr. Ashburnham to-day at dinner told how the rich fortune Mrs. Mallett reports of her servants; that my Lord Herbert would have had her; my Lord Hinchingbroke was indifferent to have her; my Lord John Butler might not have her, my Lord of Rochester would have forced her; and Sir Popham, who nevertheless is likely to have, would kiss her breach to have her. . . . I to see Mrs. Martin, who is very well, and intends to go abroad to-morrow after her childbed. She do tell me that this child did come la meme jour that it ought to hazer after my avoiye ete con elle before her marie did venir home . . . (the same day that it ought to have after my having been with her before her husband returned home). . . . Thence to the Swan, and there I sent for Sarah, and mighty merry we were. . . .

. . . He says that to this day the King do follow the women as much as ever he did; that the Duke of York hath not got Mrs. Middleton, as I was told the other day: but says that he wants her not, for he hath others, and hath always had, and that he (Povy) hath known them brought through the Matted Gallery at White Hall into his (the Duke's) closet; nay, he had come out of his wife's bed, and gone to others laid in bed for him; that Mr. Bruncker is not the only pimp, but that the whole family is of the same strain, and will do any thing to please him: . . . .

. . . and then to Mrs. Martin's, where I met with the good news que elle ne est con child, (that she is not with child) the fear of which she did give me the other day, had troubled me much. My joy

in this made me send for wine, and thither come
her sister and Mrs. Cragg, and I staid a good
while there. But there happened the best instance
of a woman's falseness in the world, that her sister
Doll, who went for a bottle of wine, did come home
all blubbering and swearing against one Captain
Vandener, a Dutchman of the Rhenish Wine
House, that pulled her into a stable by the Dog
tavern, and there did tumble her and toss her,
calling him all the roges and toads in the world,
when she knows that ell (she) hath suffered me
to do any thing with her a hundred times.

. . . Here Mrs. Pierce tells me that the two
Marshalls at the King's house are Stephen Marshall's, the great Presbyterian's daughters: and
that Nelly (Gwyn) and Beck Marshall, falling
out the other day, the latter called the other my
Lord Buckhurst's whore. Nell answered then, "I
was but one man's whore, though I was brought
up in a bawdy-house to fill strong waters to the
guests; and you are a whore to three or four,
though a Presbyter's praying daughter!" which was
very pretty.

. . . stopped at Martin's, my bookseller, where
I saw the French book which I did think to have
had for my wife to translate, called "L'escholle des
filles," but when I come to look at it, it is the
most bawdy, lewd book that I ever saw, rather-
worse than "Putana errante," so that I was shamed
of reading in it . . . (*L'Escole des Filles*, attributed
to an author by the name of Helot or Millot, was
burnt at the foot of the gallows in 1672, and the
author himself was burnt in effigy. *Putana errante*,
consisting of dialogues between two prostitutes, was
erroneously attributed to Pietro Aretino, but actually written by an anonymous author, probably
Lorenzo Veniero, a Venetian poet of the 16th
century.)

. . . We sat until almost night, and drank
mighty good store of wine, and then they parted,
and I to my chamber, where I did read through
"L'escholle des filles," a lewd book, but what do

no wrong once to read for information sake. . . .
And after I had done it, I burned it, that it might
not be among my books to my shame, and so at
night to supper and to bed.

. . . turned into St. Dunstan's Church, where
I heard an able sermon of the minister of the
place; and stood by a pretty, modest, maid, whom
I did labour to take by the hand and by the body;
but she would not, but got further and further
from me; and, at last, I could perceive her to take
pins out of her pocket to prick me if I should
touch her again—which seeing I did forbear, and
was glad I did spy her design. And then I fell
to gaze upon another pretty maid in a pew close
by, and she on me; and I did go about to take
her by the hand, which she suffered a little and then
withdrew. So the sermon ended, also, and so took
coach and home, and there took up my wife, and
to Islington with her. . . .

. . . Mr. Moor told me of a picture hung up at
the Exchange of a great pair of buttoks shooting
of a turd into Lawson's mouth, and over it was
wrote "the thanks of the house." Boys do now cry
"Kiss my Parliament," instead of "Kiss my
(rump)," so great and general a contempt is the
Rump come to among all the good and bad.

. . . after supper, to have my head combed by
Deb., which occasioned the greatest sorrow to me
that ever I knew in this world, for my wife, coming
up suddenly, did find me embracing the girl. . . . I
was at a wonderful lose upon it, and the girle also,
and I endeavoured to put it off, but my wife was
struck mute and grew angry, and so her voice come
to her, grew quite out of order, and I to say little,
but to bed, and my wife said also little, but could
not sleep all night, but about two in the morning
waked me and cried, and fell to tell me as a great
secret that she was Roman Catholique and had
received the Holy Sacrament, which troubled me,
but I took no notice of it, but she went on from
one thing to another till at last it appeared plainly
her trouble was at what she saw, but yet I did not

know how much she saw, and therefore said nothing to her. But after much crying and reproaching me with inconstancy and preferring a sorry girl before her, I did give her no provocation, but did promise all fair usage to her and love, and foreswore any hurt that I did with her, till at last she seemed to be at ease again and so toward morning a little sleep, and so I with some little repose and rest.

Rose, and up . . . , but with my mind mightily troubled for the poor girle, whom I fear I have undone by this, my (wife) telling me that she would turn her out of doors.

Thence by coach and home and to dinner, finding my wife mightily discontented, and the girle sad, and no words from my wife to her. . . and my wife full of trouble in her looks, and anon to bed, where about midnight she wakes me, and there falls foul of me again, affirming that she saw me hug and kiss the girle; the latter denied, and truly, the other I confessed and no more, and upon her pressing me did offer to give her under my hand that I would never see Mrs. Pierce more nor (Mrs.) Knepp, but did promise her particular demonstrations of my true love to her, owning some indiscretions in what I did, but that there was no harm in it. She at last upon these promises was quiet, and very kind we were, and so to sleep, and. . . .

. . . so by coach, it being now dark, I to her, (Deb), close by my tailor's and she come into the coach with me, and je did baiser (I kissed her) her. . . . I did nevertheless give her the best council I could, to have a care of her honour, and to fear God, and suffer no man para avoir to do con her as je have done, (to do with her what I had done) which she promised. Je (I) did give her 20s. and directions para laisser (to leave) sealed in paper at any time the name of the place of her being at Herringman's, my bookseller. . . , by which I might go para (to) her, and so bid her good night with much content to my mind, and resolution to look after her no more till I heard from her. And so home, and there told my wife a fair tale, God knows, how I spent the whole day.

So to my wife's chamber, and there supped, and got her cut of my hair and look my shirt, for I have itched mightily these 6 or 7 days, and when all comes to all she finds that I am lousy, having found in my head and body about twenty lice, little and great, which I wonder at, being more than I have had I believe these 20 years.

. . . I must forebear; and, therefore, resolve, from this time forward, to have it (the diary) kept by my people in longhand, and must therefore be content to set down no more than is fit for them and all the world to know; or, if there be any thing, which cannot be much, now my amours to Deb. are past, and my eyes hindering me in almost all other pleasures, I must endeavour to keep a margin in my book open, to add, here and there, a note in short-hand with my own hand.

It is well to note at this point that *The Diary of Samuel Pepys* constitutes the most reliable source of historical and psychological information among all the writers here considered. As previously indicated, Pepys made his diary entries immediately, or shortly after, the events of which he writes, which feature alone assures us of a much greater degree of accuracy than, let us say, the reminiscent type of autobiography such as that of Frank Harris, or of Casanova.

Among all the exponents of erotic realism in this book, the *Diary* contains the least amount of fantasy material and the highest percentage of almost compulsive detail. We shall see in Casanova's *Mémoires* a much greater flair for artistic literary effect and therefore a charm which is lacking in the factual reportage of Pepys. On the other hand, the artistic loss through compulsive attention to insignificant detail on the part of Pepys is compensated for by a much higher degree of authenticity.

CASANOVA—CHAMPION OF REALISTIC ROMANCE

Giacomo Casanova de Seingalt lived, loved, and rarely labored between 1725 and 1798. He wrote the world's most famous erotic autobiography. It is by no means the most erotic, yet it is more than the guardian eunuchs of the Western Temple of Morality could let pass uncastrated.

The relative mildness and sometimes even bashfulness of Casanova's *Mémoires* may not be his fault after all. Nobody has ever read the complete manuscript of his diary. Even the most complete French, German and English editions of his works have been edited to some extent.

As to the erotic content, we cannot help but feel that while it may have been difficult for Casanova to draw a clear line between truth and fiction even in his own mind, let alone for the benefit of others, his accounts show a remarkable degree of erotic realism.

The most obvious difference between Casanova's *Mémoires* and, say, Pepys' *Diary,* is that the aging Casanova was definitely writing for an imaginary audience, while Pepys was merely holding counsel with and for himself. In spite of this, Casanova's *Mémoires* remains one of the most important sources for the cultural historian, and especially for the student of sexual customs, the psychologist, and the sexologist.

Casanova furnishes us with several stories of sexual activities involving multiple partners, which are rare, if not altogether absent, even in the most realistic of the later erotic autobiographies, though they do occur occasionally, as, for instance, in *My Life and Loves*, by Frank Harris. The reason for this may be that such sexual encounters have generally been rare in the sexual behavior of modern Western civilization. However, in antiquity, and in the Orient, multiple sexual relations were frequently a part of religious ceremonial, or were taken for granted as being part of normal social rela-

tions. It may not be generally recognized that even in
Casanova's time, such sexual relations were not altogether uncommon, and that his *Mémoires* therefore
represent a point of view and report on social customs
which were not unique to the writer, but which are a
reflection of sexual customs as they actually existed.

At one point in his *Mémoires,* we find Casanova and
his agent on their way to the second rendezvous with
three beautiful young girls whom the agent had procured
for the great lover. The story goes as follows:

> We found the three girls lightly clad and sitting
> on a large sofa, and we sat down opposite to them.
> Pleasant talk and a thousand amorous kisses occu-
> pied the half hour just before supper, and our
> combat did not begin till we had eaten a delicious
> repast, washed down with plenty of champagne.
>
> We were sure of not being interrupted by the
> maid and we put ourselves at ease, whilst our
> caresses became more lively and ardent. The syndic
> (agent), like a careful man, drew a packet of fine
> French letters from his pocket, and delivered a long
> eulogium on this admirable preservative from an
> accident which might give rise to a terrible and
> fruitless repentance. The ladies knew them, and
> seemed to have no objection to the precaution;
> they laughed heartily to see the shape these articles
> took when they were blown out. But after they had
> amused themselves thus for some time, I said:
>
> "My dear girls, I care more for your honour than
> your beauty; but do not think I am going to shut
> myself in a piece of dead skin to prove that I am
> alive." "Here," I added, drawing out the three
> golden balls, "is a surer and a less disagreeable way
> of securing you from any unpleasant consequences.
> After fifteen years' experience I can assure you that
> with these golden balls you can give and take with-
> out running the least risk. For the future you will
> have no need of those humiliating sheaths. Trust
> in me and accept this little present from a Venetian
> who adores you."

"We are very grateful," said the elder of the two sisters, "but how are these pretty balls used?"

"The ball has to be at the rear of the temple of love, whilst the amorous couple are performing the sacrifice. The antipathy communicated to the metal by its being soaked for a certain time in an alkaline solution prevents impregnation."

"But," said the cousin, "one must take great care that the ball is not shaken out by the motion before the end of the sacrifice."

"You needn't be afraid of that if you place yourself in a proper position."

"Let us see how it's done," said the syndic, holding a candle for me to put the ball in place.

The charming cousin had gone too far to turn back; she had to submit to the operation. I placed the ball in such a position that it could not fall out before I was in; however, it fell out towards the end, just as we were separating. The victim perceived that I had taken her in. However, she said nothing, picked up the ball and challenged the two sisters to submit to the pleasant experiment, to which they lent themselves with the greatest interest; while the syndic, who had no faith in the virtues of the metal, contented himself with looking on. After half an hour's rest I began again, without balls, assuring them that I would be careful, and I kept my word, without depriving them of the pleasure in the slightest degree.

When it was time to part, these girls, who had formerly been scantily provided for, threw their arms around my neck, overwhelmed me with caresses, and declared how much they owed me. The syndic told them that I was going in two days, and suggested that they should make me stay a day longer in Geneva, and I made this sacrifice joyfully. The worthy syndic had an engagement on the following day, and I sorely needed a holiday myself. He took me back to my inn, thanking me almost as heartily as his charming nymphs.

(As to the golden balls which Casanova had the

girls insert into their vaginas, supposedly as a contraceptive, he had them specially made for this purpose, each weighing 2 ounces, and intended to be used as a tactful way of paying the girls who were from good, but financially-restricted families.)

On another occasion, we find Casanova in Geneva, walking in the garden and giving two young ladies, Hedvig, a pastor's niece, and Helen, her cousin, a practical lesson in sex education. The scene takes place after a dinner and some drinking of wine and liqueurs. The girls go wading in a pool and Casanova dries their legs, which causes an erection which he lets the girls feel through his trousers. He then leads the girls into a summer house, and sitting down between them, continues his lecture on male anatomy.

. . . as I caressed them I told them that I was going to show them something they had never seen before, and without more ado, I displayed to their gaze the principal agent in the preservation of the human race. They got up to admire it, and taking a hand of each one I procured them some enjoyment, but in the middle of their labours an abundant flow of liquid threw them into the greatest astonishment.

After some further mutual exhibition and fondling, Casanova reports:

Placing them in front of me I gave them another ecstasy. We then sat down, and while I felt all their charms I let them touch me as much as they liked till I watered their hands a second time.

We made ourselves decent once more, and spent half an hour in kisses and caresses, and then I told them that they had made me happy only in part, but that I hoped they would make my bliss complete by presenting me with their maidenheads. I shewed them the little safety-bags invented by the English in the interests of the fair sex. They admired them greatly when I explained their use, and (Hedvig) remarked to her cousin that she would think it over.

This story is significant as a specimen of erotic realism in Casanova, for he is one the very few writers who mentions not only contraceptives and their use, but who also describes an ejaculation, complete with reference to the semen and the girls' reactions to it.

A few days later, Casanova reports that during his second bout with the same two girls he made up for what he had not been able to accomplish during their first meeting. The scene takes place in the girls' home:

"Do you two go to bed," said Helen, "I will sleep on the sofa."

"No, no," cried Hedvig, "don't think of it; our fate must be exactly equal."

"Yes, darling Helen," said I, embracing her; "I love both with equal ardour, and these ceremonies are only wasting the time in which I ought to be assuring you of my passion. Imitate my proceedings. I am going to undress, and then I shall lie in the middle of the bed. Come and lie beside me, and I will show you how I love you. If all is safe I will remain with you till you send me away, but whatever you do, do not put out the light."

In the twinkling of the eye, discussing the theory of shame the while with the theological Hedvig, I presented myself to their gaze in the costume of Adam. Hedvig blushed and parted with the last shred of her modesty, citing the opinion of St. Clement of Alexandrinus that the seat of shame is in the shirt. I praised the charming perfection of her shape, in the hope of encouraging Helen, who was slowly undressing herself; but an accusation of mock modesty from her cousin had more effect than all my praises. At last this Venus stood before me in a state of nature, covering her most secret parts with one hand, and hiding one breast with the other, and appearing woefully ashamed of what she could not conceal. Her modest confusion, this strife between departing modesty and rising passion, enchanted me.

Hedvig was taller than Helen; her skin was whiter, and her breasts double the size of Helen's; but in Helen there was more animation, her shape was more gently moulded, and her breast might have been the model for the Venus de Medicis.

She got bolder by degrees, and we spent some moments in admiring each other, and then we went to bed. Nature spoke out loudly, and all we wanted was to satisfy its demands. With much coolness I made a woman of Hedvig, and when all was over she kissed me and said that the pain was nothing in comparison with the pleasure.

The turn of Helen (who was six years younger than Hedvig) now came, but the finest fleece that I have ever seen was not won without difficulty. She was jealous of her cousin's success, and held it open with her two hands; and though she had to submit to great pain before being initiated into the amorous mysteries, her sighs were sighs of happiness, as she responded to my ardent efforts. Her great charms and the vivacity of her movements shortened the sacrifice, and when I left the sanctuary my two sweethearts saw that I needed repose.

The altar was purified of the blood of the victims, and we all washed, delighted to serve one another.

Life returned to me under their curious fingers, and the sight filled them with joy. I told them that I wished to enjoy them every night till I left Geneva, but they told me sadly that this was impossible.

"In five or six days time, perhaps, the opportunity may recur again, but that will be all."

"Ask us to sup at your inn tomorrow," said Hedvig; "and maybe, chance will favour the commission of a sweet felony."

I followed this advice.

I overwhelmed them with happiness for several hours, passing five or six times from one to the other before I was exhausted. In the intervals, seeing them to be docile and desirous, I made them execute Aretin's most complicated postures, which amused them beyond words. We kissed whatever took our fancy, and just as Hedvig applied her lips to the mouth of the pistol, it went off and the discharge inundated her face and her bosom. She was delighted, and watched the process to the end with all the curiosity of a doctor. The night seemed short, though we had not lost a moment's time, and at day-break we had to part. I left them in bed and I was fortunate enough to get away without being observed.

At one time Casanova meets by chance a nun who turns out to be not only pregnant, but apparently is also related to one of Casanova's former sweethearts. Incredible as this may seem, Casanova vouches for the veracity of the story, which is, in any event, a true example of erotic realism.

Almost immediately after the young nun has been secretly delivered of her child (she had managed to get away from her convent under some pretext), Casanova, who has become her benefactor, visits her at the rustic guest house where she has been staying during her confinement. As usual, Casanova makes sure they are served a good supper with plenty of good wine, after which he finds himself close to the aim of all his efforts.

Casanova says about this event in his *Mémoires:*

When we were alone I congratulated her on her high spirits, telling her that my sadness had fled before her gaiety, and that the hours I could spend with her would be all too short.

"I should be blithe," she said, "if it were only to please you."

"Then grant me the favour you accorded me yesterday evening."

"I would rather incur all the excommunications in the world than risk of appearing unjust to you. Take me."

So saying, she took off her cap, and let down her beautiful hair. I unlaced her corset, and in the twinkling of an eye I had before me such a siren as one sees on the canvas of Correggio. I could not look upon her long without covering her with my burning kisses, and, communicating my ardour, before long she made a place for me beside herself. I felt that there was no time for thinking, that nature had spoken out, and that love bade me seize the opportunity offered by that delicious weakness. I threw myself on her, and with my lips glued to hers I pressed her between my amorous arms, pending the moment of supreme bliss.

But in the midst of these joys, she turned her head, closed her eyelids, and fell asleep. I moved away a little, the better to contemplate the treasures that love displayed before me. The nun slept, as I thought; but even if her sleep was feigned, should I be angry with her for the stratagem? Certainly not; true or feigned, the sleep of a loved one should always be respected by a delicate lover, although there are some pleasures he may allow himself. If the sleep is real there is no harm done, and if it is put on the lover only responds to the lady's desires. All that is necessary is so to manage one's caresses that they are pleasant to the beloved object. But M M was really asleep; the claret had numbed her senses, and she had yielded to its influence without any ulterior motives. While I gazed at her I saw that she was dreaming. Her lips muttered words which I could not catch the meaning, but her voluptuous aspect told me of what she dreamt. I took off my clothes, and in two minutes I had clasped her fair body to mine, not caring much whether she slept on or whether I awoke her and brought our drama to a climax, which seemed inevitable.

I was not long uncertain, for the instinctive movements she made when she felt the minister that would fain accomplish the sacrifice at the door of the sanctuary, convinced me that her dream still lasted, and that I could not make her happier than by changing it into reality. I delicately moved away all obstacles, and gently and by degrees consummated this sweet robbery, and when at last I abandoned myself to all the force of passion, she awoke with a sigh of bliss, murmuring:

"Ah, it is true then."

"Yes, my angel! are you happy?"

For all reply she drew me to her and fastened her lips on mine, and thus we awaited the dawn of day, exhausting all imaginable kinds of pleasure, exciting each other's desires, and only wishing to prolong our enjoyment.

The next night, Casanova suddenly becomes worried about the possibility of another pregnancy on the part of his libertine nun. He says:

When we were both in a state of nature, exactly like Adam and Eve before they tasted the fatal apple, I placed her in the position of the portrait, and guessing my intention from my face she opened her arms for me to come to her; but I asked her to wait a moment, for I had a little packet too, which contained something she would like.

I then drew from my pocket-book a little article of transparent skin, about eight inches long, with one opening, which was ornamented with a red rosette. I gave her this preventive sheath, and she looked, admired, and laughed aloud, asking me if I had used such articles with her Venetian sister.

"I will put it on myself; you don't know how I shall enjoy it. Why didn't you use one last night? How could you have forgotten it? Well, I shall be very wretched if anything comes of it. What shall I do in four or five months, when my condition becomes past doubt?"

As the impious sister puts the rosette-adorned contraceptive on Casanova, she remarks:

". . . There you are, hooded like a mother abbess, but in spite of the fineness of the sheath I like the little fellow better quite naked. I think that this covering degrades us both."

"You are right, it does. But let us not dwell on these ideas, which will only spoil our pleasure."

"We will enjoy our pleasure directly; let me be reasonable now, for I have never thought of these matters before. Love must have invented these little sheaths, but it must first have listened to the voice of prudence, and I do not like to see love and prudence allied."

"The correctness of your argument surprises me, but we will philosophize another time."

"Wait a minute. I have never seen a man before, and I have never wished to enjoy the sight as much as now. Ten months ago, I should have called this article an invention of the devil; but now I look upon the inventor as a benefactor, for if my wretched hump-back had provided himself with such a sheath he would not have exposed me to the danger of losing my honour and my life. But tell me, how is it that the makers of these things remain unmolested; I wonder that they are not found out, excommunicated, or heavily fined, or even punished corporeally, if they are Jews as I expect. Dear me, the makers of this one must have measured you badly! Look! it is too large here, and too small there; it makes you into a regular curve. What a stupid fellow he must be, he can't know his own trade! But what is that?"

"You make me laugh; it's all your fault. You have been feeling and fondling, and you see the natural consequence. I knew it would be so."

"And you couldn't keep it back a minute. It is going on now. I am so sorry; it is a dreadful pity."

"There is not much harm done, so console yourself."

"How can I? You are quite dead. How can you laugh?"

"At your charming simplicity. You shall see in a moment that your charms will give me new life which I shall not lose so easily."

"Wonderful! I couldn't have believed it!"

I took off the sheath, and gave her another, which pleased her better, as it seemed to fit me better, and she laughed for joy as she put it on. She knew nothing of these wonders. Her thoughts had been bound in chains, and she could not discover the truth before she knew me; but though she was scarcely out of Egypt she showed all the eagerness of an inquiring and newly emancipated spirit.

"But how if the rubbing makes the sheath fall off?" she said.

I explained to her that such an accident could scarcely happen, and also told her of what material the English made these articles.

After all this talking, of which my ardour began to weary, we abandoned ourselves to love, then to sleep, then to love again, and so on alternately till daybreak.

The above-quoted excerpt is significant in distinguishing erotic realism from hard core obscenity in that it describes sexual relations with a recently delivered woman. Preceding this in the *Mémoires,* Casanova tells of his attraction to the highly pregnant girl, which is another feature almost never found in obscene writing. Also, surrounding the quoted excerpts we find in the original text details concerning the delivery of the baby and other realistic, anti-erotic material (e.g., in connection with the condom) which any pornographer worthy of the name would never introduce into his (fantasy) story.

Before leaving Casanova and his *Mémoires,* we shall quote once more from him:

Then came the oyster-game, and I scolded Armelline for having swallowed the liquid as I was taking the oyster from her lips. I agreed that it was very hard to avoid doing so, but I offered to show them how it could be done by placing the tongue in the way. This gave me an opportunity of teaching them the game of tongues, which I shall not explain because it is well known to all true lovers.

Armelline played her part with such evident relish that I could see she enjoyed it as well as I, though she agreed it was a very innocent amusement.

It so chanced that a fine oyster slipped from its shell as I was placing it between Emilie's lips. It fell on to her breast, and she would have recovered it with her fingers; but I claimed the right of regaining it myself, and she had to unlace her bodice to let me to it. I got hold of the oyster with my lips, but did so in such a manner as to prevent her suspecting that I had taken any extraordinary pleasure in the act.

Armelline looked on without laughing; she was evidently surprised at the little interest I had taken in what was before my eye. Emilie laughed and relaced her bodice.

The opportunity was too good to be lost, so taking Armelline on my knee I gave her an oyster and let it slip as Emilie's had slipped, much to the delight of the elder, who wanted to see how her young companion would go through the ordeal.

Armelline was really as much delighted herself, though she tried to conceal her pleasure.

"I want my oyster," said I.

"Take it then."

There was no need to tell me twice, I unlaced her corset in such a way as to make it fall still lower, bewailing the necessity of having to search for it with my hands.

What a martyrdom for an amorous man to have to conceal his bliss at such a moment!

I did not let Armelline have any occasion to accuse me of taking too much license, for I only touched her alabaster spheres so much as was absolutely necessary.

When I had got the oyster again I could restrain myself no more, and affixing my lips to one of the blossoms of her breasts I sucked it with a voluptuous pleasure which is beyond all description.

She was astonished, but evidently moved, and I did not leave her till my enjoyment was complete.

When she marked my dreamy languorous gaze,

she asked if it had given me much pleasure to play the part of an infant.

"Yes, dearest," I replied, "but it's only an innocent jest."

"I don't think so; and I hope you will say nothing about it to the superioress. It may be innocent for you, but it is not for me, as I experienced sensations which must partake of the nature of sin. We will pick up no more oysters."

"These are mere trifles," said Emilie, "the stain of which will easily be wiped out with a little holy water. At all events we can swear that there has been no kissing between us."

We feel that the examples which we have given demonstrate the extreme psychological and historical usefulness of this type of autobiographical material. Granted that Casanova may have embellished his stories here and there, one cannot help but sense their intrinsic value and essentially realistic nature.

If we think, for example, of the "oyster-game" in the last cited anecdote, we are struck by the immediacy with which Casanova transports us directly into the spirit and customs of his time. On less than a page this little erotic miniature paints for us a more striking picture of the customs which prevailed in a certain group of upper- and middle-class men and women during the 18th century than a whole history text crammed full of facts and dates could possibly accomplish.

Somehow, these powdered and be-wigged figures of another era become more real to us through Casanova's *Mémoires* than our next-door neighbors, and the sole reason for this is that we have come to know them as sexual human beings, entirely like ourselves. (See W. O. Maxey, *Man Is A Sexual Being*, in which the author develops this point of view into a systematic theory of sexual behavior in terms of existentialist philosophy.)

THE MEMOIRS OF AN ENGLISH CASANOVA

At the height of the Victorian era (say, roughly between 1820 and 1890), there lived in London a curious, unknown Englishman whose fame as a lover will, we are sure, some day eclipse that of Casanova. When that happens, it may well alter the concept which other nationalities harbor about the supposedly phlegmatic sexuality of the Anglo-Saxon race. It may also shock the Nordics themselves into the realization that in erotic potential and fervor they are by no means inferior to the reputedly hotter blooded races of the South. For although Walter wrote primarily about himself, many other people were involved in his exploits, his attitudes and his behavior: indeed, his work adds immeasurably to all that is known of sexuality in the time of Queen Victoria.

About Walter himself we know that he was an upper-middle class Englishman who lived, at the time indicated, in or around London (when not travelling abroad in search of erotic pleasures); that he claimed he worked briefly for the War Ministry; that he soon resigned to devote himself more fully to the pursuit of amorous adventure; that he was enabled to do so by the inheritance of several moderate fortunes, all but the last of which he successively disposed of in the course of his erotic career; and that he was for some time unhappily married, until he became a widower. He does not speak much about his marriage, since it had little to do with his erotic life. We know furthermore, if we may trust his own estimate, that he made love to a record number of some 1,200 women (not counting those with whom he had other sexual contacts short of intercourse): and above all, that he left us his erotic autobiography, entitled *My Secret Life,* comprising eleven volumes with a total of some 5,000 pages of printed text!

These eleven volumes are today among the rarest and most costly books in the world. Only three copies of the entire eleven volume set are known to exist today: one in private hands on the European continent, one in England in a private collection which has been willed to the library of the British Museum, and one at the Institute for Sex Research (Kinsey Institute) in America.

This unique literary document bears indeed, as we are told in an Introduction by the author, "the impress of truth on every page." Such remarkable frankness becomes understandable when we realize that he used the device, very common in erotic writing, of concealing his identity by claiming that he was only the editor and publisher of the work, not its author or the person whose experiences it concerns.

Actually, the eleven volumes of *My Secret Life* represent a re-write and condensation of the author's diary and notes: "I began these memoirs when about twenty-five years old," he tells us, "having from youth kept a diary of some sort, which, perhaps from habit, made me think of recording my inner and secret life."

It is not without interest that among the motivating factors contributing to the writing and publication of Walter's erotic autobiography was the prior appearance of another book, and one which has over the past two centuries of English literary history, become the most widely read and banned book of all times, the famous *Fanny Hill, or Memoirs of A Woman of Pleasure.*

The author of *My Secret Life,* who disliked pornography because of its fantastic exaggerations and falsifications, was much impressed with the plausible, authentic descriptions of sexual relations in *Fanny Hill.* He even thought it not impossible that the book, as its title implied, had been written by the woman whose adventures it purported to recount: *"Fanny Hill* was a woman's experience," he says, "written perhaps by a woman. Where is the story of a man, written with equal truth?"

He felt, however, that *Fanny Hill* had one particular

fault, lying precisely in the quality which most others have considered to be its primary virtue—the absence of four-letter words! "That book has not a single bawdy word in it," he noted, "but bawdy acts need the full-flavored erotic expressions that even the chastest indulge in, when lust or love is in its full tide of performance. So I determined to write my private life freely as to fact, and in the spirit of lustful acts done by me or witnessed."—(Of this objective we cannot give the reader more than an inkling by occasionally bracketing the more acceptable synonyms for the expressions used by Walter.)

As if to explain the enormous amount of work and trouble to which he went in order to produce the monumental work of his memoirs, without any hope of reward or recognition (in contrast to his famous predecessor, Casanova de Seingalt) he adds the following revealing passage:

I had from my youth an excellent memory, but about sexual matters, a wonderful one. I recollect even now to a degree which astonishes me, the face, color, stature, thighs, backside, and vagina of well nigh every woman I have had, who was not a mere casual, and even of some who were. I had before me mentally as I wrote, the clothes they wore, the houses and rooms in which I had them, the way the bed and furniture were placed, on what side of the room the windows had been, and so forth. Besides, I was able to fix by reference to my diary, in which the contemporaneous circumstances of my life were recorded, just about every incident sufficiently nearly with regard to time.

I also recollect by and large not only what was done, but also what was said between the women and myself, and in those few instances where my memory did fail me, I have preferred to leave out details of our conversation or bawdy amusements, rather than attempting to make the story more coherent by inserting that which was merely probable.

For the same reason, I have refrained from trying to explain my course of action, or why I did this, or said that, even though my conduct very frequently seems strange, foolish, and absurd to me now, and that of some of the women equally so. Only in a few cases where the facts by themselves seemed in restrospect even to me very improbable (though I have wilfully exaggerated nothing), have I suggested reasons or causes for my own or other people's actions.

I may occasionally have been in error where I have mentioned the number of times that I made love to one or the other woman in my youth: it is difficult to be quite accurate on such points after a lapse of time. But, as before said, in many cases, the incidents were, during that period, written down a few weeks, and often within a few days after they occurred, and in these instances, are quite reliable. Still, I do not attempt to pose as a Hercules in copulation. There are quite sufficient braggarts on that head, though much conversation with gay women and doctors makes me doubt the wonderful feats in coition that some men like to tell of.

As a matter of fact, one of the features which distinguished the English Casanova from some of the other lovers famous in history is precisely this absence of any sexual braggadoccio. Casanova de Seingalt, for instance, was never reluctant to celebrate and revel in his own feats of sexual prowess, and was proud of his reputation as "Monsieur Six-fois" (Mr. Six-times). In the same manner, Frank Harris enjoyed singing his own praises in his autobiography *My Life and Loves*. But the author of *My Secret Life,* although far from putting his light under a bushel, seems, like Henry Miller, to have had no need for self-aggrandizement along these lines.

So much, in fact, was the English Casanova concerned with the veracity and completeness of his autobiography —again, in notable parallel to Henry Miller—that he refused to delete incidents from the manuscript which were not apt to put his character in the best light even with those who might have shared his tastes. He made scrupulous efforts to be honest even though he was far from indifferent to the criticism and moral censure of his fellow men: "I have one fear about publishing my memoirs," he confesses, "and that is of having done a few things by curiosity and impulse which even professed libertines may cry fie on. Yes, I know they will cast stones at me, even though they themselves may habitually have done all that I have done, and worse. But crying out at the sins of others has always been a way of hiding one's own iniquities."

Fortunately, Walter, or the English Casanova, as we have come to call him almost automatically in the course of our thorough immersion in his memoirs, did not allow his fears to get the better of him and thus destroy so valuable a record. (We intend to discuss these memoirs in greater detail in subsequent publications.) *My Secret Life* is certainly a remarkable piece of work in at least three respects.

First, it is *the only genuine erotic autobiography* published that has come to our attention. All other autobiographical writings which *include* sexual experiences (and even these are rare enough) are written from other points of view, and contain much material that has nothing to do with sexual matters. These works therefore, cannot strictly speaking be considered as erotic autobiographies. In contrast, *My Secret Life,* focuses directly on the author's sexual experiences with the deliberate purpose of recording all of his thinking, feelings and actions in this area. This of course enormously enhances its scientific value as a psychological document.

Second, the English Casanova's autobiography furnishes, like those of Pepys, Casanova de Seingalt, Harris, and, some day, undoubtedly the writings of Henry Miller and those of other contemporary writers, a faithful mirror and useful yardstick of comparison for the changes in sexual customs and social attitudes concerning sexuality that take place from century to century and from generation ot generation. This is undoubtedly the reason why *The London Sunday Times* of February 16,

1964, speaks of this work as "The . . . extremely valuable eleven volume Victorian work *My Secret Life,* a treasure house of information about nineteenth century sexual mores."

Third, and perhaps most important of all, the life of the English Casanova, as reflected in his autobiography, represents by its diametrical reversal of all the values and standards concerning sexuality which are commonly held or professed by Western society, a most serious challenge to those social values and standards themselves.

For that reason we have placed less emphasis on the sexual pathology that was, in certain respects, quite obviously involved in this case. Instead, we have taken the existentialist approach to the problem of evaluating so absolutely unique and—to our common ways of thinking—unsettling a life and personality as that of the English Casanova. For here was a man who, unlike most of his fellow men, did not place family, business, profession, security or "future" first, that is, the commonly accepted values and goals to be striven for in our kind of society. Instead, be reversed the normal order of things by placing all such considerations second, and his sexual happiness first and foremost in his life.

Two representative episodes from *My Secret Life* will demonstrate perhaps better than any amount of theoretical discussion the points we have been trying to make about this extraordinary work. The incidents selected illustrate the times and mores of the England of *Fanny Hill* and well into the following century, and are therefore relevant and applicable to our discussion of that work as well.

The first incident concerns the English Casanova's relationship with two young girls of about "Fanny's" age when she started her career as a London prostitute and who, like her, were obliged through economic hardships to supplement the family income by selling their special youthful sex appeal. Thus, we read in Volume III of *My Secret Life:*

I don't know why my erotic fancies took the desire for a young lass, but they did. My tastes had for the most part run upon the big, fleshy, fat and large-arsed; now perhaps for contrast, perhaps from sheer curiosity, the letch took possession of me. A small one, tight and hairless perhaps—I wondered how it looked, felt, and if pleasure would be increased by it. I had never had a very young girl —Nellie and Sophie had both a little hair on their mottes, so I would try for a youthful quim and one if possible with no hair on it.

I was not versed in the walks and ways of little ones, and looking about at night saw none. Talking about it at my club, I heard they were to be seen mostly in the day time, so I looked out in the Strand for what I wanted, and during daylight.

(Note that he is quite matter-of-fact about openly, even casually, seeking advice on this seemingly special interest, indicating that it was not, in fact, so unusual at the time, and was certainly totally acceptable to his social peers.)

On a blazing hot afternoon in June I walked about a long time thinking of youthful harlots, but saw none, or if I did, could not distinguish them. At length I saw two young girls idling about, looking in at the shop windows on the other side of the way. One was dressed all in black, and was taller and stouter than the other. They were not got up in any showy way, but looked like the children of decent mechanics.

They took no notice of anyone, nor was anyone taking notice of *them*. They stopped at a shop, and I noticed that the biggest one had the largest legs. A plump form had, as said, attractions to me almost superior to face. Crossing to the other side of the way, I passed them, looking them full in the face. The taller one was good looking, white faced, and had goldenish hair, a colour I could not bear. They looked at me, but there was nothing to indicate fastness. Returning, I met them again, and again they gave me the same stare, the same indifference. So, thinking of their little vaginas, and getting randy and reckless, I determined to try. They stopped at a sweetmeat shop; going to their side, and looking into the shop, not at them, so as to prevent my being noticed, I said, "I'll buy you whatever you want if you will come with me." The bigger of the two edged away from me, after looking up in my face, whispered something to her companion, and they both moved along the street, without seeming to pay any further attention to me.

I was disconcerted, and went over to the opposite side of the way, again watching them. They went to a print shop and looked in: then the big one looked in the direction of the sweet shop and up and down the street. She was looking after me evidently, so I crossed over, met them full face, and as I passed said, without stopping, "Come with me, and I'll give you money."

I turned the corner, and looked, they were at another shop, the bigger girl with her arm round the smaller one's neck. I again passed them, going back to do so, and saying "I'll give you three and sixpence." That was the exact sum, and then turned up a street which led to a bawdy house, and waited at the turning into the street.

The two girls turned the corner, stopped, and talked. The bigger one laid hold of, and slightly pulled the smaller, and seemed to be trying to persuade her. Failing apparently, she left her, but turned back, spoke to her again, and both came on together. Then I turned into a back street, the two girls appeared at the corner of that, and then stopped and talked for a minute. Tired of waiting, I thought I had made a mistake, and going slowly back heard the bigger one say, "You are a fool! Oh! You fool! Come, he wants us."

"I don't want her," said I. "But you, come," and returning, entered a bawdy house, the outer door of which stood open, thinking the bigger one would follow, and sure now that she was a harlot. I then passed through the inner door which, as was usual, had a glass window covered with a red curtain.

A minute elapsed, the bawdy house keeper had been spoken to, but the girl not coming, I opened the door to look out. The bigger girl was just inside the outer door, and was pulling in the other one. "Come you fool—you said you would—he'll give you money as well as me, and I'll give you some of mine too—well, you are a fool," quite bawling it out. There was not much secrecy needed in such things at those times, in those streets.

"I don't want her," said I hurriedly, "it's you. Come in, or I won't wait." She came in, the other girl disappeared, and we were soon in a bedroom together.

It was the first house at that end of the street, had been newly opened, and was furnished in a style not like a bawdy house; no show, neat and clean, but cheaply; no bed hangings (and in those days most bawdy houses had bed hangings), the blinds were new and white, the beds quite clean. The top floor room where I went for economy was two shillings and sixpence. The woman of the house was tall, homely, and middle aged. As I paid her, I noticed she had fat red cheeks. How curious that I should recollect those red cheeks. She had a white apron on, and was civil sort of creature.

The girl stood still staring at me. Sitting on the edge of the bed I stared at her, filled with bawdy curiosity and appreciation of novelty. "Why don't you have the other girl?" said she. "I don't want her, nor want two—and she is a dirty little imp." "No she ain't dirty, she washes herself like me. Let her come up." "No—come here." "She is quite clean, I wash her myself sometimes." "No—come here I tell you."

The girl came to me dawdling. I put my hand up her clothes. A fleshy little bum met my hand, then, in the front, a smooth belly, and a motte, almost hairless as it seemed. She said not a word, but gave a sort of jerk of her body, and as my hand touched her bum, it jutted forward. In the same manner, as I drew my hand round to her belly, she pulled her belly back. It did not seem like shame. She did not utter a word. "Take off your things," said I.

She drew away from me, and took off her bonnet, then she stood still. "Off with your things," I said, throwing off some of mine. "I can't take them off. If I do I can't fasten them again, they are in a knot." "Take them off." "If I do, you will have to fasten me." "So I will." Slowly she stripped to her chemise. "Take that off." "I won't." "Come here then." She came. Laying hold of her, I lifted her bodily, and threw her with her back on the bed, throwing up her chemise and stretching open her legs quickly. She gave a suppressed "hoh"—put her hand down to her vagina, and felt her mons nervously.

"Take away your hand, dear." She took it away . . . such a delicious little gap it was, with the smallest possible quantity of golden hair just show-ing on it; such a smooth white belly and thighs, and also plump, though I was wonderstruck at a young girl being so round and fine. I had not expected under that shabby black clothing any-thing so nice. I was charmed with her head also; in her big black and shabby bonnet I had seen nothing but a white face and large blue eyes. Her hair was golden in tone, bright and flowing.

Whilst pulling off my trousers, she sat up and asked, "Is it big?" For the instant I did not quite know what she meant. "Is what big?" "Your thing." "Measure it." I went up to her, pulling out my pego. "It is big" said she. "It's little," said I. "It ain't—it's big." "No." "Yes, don't push hard sir, will you now?" "No, my dear, I won't. Is it bigger than other men's [penises]?" "Shan't tell yer." "Well, lay down and open your thighs," said I, lifting her onto the bed. "Don't do it hard," said she, getting up again, "or I won't let you." "Then I won't pay you." Back she fell, I wetted my machine, put it to the notch, and with a shove or two was well up her. She gave a "oh!—oh!" and then lay quiet. Grasping her fat little bum, I began, then stopping, pulled out my penis, and looked at her vagina. "What are you goin' to do?" she said in an astonished way.

"Get quite onto the bed, dear." Slow at obeying, I helped her into the posture, and got onto her, and got my pleasure to an end, lying on top of the pretty little girl.

I lay on her long afterwords, and tried by the muscular contraction of my backside and bollocks to stiffen my pego again. She lay quiet all the time . . . but I could not manage it, and my machine shrunk.

A second erection without withdrawing being impossible, I got into a kneeling posture between her open legs, and checked a slight movement on her part saying, "Now lie quiet—don't move." There was I, kneeling between her thighs . . . [There follows a brief description of her vagina, the seminal fluid and manipulation of the flaccid penis]. She lay quite quiet, looking at me, her yellow hair falling all around her head as it lay on the pillow. Now I was astonished at her beauty, I had not noticed it fully before.

"You are very handsome—how old are you?" "Fifteen and a little." "You must be more." "I don't know, but mother said so." I looked at her quim, the hair on it was not an eighth of an inch long, there was scarcely any, and of course showing no intention of curling, but her form was so round that I could not believe she was so young. "Fifteen and a little," she repeated, her aunt and mother had been disputing the day of her birth; her mother was out of her mind when she gave birth to her. "Aunts says I ain't fifteen."

"Give the other gal a shilling—do," she broke in, whilst I was questioning her about age. "What are you so anxious about the other girl for?" "She lives over us, and is my friend, will you give her a shilling? Do." "Why?" "Do. If you don't, I shall give her a shilling of mine, and give her some of mine anyhow—you said you'd give me three and sixpence, didn't you?"

Curiously amused, I laughed. "I'll give you a shilling for her, if you let me do it to you again." "Oh! Do," said she.

It was hot, I had not reposed after my pleasure, so quitting my kneeling position, I lay down beside her, and began feeling her breasts. She turned her head towards me. "You have not washed yourself," said I after a minute's amusement with her bubbies. "It ain't no good if you are going to make a mess in it again. When you've done it, I'll wash it all off together." I thought from that speech she was not an old one at the game, but after all she only behaved as every young girl I have subsequently had usually behaves; they have mostly objected to washing themselves directly afterwards, I think they rarely wash until requested. There must be some sweet tranquilising pleasure that it gives to them and makes them undesirous of washing it out. It is only when a woman knows it is good for her health, if she be gay, that she ever does it. No married woman washes it out of her, yet in the morning after a night, you never find it there. Where does it go? It is absorbed I suppose.

We lay thus and talked. "How old are you really?" "Fifteen and two months, as I told yer. I always was fat, but ain't so fat as I was; father used to say I should get fat on gruel." I should have guessed her full sixteen, had it not been for the little hair there was on her motte, and the delicate pink small cut and tight penis hole. "How long have you been gay?" "I ain't gay," said she astonished. "Yes, you are." "No, I ain't." "You let men [make love to you], don't you?" "Yes, but I ain't gay." "What do you call gay?" "Why, the gals who come out regular of a night, dressed up, they get their livings by it," she said. I was amused.

"Don't you go out at night?" I asked. "No, mother keeps me." "What is your father?" "Got none, he's dead three months back, mother works, and keeps us. She's a charwoman, and goes out on odd jobs." "Don't you work?" "Not now," said she in a confused way. "Mother does not want me to, I take care of the others." "What others?" "The young ones." "How many?" "Two, one's a boy and one's a gal." "How old?" "Sister's about six, and brothers nearly eight, but what do you ask me all this for?" "Only for amusement—then you are in mourning for your father?" "Yes, it's shabby, ain't it? I wish I could have nice clothes, I've got nice boots, ain't they?"—cocking up one leg—"a lady gived 'em to me when father died, they are my best."

"Are you often in the Strand?" "When I gets out, I likes walking, and looking at the shops I do, if mother's out for the day." "Does she know you are out?" The girl, who had been lying on her back with her head full towards me, turned on her side, and giggling said in a sort of confidential way, "Bless you, no! She'd beat me if she knew—when she be out, I locks the young 'uns up, and takes the key, and make sure to be home before mother—she is out for the whole day."

"Do the children know you are out?" "No, I says to them, you be quiet now, I'm going to the yard." "What's the yard?" said I, not reflecting. The girl thought a minute, chuckled, turned her head, was silent and actually blushing. "What's the yard?" I repeated. Suddenly it struck me, "Going to the privy?" She burst out laughing. "Yes, that's it, I say I'm going to the privy. They can't get out so they are all right." She stopped satisfied with her explanation. "They may set fire to themselves," said I. "There ain't no fire after we have had breakfast, I puts it out, and lights it at night, if mother wants hot water."

"What do you do with yourself all day?" "I washes both of them, I gives them food if we've got any, then washes the floor and everything, and then washes myself, then I looks out the winder." "Wash yourself?" "Yes I washes from head to foot allus." "Have you a tub?" "No, we've only got a pail and a bowl, but I'm beautiful clean, mother tells everyone I'm the beautifullest clean gal a mother ever had—I wash everything, mother's too tired. Sometimes we all go out and walk, but that's at night; sometimes I lay abed nearly all day."

She was beautifully clean in her flesh, her linen was clean, its color awful; but what could be expected from a pail, a bowl, and one room to dry things in. "You can't always be washing." "No I do all the mending and making—look how my finger is pricked," said she, showing it.

I had been smoothing and feeling her all over . . . we turned to the never failing and always charming theme, I got close to her, I kissed her, my fingers sought the innermost recesses of the tight little orifice. "Don't you like [making love]? Does it give you pleasure?" I asked. "It never gives me much pleasure that I know of," she replied. "But you don't dislike it?" "No, if they don't hurt me." "Do they ever?" "One or two have, if they pushes hard, but I shan't say no more—so!"

There was a frankness, openness, and freshness about this girl which delighted me. Question after question I put, and would be answered; if evaded, I put it in another shape, but she seemed willing mostly to reply. I put into her little head things she had never dreamed of, and all the time kept rubbing her clitoris, probing her little quim, distending it, tickling it, and exciting her till she wriggled her little fat bum.

"Do I hurt you?" "Oh! No—" "Let me then—" "Oh! Don't sir—I wish you would not." "Did you never enjoy [making love]? You shall enjoy it with me." "Don't now," said she turning herself around as I kept on playing with her . . . I talked on, rubbing and tickling, my penis throbbing, but restraining myself, for instinct told me she was about to enjoy a pleasure she had never enjoyed yet. All at once she relinquished my penis, a slight heaving of her belly, her eyes closed, and she was ready to discharge.

I ceased playing with her, her eyes opened, her thighs which had closed, opened again. I joined my body to hers, and we were one. Thus I started making love to her, she being passive at first, but soon answering my thrusts with her own wriggles, and in a minute or two the little lass was dissolving in pleasure, whilst I was ejaculating in her, groaning as the tightness of her little vagina squeezed my sensitive penis. And I know for a cert, if Kitty had not been a harlot before, she was from that minute she had her spend with me.

She lay quite quiet till nature dissolved our fleshy union, then I lay by her side, she on her back, her thighs wide open, and her eyes closed. "Don't it give you pleasure?" After repeating that half a dozen times, she said, "I don't know." "Yes you do; did you spend?" "I don't know what a girl spending is," said she. "Did my pego give you pleasure, tell me please?" At length she said yes, and she never had had pleasure with men before. (Two years afterwards she repeated that the first pleasure she ever had with a man was with me). "Wash yourself." "I wash when I go home." "Wash now, you little beast." "What does it matter to you?" "Wash, you little devil." She washed carefully . . .

The Victorian era was a time when the double standard was in full flower. The false front of preposterous rectitude maintained by professedly respectable people flourished beside, and indeed fed, innumerable bawdy houses, bagnios, brothels and establishments of sexual commerce which abounded in London. Class differences were distinct and the working classes poor indeed. The prostitution of young girls was common; in fact, the proprietor of the bawdy house makes only the revealingly matter-of-fact condition that the English Casanova pay double fee when coming with two girls. Incidentally, the passage also throws an interesting light on the nature and function of these houses of assignation, making their description in *Fanny Hill* all the more credible as they coincide in every detail with those given in *My Secret Life*.

As far as the sexual precocity of many girls of that age is concerned, the descriptions in both *Fanny Hill* and in *My Secret Life* are entirely in keeping with the findings of the Kinsey group of researchers, as well as our own and those of others (see F. K. Vigman's study, *The sexual precocity of young girls in the United States*: International Journal of Sexology, 6: 90-91).

The second episode from *My Secret Life* which we are about to quote concerns a humorous scene in a London bagnio, or bath-house, in which the English Casanova attempts intercourse under water and finds the task a great deal more difficult than he had expected.

ON MAKING LOVE UNDER WATER

As was his habit, the English Casanova liked to discuss matters relating to sex with women who had more than average experience and did not mind talking about them. So, one day, while engaged in that kind of discussion with a woman by the name of Betsy, he says, "the subject turned to baths, and she asked if I had ever had a woman in a bath. 'It takes a good man to make love under the water,' she said."

Walter's curiosity was, of course, immediately aroused. He enquired further into the matter from the girl and, when she told him that she knew of a place where he could try, he immediately made an appointment with her for "soon after."

In James Street, not far from my favorite bawdy house, there was a small building, on the outside window of which there was written in large letters the word "BATHS." There were indeed public baths in that place, but I expect that the paying part of the business was really the double bath to which only the initiated had access.

Betsy told me not to go in with her, for men and women never went in together, but to wait a few minutes, as she had to see if a bath was ready, and let the keeper know who to expect. I did as told, and was soon in a comfortable little room, where Betsy was awaiting me.

Against the wall was a bath like any other bath, but large enough for two. Hot and cold water could be turned on at pleasure. There were several different-sized, large, flat cushions, covered with soft leather and something smooth, intended to be placed at will on the bath, for bum, back, knees, or head.

We soon stripped and filled the bath to a height just enough to cover our bodies, and got into it together. Having heard from Betsy of the difficulty, I had kept myself from making love for a few days. Lying by her side, I began to feel her. She told me the more I let the water up the more trouble I might have.

I soon began the work, but to my annoyance, could not get up her comfortably, for though she had felt well moistened before, she now seemed all dry inside. She laughed, reminding me of what she had said before about this sport.

I now arranged the cushions differently, raising her up higher, and ran in more water, so that I might get at it more readily. But I found that I had to let some water out, then run more in again, for either it covered her too much, or it covered me too little. Then her head was too low, and so on and so forth.

At length, all being carefully adjusted after much time and trouble, I again tried to mount her under the water. But this time, the motion sent the water up in waves, slopping all over my face, and directly afterwards, one of the pillows slipped away from under us, sending her head clean under the water and my face into it as well, filling my nose, and I slipped right out of her, for as little as I had been inside of her to begin with.

We got out, dripping wet and both annoyed— Betsy, because she didn't want her hair wet, and I because I hadn't succeeded in my task. So we went in again and tried this and that for a longish time, but nothing seemed to work. Finally, I got out again, this time angry and swearing, while she rose too, laughing. But having come to make love under the water, and not out of it, I began readjusting the water level, so as to cover both of us.

The problem now was to get the water at the right temperature, for it was either too cold, or too hot, and it was not easy to regulate, but at length it was right. With difficulty I then got up her under the water, when the cushion on which her hands were placed as she knelt, slipped away. It had shifted only a little bit, but anyone floats so easily, that directly she had lost her pose, down she went on her belly, her head clean under the water again, down I sank on top of her, and out I slipped, of course, as before.

We both got out of the bath, and I thought how next to proceed. "I told you, it took a good man to do it in the water," said she, and so I had found out. But I was determined to do it, and knew that I should be able to accomplish it. Again I tried various positions, but the water, acting prejudiciously, had caused her to lose all lubricity, so that at length it was impossible for me to get into her at all when under the water.

She began to feel chilly, and so did I. We therefore stirred the fire and made the water hotter. When it was all ready, we got in again and tried, but no luck either. I got furious. Betsy suggested she do me under the water, but I would not hear of it. I asked her, however, whether she had ever masturbated herself under it. She said no, but she would try, and she began, the water surging all about, as her hand moved under the surface. "You see, I can," said she, wanting to continue, but I pulled her hand away and suspended the operation, for I wanted her to spend with me.

At length, determined to do it somehow, we put the water very shallow, and did it kneeling, until our mutual pleasure was just increasing. Then I turned her on her back (for she wanted to do it under water as well as I), and she raised her behind slightly up, lifting me with it. I quickly withdrew the pillow beneath her, she sank under the water, which just covered her and me now, and so we made love with our organs in the water, only her breasts and my back remaining out of it.

Afterwards, we rapidly dried ourselves and jumped into a bed that was placed in the room and which had had a warmer in it. Then we rang the bell and ordered some warm brandy and we lay in bed talking over our odd adventure and the difficulties of aquatic copulation.

"Good lord," said Betsy, "one time in a bed is worth fifty in a bath, my dear, but you did manage and finished in it. You're the fourth man who has been in the water with me, but the only one who spent under the water; the others were just outside of it. You've got something to be proud of. I'll have to tell Mary S. (a colleague)."

Thus ended Walter's "underwater poke." Apparently he did not try to repeat the performance, for he makes no further references to this method in his memoirs.

The English Casanova's bagnio story is again reminiscent of a similar passage in Cleland's *Fanny Hill* which describes a love-bout of Fanny's in the water, but that incident takes place outdoors in natural surroundings rather than in a bath house, and is, moreover, unsuccessful.

There are many other parallels between the two books, too numerous, in fact, to be discussed here. Suffice to say that the sexual mores had not changed very significantly between Cleland's time and that of the English Casanova "Walter." This is all the more remarkable since the same time interval had seen the enormous social changes that accompanied the industrial revolution. In fact, however, English sexual mores did not change radically until after the first World War.

It is in this historical perspective that we must try to understand both *My Secret Diary* as well as Cleland's realistic background descriptions to *Fanny Hill*. If we do this, the behavior of the people concerned, regardless of whether set forth in the context of historically realistic fiction, or in the form of a factual diary, is not only totally credible, but becomes a source of valuable information on various levels of social or psychological enquiry.

FRANK HARRIS—UNHOLY FIGHTER FOR THE HOLY SPIRIT OF TRUTH

In the foreword to his autobiography, *My Life and Loves,* Frank Harris explains what motivated him to write his memoirs in the way he did, without pulling any punches, and without regard to his own or anybody else's reputation. The only stipulation he made was that the separate volumes of his chronologically arranged autobiography should be so published that none of the other persons involved in his most personal experiences should still be alive at the time of their publication.

In regard to identity of purpose, many of the reasons which Frank Harris gives for writing his autobiography as he did could well have been included in the preface to this book. We shall therefore quote from his writing the portion which is most directly to the point:

I have always fought for the Holy Spirit of Truth and have been, as Heine said he was, a brave soldier in the Liberation War of humanity: now one fight more, the best and the last.

There are two main traditions of English writing: the one of perfect liberty, that of Chaucer and Shakespeare, completely outspoken, with a certain liking for lascivious detail and witty smut; a man's speech; the other emasculated more and more by Puritanism and, since the French Revolution, gelded to tamest propriety; for that upheaval brought the illiterate middle-class to power and insured the denomination of girl-readers. Under Victoria, English prose literally became half childish, as in stories of "Little Mary," or at best, provincial, as anyone may see who cares to compare the influence of Dickens, Thackeray and Reade in the world, with the influence of Balzac, Flaubert and Zola.

Foreign masterpieces such as *Les Contes Drolatiques* and *L'Assommoir* were destroyed in London as obscene by a magistrate's order; even the Bible and Shakespeare were expurgated and all books dolled up to the prim decorum of the English Sunday-School. And America with unbecoming humility worsened the disgraceful, brainless example.

All my life I have rebelled against this old maid's canon of deportment, and my revolt has grown stronger with advancing years.

In the Foreword to *The Man Shakespeare,* I tried to show how the Puritanism that had gone out of the morals had gone into the language, enfeebling English thought and impoverishing English speech.

At long last I am going back to the old English tradition. I am determined to tell the truth about my pilgrimage through this world, the whole truth and nothing but the truth, about myself and others, and I shall try to be at least as kindly to others as to myself.

Bernard Shaw assures me that no one is good enough or bad enough to tell the naked truth about himself, but I am beyond good and evil in this respect.

French literature is there to give the cue and inspiration; it is the freest of all in discussing matters of sex and chiefly by reason of its constant preoccupation with all that pertains to passion and desire, it has become the world literature to men of all races.

"Women and Love," Edmond de Goncourt writes in his journal, "always constitute the subject of conversation wherever there is a meeting of intellectual people socially brought together by eating and drinking. Our talk at dinner was at first smutty (polisonne) and Tourgueneff listened to us with the open-mouth wonder . . . of a barbarian who only makes love . . . very naturally . . ."

Whoever reads this passage carefully will understand the freedom I intend to use. But I shall not be tied down even to French conventions. . . .

I intend to tell what life has taught me, and if I

begin at the ABC of love, it is because I was brought up in Britain and the United States; I shall not stop there.

Of course I know the publication of such a book will at once justify the worst that my enemies have said about me. . . . In itself the book is sure to disgust the "unco guid" and the mediocrities of every kind who have always been unfriendly to me. I have no doubt, too, that many sincere lovers of literature who would be willing to accept such license as ordinary French writers use, will condemn me for going beyond this limit. Yet there are many reasons why I should use perfect freedom in this last book.

W. L. George in *A Novelist on Novels,* writes: "If a novelist were to develop his characters evenly the three hundred page novel might extend to five hundred, the additional two hundred pages would be made up entirely of the sex preoccupations of the characters. There would be as many scenes in the bedroom as in the drawing-room, probably more, as more time is passed in the sleeping apartment. The additional two hundred pages would offer pictures of the sex side of the characters and would compel them to become alive: at present they often fail to come to life because they only develop, say five sides out of six. . . . Our literary characters are lop-sided because their ordinary traits are fully portrayed while their sex-life is cloaked, minimized or left out. . . . Therefore the characters in modern novels are false. They are megalocephalous and emasculate. English women speak a great deal about sex. . . . It is a cruel position for the English novel. The novelist may discuss anything but the main preoccupation of life. . . . We are compelled to pad out with murder, theft and arson which, as everybody knows, are perfectly moral things to write about."

Pure is the snow—till mixed with mire—
But never half so pure as fire.

There are greater reasons than any I have yet given why the truth should be told boldly. The time has come when those who are, as Shakespeare called them, "God's spies," having learned the mystery of things, should be called to counsel, for the ordinary political guides have led mankind to disaster: blind leaders of the blind!

Over Niagara we have plunged, as Carlyle predicted, and as every one with vision must have foreseen, and now like driftwood we move round and round the whirlpool of impotency without knowing whither or why.

One thing is certain: we deserve the misery into which we have fallen. The laws of this world are inexorable and don't cheat! Where, when, how have we gone astray? The malady is as wide as civilization. . . .

Harris begins the sexual part of his autobiography with a reminiscence from his fourth year. He remembers accidentally catching the maid in bed with a man and then using his knowledge to blackmail the maid for childish favors, such as more sugar on his bread and butter.

Between four and five, Frank Harris was sent to a girls' boarding school and put in class with the oldest girls, because of his proficiency in arithmetic. He remembers how the nearest girl used to lift him up into his high-chair, how he used to hurry through the long lines of division and multiplication, "and then turn round and climb down out of my chair, ostensibly to get it (a pencil) but really to look at the girls' legs. Why? I couldn't have said."

Harris tells how he used to be at the bottom of the class, but that the girls' legs got bigger and bigger towards the end of the long table, and how he preferred to look at the big ones. In order to get a good look at them, he had invented the little game described above, in which he would drop his pencil and then look for it under the table.

"One day," Harris recalls, "I noticed a beautiful pair of legs on the other side of the table, near the top. There must have been a window behind the girl; for her legs up to the knees were in full light and they filled me with emotions giving me an indescribable pleasure. They were not the thickest legs, which surprised me. Up to that moment I had thought it was the thickest legs I liked best; but now I saw that several girls, three anyway, had bigger legs, but none like hers, so shapely, with such slight angles and tapering lines. I was enthralled and at the same time a little scared."

Young Harris was so impressed by this experience that he could think of nothing else, but devised a further plan to get another close-up view of these wonderful legs and possibly to get to touch them. He says, "Next day I again crouched before the girl's legs, choking with emotion. I put my pencil near her toes, and reached round between her legs with my left hand as if to get it, taking care to touch her calf. She shrieked, and drew back her legs, holding my hand tight between them, and cried: 'What are you doing there?'—'Getting my pencil,' I said humbly, 'it rolled.' 'There it is,' she said, kicking it with her foot. 'Thanks,' I replied, overjoyed for the feel of her soft legs was still on my hand. 'You are a funny fellow,' she said, but I didn't care; I had had my first taste of Paradise and the forbidden fruit—authentic heaven!"

Harris says he did not remember this girl's face, nor did any of the other girls make any deep impression on him. But he clearly remembered the thrill of admiration and the pleasure which her shapely legs gave him.

Frank Harris comments, "I record this incident at length, because it stands alone in my memory, and because it proves that sex-feeling may show itself in early childhood."

This, and the next remembrance, almost read like voluntarily submitted case studies in support of Sigmund Freud's *Three Contributions to the Theory of Childhood Sexuality*. We hold them to be genuine recollections, and if anything, more trustworthy than some of Harris' later accounts of sexual experiences because they are clearer by reason of their isolation in memory. To us, they seem totally credible and make Frank Harris' orientation toward women and the important role which sexuality played throughout his life much more understandable.

Harris says he did not have another sensation of sex until nearly six years later, when he was about eleven. At that time, his sister Annie—or Nita, as she liked to be called—had just undressed their little sister Chrissie for bed, when, as Harris recalls, "she opened her own dress and showed us how her breasts had grown while Chrissie's still remained small, and indeed 'Nita's' were ever so much larger and prettier and round like apples. Nita let us touch them gently and was evidently very proud of them. She sent Chrissie to bed in the next room while I went on learning a lesson beside her. Nita left the room to get something, I think, when Chrissie called me and I went into the bedroom wondering what she wanted. She wished me to know that her breasts would grow too, and be just as pretty as Nita's. 'Don't you think so?' she asked, and taking my hand put it on them, and I said, 'Yes' for indeed I liked her better than Nita who was all airs and graces and full of affectations."

Harris somewhat contradictorally claims that he learned nothing from this incident. He professes that he had "hardly any sex-thrill with either sister, indeed, nothing like so much as I had had, five years before, through the girls' legs in Mrs. Frost's school. . . ." Apparently, the incest taboo was sufficiently strong even in Harris' case to block out the erotic feelings in connection with his own sisters which must have been present for the incident to impress itself so vividly upon his memory.

About the same time—Harris was still eleven—two of his older friends, Howard and Strangways, gave him some theoretical and practical sex education. His friend Howard told him of the pleasures of masturbation, but Harris says that "in spite of his novel reading," he was still too young to get much pleasure from the practice. However, he says, he was delighted to know how children were made and to hear a lot of new facts about sex.

Harris recalls that both of his friends had hair about their genitalia, and that when Strangways was masturbating and the orgasm came, "a sticky milky fluid spurted from [his penis] which Howard told us was the man's seed, which must go right into the woman's womb to make a child."

A week later, Strangways astonished both Harris and his friend Howard by telling them how he had made up to the nursemaid of his younger sisters and had managed to get into bed with her. His realistic description of what had transpired between him and this girl so fired the imagination of his listeners, that, as Harris says, they gave themselves "to a bout of [masturbation] which for the first time thrilled me with pleasure." Harris says that while he and his friend Howard were "playing with themselves," he "kept thinking of Mary's [sex organ] as Strangways had described it, and at length a real orgasm came and shook me; the imagining had intensified my delight." Adds Harris, "Nothing in my life up to that moment was comparable in joy to that story of sexual pleasure as described, and acted for us, by Strangways."

The above quotations from Harris' early sexual reminiscences are of importance to us from several points of view. As already indicated, it seems as though Harris was volunteering his own early recollections in support of the Freudian theory of infantile sexuality, though he never mentions Freud anywhere in his autobiography, nor did he seem in the least influenced by the new psychoanalytic movement which was just beginning to make itself strongly felt about that time.

It is also of interest to note that the early sexual experiences of Frank Harris were in no wise out of the ordinary and that in spite of Harris' interest in sexuality, the variety and frequency of his sexual activities was by and large well within Kinseyan norms. For example, outside of the cited instance during his adolescence, Harris does not speak of any other homosexual experiences. On the other hand, his intellectual curiosity in general and for sexual matters in particular, as well as his unusual degree of sexual freedom, caused him to experiment with some varieties and techniques of sexual behavior which are not within the range of most people's experience.

Let us then consider some of the adult sexual experiences of Frank Harris. He tells us, for instance, about his relationship with a certain uneducated, but very pretty girl, Rose. As he was driving to the theater with her, he tried to kiss her in the buggy. Rose told him that she didn't care much for kissing, adding that she felt all men were alike, wanting a girl only "for the same thing."

Harris patiently informs her that with men physical desire usually comes first, with love and affection following, while with the woman liking and affection come first.

We hear how, on succeeding dates, Rose began to allow Harris, bit by bit, the little familiarities of love, until one day he took her out for a picnic and suggested the two play a little game in which Harris would be a sultan and she a harem girl, bringing him goodies and waiting on him, while he was stretched out on a blanket under a lovely tree.

In such seductive circumstances, we are not surprised to hear that:

> . . . at length, as she stood close beside me, I couldn't control myself; I put my hand up her dress on her firm legs and sex [Harris' pet term for the female genitals]. Next moment I was kneeling beside her: "Love me Rose," I begged, "I want you so: I'm hungry for you, dear!"

But the girl was not yet ready to yield to his passionate advances. He tells how she looked at him gravely with wide-open eyes, affirming her love for him, but confessing that she was afraid and asking him to be patient with her. Harris was patient, but did not forget to keep pressing his attack. He went on caressing her until, he says, her hot lips told him that he had really excited her and she was ready for intercourse.

Harris seemed to have felt himself well rewarded for his patience and continued efforts, for he adds:

> . . . in her yielding there was the thrill of a con-

scious yielding out of affection for me, which I
find it hard to express.

There were other times with Rose, but while always
praising her beauty and physical perfection, Harris was
continually comparing every one of his women with
their predecessors. He never failed to find at least some
flaw in body or personality which made him ever look
for the still more perfect model of his female ideal.

About Rose, he said in this connection:

She had the best figure I had ever seen and that
made me like her more than I would have thought
possible; but I soon found when I got into her that
she was not nearly as passionate as Kate even, to
say nothing of Lily.

Another time, Harris was the student and the woman
his teacher. He tells how he met a charming girl in
Paris whom he wined and dined lavishly before taking
her home. He surmised that the girl, far from being
prudish or virginal, was a professional. He says:

I thought I might risk connection; but when I got
her to take off her clothes and began to caress her
sex, she drew away and said quite as a matter of
course: "Why not 'faire minette'?" [French collo-
quialism for cunnilingus.]

Harris was not prepared for this turn of events and
hesitated. Thereupon the girl lectures him:

"We women do not get excited in a moment as
you men do; why not kiss and tongue me there for
a few minutes then I shall have enjoyed myself and
shall be ready. . . ."

But Harris was not ready, and after some little argument, he finally said, " 'No, little lady, your charms are
not for me'," sat down at the table and poured himself

some wine. He admits that he still had "the ordinary English or American youth's repugnance to what seemed like degradation. . . ."

A few years later, Harris met another girl, this time in Greece, who had similar tastes, but by this time he was equal to the challenge. He tells how he first wanted to have his normal form of intercourse with her, but found resistance to this on the part of the girl. Here is how Harris tells of this experience in the second volume of his autobiography:

She had dropped her dressing-gown, had only a nightie on and in one moment my hands were all over her body. The next moment I was with her in bed and on her; but she moved aside and away from me. "No, let's talk," she said. I began kissing her but acquiesced: "Let's talk." To my amazement she began: "Have you read Zola's latest book, 'Nana'?" "Yes," I replied. "Well," she said, "you know what the girl did to Nana?" "Yes," I replied with sinking heart. "Well," she went on, "why not do that to me? I'm desperately afraid of getting a child, you would be too in my place, why not love each other without fear?" A moment's thought told me that all roads lead to Rome and so I assented. . . .

As one may have expected, Harris subsequently persuaded this girl to also try vaginal intercourse with him, and he vividly describes his activities and the girl's reactions to her first complete coitus. But, as Harris says, the couple—

. . . always practiced the game she had been the first to teach me; for some reason or other, I learned more about women through it and the peculiar ebb and flow of their sensuality than the natural love-play had taught me; it gives the key, so to speak, to a woman's heart and senses and to the man this is the chief reward as wise old

Montaigne knew, who wrote of "standing at rack and manger before the meal."

Harris was apparently more curious than even most psychologists about women's sexual attitudes, for he says he was always trying to win confessions from his girl friends about their first experiences in sensuality. To his regret, he was not very successful in that respect, except for a few French girls and an occasional actress. "What the reason is," Harris shrugs, "others must explain; but I found girls strangely reticent on the subject."

We must, however, give Harris credit for trying, because he kept asking the same girl, Eireen, who had taught him to overcome his prejudice against cunnilingus, about her earlier sex life "time and time again" when in bed with her. Finally, she did tell him of one adventure which took place when she was about twelve. One day her governess came into the bathroom, offering to help her dry herself. "I noticed," said Eireen, "that she looked at me intently and it pleased me. When I got out she wrapped the robe about me and then sat down and took me on her knees and began to dry me. As she touched me often there, I opened my legs and she touched me very caressingly and then of a sudden kissed me passionately on the mouth and left me. I liked it very much. . . ."

When Harris wanted to know whether and how often she had repeated the experience, Eireen turned coy, and merely said, "You want to know too much, Sir," and would not reveal any more about it. It is surprising, though, that it never occurred to Harris that there might have been a connection between this girl's preference for cunnilingus and her earlier Lesbian experiences which she had admittedly enjoyed.

Anyway, Harris says he "found several unlooked-for and unimaginable benefits in this mouth-worship." (He had previously commented that he experienced in kissing and orally caressing the girl's vulva only another lovely mouth.)

He continues:

First of all, I could give pleasure to any extent without exhausting or even tiring myself. It thus enabled me to atone completely and make up for my steadily decreasing virility. Secondly, I discovered that by teaching me the most sensitive parts of the woman I was able even in the ordinary way to give my mistresses more and keener pleasure than ever before. I had all the joy of coming into a new kingdom of delight with increased vigor. Moreover, as I have said, it taught me to know every woman more intimately than I had known any up to that time and I soon found that they liked me better than even in the first flush of my inexhaustible youth.

In the above quotations, Frank Harris first openly admits his difficulties in overcoming his strong initial prejudice against the practice of cunnilingus. Later, he anticipates our modern marriage manuals from Dr. van de Velde's *Ideal Marriage* to Dr. Eustace Chesser's *Love Without Fear,* by accepting this mouth-genital technique as a natural and enjoyable variation or as a form of foreplay in sexual intercourse.

Harris' self-commitment to absolute honesty in his autobiography obliged him to tell of his failures as well as of his successes with women. We hear, therefore, of his vain attempts to seduce an Irish girl by the name of Molly, because she could not face the prospect of having to confess her sin to the priest, besides being afraid of becoming pregnant in spite of the fact that Harris had demonstrated to her the use of the syringe. These scruples did not, however, prevent her from permitting Harris to admire and fondle her many times in the nude and to allow him every intimacy, "except that."

One cannot help but be amused when Harris tells us of how he used all of his considerable sexological knowledge without moving Molly to give in. He observed her behavior so closely that he discovered the girl was especially excitable every month about the eighth day after her menses had ceased. But even this intimate knowledge of Molly's physiological response did not bring him the final victory:

> One night I was half insane, so I promised to do nothing and thus got permission to lie on her, intending if necessary to use a little force. "That's nothing," I repeated, "nothing," as I rubbed my sex on her clitoris; "I'm not going in." But suddenly she took my head in her hands and kissed me; "I trust you, dear, you are too good to take advantage of me," and as I pressed forward, she said quietly, "You know, I'd kill myself if anything happened." At once I drew away; I couldn't speak, could hardly think!

In another place, Harris tells how, after seeing his long-time sweetheart in the company of another man, he went into a mad frenzy of jealousy and self-accusation for having somehow failed her in his affections. In this state of despair, his pretty Irish maid Bridget finds him sulking in his study. She gives him sympathy and interests him in a supper of cold grouse, one of his favorite dishes.

> As she stood by me after helping me to something, I put my arm around her, and nothing loth, our eyes and then our lips met. Soon I found she cared for me and this spontaneous affection did me good, took the unholy rage and bitterness out of me and brought me back to quiet thoughts and sanity. To cut a long story short, I consoled myself with Bridget's affection and fresh prettiness. . . .

We submit that not many men would admit to such unflattering experiences as the last two. In Molly's case, the author describes himself as utterly selfish until the girl had so cornered him emotionally that he was not able to complete his designs on her. In the second instance, he risks the accusation of fickleness and poor taste by consoling his wounded masculine pride with the maid. We therefore have to give Harris much credit for this kind of ego-deflating honesty which balances the many equally self-complimentary references in his books.

In another place, we find a perfectly delightful story about a discussion on love and love-making which he had with the great French novelist, Maupassant. The latter claimed that writers or artists make better lovers than laboring men, provided the "eggheads" keep themselves in good health. "It needs brains," Maupassant argued, "to give another the greatest possible amount of pleasure."

Harris advanced the idea that youth was the chief condition of success, but Maupassant would not hear of it. He claimed that "a dozen consecutive embraces" were nothing extraordinary. When Harris jokingly reminded him of Monsieur Six-Times in Casanova, the famous Frenchman would not accept even that authority. "Six times!" he cried contemptuously, "I've done it six times in an hour."

We also hear that in 1923 in Nice another French writer, George Maurevert, told Harris that Maupassant, upset by Flaubert's doubts, went once with a witness to a brothel in Paris and had six girls in an hour. This was, apparently, in an effort to convince Flaubert of his prowess, in which his ascetic friend took a strange interest.

Harris continues:

> Time and again Maupassant told me he could go on embracing as long as he wished.
>
> "A dangerous power," I said, thinking he was merely bragging.
>
> "Why dangerous?" he asked.
>
> "Because you could easily get exhaustion and nervous breakdown," I replied, "but you must be speaking metaphorically."

"Indeed I'm not," he insisted, "and as for exhaustion I don't know what you mean; I'm as tired after two or three times as I am after twenty."

"Twenty!" I exclaimed laughing, "poor Casanova is not in it."

"I've counted twenty and more," Maupassant insisted.

I could do nothing but shrug my shoulders.

"Surely you know," he went on after a pause, "that in two or three times you exhaust your stock of semen, so that you can go on afterwards without further loss?"

Harris kept thinking about Maupassant's story, not being able to make up his mind whether to discount the whole thing as an example of erotic braggadocio, or whether to take Maupassant seriously. During these reflections, it occurred to him that Maupassant might have had a late sexual start in life, which, he felt, could have accounted for his unusual virility. He therefore determined to ask Maupassant about this at the next chance, which presented itself two or three days later.

When Harris asked the question concerning the onset of Maupassant's sexual experiences, suggesting that he might have been older than most boys, the former denied this vehemently.

"No, no," he cried. "I learned to excite myself by chance; when I was about twelve a sailor one day practiced the art before me, and afterwards, like most healthy boys, I played with myself occasionally. But I did not yield to my desires often."

In the following conversation Maupassant tells of how he had a girl when he was about sixteen, and that the delight which she gave him cured him of masturbation.

Thoughtfully, as if speaking to himself, Maupassant went on (and this made a deep impression on Harris):

"I suppose I am a little out of the common

sexually, for I can make my instrument stand whenever I please!"

"Really?" I exclaimed, too astonished to think.

"Look at my trousers," he remarked laughing, and there on the road he showed me that he was telling the truth.

"What an extraordinary power," I cried. "I thought I was abnormal in that way, for I always get excited in a moment, and I have heard men say that they needed some time to get ready for the act; but your power is far beyond anything I have ever seen or heard of!"

"Have you always had that power?" I could not help asking.

"Always," he replied. "They used to wonder at it in the Navy when I was a youth."

"But fancy keeping it right up to thirty-five or thirty-six. You must be an ideal lover for a sensuous woman."

"That is the worst of it," he remarked quietly. "If you get a reputation, some of them practically offer themselves. But one often meets women who don't care much for the act. I suppose you meet that sort oftener in England, if what one hears is true, than in France. Here the women are generally normal. But it's seldom they feel intensely: however, some do, thank God."

"Naturally, I spent a great deal of thought on his abnormality," adds Frank Harris, concluding with a comparison of Maupassant's attitude toward women with that of his own, which he found to be quite different.

But the last discussion between Harris and Maupassant is especially instructive, both from a psychological and from a sexological point of view. Maupassant apparently had a chronic hyperexcitability of the penis, clinically known as satyriasis, which, in extreme cases, can produce permanent, and sometimes extremely painful, erections.

The Maupassant incident also emphasizes the point

which we have already made, namely, that Harris' sex life was not out of the ordinary, whereas Maupassant's certainly was. Nevertheless, we note that these two great men of very different cultural backgrounds found a common denominator in their sexuality.

Only occasionally did Harris engage in sexual activities which are more unusual in contemporary Western society; as, for instance, during a short period in his later life when he lived in a rented villa at San Remo on the Riviera. While at San Remo, Frank Harris had what he called "the greatest amatory experience of my life." Actually, it was his gardener who was the key figure in that experience, or series of experiences, for it was he who seduced Harris into inviting several local beauties for a private "beauty contest" at the villa. Out of this grew orgiastic experiences, involving at times several girls and male friends of Harris':

> I shall never forget one occasion when we all went bathing in a state of nature—half a dozen girls and four men. After the bath we all came up and lay about on the grass and soon the lovely girl-forms seduced the men, and the scene turned to embracing, which the beauty and abandon of the girls made memorable.

At another time, Harris writes of an episode which is rich in insights concerning sexual psychology. He had married and confesses that after six months his honeymoon had begun to weary him. Just at this strategic time, "Laura," the same girl who had once driven him into the arms of his maid (see p. 138), unexpectedly appeared, to visit him in the bachelor's apartment which he had retained as a kind of "home away from home." After some preliminary sparring they confessed their love for one another and Harris carried the lady to his bed. He comments on his feelings for her as follows:

> "I had never felt such passionate admiration for any other woman; the beauty of her figure appealed to me intensely, and the mere touch of her firm

flesh thrilled me as no one else had ever done. I cannot explain the magnetism, the intensity of the attraction and the passion she inspired in me. Life would have reached its highest point through my connection with her if it hadn't been for one thing.

"I don't know why but I was never sure of Laura's love; and that caused in me a curious reflex action; I never tried to give her the greatest sum of pleasure that I possibly could. *I often stopped embracing just when she was most passionate, out of a sort of revenge that sprang from hurt vanity.*" (Italics supplied.)

Here Harris showed rare insight into a psychological mechanism by which many men (and women) take revenge on their sex partners for real or imagined hurts. This tendency frequently manifests itself in partial or total impotence of the man, in premature ejaculation, and, paradoxically, in its opposite—a spurious hyperpotency and prolonged erectability of the penis, with often painful effects on the partner. In a woman, resentment toward a man may manifest itself in avoidance reactions and varying degrees of frigidity during intercourse. Inability to achieve orgasm is not necessarily related to general sexual inhibition but to (often subconscious) animosity toward a specific partner. Failure to achieve orgasm may thus be a means of humiliating the other person.

Immediately following a quarrel during the affair just mentioned, Harris consoled himself with his pretty maid, but ". . . as soon as my passion was satisfied and I knew all her past, I lost interest in her: there was nothing extraordinary in her, either in face or figure or mind, and so I quickly grew to indifference."

Harris frequently started a new affair with great enthusiasm, only to cool off within a comparatively short time. This was not due simply to the fact that sexual desire was, for him, at least partially dependent upon the newness of the stimulus but was, much more importantly, a symptom of psychological sex fatigue which in Harris's case was extremely marked or conspicuous.

Typically, he rationalized this tendency by finding fault with some character trait, or still more often with some physical imperfection in his partner.

In an introduction to the first volume of *My Life and Loves,* Harris confesses that as a youth he made hideous blunders and had seen even worse blunders made by others, out of sheer ignorance. For that reason, he wanted to warn the young and impressionable against the hidden traps and dangers which lie in misinformation, or in the lack of information.

Harris also states that he felt he had missed indescribable pleasures because the power to enjoy and to give delight is at its peak early in life. On the other hand, Harris laments that knowledge and understanding of how to give and receive pleasure usually come later in life when the physical body is already in its decline. In that respect, he reminds one of Anatole France, who once made a similar statement, saying, "If youth only knew, and old age only could."

In order to bring biological readiness and understanding into closer harmony, Harris wished to share his experiences with others, especially younger people. In that respect his aim was mainly educational, and to our way of thinking it seems regrettable that many years were lost before readers in this country could have ready access to this autobiography, which, in spite of its obvious shortcomings, errors, and limitations, constitutes a veritable gold mine of general and sexological information.

Another motivating factor for the inclusion of erotically realistic detail in his autobiography was Harris' almost fanatical hatred of hypocrisy and of puritanical denial of reality. He felt very deeply about these matters. Is is sad, indeed, that he met with so much ill will and was so cruelly persecuted in many quarters that this unholy fighter for the holy spirit of truth had to pay a high price for his attempt to speak plainly, directly, and unblushingly about the "taboo" aspects of his personal life. In so doing he could not help but expose his fellowmen who are less willing than he to shed their masks of hypocrisy, and that the puritans could never forgive him.

It is our hope that a new generation of Americans, with whom Harris so strongly identified and whose nationality he voluntarily adopted, may give this courageous writer and his autobiography another and fairer day in the court of public opinion. Had he written in post-Kinseyan America, he might have had a better chance to be understood and appreciated. As it was, he died lonely and discouraged, warning those who would come after him of the intolerance they would meet with in those who have a high personal stake, and often economic and political investments, in the sexual misery of mankind. But the fact remains that he did believe there would be others after him who would take up the fight for sexual freedom, and that the ultimate victory would be on the side of science, progress, and enlightenment. After so many years of suppression, the successful publication and wide critical acclaim of *My Life and Times* would undoubtedly have pleased Harris very much.

HENRY MILLER—APOSTLE OF THE GORY DETAIL

On the frontispiece of Henry Miller's *Tropic of Cancer* there is a quotation from Ralph Waldo Emerson:

> The novels will give way, by and by, to diaries or autobiographies—captivating books, if only a man knew how to choose among what he calls his experiences that which is really his experience, and how to record truth truly.

Miller tried to follow Emerson's advice, so that most, if not all of his books are autobiographical in nature. They are more than that, they are also truthful, as Emerson suggested such books should be. Several of his works have been published in France, and are sold all over the world. Until recently it has been necessary for Americans to purchase some of Henry Miller's books abroad and to sneak them into this country, hidden from the eyes of customs inspectors.

In a preface to *Tropic of Cancer*, Anais Nin expresses the hope that Miller's book "might restore our appetite for the 'fundamental realities'." She also feels that we live ". . . in a world grown paralyzed with introspection and constipated by delicate mental meals," into which Miller's "brutal exposure of the substantial body comes as a vitalizing current of blood."

What do we find in Miller's books? Nin says, "It is blood and flesh which is here given us. Drink, food, laughter, desire, passion, curiosity, the simple realities which nourish the roots of our highest and vaguest creations."

The erotic realism of Miller's books is in the same tradition as, for instance, that of Mark Twain's fantasy, "1601," Pepys' *Diary*, Cassanova's *Mémoires*, or *The Life and Loves of Frank Harris*. There is, perhaps, more concern about food in Miller's books than in the autobiographies of other writers. The reason is, most likely, that Henry Miller went hungry more often than his confreres.

There is also a good deal of sleeping with whores in Miller's books, more so than in Casanova's *Mémoires* or in Frank Harris' autobiography. However, the former Secretary of the British Navy, Samuel Pepys, runs Miller a close second in this regard, if only as much as fifty percent of the ladies whom he calls "strumpets," "whores," and "sluts" could lay legitimate claim to these titles.

Sometimes it does take a rather healthy stomach to digest Henry Miller's realism, as for instance when his free associations lead him from his roommate's goatee (with a little egg from breakfast hanging down from it), to the pubic hair of Tania, to the awareness of a desire to tear off a few hairs from it and paste them on his bearded roommate's chin, to a fantasy of biting into her clitoris and spitting out two-franc pieces. But, undoubtedly, this is what went on in Miller's mind when, as he says, one night while looking at his friend's goatee

lying on the pillow, he got "hysterical." As psychotherapists, we realize that the things which we hear
from our patients behind the closed doors of our consultation room are not a particle less objectionable than
this, nor can we say that our own experiences and
fantasies are on a higher plane than those of Henry
Miller. The only difference is that most of us would
not dare to admit to this side of our life as Miller does.
Therapeutically this is unfortunate, since such frankness
is reassuring to most people, not necessarily in psychiatric treatment by any means, who have similar
fantasies and who carry a shameful, and needless, load
of guilt as a result. Such thinking is not unique, nor
even unusual.

The growing movement of group therapy in America
is based on this principle. In the therapeutic group, one
shares one's most private world with a number of fellow
humans, not only with one other person, or therapist,
or analyst (whom it is so easy to put in a different
category of beings so that there is little carry-over from
the consultation room to the outside world). But from
the therapy group it is only a small step to one's intimate circle of friends and family members, and from
there to the larger community of men. If absolute honesty with oneself and loss of false shame toward one's
fellow men is the rule in the one situation, it may well
come to permeate all our human relations in due course,
so that twenty years from now, anything we or Henry
Miller are saying today will probably be nothing out
of the ordinary.

Henry Miller's realism does not exclude his concern
over his bowel movements, his bleeding hemorrhoids,
his constipation, and vomitings. Here again, he reminds
us more of Sampel Pepys than of any of the other
realistic autobiographers, for Pepys, too, makes diary
entries about his "shitting" and "spewing" when he has
overindulged in drink or food, or when ill for other
reasons.

There is a scene in *Tropic of Cancer* which mixes
sex and excretion with stark realism. But, as in Mark

Twain's "1601," the humor of the situation relieves the incident from being merely sordid. We are referring to the time when Henry Miller and his Indian friend visit a Paris whorehouse and the Indian, mistaking the bidet for the toilet, voids his stools into it. The girls are outraged, the Madam demands an explanation for the *cochonerie*, and Miller has to do some fast talking to get himself and his paying friend out of the embarrassing situation.

One could go on at great length in this vein with Henry Miller's writings. But we shall give only one example from the same book, though his other books contain similar scenes of which some are even stronger than the following one. However, the reader will get a sufficiently clear feeling for Miller's style, even from this single passage.

Henry Miller tells how one day he unexpectedly meets one of his old girl friends again. Her name is Mona. They can celebrate their reunion through the courtesy of Miller's friend, Eugene, in the same hotel room which formerly had been their love-nest, if we can call it that.

> The trunk is open and her things are lying around everywhere just as before. She lies down on the bed with her clothes on. Once, twice, three times, four times . . . I'm afraid she'll go mad . . . in bed, under the blankets, how good to feel her body again! But for how long? Will it last this time? Already I have a presentiment that it won't.

In the next paragraph, Miller tells of the two "breathing warmly into each other's mouth," and of his happiness in having this girl in bed with him, "her hair in my mouth."

But immediately after this, we read how in the pale light of the morning, while admiring Mona's "beautiful, wild hair," he suddenly feels something crawling down his neck.

I look at her again, closely. Her hair is alive! I pull back the sheet—more of them. They are swarming over the pillow.

And so the pair hurriedly pack and sneak out of the hotel, looking for a café that is open at this early hour, walking, and as they walk, scratching themselves.

There is no doubt that Henry Miller's erotic realism is several degrees starker than that of the other writers considered here. However, in his descriptions of violence he is mild compared to many contemporary authors. There is, for instance, nothing comparable in his books to the scene in Remarque's *All Quiet On The Western Front,* in which a soldier digs his way in the trenches through the innards of buried comrades. Nor is there anything in Miller even faintly resembling the brutality of Steinbeck's *Grapes of Wrath,* or Hemingway's story about a drunk biting out the eye of another man with his teeth, or the cannibalism in Tennessee Williams' *Garden District,* and the medieval-like castration scene in *Sweet Bird of Youth.*

But from a mental hygiene point of view, Henry Miller's relentlessness in facing the harsh detail of the sexual situations he encounters is much more preferable than the current literary tendency to mix sex with strong doses of sadism and hostility. In Henry Miller's books sex is there for its own sake. He neither apologizes for nor glorifies its expression.

It is true that much of what he discusses in his books strikes initially with the force of shock. However, such is the nature of life itself, which does not shelter us from unexpected harshness in human experience. On the other hand, we will not find in Henry Miller's writings any erotic presentation which describes beating a woman over the breasts and winding up the romantic encounter by shooting her in the belly. As psychologists, we therefore regret that the American reader, and especially the younger reader, is presented with literary sex in a style which, while evading the onus of obscenity,

confuses healthy genital sexuality with infantile pre-
genital sadistic perversions of the sexual impulse.

The legal debate as to the acceptability of Miller has
been a major censorship issue over the last ten years.
Miller has almost won. Hundreds of writers, artists,
educators, lawyers and literary critics have testified in
Miller's defense or written opinions on the merit of
giving his books free circulation. In court after court
the argument that Miller writes erotic realism was used
to defend his work. Frequently direct reference was
made to *Pornography and the Law* as the source of the
concept of erotic realism. The authors cannot help but
believe that their book and its many readers have played
an important part in securing for Henry Miller the
recognition in the country of his birth that he so richly
deserves.

What is a dirty word, a word that is capable of arousing the hue and cry of censorship? Since the prudish Victorian era, many so-called mature adults have been upset by seeing the four-letter vernacular words for sex and excretion and they have forced their standards on the rest of humanity who are capable of taking life as it is rather than having to pretend it is - - - -, or f - - k, or ****.

Scott Fitzgerald's courageous use of realistic language in the 1920's symbolized the beginnings of the march back to reality and truth, and away from denial and prudishness.

Truth and reality force us to admit that dirty words are a vital, integral part of the everyday conversation of many people. When writers attempt to depict this group of people as they really are, they must use the words in the same way as the prototypes of the people in their stories do. Literature, inhibited by - - - -, and ****, has frequently been artificial and misleading.

Erskine Caldwell, in his article *My Twenty-five Years of Censorship,* rightly points out that the courts have declared that " 'coarse' language was not necessarily 'obscene.' " Caldwell goes on to state:

> . . . Greenspans' general conclusions were given wider scope when Random House was hauled into Federal Court for importing James Joyce's *Ulysses.* Judge John Woolsey exonerated *Ulysses,* noting that although it contains . . . many words usually considered dirty, I have not found anything that I considered dirt for dirt's sake . . . I do not detect anywhere the leer of the sensualist."
>
> *Since Joyce used every four-letter word in the English language, that language taboo was shattered once and for all.* Woolsey also agreed with

Greenspan that a book must be judged by its effect as a whole, not upon the easily inflammable or the disordered, but "on a person with average sex instincts." A few months later, Woolsey was upheld by the Court of Appeals, thus erecting a "nation-wide standard to which the liberal could repair." [Emphasis supplied.] (*Esquire,* October 1958.)

Unfortunately, Caldwell's conclusion concerning the shattering of the language taboo in literature is some-what optimistic. Logically, it should be true after such a decision on a book which does contain almost all the taboo words. However, people are not completely logi-cal or consistent. Writers are still being dragged into court or having their books banned because of the use of these taboo words, Henry Miller's books being the best examples. (Some of Miller's books are undoubtedly banned only because of the use of certain words and not because he is presenting *ideas* which are unaccept-able.)

Paradoxically, many novels which are accepted by the public do contain the taboo words, once, twice, or several times throughout their pages. The following list, which was compiled from about a dozen popular books, such as *Peyton Place, Studs Lonigan,* and *No Down Payment,* indicates that every taboo word and quite a few "strong" phrases do now appear in print, without - - - - and ****.

Here is the tabulation of "obscene" words and phrases in some currently popular novels and plays:

son of a bitch	plump hillock	spread-eagled
bastard	bullshit	prick
fucking	shit	fag
cock	fart	butch
screwing	cherry	queer
peeping	crotch	circumcise
fornication	safe (condom)	clap
pubic floss	pussy	tits

butts
ass
suck the breasts
host lay
hard-on
mother-lovin'
mother-lovin'
    dog
fuck you
getting into your
    pants
dropping your
    pants
hot pants
had me a piece
escapement of
    wind from his
    breech
feeling up both
    dames

make me a baby
hidden tumor
    (erection)
goddam whorin'
    little slut
is it up good and
    hard?
dildos
"French"
mounts her
so hot
good pounding
getting enough
knock her up
tongue-in-ear
    play
canters her for
    long
knocking her off
    hard and fast

hard body
    thrusting and
    pounding
shove it in
went down
down there
I feel it like a
    hard finger
between his legs
    pressing into
    my thighs
letting boys feel
    her
ride the livin'
    hell out of her
unzip his trou-
    sers
got his nose in a
    white man's
    ass

Yet, the fact that all these words are being used in modern fiction does not mean that the language taboo is broken. It only means that language censorship is now being applied in a different way. One cannot publish a sentence composed only or mainly of obscene words, even if it is appropriate to the book as a whole and is written to convey an important idea or characterization. Only banned, "hard core obscenity" enjoys this "freedom."

To illustrate the point, we invite the reader to conduct a little experiment of his own and make up in his mind a sentence from the words in the above list. It will immediately become apparent that whatever sentence he may have made up would be unprintable, even though all the words used have appeared in books which are accepted by the public, some of which are best sellers, have won literary prizes, or have been made into movies.

The taboo surrounding dirty words makes the use

of them all the more attractive to everyone. This attraction may be expressed either by using the word whenever one feels like it, or by its opposite: staunch avoidance of all obscene language, a reaction-formation which gives away the underlying preoccupation.

To understand the psychology of four-letter words, one only has to observe children when they are going through the phase of experimenting with "dirty" words. Children quickly pick up tabooed words, even (or especially!) if they are not used in the parental home. At times, it is carried to the length of learning a considerable amount of foreign vocabulary; the only foreign words they might ever come to know! Children enjoy using these words for all the dramatic effect they are worth. The adults in the child's environment are generally shocked to hear that the child knows and uses these words. This is true in spite of the fact that the adults may have used these very same words in the child's presence. More often than not, the child, displaying great dramatic "know-how," has dropped the bombshell in front of those guests who would be the most shocked. The flustered parents usually manage to mumble that they have no idea where their child heard such language. Not a few of these parents would rather have had the child have an accident in its pants instead of spewing forth dirty words in front of guests.

Freud, of course, pointed out the connection between our intense reaction to "dirty" words and toilet training. Mothers are as quick to wash out their children's mouths with soap as to give them enemas. Disturbed children, and even disturbed adults, reflect these stringent disciplinary measures by being preoccupied with both excretion and "dirty" words.

One little boy, during therapy, filled a whole notebook with the word "fuck." The therapeutic permissiveness gave him an opportunity to abreact his trauma around the word. After writing the word many, many times, it did not seem to be as terrible as he had been led to believe. It was just a word in our language and not a dangerous monster which would destroy him.

Clinically, therefore, there is obvious therapeutic value in accepting the use of "forbidden" words. From the preventive point of view of good mental hygiene, however, (and that is what is really important), if the use of these words did not provoke a "horror" reaction in the first place, they would not assume a disproportionate value in creating fright and guilt.

Adults who find themselves incapable of reading or hearing a "dirty" word without becoming upset have never overcome their severe childhood training. Even if one does not want to use these words, one should be able to tolerate hearing them or seeing such expressions in print.

In a foreword to Bourke's *Scatologic Rites,* Freud remarked about the manner in which civilized people today deal with the problems of their corporeality:

They are annoyed by anything which reminds them unequivocally of the animal nature of man. They would rather compare themselves with the "more perfect angels" who, in the last scene of *Faust* complain:

Some earth-taint we still bear
And find it painful.
Though of as best it were,
'Twere a taint baneful.

But since they can never attain such perfection, they have chosen an expedient. This is to deny, as far as possible, one's uncomfortable earthiness, refusing it the attention and care to which, as an integral part of one's nature, it is entitled. Civilized people conceal their sexual and excretory functions from their fellow-men, though every one is aware of their existence in others. *Assuredly, it would be wiser to recognize their presence candidly and to devote to these earthy parts of our person as large a measure of refinement as their nature permits.* [Emphasis supplied.]

The concealment of sexual and excretory functions of which Freud here speaks is very evident in the way that virtually every civilized language refers in two or three different ways—primitive, refined and scientific—to the organs of sex and excretion. The English language has, for example, two entirely different sets of vocabulary for these matters. One set of words is derived from the Latin and serves us for polite and scientific discourse. The other set of words is of Anglo-Saxon origin and is used for informal talk, and especially when we want to express ourselves more emphatically.

The Anglo-Saxon vocabulary is learned much earlier than the Latin synonyms and therefore remains the preferred language of the emotions. These "primitive" terms remain closely connected with the things and actions for which they stand, while their "refined" verbal supplanters have undergone the process by which they have become further removed and of lesser emotional value than the things they signify. For that very reason, the vernacular terms are more subject to self-or-socially-imposed censorship than their scientific equivalents.

It is not surprising that when we do transgress the language taboo in spite of all these barriers and use the forbidden words for which we once used to get our mouths washed with laundry soap, we often feel a sort of sudden exaltation in at least temporarily overthrowing and defying our own inner conscience and the outward repressive forces of society. (See J. C. Fluegel, *Man, Morals, and Society*.)

The language taboo can become especially cumbersome in certain areas of social research, of which the present study is a case in point. Again and again we shall find in the second part of this book, dealing with "hard core obscenity," how we have had to circumscribe, transliterate, paraphrase, and excise the original material from the "obscene" books in order not to endanger our own discussion of the problems here involved.

Maria Jahoda refers to the same situation in her report, *The Impact of Literature: A Psychological Discussion of Some Assumptions in the Censorship Debate*. In that case, a Congressional committee which had been studying a large number of "obscene" books felt unable to communicate their findings because if they had used the terminology of the "obscene" books studied, it was feared that the committee itself might have been accused of disseminating "obscenity."

Any scientist who has interviewed individuals of certain groups, for example among the laboring class, farmers, members of certain ethnic groups, or disturbed people such as delinquents, criminals, and prostitutes, can testify to the fact that some of the material thus obtained is rendered useless because very "obscene" language, which is not unusual for these cultural subgroups, cannot be freely used in reports dealing with these groups. Social scientists are thus expected to accept this limitation in reporting their findings, while modern society would scarcely expect its physical scientists to change their research data in order to make them socially more acceptable.

Indeed, the ban on the use of certain words extends itself even into the professional work of men and women trained to deal with problems which are themselves created in part by these very taboos.

Dr. Hyman Spotnitz, a psychoanalyst, found it necessary to remind his colleagues that this type of intolerance was neither complimentary nor appropriate for adults who are supposed to be scientists. Dr. Spotnitz presented his remarks in a discussion concerning the research of Dr. John Rosen in using his technique of direct analysis to treat schizophrenics. Actually, much of the hostility and resistance to Dr. Rosen's treatment grew out of the fact that he used the peculiar language of the mental patient to communicate with him, and this language was often composed of a large assortment of "dirty" words. Few of Dr. Rosen's colleagues were sufficiently free or mature to listen to such a conversation, to say nothing of participating in it, without becoming anxious and hostile. Thus, by sheer prejudice many clinicians attempted to discredit the usefulness of Dr. Rosen's particular method of treatment, without investigating it more carefully.

In the same issue of *The Psychiatric Quarterly* (then edited by Dr. Richard H. Hutchings) which contained the discussion of Dr. Rosen's method, the editorial commented as follows:

"Ode to the Four-Letter Word"

Anonymous.

Oh perish the use of the four-letter words
Whose meanings are never obscure;
The Angles and Saxons, those bawdy old birds,
Were vulgar, obscene and impure.
But cherish the use of the weaseling phrase
That never says quite what you mean.
You had better be known for your hypocrite ways
Than vulgar, impure and obscene.

The "vulgar, impure and obscene" words which English has inherited from the Angles and the Saxons loom large in the vocabularies of psychotic patients. But when an investigator and earnest student attempts to rescue a deteriorated patient sunk in the morass of catatonic stupor by interpreting his delusions and hallucinations and speaking to him in the same infantile words flung at him by accusing voices—thus to draw out his mental content, to be understood, and to gain a response— he must watch his step or he will be misunderstood by the uninformed and suspected of evil-mindedness. . . .

The unconscious, when coming to verbal expression, does not choose the "weaseling phrase" but the hearty Anglo-Saxon words which mean just what they say. Every experienced psychiatrist has heard from the lips of patients known to come from homes of culture and refinement, torrents of vulgarity and obscenity when in a maniacal rage. One is prompted to exclaim: "Where *could* she have learned such words!" And the deteriorated hebephrenic or catatonic, without the spur of rage or excitement, without any appearance of shame, uses words and phrases that *so shock the prudish that interns and nurses have asked to be excused from service on certain wards.* [Emphasis supplied.]

The editor and his associates feel that a keen sense of clinical duty makes it imperative upon them to quote—when quotations are essential to an unbiased presentation of clinical material—patients' and therapists' remarks exactly as they are made. *An attempt to "purify" the clinical record by substituting parlor or scientific phraseology of the twentieth century for four-letter words known to everyone would be a species of prudish hypocrisy unworthy of a medical publication.* The members of the editorial staff are not addicted to the employment of scatology in their own conversation. They regret that prudes may find on the pages of the Quarterly words employed—when essential to the context—that *may give offense to the Miss Nancies of both sexes, but the regret is wholly for the state of mind of such prudes, and there is no intention whatever of modifying the editorial policy of truthfulness to details in quotations.*

We submit here and now that psychiatry is a profession for adults and that it is time for psychiatrists in general to act adult. It is not a profession for the sort of lady, male or female, who shudders at four-letter words and the mental images they invoke. [Emphasis supplied.]

. . . We all know what the deteriorated schizophrenic may occasionally say or do. To point out the A, B, C's of psychiatry—he often speaks of things in the "dirty words" which a child would use in a tantrum. It is sometimes necessary, if one is to meet the regressed schizophrenic on his own level, to employ words he hears in his hallucinations. These may comprise the only vocabulary that will make an emotional contact with his distraught self-absorption and gain a response.

All of us know what those words are. Most of us learned them as children. All of us have seen them

*in public or school toilets. Anybody so squeamish
as to shudder at them or at the desires or actions
toward which they point has no business in psychiatry and psychotherapy.* [Emphasis supplied.]
Psychiatric Quarterly, January, 1947.

The authors recently experienced the voluntary censorship of verbal "obscenity" at a national meeting of
psychotherapists at which they were resource participants. A talented and experienced psychoanalyst presented the case of a high-school boy who had been his
patient over a period of three years. During his treatment, the young man was involved in a traffic incident
in which he cursed the other party, or as the therapist
stated: "He called the other motorist by an obscene
term."

In the discussion that followed the case presentation,
we emphasized the importance of knowing the *exact*
words which the patient used. In this particular case
it would have been clinically significant and of diagnostic importance whether the patient had used an anal
or oral expression, and to get a feeling for the emotional
tone conveyed by the words used. In short, it is our
contention that one cannot understand the dynamics of
an individual, nor actually help a patient therapeutically,
without being familiar with his vocabulary.

In our experience we have yet to find the patient who
cannot tolerate direct expression of sexual acts or ideas,
if he is sure of the therapist's understanding and support.
In our opinion, the use of "it" or other vague, ambig-
uous terms can only lead to *confusion,* because the
patient is required to guess what the therapist really
meant to say; this leaves a dangerous opening for the
patient to give the therapist's words a meaning other
than the one intended; it may give rise to suspicions
concerning the sincerity of the therapist and his intentions; and finally, the patient is deprived of a unique
opportunity in emotional re-education which could have
resulted in his acquiring greater freedom of thought and
expression.

We have been discussing the therapeutic value to disturbed patients of accepting the use of "dirty" words. But the same thinking applies equally well to perfectly normal and healthy people. During the war, it was a well-known and completely acceptable fact that men in the armed forces, bound by unaccustomed restrictions and under the pressure of prolonged tension, habitually used "dirty" language, which provided a greater release than they were perhaps aware of; nor were those women who were in the armed forces far behind the men in using this basically healthy device for the release of tension.

Confirmation of our theory concerning the therapeutic value of verbal "obscenity" has recently come from a psychiatric report dealing with the experience of naval personnel in the Antarctic which bluntly states that being confined in the close quarters of their "tight little world," the men were prone to develop severe tension-headaches which they relieved by violent swearing, vigorous horseplay, and "an interesting technique of exchanging frank and fearful insult, often quite personal and to the point, but apparently rarely reacted to with much if any anger."

The cartharsis of expressing hostile and aggressive feelings by such self-instituted techniques as the above report describes is certainly to be welcomed from a mental health point of view.

As a matter of mental hygiene, it is therefore important that these avenues of communication, vicarious release, and tension-reduction not be closed by moralistic or censorial attitudes on the part of society. To the contrary, a wise social organization should encourage such harmless expressions of otherwise taboo ideas, preferring them by far to the only alternatives: mental illness, and violent acting out to the actual damage of the individual and of society as a whole.

Another danger in the repression of "bad language" is that it tends to perpetuate censorship. In fact, the concept that certain words are so bad or dangerous that they simply cannot and must not be used is at the core of many attempts to limit the free expression not only of words, but of ideas in speech and writing. If it were recognized that the words themselves are no more than verbal symbols and cannot work magic by forcing people to commit sexual or other acts, this would go a long way toward solving the problem of censorship.

The naïve belief in the potency of words has its basis in an archaic leftover from the period of animistic worship, a stage of development which we have apparently not fully outgrown.

Contrary to our intentions, we still lend to "obscene" words a mysterious power by maintaining the taboo against their use, particularly in print. Modern recognition of the realistic value of these words has not yet removed our basic fear of them. Thus, censorship turns out to be essentially an anxiety operation on the part of society. As long as society feels itself threatened by the use of "obscene" words, it will continue to exert some degree of censorship on this basis alone in literature and in speech.

In the daily life of the individual, the judgment that the use of a particular word, or group of words, is obscene, depends on the surrounding circumstances. Writing or printing the words implies that they may appear in a variety of circumstances, which may include instances where the individual would censor his or her own language. But with changing community standards, what may once have been considered obscene is now regarded at worst as in bad taste.

Nevertheless, the individual may, while accepting that some uses of words are not censorable, have the uneasy feeling that a line needs to be drawn somewhere without knowing where it should be placed.

Since legal decisions have on the whole seemed to support the broad circulation, sometimes in multimillion copy editions, of books that would have been thought of as going too far just a generation ago, the individual finds in his own reading the use of words and descriptions of acts which might once have been considered obscene. This individual may feel that the legislature and the courts have come close to abandoning the control of obscenity. This is not so. Cases of great importance have recently increased the scope and refined the distinctions made under the obscenity statutes even though these court decisions point up as many questions as they answer. What is involved here is a question of degree, and in the end, in a free society, this must become the choice of the individual. In a democracy, this is a person's privilege, and rightly so. The essence of democratic thinking is the free right of the individual to choose. But no free, intelligent choice can be made if the chooser himself is ignorant, through prejudice, latent fear, or imposed restriction, of the psychological and social implications of his choice. If freedom of expression is a sign of a mature society, then the fearful suppression of words and/or ideas by certain censorious groups must be recognized for what it is: the symptom of a social neurosis defending its own illness, and thereby contributing to a continuance of that illness for the society as a whole.

We have shown that the paradoxical title of this chapter is fully justified; there may be foul language in clean books, depending on the intent, the over-all purpose, and the ultimate psychological effect of the book as a whole.

In Mark Twain's "1601" a large number of four-letter Anglo-Saxonisms are used in the context of a social satire. In some of the autobiographical writings, especially in Pepys, Henry Miller, and Frank Harris, we again found a number of "dirty" words, though these writings themselves are certainly not "obscene." We have also seen how even the talk and writings of religious leaders like Martin Luther contained unblushing erotic and excretory references, though nobody would contend that these individuals and their works were "obscene," "lewd," and "lascivious."

For the individual, for the legislature, and for the courts, we shall endeavor in the following sections of this book to show that there are reliable criteria of obscenity which govern both words and ideas.

PART II

OBSCENE BOOKS AND THE LAW

THE SUPREME COURT DEFINITION OF "OBSCENITY"

In order to set our study within a framework of present legal practice and to give it thereby more direct applicability, it is necessary to know what standards the law uses to determine whether a particular book is "obscene" or not.

In order to avoid errors in those areas which are, strictly speaking, outside our range of competence as behavioral scientists, we consulted at great length with several people in the legal profession who are specialists in this area of law, notably attorney Stanley Fleishman of Hollywood, California.

The Supreme Court of the United States has stated in the first place negatively what obscenity is *not*. In trying to make a distinction between sex and obscenity, the Supreme Court stated that *"sex and obscenity are not synonymous."*

Having expressed itself thus, that sex and obscenity are not the same, the Supreme Court informs us that "the portrayal of sex, for example, in art, literature, and scientific works, is not in itself sufficient reason to deny material the constitutional protection of freedom of speech and press."

When talking about the "constitutional protection of freedom of speech and press," the Supreme Court is referring to the first and fourteenth amendments to the United States Constitution. The first amendment provides:

> Congress shall make no law respecting an establishment of religion, or prohibiting the free exercise thereof; or abridging the freedom of speech, or of the press; . . . .

The fourteenth amendment provides:

> No state shall . . . deprive any person of life, liberty or property, without due process of law; nor deny to any person within its jurisdiction the equal protection of the laws.

The first amendment furnishes the basic elements out of which have grown the current discussions regarding the constitutionality and limitations of any obscenity legislation. The fourteenth amendment becomes meaningful mostly with regard to "due process" and similar considerations.

Further, the highest court in the land says that "sex, a great and mysterious motive force in human life, has undisputably been a subject of absorbing interest to mankind through the ages; it is one of the vital problems of human interest and public concern."

Again, the Supreme Court admonishes that the "fundamental freedoms of speech and press have contributed greatly to the development and well being of our free society and are indispensable to its continued growth." We are told further that "the door barring federal and state intrusion into this area cannot be left ajar; it must be kept tightly closed and *opened only the slightest crack necessary* to prevent encroachment upon more important interests." [Emphasis supplied.]

To repeat, the Supreme Court recognizes that a mere discussion or portrayal of sex in literature will not automatically stamp such writing as "obscene." On the contrary, the Supreme Court recognizes that books dealing with problems of sex are an essential part of the exposition of ideas protected by the Constitution, and that essentially only those writings which do not have ideas in them, which do not have the "slightest redeeming social importance," are outside the protective arms of fundamental law. But unorthodox ideas, controversial ideas, even ideas hateful to the prevailing climate of opinion have the full protection of the first amendment.

But how are we to determine when a writing contains no ideas of redeeming social importance? Put in other words, what is the test for determining that a certain book is obscene?

The Supreme Court gives us the following answer:

Whether to the *average* person, applying contemporary community standards, the dominant theme of the material taken as a whole appeals to prurient interest." [Emphasis supplied.]

This is the test which the Supreme Court has used, and this is the test with which lawyers and judges and juries have to wrestle in the countless obscenity cases which come before the courts.

The thinking of the Supreme Court parallels in this respect that of the American Law Institute in their definition of obscenity. The American Law Institute consists of a body of judges and lawyers which devotes itself to making suggestions for restating and bringing the law up to date. It is at present working on what is known as a Model Penal Code, and in the course of its preparation the Institute has tentatively defined "obscenity" in the following way:

A thing is obscene, if, considered as a whole, the predominant appeal is to prurient interest, for example, a shameful or morbid interest in nudity, sex or excretion, and if it goes substantially beyond customary limits of candor in description or representation of such materials.

To follow the thinking of the American Law Institute in arriving at its definition, here is the basis of the Institute's position:

Everybody is subject to *two conflicting forces: sexual drives, sexual curiosity* on the one hand and universal social repression of that on the other hand. This creates a certain sense of shame, of embarrassment, or wrongness that sexual aspects of our life involve, and people who want to make a living by exacerbating that, by *rubbing the sore,* as one author put it, we say are out of bounds. [Emphasis supplied.]

In accordance with this thought, the Supreme Court advises us that material appealing to prurient interest is "material having a tendency to excite lustful thoughts." It also adopts the dictionary definition of "prurient" as follows:

Itching; longing, uneasy with desire or longing; of persons, an itching, morbid or lascivious longing; of desire, curiosity, or propensity, lewd. . . .

It would appear then that the Supreme Court and The American Law Institute intend to test the obscenity of a book or writing first by the content of the material in it, and second by the over-all appeal of that content. They appear to be saying, if you take any piece of literature as a whole, does it predominantly appeal to that itching, morbid, shameful interest that all persons seem to have in greater or lesser degree? Or does the book as a whole appeal primarily to some other interest— educational, entertaining, scientific, humorous, moral, etc.? But if we once determine that the writing taken as a whole does have an appeal to anything other than the aforesaid prurient interest, then unquestionably it does contain ideas which deserve constitutional protection.

The reader will recognize that this has nothing to do with whether the book is well or poorly written. Nor does it have any bearing on whether the ideas contained in the book are acceptable or disagreeable to the reader, nor whether they involve any other element of personal taste normally involved in the criticism and analysis of any literary or scientific work.

In these obscenity cases, the law attempts to determine whether or not a particular piece of writing, let us say the unexpurgated version of *Lady Chatterley's Lover* by D. H. Lawrence, will have a substantial tendency to appeal to "prurient interest."

We can now approach the problem of identifying the hypothetical reader in whom an "obscene" piece of writing is said to appeal to "prurient interest." In the first place, we must keep in mind that the Supreme Court is referring to the *"average person."* That means the law is not testing the writing with respect to its appeal to a particular segment of the community—the young, the immature, or the highly prudish, nor yet the scientific and highly educated, nor the so-called worldly-wise and sophisticated. The test is the impact of the book on the "average" person in the community.

In the next place, the Supreme Court stresses the point that the writing must be judged as a whole in its entire context. We are not to consider detached or separate portions of the book in reaching a conclusion.

There are still other considerations. We must, for example, concern ourselves with what is known as the "dominant theme" of the writing. It is not always easy to tell whether this means the "lesson" which the book teaches, or whether it means the predominant appeal of the book to a particular interest of the reader. It seems to us there is a distinction between these two facets of the problem.

We shall attempt to resolve the question by exploring both aspects of the issue. First, what is the dominant theme of the writing taken as a whole, and second, what is the predominant appeal of this dominant theme to the average reader? If the story is about a prostitute or a Lesbian or a homosexual, does the theme essentially show that the life involved is sordid and leads in the end only to disaster? Or is the theme one which requests us to have sympathy and understanding for the position of these sex variants in society? But underneath this so-called moral theme there may be involved studies in human relations, recognition of the fact that a background of broken homes and poverty will twist personalities and lead to thoughts and actions commonly looked upon, perhaps, as perverted or not acceptable, and yet requiring sympathy and understanding.

Underlying these themes there may be still another question, namely, that of why the piece was written. Is the author asking the reader, in effect, to disregard the plot, to disregard the theme and merely to keep on turning the pages to look for "dirt for dirt's sake"? Or did he intend to awaken in the reader a desire to pursue the story because of sobering and provocative thoughts of one nature or the other—including reflections upon sex and sexual relations?

Assuming that even these many questions have been dealt with successfully, there are still other aspects of the legal definition to be taken into account. Does the hypothetical piece of literature under examination go substantially beyond customary limits of candor in description or representation of such matters?

Here, for the first time, the investigation is going beyond the *corpus delicti*—in this case the particular book or writing—itself. We are, at this point, beginning to compare it with other writings of comparable subject matter which apparently have been accepted by the community at large. Proof of such community acceptance would be the general public's familiarity with similar writings, their presence in the public libraries, their ready availability in book shops, on newsstands, and other outlets.

In dealing with obscenity cases within the definitions set by the Supreme Court, the lower courts thus have to consider the question of what constitutes "contemporary community standards." This question necessitates an examination of the overt sex mores of the community, as well as the covert sexual behavior of large segments of its citizens. And this, of course, poses new problems of legal interpretation which are, indeed, formidable.

The technical problems of the law, it is evident, are

so complex as to make themselves virtually insoluble, at least on any consistent basis. Let us turn then, for a moment, to the psychological and philosophical aspects of the basic issue, namely, sex life in our society.

The human animal is motivated by two basic drives—self-preservation and procreation. Basic to self-preservation is the need to eat. Although in the course of history, there have been times when eating and drinking for any reason except the preservation of life was condemned as a sin of the flesh, few humans indeed are now ashamed of eating; nor, in our society, does the average human confine eating to the primitive acts of kill and consume. On the contrary, civilized man has surrounded this basic act of self-preservation with a complex ritual of delight, pleasure, and pride in the diversity of preparation and the variety of foods he now consumes.

Basic to procreation is sexual intercourse: primitive man, in seeking to satisfy this urge, did so as an animal, without, very probably, even connecting the sexual act with procreation, responding only to a violent need which could not be denied. The *dominant power* of the sexual impulse was once absolutely necessary to continued procreation. Again, civilized man has introduced into the act of sexual intercourse gentler emotions and more sensuous refinements than simple procreation now demands, *but without removing the power of procreative force:* thus, love, humor, tenderness, and a variety of sexual techniques have come to surround the basic sexual impulse of mankind.

Yet there are still segments of our society which adhere to the principle of indulgence in intercourse solely for the purpose of procreation, and condemn what has become pleasurable interest in sex as "obscene"; to such effect, indeed, that many otherwise enlightened people are still ashamed of that primitive urge and attempt to deny its importance by clouding it over with a shadowy and mysterious form of "romantic" love. They then have to perpetuate a basically confused position by also frowning on anything which is liable to stimulate the sexual drive. In so doing, society is apt to destroy, not the basic drive, which *cannot* be eradicated, but the real, healthy and rewarding joys of a mature, civilized attitude toward sex which acknowledges its fundamental physiological power as an integrated aspect of the whole.

It seems to us highly debatable, from a mental hygiene point of view, whether the mental health of the individual or the group is furthered by the social repression of the sexual drive and of sexual curiosity, particularly in the young. There is good clinical, anthropological, and historical evidence to the effect that quite the opposite may be the case.

We know from clinical practice that neuroses and psychoses are nourished by a sense of guilt and shame which is usually anchored in the person's feelings about his body, its functions and appetites, on the one hand, and his need for social acceptance and self-esteem, on the other. In other words, the conflict between the sex drive and sex repression results, exactly as the American Law Institute defines it, in a sense of ". . . shame, of embarrassment, or wrongness. . . ." However, we do not think this conflict can be remedied by increased "social repression." Attempts at social control of an instinctual force which has as strong a basis in biology as the sex drive must be in keeping with the realities of human nature if they are not to be harmful to the development of the individual and the progress of society.

According to one point of view, "obscene" literature is apt to intensify the internal conflict between man's sexual desires and ("prurient") curiosity as opposed to his need for achievement, self-esteem and social recognition. At the same time, it is apparently feared that a lessening of sexual repression may lead to the breakdown of all social controls and result in unbridled instinctual living-out.

The reader will recognize that this is the same argument which was originally brought to bear against Freud and the psychoanalytic movement, before it became sexually tame and house-broken. The hue and cry against Freud and his early followers was that psychoanalysis would loosen the "social repression," cut down inhibitions, bring with it the breakdown of the family, and finally result in total sexual anarchy. The furor only abated when Freud himself came out with his theory of "sublimation" of the sex drive, the necessity for which he advocated in the interest of "civilization."

Immediately after these pronouncements of Freud's, his theories and the psychoanalytic movement met with much less public resistance and became almost universally accepted, even to the extent that the present day movement of "pastoral psychiatry" operates with many of Freud's concepts and does not hesitate to apply the very techniques which only thirty years ago were thought to be the devil's invention for leading mankind into perdition.

Freud's theory of sublimation is, however, by no means a one-sided argument. Theodor Reik has stressed that the crude sex drive, while easily satisfied, "is entirely incapable of being sublimated. . . . The satisfaction of this particular urge cannot be fulfilled by the substitution of another goal." Reik feels so strongly about this matter that he adds,

> I should like to drive this point home because it is time to make an end to the general confusion now current. I am speaking of the crude sex-drive, not of those forms in which it is fused with other drives. [Theodor Reik, *Psychology of Sex Relations.*]

Reik argues that it would make as much sense to try to convince us that the urge of thirst or excretion could be deflected to the accomplishment of cultural achievements, as to suggest that the sexual needs of the human animal could be put to such use. "All evidence," he says, "discredits the theory that the crude sex-drive can be sublimated." What can be used for cultural achievements is, much rather, the energy of ego-drives, says Reik, of which love itself is one of the main ingredients, and the need for social recognition, competitiveness, vanity, and vainglory its less glamorous relatives.

Another psychoanalyst, Wilhelm Reich, went even

further in his criticism of Freud's sublimation theory. He said,

> Sublimation, as the essential cultural achievement of the psychic apparatus, is possible only in the *absence of sexual repression*. [Wilhelm Reich, *Sexual Revolution*. Emphasis supplied.]

For Wilhelm Reich, repression, deflection, or sublimation apply in the adult only to the *pre-genital,* but not to the *genital* impulses. He felt that genital gratification is one, if not the most, decisive factor in prevention of emotional disturbance and the establishment of cultural achievement, both for the individual and for the group.

We readily admit that sexual reform may bring about far-reaching social change. Intellectual honesty demands the admission that if our sexual mores were to change in the direction of greater acceptance of sexuality, this might very well entail social changes on a broad front. That the conservative elements of society, backed by the precepts of our religious tradition, will shy away from such moral radicalism goes without saying. On the other hand, the social changes occasioned by two world wars and other factors have already so affected the repression of sexuality that suppression is today no longer nearly as "universal" as even in the most recent past.

The conflict between the repressed and the repressing forces in Western society is therefore more keenly and painfully felt at present than at any previous time in our history. Nothing is a better barometer of this heightened tension than the back-and-forth war of censorship in our day. On the one hand we witness the ever-increasing demand for greater freedom of expression and communication in the area of sexuality; on the other hand the clamor for more vigilance and stricter enforcement of sex-repressive legislation.

The fact is that we are already in the midst of a "sexual revolution" which is welcomed and lauded by one segment of our population, while it is deeply feared by others who—correctly—see in it the beginning of the end of many of their cherished values. Social institutions and the law tend to lag behind the rapid change in sexual mores in the community—a situation which we are presently witnessing to an extent never before experienced, because of the highly accelerated rate of change in our living patterns. The findings of the Kinsey report as to *behavioral sexual patterns* in our society was a quiet bombshell whose full significance is so revolutionary that it has been tacitly ignored after the first flurry of excitement subsided.

Seen in the light of Kinsey's findings, the social repression of sexuality, of which censorship is the chief weapon of attack, takes on a new and broader meaning. It raises, among other things, the question as to whether, by suppressing publications of an erotic nature, certain segments of society may not be exercising a censorship of ideas and beliefs which are entitled to constitutional protection.

THE CONCEPT OF "CONTEMPORARY COMMUNITY STANDARDS"

There appears to be a vast difference between the actual sex behavior of many people and what these people think they ought to be doing. This in itself is nothing particularly new or startling. A century and a half ago, the German poet, Goethe, had his conflict-ridden Dr. Faust cry out, "Two souls, alas! are vying in my breast!" But that did not prevent him from seducing, impregnating, and then abandoning his sweetheart, Gretchen.

Only this year, in the preliminary report of the California State Subcommittee on Pornographic Literature, there appeared the following statement:

It is still the principle of our nation that premarital or extramarital sexual activity is an undesirable thing, and anything that incites or lures or glorifies premarital or extramarital activity is objectionable.

One wonders, and hurries to the Kinsey studies to get the facts about the actual sexual behavior of the American male and female *as it is*. Doing so becomes all the more imperative since we must know what "contemporary community standards" really are if we are to form a guided opinion as to which books are in accord and which are clearly not in accord with what goes on in the community. Here, then, are the facts.

As to premarital sex activities of one kind or another, we learn that 64 percent of American females had "responded to orgasm" prior to marriage, while *all* of American males at marriage "had not only long since had their first experience in orgasm, but had already passed the peak of their sexual capacity." (Kinsey, *Sexual Behavior of the Human Female*.)

As to extramarital sex activity, Kinsey, *et al.,* report that by age forty, 26 percent of American females *had had coitus* with males whom they could not call their husbands. Add to this the 16 percent of wives who told Kinsey they had engaged in extramarital *petting* although they did not believe in extramarital coitus.

But what about the extramarital experiences of the husbands? Kinsey says about that:

> . . . allowing for the cover-up that has been involved, it is probably safe to suggest that about half of all the married males have intercourse with women other than their wives, at some time while they are married.

The American Law Institute must be credited with recognizing these facts concerning premarital and extramarital relations. In its recommendations for legal reforms (the Model Penal Code), it calls attention to the fact that,

American penal laws against illicit intercourse are

generally unenforced. . . . There is some indication that these laws, like other dead letter statutes, may lend themselves to discriminatory enforcement, e.g., where parties involved are of different races, or where a political figure is involved.

The American Law Institute goes on to say:

Pre-marital intercourse is also very common and widely tolerated so that prosecution for this offense is rare.

Further on, the Institute, in its Model Penal Code, states:

. . . [We do not] attempt to use the power of the State to enforce purely moral or religious standards. We deem it inappropriate for the government to attempt to control behavior that has no substantial significance except as to the morality of the actor. Such matters are best left to religious, educational and other social influences.

We now have to face two other problems in this connection: one concerns the *feelings* and *attitudes* of those Americans who engage in premarital and extramarital activities; and the other problem concerns the split between our overt sex mores and covert sexual behavior as, for instance, revealed in the Kinsey studies.

As to the feelings and attitudes of those who engage in premarital and extramarital sex activities we have of necessity less accurate information than on their behavior itself. It is much more difficult to ascertain people's sex attitudes than it is to find out what they are actually doing in this area (though this in itself is by no means an easy task!). We have to rely here on anecdotal material, and—to make things more difficult —sometimes we have to *infer* the attitudes from what people tell us.

Even though a rather large percentage of the American people engage in premarital sex activities, it would be unwise to assume that such behavior is not attended with considerable guilt and regret, at least on the part of *some* individuals. For this reason, Kinsey and his co-workers have included the factor of "regret" in their investigations.

For a meaningful estimate of "contemporary community standards," we shall therefore have to consider not only sexual behavior, but we must also try to arrive at some kind of understanding of the emotional climate in which premarital and extramarital (and even marital) sex activities take place.

As to premarital coitus, the Kinsey study suggests that between 69 to 77 percent of the women in their sample did not have the slightest regret about their experiences. Interestingly enough, the married women regretted their premarital experiences least. This fact should, as Kinsey notes, put big question marks behind the rash statements of all those who, for years, have claimed (and keep claiming) that married women usually regret such experiences because of the far superior quality of their marital relationship!

Kinsey also remarks that those whose regrets are deepest are also the *most disturbed* persons, who go to professional counselors for help. This, possibly, could account for the bias of these clinicians, who do not, in their practice, encounter the relatively guilt-free larger group.

As to men, the Kinsey studies show that attitudes about premarital intercourse follow economic class lines and educational levels rather closely. Kinsey found that some of the younger generation "find it modern" to deny that they have moral inhibitions against premarital intercourse. They insist, instead, that sexual relations are "too precious" for them to have with anyone except the girl that they marry, or that they hold certain convictions about marriage having a better chance for success if there was no premarital intercourse. Kinsey dryly observes, "to this extent the younger generation is 'emancipated'; but the change in the form of its rationalizations has not affected its overt behavior one whit."

The other 85 percent of the male population, which does not attend college, takes premarital intercourse for granted as the most normal and natural thing in the world. Kinsey insists that for this group there just is no question of right or wrong involved. We are told that even some lower-level clergymen seem to share these convictions. They do preach against profanity, smoking, drinking, gambling, and extramarital intercourse, but will not consider premarital intercourse as sinful.

As a matter of fact, premarital intercourse is so nearly universal in the lower economic and educational group that in the two or three lower-level communities in which the Kinsey researchers worked, they were "unable to find a solitary male who had not had sexual relations with girls by the time he was 16 or 17 years of age." In these communities, the occasional adolescent boy who does not "make out" with girls by that age is either physically handicapped, mentally retarded, homosexual and/or on the way out of his community.

The inconsistency of these "lower class" juvenile Romeos is revealed in their professed attitudes concerning virginity. Here they suddenly insist (41 percent of them, at least) that they would not want to marry a girl who was not a virgin on her wedding night. But, as Kinsey wisely assumes, "This may be more of a profession than a matter on which they will stand when it comes to the actual choice of a mate."

Young lower-level men not only start sexual relations rather early by American middle-class standards, but they are often also highly promiscuous. Many know of nothing but "one-day stands," changing their partners with each new experience. Says Kinsey, "This strikingly parallels the promiscuity which is found among those homosexual males who are 'oncers,' as the vernacular puts it." He goes on to say, "Some lower level males may have pre-marital intercourse with several hundred or even a thousand or more different girls before marriage,

and here their behavior is most different from the behavior of the college-bred males."

With regard to extramarital intercourse, there is "a
somewhat bitter acceptance" in the lower social levels of
the fact that most men don't seem to take kindly to
monogamy, but will have extramarital relations if, when,
and as often as opportunity presents itself. There is apparently a carry-over here of the group attitudes about
premarital sex relations, at least as far as the first five
or ten years of marriage are concerned. Later, the group
mores tighten up considerably, and lower-level men
"run around" less and stay home more as the years
go by.

With upper-class men, things work out quite differently. If, as Kinsey points out, they have been "hetero-
sexually restrained" for the past ten or fifteen years
before marriage, just getting married does not transform
them overnight into Don Juans. In fact, a good many of
them have a difficult enough time working things out
sexually with their wives, to say nothing about looking
for mistresses and "extracurricular" sex activities. But
this does not mean that these upper-level individuals are
harshly condemnatory of such practices.

In terms of censorship, this means that allegedly "obscene" books, dealing primarily with premarital and
extramarital relations are, by and large, faring better in
the courts than those books focusing on less widely accepted sex practices or deviations.

As far as community attitudes toward *homosexuality*
are concerned, we find much less tolerance toward the
male homosexual than toward unorthodox heterosexual
practices or toward homosexuality in women. This is so
in spite of the fact that, as Kinsey reports, about 46
percent of American males have had both homosexual
and heterosexual items in their histories.

The incidence of homosexuality in women is roughly
about *half* of that found in the male population. In spite
of, or perhaps because of, this and a variety of other
reasons, female homosexuality is much more tolerantly
accepted.

Female homosexuals are less often molested by the police, and still more rarely brought into court. On the other hand, male homosexuals are constantly being rounded up and not infrequently "roughed up" by the strong arm of the law, and thousands of them are annually fined and imprisoned.

This does not mean that female homosexuals do not often suffer rather severe indirect punishment through social reactions, employment difficulties, or by direct disciplinary measures in branches of the U. S. Armed Forces, in penal institutions, etc. But on the whole, female homosexuals in our culture are better off than their male counterparts, and the same principle can be expected to hold by and large, for books dealing with Lesbian activities.

None of this need surprise one, for it is much easier for a man who is heterosexual to be tolerant toward female than male homosexuals. There is ample psychological reason for this, aside from the Judeo-Christian prejudice (both Biblical and Talmudic tradition is more lenient toward female homosexuality). One of the psychological reasons is undoubtedly that many completely "normal" heterosexual males are erotically roused by watching female homosexuals in action, by reading about them, or by merely weaving fantasies and "thinking" about such activities. Moreover, the average man's sexual enjoyment in watching Lesbian activities, or indulging in fantasies about such activities, need not be dimmed by the arousal of homosexual anxieties which would be unavoidable if such actions or fantasies concerned members of his own sex.

For the male part of the community, Kinsey found least objection to homosexual practices at the very bottom of the socio-economical scale, and also at the top. It appears that the poorest and the wealthiest men are the most tolerant in this respect. The poor just have been less restrained sexually during their maturing years and seem to carry this tradition into adult life. They apparently extend this "liberal" attitude (if we can truly call it such) to sexually deviant behavior, such as homosexuality.

With upper-class men, Kinsey feels, their greater acceptance of, and tolerance toward, homosexuality is due to a more realistic understanding of man's sexual nature, better comprehension of the factors involved in the development of homosexuality, and a greater appreciation of the intellectual and social capacities of a person, quite aside from his sexual history and behavior.

The loudest protest against homosexuality and the most determined persecution of homosexuals comes from the group "that goes into high school, but never beyond in its educational career." Ironically, though not surprising to the psychologist, this is also the group in which Kinsey found the largest amount of overt homosexual activity! The watchword with this "solid" group of middle-class citizens apparently is "cry thief!" in the hope of avoiding suspicion in so doing.

What Kinsey suggests, not only with regard to homosexuality, but generally in the area of sex, is that the "upper-level rationalize on the basis of what is right or wrong." The lower level, on the other hand, rationalizes sexual behavior according to what is "natural or unnatural." In the lower economic levels, premarital sex, and to a certain point also extramarital sex and even homosexual acts, are only examples of doing "what comes natur'ly." However, when it comes to masturbation, petting (even marital petting before coitus), and certain other sex activities, their tolerance quickly comes to an end.

What interests us most about all these matters are, of course, their *social implications,* for what people do about their sexual needs and how they feel about them becomes a matter of passing one law rather than another, enforcing or not enforcing them, returning a verdict of "guilty" or "not guilty." And since most of those individuals administering the laws represent the morals of the conservative middle-class (with a few exceptions in the lower echelons of the law-enforcement group or an occasional judge of "lower-class" background who is elected to the bench), we must be prepared for—and in fact are used to—a strong bias toward sex suppression.

Kinsey, who had a keen eye for the differences in the sex mores of the different cultural levels in the American community, again and again calls our attention to these differences and their significance in terms of behavior. For the purposes of our investigation, social differences in sex attitudes are of crucial importance. We cannot meaningfully talk about "contemporary community standards" without taking these factors into account.

From all the evidence, it appears that those lower-level individuals who do see moral issues in sexual behavior are decidedly in the minority. This does not mean that the majority of such men (and women) are without any sex guilt. Quite the contrary! Even for them puritanical inhibitions and qualms cast a shadow over their "happiest moments." Says Kinsey, "They 'know that intercourse is wrong,' but 'they expect to have it anyway, because it is human and natural to have it.'"

If the upper-level male breaks his class code and has intercourse, it is probably with a girl whom he considers his fiancée. He rationalizes, "It's all right because we love each other." Again and again, statements like these appeared in the sex autobiographies of the college men about whose sex life and attitudes one of the authors is going to report elsewhere. (See Phyllis C. Kronhausen, *The Sex Life of the American College Male*.)

This attitude of the upper-level men is diametrically opposed to that of the lower-level males, whose feelings can be summed up in statements such as, "I didn't think much of her, so I went ahead and had intercourse with her. But when I find the 'right' girl, the one I really love and want to marry, I won't touch her until we're married." But, as was said before, more often than not these resolutions do not stand the test of reality.

Now, for our purpose, it is again necessary to remember that the upper (middle) class males who exercise jurisdictional control and run the judicial machinery come from the most sex-suppressive backgrounds in our community. In their thinking, morality and sexual purity are one and the same thing: "Many persons at this level believe that there are few types of immorality which are more enormous than sexual immorality," as Kinsey says.

In other words, many of the men who wield the widest power on a community level equate everything that is good, upright, desirable, ethical, clean and decent with abstinence from sexual relations. They will accept marriage and limited sexual expression within a life-long monogamous relationship (broken up only by the convention-time or sales-trip adventures). But—outside of such rare exceptions—their concept of themselves as self-respecting, honorable citizens is bound up with their ability to completely absorb their sexual urge in coitus with their wedded wives. There is, as Kinsey found, "nothing of which persons at this level are more afraid than a charge of immorality, as immorality is defined by the group. There is no disgrace that is more feared than that which may result from sexual scandal. Sex is so clearly a moral issue that *many persons in the group consider it a religious obligation to impose their code upon all other segments of the population.*" [Emphasis supplied.]

There are still certain other matters to consider if we are to gain at least a bird's-eye view of so-called contemporary community standards in the area of sex practices and sex attitudes. The first of these concerns the *positions in intercourse* and the shift in attitudes about *sex technique* over the period of the two world wars, and the second involves the most frequent sexual abnormalities, deviations, and perversions in our society.

With regard to intercourse positions, the prevailing attitude in the community is by and large still that there is one coital position (female lying down, face upward, with the male outstretched over her) which is biologically natural. All other positions are held by a considerable number of Americans to be man-devised variants. If excessively engaged in, that sizeable group feels, these different techniques will turn into perversions.

The Kinsey studies and the various reports of anthropologists describing the sex habits of other societies have largely dispelled the myth about the "naturalness" of what South Sea natives like to call the "missionary position." Taken on a global scale, "the beast with two backs" (as the French see it and as Shakespeare refers to it in *Othello*) is rather a rare specimen and somewhat of a laughing matter to members of other cultures who are equally convinced about the "naturalness" of their preferred coital positions.

The origin of our present custom is tied up, like so many of our sex standards, with Christian theology. After all, there was a time—and it is not so far back, either—when engaging in any other than the presently still most common position was a matter for religious confession. No longer aware of its connection with theology, people have just come to regard as "natural" what started as an expression of the "supernatural."

The second most prevalent coital position in America is the one with the female above, a factor for which the upper educational levels are largely responsible; that same group which, however, is most strongly repressive otherwise. The lower levels (and some clinicians) consider this position as highly perverted and objectionable, because it conveys to them the idea that the sex roles are reversed and raises in these people anxiety over homosexuality. Still, this position is used occasionally by about one third (34 percent) of Kinsey's upper-level males and in lesser degrees by the others. Next in line follows the position in which the partners lie on their sides, facing each other (26 percent of the college, and 16 percent of the high-school and grade-school men). Rear entrance into the vagina comes last (only 11 percent of college and high-school, and less than 8 percent of grade-school men practicing it at times). In other words, the more money and more education, the more variety in coital positions.

Kinsey found that the generation born about 1900

were loosening up in their restricted attitudes about positions in intercourse. For instance, over half (52 percent) of the younger-generation females reported that they had frequently been in a position lying above the male. But we must not forget that Kinsey's sample was slightly top-heavy with upper-level individuals, so that for the American community as a whole these percentages would be somewhat lower and give us a slightly more conservative picture.

All of this is of great importance for the problems of censorship, because the people who are to decide on such matters—for instance our jury men and women— each holding to the individual sex myths of their social class and generation, are likely to condemn as "immoral," "indecent," or "obscene" anything which runs counter to their cherished beliefs and deep-seated prejudices. The issue of community attitudes about coital positions may, for example, become vital in "obscenity" cases involving books describing a variety of sex techniques which are, notwithstanding their widespread popularity in the community, still unacceptable to many people on an emotional level.

Foremost among controversial sex techniques are mouth-genital contacts. It is astounding that mouth-genital activities are still so generally disavowed in public, while we know from the Kinsey studies that they "occur at some time in the histories of 60 percent of all males." And even among married females, stimulation of the male genitals by mouth occurs in about half of the number of cases. Nevertheless, books dealing with, or containing descriptions of, mouth-genital activities frequently encounter reactions of loathing on the part of the public which single out such writings for suppression.

Anal intercourse is much rarer than mouth-genital play. Still, it occurs in about 17 percent of those pre-adolescent boys who have any homosexual play (and 44 percent of all pre-adolescent boys do have some kind of homosexual experience). Its significance decreases in later years, except for those individuals who prefer this type of activity to the more common homosexual techniques—mutual masturbation and fellatio.

For the female, anal penetration is statistically insignificant. Nevertheless, a number of men practice occasional heterosexual anal intercourse in and out of marriage, mostly as a matter of variety. Also, some women (though their number is too small to make a statistical impression) prefer anal penetration to vaginal intercourse. It should be kept in mind, however, that anal erotism (anal masturbation, the insertion of objects into the anus, and homo- and heterosexual anal play) does have an important function in the psychosexual development of the individual during early childhood and pre-adolescence (see, for example, Freud's discussion of anal erotism in *Three Contributions to the Theory of Sexuality*).

There is sufficient evidence to suspect that the severe repression of anal erotism in our society accounts to a large extent for the development of feelings of "embarrassment, shame, and wrongdoing," which feelings are then connected with the much wider variety of acceptable sexual patterns not necessarily directly concerned with anal erotism. By instilling extreme feelings of aversion against "dirt" during the early years of life, Western education is conditioning the individual to associate sexuality with the excrementitious. In this way both scatological and genital-erotic interests are condemned to share the same subterranean existence in the limbo of repression. The same deep-seated cultural aversion to anal erotism is undoubtedly at least partially responsible for the severity of our sodomy acts, which extend also to marriage partners, and the penalties for which in some jurisdictions are only surpassed by those for murder, kidnapping and rape.

With regard to books, we find that otherwise rather broadminded individuals who would defend other types of erotic art and writings become intolerant of scatological works dealing with the organs and products of excretion. This intolerance is so profound that it extends itself on occasion, and quite unreasonably, to people who are in no way responsible for the production of such writings.

Booksellers, for instance, who find it impossible to be familiar with the contents of every title they offer for sale, can find themselves severely criticized, and even ostracized, by some members of the community who have discovered personally offensive passages in the titles of nationally recognized publishers.

Prostitution, as practiced and "enjoyed" in the community, likewise deserves our attention. It is significant not only in a general sociological way, but particularly so for our study. Literally hundreds of books with prostitution as one of their main themes make their perennial appearance on the American book market. Besides, hardly a theatre season goes by without at least one or more major plays being offered on Broadway stages dealing in one form or another with prostitution or the life of prostitutes.

The popularity of prostitution as a theme for writers of books and plays is, as we shall soon show, strictly out of proportion with its social significance in contemporary America; not that there are less females in our communities today who sell their sexual favors for stipulated amounts than there were a generation or two ago, nor that a smaller percentage of men than before World War I finally do have some sort of experience with prostitutes (most of them do). But "the mean frequency of prostitute contacts for the entire male population of all ages and of all educational and occupational groups is 0.093 per week, or approximately 5 times per year," (Kinsey). This is not very much, if seen in the context of men's total sexual outlet, and is certainly less impressive than the much higher frequencies for male homosexual experiences.

However, it is a well-known and fully attested fact that considerably more lower-level than upper-level men frequent prostitutes. So again, in connection with prostitution, there are significant class differences which enter into problems of censorship.

Having considered the more common types of sexual

behavior, i.e., heterosexual vaginal coitus, homosexuality, extra- and premarital sex activities, mouth-genital contacts, and prostitute contacts, we are ready to examine those sexual activities which are less commonly engaged in. As Kinsey observes, men have shown an entirely disproportionate amount of interest in the rarest, and not infrequently in "the most fantastically impossible," sexual acts. Consequently, we find this kind of inordinate interest reflected not only in the huge amount of scientific discussion, but equally in the scores of fictional accounts of such things as incest, transvestism, necrophilia, fetishism, sado-masochism, and animal contacts.

Though it may come as something of a shock to the average person, who has had no occasion to become aware of the more deviant forms of sexuality, and rare as these sexual activities may be among humans, we must here deal with them, precisely because they enter prominently into the question of "obscenity" in art and literature. Intercourse between humans and various animals is, in effect, one of the characteristic features rarely missing in "obscene" books.

Actually, the total sexual outlet through *animal contacts* is very low for both males and females in the U. S., if we use the total population as our yardstick. The reason for this is obvious: a rather large percentage of our city population has no, or minimal, contact with animals. The absence of appropriate animals in our large urban centers simply rules out this particular source of temptation.

In the country, however, where farm animals from sheep and goats to cows and horses are readily available, and suitable human sex partners are not, the picture is quite different. According to Kinsey, in these areas of the country, about every other farm lad has had some kind of sexual contact with animals at some time or another, and quite a few of them for several years of their life. For these men who were raised on farms, sexual activities with animals rank about equally in numerical importance to contacts with prostitutes or homosexual experiences in the population as a whole. In fact, in some parts of the West, Kinsey found that as many as 65 percent of the male population has had animal contacts in their sex histories, and indications are that in some communities sexual relations with animals are even still more common.

There are other aspects of these relations with animals which are, from a psychological point of view, still more significant. First of all, we find that quite a few individuals are erotically aroused by thinking about animals copulating or by watching them do so, a factor which "obscene" books often include for precisely that purpose. Kinsey suggests that observing animals in sexual activities stimulates at least many of the boys and men and leads them to identify their own sexual desires and capacities with those of the animals in their environment. It is therefore not surprising to find that some of these animal contacts do not lack the element of affection; but the significance of these animal contacts is that they are a proof that the sex drive is so powerful that it will find an outlet, no matter what the circumstances of deprivation.

Here again, the entirely different attitudes and experiences of the city—as against the country—in our communities make for trouble in the legal scene. The law calls these animal contacts "sodomy" or "bestiality," and punishes them (if brought to the attention of the courts) under the same provisions as homosexuality and mouth-genital contacts (between humans). In fact, men who are convicted of such "crimes" usually face the harshest and most cruel treatment, both from the prison administration and from the other inmates. As Kinsey points out, "All in all, there is probably no type of human sexual behavior which has been more severely condemned by that segment of the population which happens not to have had such experiences and which accepts the age-old judgment that animal intercourse must evidence a mental abnormality, as well as an immorality." Animal contacts as a sexual outlet for women, says Kinsey, "are obviously a minute fraction of what most human males have guessed them to be." And he concludes correctly that this fact may illuminate "some of the basic differences between the sexual psychology of the human female and male, and show something of the effects that such differences in psychology may have on the overt behavior of the two sexes."

Books dealing with, or containing descriptions of, sexual contacts between humans and animals (or, as the biology-oriented Kinsey liked to put it, between the human animal and animals of other species) are of course liable to be censored.

Another troublesome spot in literary obscenity cases is the area of incest. Here we run head-on into the most powerful, and one of the oldest, taboos of mankind. From the standpoint of contemporary community standards it would therefore be all the more important to know to what extent incestuous relationships exist in our society and to try to understand the nature of these relations. However, at this point, even the Kinsey studies forsake us in our inquiry, and one is forced to speculate and make inferences from clinical observation, court records, and the reports of a variety of social agencies. (We understand that the forthcoming study of "Sex Offenders," undertaken by the Kinsey group of researchers, will shed further light on this subject.)

For the present, nobody is able to quote meaningful figures on the prevalence of incestuous sex activities in the American community. By methods of indirect proof, one can only arrive at the conclusion that it is not nearly as uncommon as is usually assumed. One of the few statistical datum which we do have on the matter does originate in the Kinsey studies. From this source we learn that approximately 16 percent of all sexual approaches by adult males toward pre-adolescent girls were made by relatives, among whom uncles were the most conspicuous single source of contact.

From another source we learn that at one time in Chicago, out of 72 cases of delinquent girls brought before the Juvenile Court, 32 had had incestuous relations with the fathers. (Kirsen Weinberg, *Incest Behavior*.)

It appears that incest behavior in the American community is connected with lower social status and delinquency. Some writers (e.g., Judge Murtagh and Sara Harris in *Cast the First Stone,* and psychologist Harold Greenwald in *The Call Girl*) have found incestuous relations in the backgrounds of some prostitutes. The implication is that this kind of "sexual trauma" (among a number of other things) may lead to, or contribute to, prostitution, delinquency, neuroses and psychoses.

This is not the place to discuss the causative factors of prostitution, which—most experts agree—are partly social and partly psychological. It is certain, however, that the *guilt* engendered by the family's and the community's reaction to such behavior is indeed sufficiently traumatic to lead to serious emotional complications.

For our purposes, it is sufficient to keep in mind that incest behavior is not as uncommon in certain (lower-level) segments of the community as one might be led to believe, even though accurate statistics are at present lacking. The case files of social agencies, of welfare departments, public health clinics, etc., all give testimony to this fact. It also appears, from the clinical experience of psychoanalysts, working mostly with individuals from the highest socio-economic levels of society, that incest behavior of one kind or another (for example, fondling, "sexy" kissing, manipulation of the genitals, petting, and, in some instances, complete coitus) is frequently present in the histories of these upper-class individuals.

As far as censorship of books is concerned, no other single factor in literature lends itself to quite as much legal complication as the description of incestuous relations. Judges and juries uniformly reflect the deep cultural taboo on all such relations and usually consider their realistic description in a book sufficient grounds for its condemnation.

Books in the "hard core obscenity" group (as defined) accentuate incestuous relations by stressing their overt, *physical* side, while classical literature deals mostly with the covert and *emotional* aspects of such relations. In so doing, "obscene" books prejudice censorial

, let us say, a novel about sexual practices in Samoa. It would simply have no relevance. One cannot escape the facts of life itself. That which is real and acceptable in one segment of a community loses none of its reality by being unacceptable to, or not practiced by, another group or individual. "Obscene" books, on the other hand, are straight fantasy and as such cannot be said to be based on the reality of any community in any part of the world. It would therefore be impossible to apply even an artificial norm or community standard to such writings.

The distinction between these two forms of writing can only be sensibly made in terms of intent, content, and structure.

A CRITIQUE OF CURRENT LEGAL THEORY AND PRACTICE CONCERNING "OBSCENITY"

As we have seen, the Unted States Supreme Court has set up several standards by which the 'obscenity' of a book is to be judged. Likewise, the courts in various European countries have set up certain standards for the same purpose and, though these differ in some instances from the wording of the United States Supreme Court (and still more in the manner of their enforcement), they reflect a basically similar line of argument and manner of thinking. We therefore feel that an analysis of the standards laid down by the United States Supreme Court will also cover the essentials of European obscenity legislation, without going further into the subtler differences in the wording of the various national obscenity laws, as they apply to one country or another.

Briefly, the standards set up by the United States Supreme Court for the determination of the obscenity of a book are the following:

bodies still more by raising before them the specter of physical incest. Stories about incestuous relations, especially those going into physical detail, are certainly "rubbing the sore" by stimulating incestuous fantasies which most of us would rather keep in repression. However, the fact that both classical and "obscene" literature apparently cannot do without the inclusion of incest gives testimony to the universality of incestuous fantasies and desires, as indeed Freud and the psychoanalytic school have amply demonstrated.

In classical and non-obscene literature, incestuous relations are usually handled by stressing the emotional conflict which such relations bring about. We also find that in such works as Sophocles' *Oedipus Rex*, Thomas Mann's novel *The Holy Sinners* and his short story *Blood of the Wolsungs*, as well as in several of Shakespeare's dramas, or Schiller's *Don Carlos*, those engaging in incestuous relations, or even contemplating them, are generally punished in one form or another. In "obscene" books, however, as we shall see, incestuous relations are freely enjoyed by the participants.

It will also become clear that any or all of the rarer sex deviations are a *necessary* part of "obscene" books. It is obvious that erotic realism in literature must deal with these phenomena too, but we shall note the distin differences in the presentation of such material in ero realism as against hard core pornography.

As to "contemporary community standards": we h demonstrated that there is such an enormously variation in what is more commonly practiced, that fect there is no such thing as a contemporary comn standard to relate to erotic writings. But even if uniform standard could, in fact, be said to would actually not be relevant with regard to erotic realism, nor with respect to "hard core o Erotic realism presents life as it is, wherever ever the setting may happen to be, in wha the artist chooses to present it. If there we thing as a community norm in the Unit America, it would still be manifestly impos

1. The "social value" test. ~~...~~ threatening
2. The "prurient interest" test.
3. The "patently offensive" or "contemporary community standards" test.
4. The "hard core pornography" test.

To these tests which have been variously applied by the Court, we may add still another which has been proposed as an alternative to the constant or static "hard core pornography" test, namely:

5. The "variable obscenity" test.

We shall now proceed to examine these standards critically, though sympathetically, and with all due respect for the thinking of the United States Supreme Court, the American Law Institute, and of individual jurists on these matters, and with the view of trying to clarify still further the complicated and troublesome issues at stake.

1. *The "social value" test.*

As previously pointed out, the United States Supreme Court feels that hard core pornography is devoid of any serious social value and therefore is not entitled to the constitutional safeguards concerning the free communication of ideas. Likewise, Professors Lockhart and McClure state, in their excellent articles *Censorship of Obscenity: The Developing Constitutional Standards* (Minnesota Law Review, Vol. 45:5, 1960), to which we shall return for reference or exception: "For hardcore pornography is so foul and revolting that few people can contemplate the absence of laws against it—that would be unthinkable."

Reduced to its simplest formula, this is the theory, variously brought to bear by the courts, that holds pornography to be "dirt for dirt's sake," without any other "redeeming social value," such as artistic or literary merit, or the communication of socially or philosophically important ideas. As a corollary to this standard, it is declared that such material has as its sole and obvious object the stimulation of "lustful thoughts and desires," that is, the sexual arousal of the reader.

Now, one may still grant that argument (though not without some very serious reservations, discussed in more detail in the chapter "The Psychological Effects of Erotic Literature") at least with regard to the communication of ideas (other than sexual), and as far as the most clear-cut and indisputable hard core pornography is concerned. We therefore agree that some kind of social control of this type of material is probably in order, especially as its accessibility to young people is concerned—a purpose which can perhaps best be served by restricting its sale to "adults only". We are, however, in no wise convinced of the presence of a "clear and present danger" to society or even to "the young and most susceptible" with regard to hard core pornography. At the present stage of our scientific knowledge about the effects of such material, there is no proof that contact with hard core pornography tends to lead the individual to the commitment of anti-social acts (see "The Psychological Effects of Erotic Literature.") Our suggestion to restrict the sale of hard core pornography to adults is rather a *concession* to the conservative opinion, than a recommendation based on positive evidence of any irreversible damage resulting from exposure to such material.

Furthermore, it is not nearly as "unthinkable" as Professors Lockhart and McClure take it to be, that there ought not to be *any* "obscenity" legislation at all. At least two Chief Justices—Douglas and Black—favor precisely that position.

The legal definition of what constitutes pornography is complicated further by the fact that not only hard core pornography, but also erotica of indisputable artistic or literary merit may have as their *sole* or *main* *purpose* the sexual stimulation of the reader. Of course, it can be argued that the superior writing or "quality" of these erotica constitutes such a "socially redeeming" value. However, one must face the fact that even hard core pornography may at times be extremely well written and still conform in every respect to our criteria for such writing in structure, content, and intent.[1]

Plainly, then, one has to approach the problem of "socially redeeming value" from a still more basic point of view, and ask oneself why it has not been assumed that erotic stimulation is, in itself, a "socially redeeming value?" Obviously, legal thinking has thus far not even considered the problem from this premise, though the United States Supreme Court has decided that "sex and obscenity are not synonymous," and that, "The portrayal of sex, in art, literature and scientific works, is not itself sufficient reason to deny material the constitutional protection of freedom of speech and press."

On the other hand, it is not within the Western cultural tradition to consider sexual stimulation a positive social value. Thus, even the progressive-minded American Law Institute in its drafting of a Model Penal Code speaks of a *necessary conflict* between sexual and social interests and wishes to penalize those who, as the Institute puts it, "want to make a living by exacerbating that [conflict], by rubbing the sore . . ."

In criticism of this position, we would like to point out that it is *not* an established scientific fact that sexuality is necessary in conflict with other social aims, and that in fact quite the contrary may be the case. Furthermore, it would seem more reasonable to reduce the presently undeniable conflict between sexuality and attempts at its social control by reducing the rigor of some of the efforts at control (a purpose which would be served by the legal reforms proposed by the American Law Institute itself), rather than by attempting to regulate the amount of sexual stimulation allowed in the culture. (In actual fact, the amount of stimulation supplied by hard core pornography can only be considered minimal in comparison to other sex stimuli, such as advertising, fashions, and many other powerful sex

[1] See *The Psychology of Pornography* especially pp. 220-237. Our sample *The Lascivious Hypocrite*—in the original French, *Le Tartuffe Libertin*—is a case in point.

stimuli which are today perfectly accepted and integrated into our culture.)

Finally, it can hardly be considered fair to bring the economic profit motive into the field against the producers of erotica (including hard core pornography) when virtually any commodity one can name is sold by the exploitation of sexual stimuli, and where the profit motive, being one of the declared values in our type of free enterprise society, is bound to play a prominent role even in the loftiest artistic and intellectual pursuits.

We would therefore urge that the concept of "redeeming social value" be reconsidered from the point of view that erotic stimulation as such can be said to constitute such a value itself, without the need for further 'redeeming' features, such as the superior aesthetic quality of the work, its philosophical message, or any other aspect beyond its erotic appeal per se. In considering this question in the most objective manner possible, we would suggest that it be abstracted from the immediate concern with hard core pornography, and that it not be confused with the concept of "erotic appeal" to unusual ("perverted") sexual interests, that are typical for a special kind of erotics, though not of deliberately erotic writings as such.

It is also clear that in reconsidering the problem of "social value," prejudices arising possibly out of certain religious preconceptions must be excluded, so as to facilitate an impartial study of the question and, further, to protect dissident philosophical minorities in the culture from the imposition of religious standards and value judgments which cannot be binding for the entire population of a complex modern society, nor form the basis for its legislation. But we are afraid that nothing short of such fundamental re-thinking of the question of social value will result in a resolution of the present confusion in legal theory and practice: for if erotic stimulation can be considered a "socially redeeming value" (and there is very good reason to feel that this may objectively turn out to be the most logical and scientific answer), then even deliberately erotic writings and pictorial representations would automatically come under the constitutional freedoms of expression and would require no further "redeeming" features in order to make themselves acceptable before the law.

2. The "prurient interest" test.

As we have previously seen, the United States Supreme Court specifies that, "Obscene material is material which deals with sex in a manner appealing to prurient interest." As a corollary to this statement, the Court declared, as we have previously discussed, that this in effect meant that, "Whether to the average person, applying contemporary community standards, the dominant theme of the material taken as a whole appeals to prurient interest."

Leaving aside for the moment the question of "contemporary community standards" to which we have already devoted a special chapter and to which we shall return in our discussion of the "patently offensive" test, we shall now examine the problems connected with the concepts of "prurient interest" and the "average person" to whom this test is to apply.

As Professors Lockhart and McClure observe, "The phrase 'appeal to prurient interest' is relatively rare in the law of obscenity. Even the word 'prurient' is not common and, when used, is usually used to describe a type of abnormal person who is not a suitable hypothetical person for judging the material. In the Roth-Alberts opinion the Court borrowed the phrase 'appeal to prurient interest' from a tentative draft of the American Law Institute's *Model Penal Code,* which in turn had lifted it from a 1915 opinion of the Supreme Court. But the Court and the American Law Institute did not agree upon the meaning of the phrase.

"To the American Law Institute, 'prurient interest' is a 'shameful or morbid interest in nudity, sex or excretion;' it is 'an exacerbated, morbid, or perverted interest growing out of the conflict between the universal sexual drive of the individual and equally universal social controls of sexual activity. . . .' "

On the other hand, the American Law Institute rejected, "the prevailing tests of tendency to arouse lustful thought or desires because it is unrealistically broad for a society that plainly tolerates a great deal of erotic interest in literature, advertising, and art, and because *regulation of thought or desire, unconnected with overt misbehavior,* raises the most acute constitutional as well as practical difficulties." As Professors Lockhart and McClure point out, The American Law Institute likewise rejected the test of "tendency to corrupt or deprave" because of the lack of evidence of any connection between obscenity and misbehavior and because of "the wide disparity of strongly held views as to what does tend to produce that result." And Lockhart and McClure continue "it seemed obvious [to the draftsmen of the *Model Penal Code*] that inquiry as to the nature of the appeal of a book, i.e., the kind of appetite to which the purveyor is pandering, is quite different from an inquiry as to the *effect* of a book upon the reader's thoughts, desire, or action."

"But what seemed obvious to the draftsmen of the *Code* was not obvious to the Court. For after borrowing the phrase 'appeal to prurient interest' from the *Model Penal Code,* the Court went on to say that 'material which deals with sex in a manner appealing to prurient interest' is 'material having a tendency to excite lustful thoughts.' " Thus, we are right back to the kind of "sexual thought control" without clear relation to overt misbehavior to which the American Law Institute specifically objected.

The American Law Institute, furthermore, seems to be aiming with their definition of "prurient interest" as much at the manner of distribution, the advertising, and "merchandising" of the erotic material, as at its psychological or mental *effect*—if we read their wording as to "the kind of appetite to which the purveyor is pandering" correctly. This interpretation would seem to imply a "variable obscenity" concept, depending on how the erotic material is presented to the public, a proposition favored by some leading American jurists (including Professors Lockhart and McClure, as well as Chief Justice Warren), but presenting serious problems of its own, of which its proponents seem to be aware and which we shall discuss more fully below.

Needless to say, we do not think that the "prurient interest" test, as presently applied, has much scientific validity by which to recommend itself. Rather, it represents an emotional concept, arising out of a certain tradition of anxiety surrounding sexuality, of which even the American Law Institute's narrower definition is not entirely free. Still, the latter's attempt to define "prurient interest" as a "perverted, shameful, morbid, exacerbated" interest in matters pertaining to sex or excretion is generally in line with the United States Supreme Court's distinction between sex and obscenity as separate entities. Both seem to be aimed primarily at certain sado-masochistic and other "perverted" material (such as the "bondage photographs" to which Professors Lockhart and McClure allude and which apparently constituted the bulk of the evidence in the *Alberts* case).

However, even if the courts were to interpret "prurient interest" in this narrower sense of the "morbid" and the "perverted", judges and juries would find themselves suddenly in the unenviable and totally impossible position of having to play the role of psychiatric watchdogs for the mental health of the citizenry, or of having to employ expert testimony as to the degree to which the erotic material in question or the manner of its presentation constituted an appeal to "morbid, exacerbated, perverted, etc." sexual interest.

Obviously, here again we have arrived at an impasse, for the opinions of the experts differ considerably (as in the case of the *effects* of erotic material), with regard to what they consider "normal" and "abnormal," or "perverted" in sexual behavior. Many—perhaps most—clinicians consider, for instance, that homosexuality is a kind of "mental disease" or "perversion" (thus agreeing with the current legal opinion and language in this matter, though not necessarily with the *application* of the law). But a substantial minority of social scientists, including the Kinsey researchers, hold a very different point of view.

Further, sado-masochism and "bondage" themes, as well as other sexual deviations, can be a feature not only of hard core pornography, but also of other literature of undeniable artistic or other "socially redeeming" value. Similarly, in the arts, one cannot say that "normalcy" of content or subject matter has been a characteristic feature of some of its greatest examples, as any casual inspection of an art museum or study of art history would show. If great art occasionally manifests unhealthy erotic tendencies, controlling the arts seems even more disastrous, as the example of art in the Soviet Union amply demonstrates: there, literature and the arts have come under the most rigorous control of the State, with the result that Soviet art and literature, with few exceptions, has become morally and perhaps even clinically unobjectionable—but also dead!

Clearly then, the application of any standards of "normalcy" in the judging of literature and the arts—even more so than in actual behavior—can only lead to compounding of the present confusion and to the most absurd situations in actual legal practice. The position of, equating 'prurient interest' with 'lascivious' or 'lustful' thoughts and desires, having a 'tendency to deprave or corrupt' is equally untenable. The whole language of this portion of the Supreme Court's definition of "obscenity"—like the term "obscenity" itself—is so clearly colored by emotional prejudice, and its thinking so patently unscientific, that it seems beyond doubt that the whole concept of "prurient interest", either in its narrower or its wider interpretation, will ultimately have to be abandoned in any new attempt to re-define the area of sex-censorship unless, as one may hope, the opinion of some members of the Supreme Court that there is no place whatever for censorship in a truly free society, should ultimately prevail.

Meanwhile, the courts will have to struggle not only

with the foggy concept of "prurient interest," but also with that of the "average person" to whose prurient interest the obscene material is supposed to appeal. This "average man" has been variously described as "the man in the street," "the person with average sex instincts," "the reasonable man," and similar generalities.

Professors Lockhart and McClure point out the various defects in the "normal person test," of which perhaps the most serious one is that the average or "common" man may care little about the intellectual or artistic aspects of a given book or art object, while reacting only to its erotic appeal, and they ask "what is to be done with material of substantial aesthetic value that the common man peruses for his own private titillation, oblivious of its artistry?"

However, Professors Lockhart and McClure see still another puzzling problem in the "average person" test which has, we cannot help but feel, arisen out of a misunderstanding about the nature of the appeal of hard core pornography. For if—as the Professors argue —hard core pornography were to appeal solely to the "sexually immature," while being merely "repulsive, not attractive" to the "sexually mature person," then it cannot at the same time be of "prurient interest" to the "average person."

It is readily enough seen how a confusion of this kind could have arisen: for Professor Margaret Mead's definition of pornography, to which Lockhart and McClure refer, makes, indeed, this kind of implication: (*Sex and Censorship in Contemporary Society*, New World Writings 7, 18: Third Mentor Selection, 1953). Furthermore, our own findings concerning the basic nature of hard core pornography as erotic fantasy material, which up to that point coincide with Professor Mead's definition, seem to lend further substance to the notion that only the "sexually immature" might react postively to this type of stimulation (to say nothing of the vulgarity of the bulk of hard core pornography to which Professors Lockhart and McClure, as well as

Professor Mead seem to have reacted with understandable "shock").

Be that as it may, we wish to differentiate our own view from those expressed by Professor Mead and all other moralistic or philosophical interpretations of deliberately erotic art and literature (pornography), including those voiced by some of the writers (such as D. H. Lawrence) who themselves have been accused of pornographic intent. Indeed, we wish to emphasize that in our opinion hard core pornography—even when vulgar and offensive in character—can and does have an appeal to the "average", "normal" person.

At the same time, we wish to state with equal emphasis that *we hold no brief in favor of hard core pornography*. We think, as we have stated over and over again, that hard core *pornography bears the stigmata and carries with it the unsavory odor of the sexual neurosis of our civilization.* It frequently does "degrade sex" and offers an "insult to the human spirit," as D. H. Lawrence remarked. But it is *not* true that deliberately erotic art and writings always and invariably do so, nor does it lie in the *nature* of erotic fantasies or day-dreams (Mead's "reveries"), that they should be "infantile," "immature," and "pathological" in the clinical sense, or "disgusting," "degrading," and "shocking" in the moral or aesthetic sense. If deliberately erotic art and writing in general, and hard core pornography in particular, are today often characterized by pathological and aesthetically offensive features, this is, to our minds, an indictment not only of such products, but of the sick culture, with its unreasonable sexual anxieties and taboos, which produced it.

Seen in this light, it becomes at once clear and perfectly understandable why hard core pornography, with all its admittedly unsavory features, should nevertheless have a much more general appeal than one might have thought. If this were not so, and if hard core pornography had an appeal only to a relatively small subgroup of sexually immature individuals, "perverts," and "degenerates," it would be difficult to explain the historical role it has played from one generation to another or the continued, insistent demand for this type of material.

It is also our experience that persons of considerable aesthetic sensibility and high ethical standards, but with more than "average" exposure to erotic materials, may have a more relaxed attitude toward erotica (including hard core pornography), that they may show no signs of "shock" or "revulsion," and that they may either react positively but *differentially* to such material, or fail to react to it at all, being, as it were, inured to its influence.

At the same time, it is typical for members of the more conservative segments of society—as we have pointed out in our discussion of "Contemporary Community Standards"—to project their feelings and attitudes onto those persons of different social background or different psychological make-up, and to judge too harshly in these matters. Also, it must be borne in mind that the majority of those, who as judges, jurors, or lawmakers are generally called upon to make decisions on matters of social control of sexuality and its literary or artistic expressions, have had relatively little contact with the problems under consideration, nor can they reasonably be expected to be experts in such highly specialized professional disciplines as the psychology and sociology of sexual behavior, or in the history of erotic art and literature. On the other hand, these circumstances would point to the necessity for the most careful evaluation of these matters on the part of those entrusted with the interpretation and the enforcement of laws pertaining to sexual conduct or to the exercise of the freedom of expression in these areas.

3. *The "patently offensive" or "contemporary community standards" test.*

We have already indicated some of the serious problems connected with present judicial reliance on the test of what is "patently offensive" to public taste, that is, whether or not a book or pictorial representation is objectionable in terms of "contemporary community standards." To these standards we now wish to add the following objections:

1. The application of the "patently offensive" or "contemporary community standards" test lends itself to the down-grading of the arts and literature. Here again, Lockhart and McClure have correctly pointed out that even if national instead of local or state standards of public approval are applied, such procedure would "invite triers of fact to apply Philistine standards in judging material for obscenity."

Contrary to any such process of evaluating and legally judging the merits of literary and artistic production, it is to be noted that vital art and literature are by definition invariably *ahead* of their times and therefore frequently not appreciated by contemporary society. If the law therefore sides on these occasions with a hypothetical "public" opinion, the result can only be the killing of creative initiative (such as is indeed the case under authoritarian governments).

2. By the same token, we must reject Lockhart and McClure's unquestioning assent to the fact "that contemporary American society rejects and will not tolerate the dissemination of hard core pornography." Even if this should be so (and we do not doubt that the majority of the people in the United States and in most European communities would *officially* go on record along these lines, though many people may *privately* hold quite a different view), we are not convinced that such rejection by the majority should necessarily *form the basis of the law,* (a comparable case in point would be the rejection by the majority of the people in some of the southern areas of the United States of the concept of racial equality). Here, we feel, the law and the lawmakers—just as the artist, the writer, and the scientist —should be *ahead* of the time and *above* the pressure of public opinion. This is especially important in those areas of public life where personal feelings and prejudice

run high and where, as in matters of sexual conduct and censorship, questions of fundamental constitutional freedoms, far beyond the immediate issues at hand, are so clearly involved.

3. The "patently offensive" or "contemporary community standards" test is incompatible with the fair and equitable administration of the law because of the *greatly accelerated* process of change in these standards themselves under present social conditions. In other words, a given community may find a certain book or pictorial representation "patently offensive" today and the courts will convict the offender of public taste and morals—only to find that a few years later, in a similar case, the same community no longer finds a book or pictorial representation of this kind "patently offensive." In all these cases—and they are far from being merely "hypothetical," as the rapidly succeeding reversals of legal opinion and decisions amply indicate—the injustice of the prior conviction is too obvious and painful to be tolerated by an enlightened judicial machinery.

We would therefore agree with Professors Lockhart and McClure when they conclude in their own analysis of the question, that in their judgment, "contemporary community standards have little place in obscenity censorship."

4. *The "hard core pornography" test.*

This is a relatively new test of obscenity and, though apparently *implied* in the more recent decisions of the United States Supreme Court and in the arguments of some of the lower courts, it has not been explicitly accepted by the United States Supreme Court itself. Briefly, it is based on the following line of reasoning: ". . . The inquiry for the court, therefore, is whether the publication is so entirely obscene as to amount to 'hard core pornography' (not necessarily dealing with deviate sex relations since, while there is a pornography of perversion, 'pornography' is not limited to the depiction of unnatural acts)." (*People* v. *Richmond County News Inc.*, 9 N Y 2d 578).

As is clear from our previous comments in "The Supreme Court Definition of 'Obscenity'" and in our efforts to analyze and identify this type of erotica, we consider this legal concept the most useful one of all, or perhaps rather the *only* useful one. It, at least, insists on a narrower definition of "obscenity," thus preventing the arbitrary application of broadly defined obscenity statutes to books and pictorial representations of erotic content or subject matter, but not clearly falling into the hard core pornography category. Thus, the concept affords, where applied, a certain amount of legal protection for the so-called borderline cases—e.g., the recent California decision in favor of Miller's *Tropic of Cancer* in which the court relied, among other evidence, upon the criteria for "hard core" pornography as outlined by the authors.

The most serious defect of the concept, however, lies in the fact that it has permitted confusion between hard core pornography and *deliberately erotic writings* in general, both of which have in common that they serve, and are *meant* to serve, as psychological aphrodisiacs or sex stimuli. It is for this reason that we have analyzed and outlined the *specific* characteristics of hard core pornography which is, really, nothing but a particular type of deliberately erotic writing, but by no means synonymous with it.

The present legal practice of equating hard core pornography with other forms of deliberately erotic writings, offers, therefore, no protection for the latter; a confusion which has, we believe, arisen out of the general unfamiliarity with the wider field of these materials on the part of those officially concerned with these problems. A distinction between hard core pornography on the one hand, and deliberately erotic writings of different types is therefore necessary, if the hard core pornography test is not to discriminate unjustly against other forms of erotica

In making this distinction, it must be emphasized that

the difference between hard core pornography and other deliberately erotic writings does not in any way depend (as is generally assumed) on the varying degrees of "rawness" that characterize the material in question. Thus, Lockhart and McClure, while aware of the necessity for a distinction between hard core pornography and other types of erotica, mistakenly formulate the problem in terms of the extent to which a given book contains "raw" or "vulgar" passages, and ask: "What test will with tolerable accuracy distinguish Henry Miller's *Tropic of Cancer* and *Tropic of Capricorn* from *Lady Chatterley's Lover?* Or if the *Tropics* are not quite raw enough to be classed obscene, what test will distinguish these novels from his *Quiet Days at Clichy,* which is rawer still?"

Now, Miller can get very "raw" (offensive) indeed, and does so with obvious deliberation to challenge certain values in our society, but that does not make his books particularly "sexy" or effective as psychological sex stimuli. Nor are his books *intended* to be erotically stimulating.

No, the real problem in the hard core pornography test, to our way of thinking, rests in the fact that hard core pornography is not the *only* type of deliberately erotic writing. By applying that test, the courts are therefore more than likely to judge anything "obscene" which is designed to act as a psychological aphrodisiac by emphasizing the physical aspects of sexual relations, that is, by the detailed description of sexual activities or sexual fantasies. They may so judge even though these descriptions (or portrayals in the arts) may be aesthetically in perfectly good taste and show none of the rawness or vulgarity that is, as we have seen, characteristic not only of hard core pornography, but also, and sometmes *even more so,* of erotic realism. Moreover, this offensive vulgarity can and does occur in surrealistic, philosophical and other types of literature, as evidenced in the work of de Sade, Apollinaire, Bataille, Genêt, and many others.

If these obstacles to the practical applicability of the

hard core pornography test seem almost insurmountable, we still think that the concept is so far the most useful one. For if one applied our analysis of the characteristics of hard core pornography to the vast majority of those writings which can and have been confused with it, one would find that even in such genuine "borderline" books as *Fanny Hill,* these writings do not really conform to the typical pattern of hard core pornography. On the other hand, the case of *Fanny Hill* shows clearly that one might find it more difficult to clear books of that type from the charge of being deliberately erotic writings (quality erotica) in the wider sense.

Here the question of "contemporary community standards" once again enters the picture: for, while it appears that the professed attitude of contemporary American (and European) society is that it does not approve of nor intend to tolerate hard cord pornography (as Lockhart and McClure have been stressing and which is likewise our own underlying assumption in favoring the hard core pornography test as an intermediary stop gap on the road to complete abolition of censorship), it is not so clear that contemporary western society also rejects quality erotica, *including* deliberately erotic writings of potent psychological sex appeal. In fact, it would seem from the wide public acceptance of *Fanny Hill* as well as of certain Oriental love classics, (such as the *Kamasutra* and the *Perfumed Garden*), that the western community is ready to appreciate psychological sex stimuli of a fairly concentrated nature. The need for a distinction between hard core pornography and quality erotica (including deliberately erotic writings of a non-pornographic nature) is therefore more than theoretical. It is a necessity, the need for which will undoubtedly become more and more acute in the near future.

At the same time, the greater acceptance of quality erotica in the western world demands a re-consideration of the hard core pornography test, inasmuch as it applies to *pictorial* representations. Here again, the public has recently become much more appreciative of good (but "strong") erotic art, as is shown by the large sale of erotic art books, such as those presenting the erotic temple sculpture of India, or the erotic art of the Greeks, the Etruscans, or the frescoes of Pompeii. But this is precisely where the hard core pornography test is *least* useful, for a single picture or art object does not lend itself to the same kind of detailed analysis of its content, as is possible (and necessary) in arriving at a reasonable conclusion concerning the pornographic or non-pornographic nature of literature.

In the case of pictorial representations one would simply have to fall back on judgments of *quality,* so that, for instance, an intercourse scene drawn by the hand of Rembrandt (his famous and often reproduced self-portrait with his wife), or by Picasso, would have to be considered "art" (and thus not *obscene*), while the same scene, shown in an amateur photograph or drawn by a lesser artist might be considered "obscene," for lack of "redeeming social value." Clearly, all such designations of "obscenity" cannot be anything but completely arbitrary and point to the limitations of the hard core pornography test in actual legal practice, particularly with regard to pictorial representations.

5. *The "variable obscenity" test.*

Under this test, a book or picture is judged, as Lockhart and McClure explain, "by its appeal to and effect upon the audience to which the material is primarily directed. In this view, material is *never inherently obscene*; instead its obscenity varies with the circumstances of its dissemination." (Emphasis supplied.)

Lockhart and McClure, who seem to favor this test (as does Chief Justice Warren) as an alternative to the constant or static hard core pornography concept, point out that this test would make it possible to prosecute persons who, like Roth and Alberts, "advertise material that is not intrinsically pornographic as if it were hard core pornography, seeking out an audience of the sexually immature to exploit their pitiful needs. When material is thus *treated* as hard-core pornography, the nature and appeal of hard-core pornography seems to furnish a reasonably satisfactory tool for separating the obscene from the non-obscene, regardless of its intrinsic nature."

However, the Minnesota jurists themselves point to the limitations of the "variable obscenity test in those cases in which the material itself "is neither hard-core pornography, nor treated as such," and suggest that, if the Supreme Court should adopt the variable obscenity concept, "it might well draw the constitutional line at the level of material that is treated as hard-core pornography."

Another problem under this test would be, as Professors Lockhart and McClure agree, that it might be difficult to draw the line between the unscrupulous advertisers of spurious erotica, promising their audience more than they intend to give, and the "come-on" advertising of certain movie-theaters, luring the gullible into their houses with adjectives such as *"red-hot," "sexsational,"* and other types of fraudulent sex-advertising.

Actually there has been at least one conviction in America of such an advertiser and, under the "variable obscenity" test, more convictions of this sort could be procured. However, as unsavory as the fraudulent sex advertisers may generally be, it seems hardly fair first to make the dissemination of hard core pornography illegal, and then convict a person for fraudulently advertising erotica which do not, upon inspection, come up (or *down*) to the level of the hard core pornography! And, in spite of the theoretical purpose of the "variable obscenity" test, that is precisely what such prosecutions would amount to in actual practice.

The most dangerous aspect of the "variable obscenity" concept in our estimation, however, is that it would open the door to the prosecution of all kinds of erotic material which are admittedly *not* hard core pornography—i.e., material that is not held to be "obscene," even by the standards of the courts! One shudders, indeed, to think what injustices and confusions the application of the "variable obscenity" test might lead to in actual legal practice—a result which could certainly not be acceptable to persons of the integrity of those now advocating such a test.

Nor do we see, as Lockhart and McClure seem to do, the necessity for a "variable obscenity" test in order to make it legally possible for social scientists to import hard core pornography for purposes of research. For, in these cases, the issue is never one of *dissemination* on the part of the purchaser or importer, but only one of the right to import, purchase, or possess such material. Actually, the right of the individual to purchase and possess erotic material (including hard core pornography) is rarely challenged by the law, either in the United States, or elsewhere (though there are exceptions to this general rule in certain localities).

The problem in most of these cases where erotica are to be used for scientific study arises either out of restrictive customs regulations, prohibiting the import of such material (as in the *Kinsey* case), or on the charge of alleged dissemination (as in the case of an American professor who was accused of 'dissemination,' because he admittedly presented erotic pictorial representations to subjects in order to test their reactions to this material). To us, as lay persons in the legal field, the most logical means of forestalling such prosecutions in the future seem to be simply the extension of existing customs regulations permitting the import of "personal items" (not imported for re-sale) to include erotic material, regardless of whether it is imported for scientific or other reasons. If this privilege is then abused by an importer by way of dissemination, existing legislation would cover this contingency as well. Likewise, the concept of "dissemination" should be narrowly defined, so as to exclude the abuses of the regulations by over-zealous law-enforcement agencies.

Such liberalization of customs regulations and the narrower interpretation of the concept of "dissemination" are badly needed, if research in this area is not to continue being severely impeded by the situation as it now prevails, both in America and in Europe. However, we feel, as before stated, that such liberalization is possible and preferable without the introduction of the concept of 'variable obscenity' which would, we fear, only invite other abuses of the law without really clarifying the issues at stake or facilitating fair legal process.

Having found serious defects in each of the legal tests of "obscenity" now in use or under consideration by the courts, one is forced to ask—"Where do we go from here?" To us the answer seems clear: *not* toward more obscenity legislation, nor toward stricter enforcement of the vague and antiquated obscenity laws, with all the unavoidable abuse and mistaken judgments to which this would lead.

Instead, we seriously suggest—in the absence of any evidence suggesting the existence of a "clear and present danger" with regard to exposure to erotica—the *abolition* of all obscenity legislation, *including* the legal suppression of hard core or any other kind of pornography, erotica, or whatever the particular terminology might be. The only possible exception we might want to make to this "hands-off" rule would be the restriction of the sale of such material to *adults only*. As previously said, we do not think that such abolition would result in an over-indulgence of the citizenry (or even of juveniles) in erotica, any more than the abolition of the "dry" laws in the United States has resulted in turning the country into a nation of alcoholics (though one sometimes might get that impression, forgetting that alcoholism was no less of a problem during the time of Prohibition!)

Having given the subject perhaps as much thought and study as anybody today, over the years we have gradually arrived at the conviction that the entire problem of pornography has been exaggerated beyond all reasonable proportions by certain hysterical and sex-obsessed segments of society. It is embarrassing to witness the enormous effort and the investment of time and resources spent in legal proceedings and debate on matters of "obscenity", which an adult society ought to be able to take in its stride. In fact, official preoccupation with these matters appears at times not only as utterly absurd and undignified, but as almost cynically misplaced and misdirected in the face of far more pressing and urgent problems facing the civilized world today. Would it not be more fitting and proper, one might ask, for government to concern itself with the grim realities of *poverty, disease*, and *war*, the devastating effects of which are well known and undisputed, rather than engage in grotesque shadow-boxing with the phantoms of "obscenity," "pornography," "smut," or whatever labels may have been attached to these scarecrows of another day and age?

We ourselves are almost apologetic for having spent as much time and effort on the subject as we have, yet we felt the necessity to delineate—once and for all, as far as we are concerned—the nature of the problem as we see it. We do not think at this point, that the problem of pornography or of erotica in the wider sense of the term should be given any official attention by an adult society, except to provide for the *impartial scientific investigation* of the *effects* of various types of erotica.

In this quest, more and more scientists in various nations have joined us since we first pointed out the need for such study several years ago. However, it seems that governments are slow to accept the responsibility for such studies, being sure of the correctness of their prejudice and perhaps wanting to protect it from the challenge of scientific evidence which might not support it.

But it is probably a mistake to expect governments to sponsor and support investigations of this sort which, at least on the face of it, seem to be contrary to their own vested interests. In a free society such official sponsorship is perhaps not even desirable in cases of this sort, and the cause of scientific objectivity might be better served by *private* sponsorship of research which, we are confident, can and will be found with the increasing tolerance for such discussion, both in the United States and in Europe.

Meanwhile, since the effects of erotic writings and pictorial representations (including hard core pornography are still not clearly known, and since no "clear and present danger" has been proved to exist, any legislation or suppression of erotica beyond the restriction of these materials to "adults only," seems to be out of line with the realities of the matter, as well as with the concept of the free individual in a free society.

PART III

THE PSYCHOLOGY OF PORNOGRAPHY

We shall now introduce the reader to a number of "obscene" (pornographic) specimen books of varying lengths, sizes, literary styles, countries and periods of origin. None of these outward, and more or less accidental, circumstances should, as we will try to demonstrate, detract from recognizing the common criteria which all these works have, of necessity, in common. The reason for this, as we have previously indicated, is that an "obscene" book, in order to fulfill its function as an erotic stimulant (aphrodisiac), must follow certain psychological principles (or "tricks of the trade" based on sound psychological theory) if the book is to stand any chance of success in arousing erotic fantasies and sexual desires in the average reader.

The "obscene" books with which we want to acquaint the reader at this time, are:

Specimen No. 1

The Lascivious Hypocrite, or *The Triumphs of Vice,* a Free Translation of Le Tartuffe Libertin. Done at Cythera: By the Keeper of the Temple, MDCCXC. 73 pages in 4 chapters.

Specimen No. 2

Fay and Her Boy Friend, Anonymous. Place and date of publication unknown, probably of British origin. The book is brief, only 27 pages in all, and "illustrated from life" with three drawings, one photograph.

Specimen No. 3

The Confessions of Lady Beatrice, sub-titled: *Showing how she kept the XIth Commandment "Thou shalt not be found out."* Anonymous. Published by the Erotica Biblion Society of London and New York. 42 pages. This edition limited to 125 copies.

Specimen No. 4

Nelly, or *Confessions of a Doctor,* by Dr. Mortimer R*** (pseudon.) Paris-London. Date of publication not given. 82 pages, no illustrations.

Specimen No. 5

The Autobiography of a Flea. Anonymous. Printed for the Erotica Biblion Society of London and New York, 1901. 274 pages, 12 illustrations. A well-known erotic "classic."

Specimen No. 6

The New Ladie's Tickler, or *The Adventures of Lady Lovesport and The Audacious Harry.* Anonymous (actual author known to be E. Sellon). The copy here used is probably the 1866 edition published by Wm. Dugdale (according to Ashbee's Index Librorum Prohibitorum). 158 pages. This edition with four privately inserted original watercolors.

Specimen No. 7

Lustful Stories. Anonymous. No place and date of publication given. Contains three separate stories, entitled, "Rosa's Maidenhead," 54 pages; "The Golden

Member," 35 pages; and "The Slave Market," 17 pages; no illustrations.

Specimen No. 8

The Strange Cult, by George Clement (pseudon.). No date. "Reprinted from the Bound Book Edition." Privately Printed, Madrid. Contemporary. 100 pages, 12 illustrations.

Specimen No. 9

The Oxford Professor, "In which L. Erectus Mentulus, Ph. D., late of Oxford College, is taken further in the narration of his adventures and misadventures, erotic, alcoholic, and otherwise; not to mention a choice accompaniment of drolleries, notes and excursions of one sort or another, metaphysical and also miscellaneously edifying and entertaining." Done by the hand of the author into a manuscript at Natchitoches, Louisiana. Contemporary. 239 pages, 8 illustrations.

Specimen No. 10

Memoirs of a Russian Princess—"Gleaned from her Secret Diary—Compiled, noted and arranged by Katoumbah Pasha"; Erotik Biblion Societe, Paris. No publication date. 300 copies issued "for private subscribers." 175 pages.

We chose these ten "obscene" books because some of them (as for example, Specimens Nos. 1 and 8, *The Lascivious Hypocrite* and *The Strange Cult*) contain most of the elements or criteria which we claim to be essential for an "obscene" book, while others (for example, Specimens Nos. 3 and 4, *The Confessions of Lady Beatrice* and *Nelly*) contain these elements barely in sufficient concentration to qualify these writings as truly "obscene" (as defined). Among all ten of them, the reader will get a bird's-eye view of the vast, and for most people still inaccessible, territory of "obscene" books. Being familiar with a cross-section of "obscene" literature, he will be able to gain a sufficiently strong personal impression about the style and special characteristics of such books so as to recognize other specimens of the species when he meets with them.

THE STRUCTURE OF "OBSCENE" BOOKS

"Obscene" books have, as a rule, a general structure or make-up by which they can be distinguished from other types of writing. They may vary in length from a few pages to several hundred. The style of writing may differ as much as that between a murder scene by Shakespeare and one by Mickey Spillane (though we are not implying that either of these writings is obscene). The setting may be ancient Rome; London of the mid-1850's; Paris of the "gay nineties"; New York in the "roaring twenties"; or Hollywood of today. But the *basic structure* or organization of "obscene" books remains fairly constant, regardless of their outward shape, size, and individual style.

A book which is designed to act upon the reader as an erotic psychological stimulant ("aphrodisiac") must constantly keep before the reader's mind a succession of erotic scenes. It must not tire him with superfluous non-erotic descriptions of scenery, character portrayals, or lengthy philosophical expositions. All these are unnecessary trimmings for the writer of "obscene" books. The idea is to focus the reader's attention on erotic word-images, and not to distract him with side issues and tangents of one kind or another.

The characteristic feature in the structure of "obscene" books is the *buildup of erotic excitement* in the course of the text. An "obscene" book may start out with a scene which is only mildly erotic and not highly stimulating. In progression, it will then become "hotter" and "hotter" until the story culminates in the description of the most sensual scenes, which are highly conducive to the arousal of erotic desires.

Before going any further with theoretical considerations, we think it best to inspect at least *one* typical "obscene" book from cover to cover and so gain a first-hand impression of the structure and organization of "obscene" books. We have chosen for this purpose *The Lascivious Hypocrite,* or *The Triumphs of Vice,* both for its convenient size (73 pages in 4 chapters), and for the fact that it gives the reader a preview of all the other criteria which we shall consider subsequently.

The book starts (contrary to the general rule for "obscene" books) with an unusually lengthy philosophical discourse of slightly over six pages about the capricious workings of "providence," summed up in the following paragraph:

Whilst wise hypocrites, lascivious deceivers, never detected, and respected by everyone, grow old in health, joy and peace, in the bosom of all the delights of love and lust, never troubling themselves about the future, which is extremely doubtful after all,—and they are right, at any rate Providence seems to approve of their conduct. [p. 6.]

However, even the first few pages contain vernacular expressions for the female and male genitals which alone would cause many people to consider the book "obscene."

The buildup of sexual excitement in this book does not actually begin until page 11. It starts with a rape scene in which the hero, Valentine, deflowers his young girl-cousin whom he has previously drugged. We read:

He at once determined to execute his project the same evening. He emptied the sleeping draught into Eugenie's glass as he helped her at supper, and towards the close of the meal she began to feel its drowsy influence. She rose from the table and said she should go up into her room to indulge in the sleep she felt creeping over her. They wished her good night, and Valentine remained some time chatting to his father and mother before going to bed himself.

When he felt sure that everyone was fast asleep, he nervously stole into Eugenie's bedroom, naked all but his drawers.

Eugenie was in a profound slumber, and had been so suddenly overcome by the narcotic, that she hadn't even pulled the clothes over her before she fell asleep.

His greedy and lustful gaze was riveted on all her charms; he lifted up the night-dress that concealed her most secret charms, her bosoms of alabaster, firm and well developed, tipped with two coral buttons; he had the daring to press them with his hand, and to twine his fingers in the curly hair that thickly shadowed her armpits; and then he made ready to consummate the greatest and blackest of outrages. [pp. 11-12.]

Here follows the detailed description of how the hero-villain deflowers his unconscious victim and, taking care to leave no traces of his deed, withdraws from her room to resume his role of hypocritical sanctimoniousness.

Well liked and respected by all, our "lascivious hypocrite" is soon thereafter made director of the "Administration of Orphanages of both sexes." He assumes the religious title "Saint Geraud." No sooner is he installed in this high office than he begins to abuse his influential position:

A buxom widow, in some money difficulties, came to consult him in her troubles. She had daughters, and she was accompanied by the eldest, a very pretty young girl . . . he gave her a large sum of money, and promised her similar aid each month. . . . He made her promise to come and see him from time to time, and had his reasons for his request. The mother was fair, fat, and forty, with splendid bosoms and hips, and her daughter was a charming unfledged little beauty, whose short petticoats nearly drove him wild with the thoughts of the beauties and immature charms they concealed. [p. 23.]

Leaving the attractive widow and her daughters for future enjoyments, the Director of Orphanages first seduces "the Lady Superioress of an orphanage for girls, who had fallen in love with him on the first interview."

A blush covered her face and showed by its crimson flush the heat of the passion within. Seizing her hand, he softly pressed it, and kissed it madly. The sister could not resist this evidence of his feelings and [showed it] by the convulsive tremor that shot through [her]. She was sitting on the sofa near his armchair; he profited by this to push her gently on the sofa. She fell back gently, stretched out, with but feeble resistance on her part. [p. 24.]

Here follows the description of various sexual activities; the hero performs cunnilingus on the Lady Superioress, while masturbating himself. He brings the woman to orgasm in this fashion, then has coitus with her twice. (pp. 24-25.)

Afterwards, the hero glibly assures the woman of his undying love for her, calms her moral scruples, and gives her "fatherly" advice on how to extinguish the flames of her passions by masturbating with fantasies of himself when he should not be available at the moment.

Not yet ready to part from each other's company, the couple "lavished fresh caresses on each other, and the tenderest kisses . . .," while Saint Geraud gives the Lady Superioress an object lesson in mutual masturbation.

Finally after an hour's dalliance thus, he gave

her a fresh proof of his vigour in one final and satisfying [vernacular for coitus]. [p. 25.]

Thus, the story follows the course of sexual activities from foreplay to intercourse and afterplay:

. . . When he retired at length from between
her thighs, she lay back with her legs wide apart,
swooning in the after-throbs of pleasure, whilst he
kissed the body of his fair conquest all over, who
abandoned herself entirely to him as he pressed his
lips in a farewell kiss on the curls of red hair under her armpits, on the nipples of her breasts, and
on the rich bush of her pretty [vernacular for
vulva]. [pp. 25-26.]

This may be the place for an "aside" to the reader,
who may be puzzled by several of the features of this
story; for example, the unusual emphasis on the hair,
especially the pubic and axillary hair. We must not
forget that this is a European story, written by a European for an earlier generation of European audiences.
At that time, and still today in Europe and other parts
of the world, the hair of the armpits and the armpits
themselves are highly eroticized. Moreover, the writers
reveal in their stories, especially in "obscene" books,
their own sexual idiosyncrasies, their fixations, and
fetishes.

But, to proceed with the demonstration of how "obscene" books use the "buildup technique" of erotic
tension just as murder mysteries build up to the final
killing of the victim or of several victims until the killer
himself is hunted down and destroyed in the aftermath,
the next erotic scene in *The Lascivious Hypocrite* concerns our hero's initial affair with the "buxom widow,"
who is visiting him at his office:

She was charmingly dressed, and soon aroused
desires in him that he longed to gratify, if he could

get the opportunity. She was alone, which was an obstacle less in the way. [p. 27.]

A little frivolous conversation at first, then a teasing bout:

He risked a caress, she laughingly evaded it. He snatched a kiss: a close tongueing kiss, which brought the colour to her face; her ample bosoms heaved.

"You couldn't dream of such a thing," said she, "with a woman of my age!"

"How many girls would give their ears to be as charming and resemble you!" he whispered, and pressed his point; he stopped her reply by another kiss; her eyes were troubled, her breath came quickly; he profited by it, and became more pressing, more enterprising.

The sofa was handy, she fell back on it; she was in the very lists of love, in the exact position; he threw up her clothes, showing two stout, and well-shaped legs and a round, white matronly belly extraordinarily attractive, with a wonderful thick black bush of hair at the bottom of it, extending its black triangle almost to her navel.

She could not resist even if she wished: there was no time to argue the point. [There follows a phrase describing how the hero's erect penis touches the widow's "pleasantly mature" genitals.]

This magic contact took all power of resistance from the lustful dame; he penetrated, she felt the beginning of the flow of pleasure from her very womb. [There follows an account of how the two lovers quickly achieve simultaneous orgasm, accompanied by the production of large quantities of seminal and vaginal fluid. The text uses the vernacular for the genitals, the buttocks, testicles, and for the genital secretions.] Their souls co-mingled, and when they regained consciousness, they were too satisfied with each other to have anything to reproach one another with. [p. 28.]

It seems anticlimactic when the widow afterward says to our hero-villain ("looking at him with eyes full of love and desire"),

> You're a very naughty boy. When I came to see you, I was far enough from thinking what was going to happen to me. [p. 28.]

The couple is interrupted by the ringing of a bell, but Saint Geraud assures the lady that nobody will be able to enter without his touching the bell-pull—and apparently he has no intention of doing so, for he says, "you shall not leave me thus; my happiness has not been perfect. I must complete it." (p. 29.)

Another intercourse scene follows, the author always using the vernacular, describing how the widow during orgasm is "clasping her well-shaped stout legs across his back, and pressing him to her capacious bosom." Again the emphasis is on their "two successive discharges," which are said to have "abated their mutual fires, without extinguishing them."

Dispatching the widow with the promise of renewing their pleasure the next day, Saint Geraud goes to see who had entered the anteroom to his offices while he and the widow were still engaged in sexual activities. It turns out to be the young Superioress with whom we are already acquainted.

The following conversation takes place between the two:

> "Well, my dearest sister, have you thought of me?"
>
> "Yes darling, and dreamed of you; and such a dream!"
>
> "And you have kept *me* awake. Why was I not next [to] you?"
>
> "If I could only have known, it would have been too sweet!"
>
> "Well dear, we can make up for lost time."
>
> "I long for it!"

Then he covers her with kisses, and revels in searching all her beauties over in a most voluptuous examination.

What a bosom, fresh and rounded, delicate and dimpled! What a [vernacular for the female sex organ] shadowed by its curly fleece; thighs perfect, a perfect leg and foot; an enchanting figure, two lovely black eyes, and a mouth, whose lascivious smile suggested a kiss; all this made Saint Geraud feel stiffish, the flesh turning to gristle and gristle to bone. He felt that a kiss below would recuperate his powers; he gently laid her back on the broad armless couch, and, kneeling down at the end. . . ." [There follows a detailed description of cunnilingus, during which the man excites himself by masturbation. He then places his penis in the woman's hand, who performs fellatio on him before the pair experience orgasm during coitus. There is again mention of the pubic hair and of the copious discharges, all expressed in the vernacular.] [p. 30.]

In the following paragraph the reader of *The Lascivious Hypocrite* is encouraged at this point to either have intercourse with a partner, if such is available, or to use masturbation, for "this is as it should be."

The discourse of our hero and the young Superioress then turns to matters of the convent, during which the girl discloses "a scandal, which," she says, "should be avoided." "What is it?" asks Saint Geraud. "Our Supreme Lady Superior sleeps every night with the Chaplain of the establishment." "Well," said Saint Geraud, "we'll have some fun with them; they ought to have had respect for appearances." (p. 32.)

Plans are made to surprise "the chaste and holy mother" the same night, during the discussion of which the young Superioress masturbates the hero to the point of ejaculation. Then follows a disrobing scene with more sexual activity.

He began to undo the strings and buttons, to pull

out pins; the holy sister seconded him to the best of her ability, and in the instant she stood in the centre of a ring of garments, slipped down, as naked as Eve in Eden. Nothing more beautiful, more perfect, had ever been seen.

His eyes wandered from her pretty face, to her lovely bosoms, to the curls of her shadowy armpits, to her snowy belly, with its thick bush at the bottom, and so on to her rounded thighs, and legs, and pretty feet; [there follows a description of his tumescent member] he stretched her on the couch, kissed her, felt every part of her body. . . . [There follows a description of cunnilingus with simultaneous anal masturbation of the woman. The new pleasure, we are told, quickly brought the woman to renewed orgasm during which the man performs coitus with her "to complete her bliss."] [pp. 33-34.]

Here follows a scatological passage in which we are told of how the couple engage in urolagnia. We read that the man dried the pubic hair both orally and "with a scented handkerchief."

After this, the couple don again their clerical robes and assume their official "dignified manner." Cries the author, "Oh cant! oh humbug! oh hypocrisy!"

Saint Geraud, the hero of our "obscene" specimen book, next prepares to entrap the Supreme Lady Superioress and the Chaplain of the Orphanage. He succeeds in catching them in *flagrante delicto* (the description of which takes up the next several pages) and, putting on airs of moral indignation, has them both arrested. At daybreak, the Second Superioress promptly enters to pay Saint Geraud her visit. He promises her the post of the deposed Holy Mother, fondles her, masturbates himself briefly, has her engage in mouth-genital contact with him, then enjoys her "divinely" on the sofa: "She lent herself to it with the best of grace in the world, and showed consummate skill." (p. 42.)

The two culprits disposed of, the Second Superioress

is installed in her new office with pomp and circumstance:

> They rang the great bell, and every one assem-
> bled in the hall, where she was installed in her new
> honors; her beautiful face was flushed and she
> looked upwards, and appeared thanking God for
> the reward of her virtue (she was, in point of fact,
> thinking of Saint Geraud and his [slang word for
> the male genital] which flushed her pretty cheeks,
> and made her [slang word for the female genital]
> throb too.) All applauded, she was loved and es-
> teemed by all the sisters; to many of them, she was
> bound by ties of more than love, and had received
> many in her bed. . . ." [p. 44.]

We read, "The sister on her promotion had assumed
the name of Holy Mother Sainte Julie." The sentence
immediately following tells of her kneeling on the sofa,
where her benefactor initiates her into the technique of
anal intercourse, "for he wished to teach her every kind
of delight."

After that, "Saint Geraud made her [slang word for
masturbate] herself, with her middle finger, whilst she
told him of all her *tribade* [female homosexual] adventures with the novices and older nuns." The woman then
makes Saint Geraud masturbate himself for her (voyeuristic) enjoyment, "but when she saw the crisis
approaching, she knelt before him and [performed fellatio on him]. . . ." (p. 44.)

The chapter ends with another bit of philosophizing,
similar to that in the introductory part of the book. But
we are told that our hero, Saint Geraud, is about "to
enter a new experience," to which the next chapter,
entitled "Adonis," is devoted.

The chapter opens with Saint Geraud setting out to
inspect the boys' dormitories. Talking to "the heads of
the places where the youths were," they inform him of
"plenty of details concerning mutual [vernacular for
masturbation], and pointed out pretty boys who could

be found in each other's beds, and had been detected in [vernacular for mouth-genital contact] and every kind of excess." (p. 46.)

He hears, especially, complaints about a certain beautiful young man with "the figure of an Adonis, who, when stripped must have looked like the Apollo Belvedere." Saint Geraud ("listening gravely") demands to have the youth sent to his office the next day for a personal interview, presumably in order to "correct" him. But, "He had his own ideas, as we shall know soon!"

Anticipating with delight what tomorrow's visit held in store for him, "he thought it a good thing to spend an hour in visiting the Lady Superioress." He finds her "surrounded by a crowd of young sisters, as pretty and fresh as roses." (p. 47.) Noticing the embarrassment of the newly appointed Holy Mother, he extracts from her the following confession:

. . . before I ever saw you, I had passions, and strong ones too; they often carried me away, and all those sisters—my favorites—that you have just seen round me, feel just as I do, and we used to mutually console each other with candles, fingers, and tongues, for the absence of the love of your sex. Night after night I have passed, with one or two of them with me, lying clasped in each other's arms, their white thighs around me [vernacular for masturbating] each other with eager fingers, or lying reversed, devouring [vernacular for mutual cunnilingus] and watching [here follows further description of Lesbian activity]; but now all my pretty *tribades* think I have abandoned them, because since I have known you, dear, you have absorbed all my desires, my fancies, and my dreams. They are all grumbling at me, and scolding me, for depriving them of their accustomed pleasures. [p. 49.]

The discussion leads into an intercourse scene, " 'Come,' said she, softly, and opened a darkened little room, where stood a bed. Casting themselves on it, their sighs and moans soon attested to a quick delight." (p. 49.)

Saint Geraud declares his fondness for watching Lesbian activities while masturbating himself. It is promised that he will see all future Lesbian activities and is told that it will make the women "twice as randy" to know that he will be looking on while they satisfy each other orally, especially if they also can watch him masturbating and see his copious ejaculation.

The Lady Superioress further shows Saint Geraud her collection of erotic books and pictures and tells him how she often used to amuse herself with them, while masturbating herself in front of a mirror, "watching every motion":

> Saint Geraud entreated to let him see her. She sat down, and Saint Geraud stood beside her, with her [vernacular for female genitals] beautifully reflected, she began to masturbate herself scientifically, staring randily at her own reflection. . . . [p. 50.]

This proves too much of a stimulus for the hero of our story, so that the two soon masturbate in unison. Mutual orgasm (in detailed description) follows, and we hear, "Nature could do no more, and they separated, enchanted with their similarity of tastes, and hoping soon to renew fresh pleasures." (p. 50.)

Now the scene changes to the hero's office, where he is interviewing the young Adonis. He "reprimands" him for his homosexual practices. The young man, far from showing remorse, lectures Saint Geraud on the "perfect naturalness" of homosexuality. Not content with that, he strips "and shows himself naked before Saint Geraud's admiring eyes; his body was a perfect model, fresh and dimpled, and his curves most seductive; his chest was well developed, a mass of curly hair underneath each armpit; downy thighs, and a beautifully curved bottom; in front a [vernacular for penis] white as ivory, with a crimson [vernacular for glans penis] and two splendid [vernacular for testes], with downy hair. . . . (p. 52.)

We read of Saint Geraud's excitement, and the youth offering himself for anal intercourse. Here follows a detailed description of the act, and afterwards the following dialogue:

> When they had finished their duet *a la sodom,* the youth said to Saint Geraud:
> "Well, what do you think now?"
> "It is a new experience for me, and I must allow it's rather nice." [p. 53.]

There follows a discourse on the attractions of vaginal intercourse as opposed to those of anal intercourse with a male or with a female, though the author of our "obscene" specimen book admits that some women enjoy the latter, particularly if the man does not fail to provide them with manual stimulation of the genitals. (p. 53.)

Adonis now proceeds to undress Saint Geraud, and takes his "maidenhead" (anally) while masturbating him "skillfully." Saint Geraud anticipates joint orgies with the Lady Superioress and her tribadic girls and with his future male lovers, though he thinks he still prefers making love to females. But Adonis is not through with Saint Geraud yet; he shows him how one man may perform fellatio on another. The episode ends with Saint Geraud keeping the young man for the night in his apartments where, "They slept together and gave themselves up to the most violent and lascivious delights of pederasty [there follows the vernacular terms for a variety of sexual activities]. . . ." (p. 55.)

However, Saint Geraud does not trust Adonis and soon thereafter "removes" him with the aid of some medicine and prussic acid (here and in many other places throughout the book we meet again with the subtheme of the story—the universal hypocrisy of mankind):

He accompanied his remains to the tomb with

every expression of sorrow, and Saint Geraud was complimented by all on his kindness and tenderness to the dear departed. These compliments he received with modesty, and said it was only his duty. [p. 56.]

Erotic action now shifts back to the "buxom widow" and her two young daughters (eleven and thirteen years of age). We hear that their mother had instructed them to masturbate and to "play [erotically] with boys of their own age." (p. 56.) They had also been encouraged to prepare themselves for coitus by stretching their vaginas with their own fingers, or to let their mother perform this service for them, in addition to having used "a candle or two" with their playmates. Therefore, it does not prove too much of a task for Saint Geraud to "take the maidenhead" of each of them "without any difficulty," as "their buxom mother held each of them naked on her belly." (p. 56.)

From this point on, the story really gathers momentum. We have already seen how it progressed from a single defloration scene in the beginning to more and more varied activities, including oral-genital contacts, Lesbianism, male homosexuality, anal intercourse, etc. Thus far, there have, however, been only two partners present in each scene (even in the last one, it appears that the mother presented each one of her daughters separately and individually to Saint Geraud). From now on, the story goes beyond these limitations and brings us orgiastic scenes in which numerous individuals engage in a large variety of sexual activities, taking place simultaneously.

After some biographical notes on Saint Geraud's further life, including the death of his parents, the inheritance of their large fortune, his marriage to the now widowed cousin whom he had drugged and raped on the eve of her wedding, the story concentrates on the "buxom widow," her experiences in the past, and Saint Geraud's sexual pleasures with her and her offspring. Says the author:

The widow had been a most lascivious woman ever since her seventh year, and gave him many accounts of the various ways she had of satisfying all her strange lusts, some of which you will find shortly detailed at more or less length. [p. 56.]

The last chapter of our specimen book is entitled, "The Widow's Story," and begins as follows:

Not long before his [Saint Geraud's] death, the buxom widow, who was always his greatest favorite, on account of her love for all that is out of the way in sensual libertinism, gave him a few sketches of her life, with which we will close this book and bid our readers farewell. [p. 59.]

The widow tells Saint Geraud salacious episodes from her past in order to excite him sexually. We learn that her mother was "the result of an amour between a charming nun in one of the largest convents of France, and an Abbé noted for his gallantries." She was smuggled out of the convent and turned over (by her father) to "one of the most noted procuresses in Paris" to bring the child up as she saw fit. In time she became a successful courtesan herself, and amassed a large fortune. But at the age of 28, at last some admirer "succeeded in giving her a big belly," and the baby turned out to be the "buxom widow" herself:

"It can easily be imagined," continues the widow, "that, with such a lineage, I was born with very strong passions. When I was seven years old, instead of being soothed to sleep by toys or sweets, my mother [coarse description of instructing her daughter in the technique of manual masturbation]; nature did the rest, and I soon [vernacular term for masturbation] myself to sleep. I have heard since [that] this is a common trick with randy nursemaids. When I was eight I used to be witness of all my mother's love encounters with her lovers, and she used to take a lascivious delight in know-

ing that I was an interested spectator. . . ."
[p. 60.]

Further, the buxom widow tells how her mother had
the little girl participate with her in the business of making her stimulate her male clients manually and aiding
them in performing coitus with her mother.

We also learn that when no man appeared, the girl
had to put her mother to sleep by satisfying her with a
dildo (artificial penis), or by bringing her orally to a
climax, while the mother reciprocated her daughter's
favors by stimulating her orally, which, the widow says,
"made me wild with delight." (p. 61.)

The mother taught her daughter the correct masturbation movements by doing it with her in unison; then
she encouraged her to play with boys a little older than
herself, to masturbate them and perform fellatio on
them, "till at ten," the woman remembers, "she had my
maidenhead taken by one of her wealthiest patrons."
(Here follows a detailed description of her defloration,
in which the mother takes an active part and which she
enjoys voyeuristically.) "From that day to the day of
her death," the story continues, "I was her constant associate in every lascivious sport. I was then twelve
years old, and was as well acquainted with everything
as a woman of thirty." (p. 61.)

The widow relates how a man whom she suspected
was her father sent her to good schools. "Here," she
said, "I became quite a goddess to the other girls, as I
instructed them in all the mysteries of tribadism," (there
follows a vernacular expression for teaching them to
masturbate themselves) "till we all became a set of the
most lascivious little devils you can imagine." (p. 61.)

At sixteen, our heroine takes "most charming apartments," but then was "fool enough to marry." Her husband died after squandering half of her fortune, leaving
her with a boy of ten and two girls of eleven and nine.

"Having still a very good income . . . I de-
              for pleasure alone. I soon had

many lovers, and educated my children to assist in my orgies and add to my income. I found that they had thoroughly inherited the lascivious disposition of their parents; they could scarcely help it, if there is anything in hereditary transmissions. The eldest girl, now thirteen, you have seen, is, as you know, called Clairette, the prettiest brunette, with rosy cheeks, and black hair, and a fine leg; the second, ten, Zilla, a laughing blonde, with flaxen hair and blue eyes; and the boy, a little Adonis of twelve, with brown eyes, red-gold hair and a perfect [vernacular terms for the penis and testicles], without a hair, whose name is Claude. I would often strip them and myself stark naked, and with closed doors and bright lamps and fires, pass half the day in instructing them in every amorous device." [p. 62.]

The widow goes on to tell how she used to make the girls masturbate themselves and their brother, and how she loved to "watch them as they all three writhed in lascivious contortions with not a single hair on their pretty little privates." (p. 62.)

Although she was very fond of men, the widow says, she "took a frantic and lustful pleasure in teaching boys and girls their first lessons in the art of love." However, she kept the girls' maidenheads intact for the "right" man, who, of course, turned out to be Saint Geraud, to whom she was so greatly indebted for having saved her by his kindness from "that dreadful financial crash," which had nearly ruined her.

"As for the boy," the mother could not resist the temptation of taking his "maidenhead" herself. She says:

"It was one afternoon, all kinds of lascivious ideas were floating vaguely in my brain; we were all together, the table was covered with fruit and silver cups of iced champagne; scattered here and there were books with illustrations of every device of lust, and with photographs from life of every attitude of love." [p. 62.]

It transpires that Saint Geraud had followed up the widow's rape of her son, in which she was assisted by her two daughters, by taking the boy's other "maidenhead" anally soon afterwards, again during one of their family orgies. "Those were the happy days," muses the widow.

The story here becomes so typically "obscene" that even attempting to transcribe the happenings in any detail into more acceptable terminology seems to become impossible. From page 62 to page 73 there is a concentration of orgiastic scenes involving mass orgies between adults and children, including parents and their own children, incestuous hetero- and homosexual relations between children, zoophilic scenes involving coitus between a woman and a dog with multiple voyeuristic participants, multiple oral-genital and oral-rectal contacts, urolagnia, incestuous child-adult and incestuous homo- and heterosexual adult activities, as well as various sexual exhibitions.

SEDUCTION

Characteristic of "obscene" books is the fact that in these seduction scenes the "victim" is, more often than not, a *willing collaborator*. In other words, the women who figure prominently in "obscene" books are generally as anxious to be seduced as the men are to seduce them. In fact, in some "obscene" stories the women are the aggressors and the men are the seduced, in which case the male "victims" are as easily "persuaded" as are the women.

Also characteristic of seduction scenes in "obscene" books is the fact that the stories emphasize the *physiological sex responses* of the participants; in this instance, particularly those of the women.

Still another distinguishing feature of "obscene" seduction scenes is their *brevity* due to the ease with which the seduction is accomplished. We will therefore not find page after page, or entire chapters, of an "obscene" book devoted to the hero or heroine attempting the seduction of his or her lover as is so frequently the case in ordinary fiction. In any "obscene" story, the hero typically meets a female (or male) to whom he is sexually attracted and in the next sentence or paragraph the couple are in the middle of foreplay, and a few lines further down the text, we find the pair already in the midst of love-making.

In our first specimen book, *The Lascivious Hypocrite,* Saint Geraud did not meet with much, if any resistance, either on the part of the Second Lady Superioress or on the part of the buxom widow or her children; neither did it take much effort for the youth "Adonis" to involve him in the homosexual activities which Saint Geraud wanted to experience anyway.

We shall now quote other examples of typical seduction scenes from some of the other "obscene" specimen books.

Our specimen book, *Fay and Her Boy Friend,* opens with an older gentleman seducing a much younger virgin girl, whom he has just met, in a railroad compartment. When she objects, remonstrating that she is a virgin, he promises to respect her virginity and offers her money in return for certain "little favors": the result is that between stations the girl has masturbated the man, has let him masturbate her, has allowed him to perform cunnilingus on her, and she has performed fellatio on him (for five pounds). The story begins:

"But there's a good deal of harm in your putting your hand up my clothes," I said.

"Well, give us one kiss and I'll be good," he retorted.

I let him have the kiss; he was a nice looking old man—and I always liked being kissed. As I expected, he put his tongue in my mouth, and I—well, I didn't jump away as I should have done; I gave the tongue just one little lick with mine.

It maddened him, as I expected it might.

"As you jolly well knew it would," puts in the typewriter.

"Nothing of the sort, you nasty minded girl"; mind you, I was still a virgin at the time.

How long, o Lord, how long?

Well, he began putting his hand up my clothes again, so I jumped away and ran to the other end of the compartment.

He came after me, and pushed me down on the cushions of the carriage seat, standing over me and trying to force his legs between mine, but I escaped him again, and I think he saw then that it was no use to try to get me by force.

The brazenness of his next speech astounded me.

"Don't be frightened of me, dear," he said, "I won't do you any harm, but I see that you are a little girl who knows her way about a bit; if you'll let me play with you a little, I'll make it worth your while."

Suddenly Eloises's contention that men were accustomed to pay for the pleasure they got from women, recurred to me. I certainly at that time needed a little ready money badly. I was tempted —and he looked like a man who was rolling in riches.

"You mean you'll give me money?" I asked, staring him straight in his face.

"Exactly."

"And what do you want me to do for it?"

"I'll show you!"

I had become quite alive to the business side of the situation by this time, also the very fact that this old man wanted to give me money for making him naughty, excited a naughty feeling in me, too.

"Mind," I said, speaking deliberately, "I'm a virgin, and I shan't let you seduce me; if you'll promise not to do that, I'll do other things with you."

He seemed delighted at my candor and the bargain was struck. I was to have five pounds for doing "a few little things." [Here follow the masturbation, cunnilingus, and fellatio scenes.]

Our next example is taken from *The Autobiography of a Flea*. In the opening pages of the book, the fourteen-year-old Bella meets her boyfriend, who is about two years older, for what turns out to be a practical lesson in sex education. She is still "innocent," but anxious to learn, and her friend is eager to teach. The curtain opens on the youthful pair, seated toward evening on a secluded garden bench.

Bella fidgeted her pretty little foot and looked thoughtful.

"When are you going to explain and show me all those funny little things you told me about?" she asked, giving a quick glance up, and then as rapidly bending her eyes upon the gravel walk.

"Now," answered the youth. "Now, dear Bella, while we have the chance to be alone and free from interruption. You know, Bella, we are no longer children?"

Bella nodded her head.

"Well, there are things which are not known to children, and which are necessary for lovers not only to know, but also to practice."

"Dear me," said the girl seriously.

"Yes," continued her companion, "there are secrets which render lovers happy, and which make the joy of loving and being loved."

"Lord!" exclaimed Bella, "how sentimental you have grown, Charlie; I remember the time when you declared sentiment was 'all humbug'."

"So I thought it was, till I loved you," replied the youth.

"Nonsense," continued Bella, "but go on, Charlie, and tell me what you promised."

"I can't tell you without showing you as well," replied Charlie, "the knowledge can only be learnt by experience."

"Oh, go on then and show me," cried the girl, in whose bright eyes and glowing cheeks I thought I could detect a very conscious knowledge of the kind of instruction about to be imparted.

There was something catching in her impatience.

The youth yielded to it, and covering her beautiful young form with his own, glued his mouth to hers, and kissed it rapturously.

Bella made no resistance, she even aided and returned her lover's caresses.

Meanwhile the evening advanced; the trees lay in the gathering darkness, spreading their lofty tops to screen the waning light from the young lovers.

Presently Charlie slid on one side; he made a slight movement, and then *without any opposition* he passed his hand under and up the petticoats of the pretty Bella. Not satisfied with the charms which he found within the compass of the glistening silk stockings, he assayed to press on still further, and his wandering fingers now touched the soft and quivering flesh of her young thighs.

Bella's breath came hard and fast, as she felt the indelicate attack which was being made upon her charms. *So far, however, from resisting, she evidently enjoyed the exciting dalliance.*

"Touch it," whispered Bella, "you may."

Charlie needed no further invitation; indeed he was already preparing to advance without one, and instantly comprehending the permission, drove his fingers forward. [After an intimate description of the foreplay, the mutual seduction is near its completion.]

With her beautiful eyes half closed, her dewy lips parted, and her skin warm and glowing with the unwonted impulse stealing over her, she lay the delicious victim of whomsoever had the instant chance to reap her favors and pluck her delicate young rose.

Charlie, youth though he was, was not so blind as to lose so fair an opportunity, besides, his now-rampant passions carried him forward. . . .

. . . he beheld the beautiful girl lying invitingly to the amorous sport, he watched the tender breathings which caused the young breast to rise and fall, and the strong sensual emotions which animated the glowing form of his youthful companion. [pp. 14-20; emphasis supplied.]

Almost identical passages could be cited from seduction scenes in many "obscene" books; as, for instance:

As the exquisite sensation began to inflame her senses, Annie opened her knees and her thighs fell apart, inviting more direct contact with her tender tissues. [*The Oxford Professor*, p. 49.]

In all these instances, the girls yield rapidly, willingly, and any objections raised by them are mere token resistance. Still, many more "obscene" books, as already indicated, show the woman as the aggressive seducer and the man as the seduced party, as in the following example.

Waiting until her mother and sister had left, Inez went to her room. Having already bathed, her toilet was simple. Stripping, she sprayed her body with a dainty love-provoking perfume, rouged her lips and colored her cheeks. Satisfied that no one was about, she slipped into a loose-fitting black, lacy dress, mules on her feet.

Having thus laid a seductive trap for the man, who happens to be the family's Negro chauffeur, the girl is now ready to move in on the not-too-reluctant male:

Inez was all smiles. Pete, the Jamaica negro, seemed peeved. Inez, all smiles, approached him, posed for a moment, then she said:

"Well, Pete, dear, aren't you going to kiss me?"

Peter stared at Inez. That he was both angry and aroused was obvious by his very look. Angry, because she had neglected him, and aroused by the simplicity of her attire. But he fought down his maddening desire. . . .

"What you make Pete wait for?" he cried. "Who-all you runnin' with?"

Inez smiled. She stepped close.

"Don't be angry, dear," she cooed, encircling his neck with her arms and pressing against him. "I know I've been neglecting you, but I couldn't very well help it. I've been awfully busy at the Club, and . . ."

"It ain't the Club," he said, trying to be angry, —a difficult task at the sight of this ravishing young girl. "It's them white boys . . ." he said. "I ain't mad about the girls; I tol' you-all that. It's them white boys . . ."

Clutching him close, Inez continued to press against him. He wasn't fooling her a particle; through his trousers and her thin dress she could easily feel . . . [equivalent for the man's tumescent member.] It thrilled her. Hot when she entered the garage, she was raging hot now.

"Kiss me!" she demanded, and, when he failed to respond, she drew his face close . . . .

"It ain't the girls," he cried. "Besides, you-all promised Pete you'd bring some of 'em here!"

She searched his eyes with hers.

"Which of them do you prefer?" she asked, spreading her legs and moving her loins against his . . . a little act which never failed to bring him to terms. [*The Strange Cult,* pp. 10-11.]

In still another "obscene" book, *The Confessions of Lady Beatrice,* written in a completely different literary style and with the action taking place in a totally different milieu from that of the two preceding stories, we find a mature woman seducing her young page-boy. Again, the "victim" does not seem to feel that he is made to suffer a hardship and injustice.

When she was gone, I rang the bell twice, which was always the signal for Alphonse, a fine boy rather over sixteen, who acted as page, and ordered him to make haste and bring me some coffee and a little bit of fish as soon as the cook could send it up.

My blood coursed like fire through my veins, but I restrained myself, telling him to return for the tray in about ten minutes. [pp. 14-15.]

When the boy returns, the mistress has him drink some aphrodisiacal liqueur with her. The page says something about what a pleasure it is for him to put his lips to the same glass that her lips had touched, to which the lady replies:

"You silly boy, Alphonse, I can't be cross with you, it's too amusing" . . . then a moment after my design on the handsome boy was materially helped by a real attack of cramp in my leg; I was just then reclining in an easy chair, simply dressed in a loose robe thrown over my chemise . . ., no stockings or drawers, and only slippers on my naked feet. In evident pain I tried to rub the calf of my leg, but Alphonse at once came to my assistance.

"Dear Madame, dear mistress, what pain you seem to be in; oh, do let me rub your leg," and without waiting for permission, commenced his self-imposed task.

"That's right, rub hard, you're a good boy, Alphonse," I almost sighed in a low voice, raising my leg over the low arm of the chair so as to place it quite at his disposal, as I reclined myself backwards.

"Rub, rub, it is a relief, it will soon feel better, there now, stop, what are you kissing my leg for?"

"Ah, Madame, I've never seen such a beauty, I couldn't help it," he said looking up, his face in a blaze of blushes.

"Why, what's the matter with you? You couldn't have seen anything to make you blush, you silly boy!"

"Indeed, dear mistress, I could have kissed it all day, the soft, white warm flesh is so delightful, and a sort of something came over me that I can't describe. It was maddening."

"Would you like to kiss it again, Alphonse, it is so amusing, and you are such a comical boy, to make such a fuss over my leg!"

"Ah, Madame, do you mean it?"

"Yes, if you like, Alphonse, it's really too funny, if it's any pleasure to you."

In an instant his hot burning kisses covered my

calf, and finding my leg entirely at his disposal, he proceeded to take possession of the thigh also; quite a delirious tremor shook my whole frame . . . I actually [vernacular for emitting vaginal secretion] in a delirium of anticipation.

Closing my eyes I leaned back in the easy chair and let him do as he pleased, feeling assured the boy did not require much teaching, or he would not have been so excited . . . [There follows a description of cunnilingus, fellatio, and two intercourse positions between the mistress and her young servant.] [pp. 14-18.]

DEFLORATION

In books which are clearly "obscene" (as defined), defloration scenes with strong sadistic elements play an important role. These defloration and rape fantasies are psychologically significant in demonstrating the fusion of erotic and sadistic impulses, although it is highly characteristic of these fantasies that no matter what the degree of agony inflicted, the girl invariably disclaims any concern over her pain. For that reason, we do not find in "obscene" books any indication of hostility on the part of the cruelly deflowered girl. Typical of such scenes is the widow's description of her own defloration in *The Lascivious Hypocrite,* in which she is strapped down while her mother sits on her head the better to voyeuristically enjoy the scene. We are unable to give complete quotations of defloration scenes because of the gruesomeness of the details involved.

The first thing which strikes the eye with regard to these scenes in "obscene" books is that defloration is here almost synonymous with rape. We had at first intended to include *"rape"* as one of the identifying criteria of "obscene" literature, but refrained from doing so upon discovering that virtually all the rape scenes in these books concerned *virgins.* Upon further reflection, the reason for this becomes obvious: since the authors of "obscene" books visualize all the females in their stories as highly sexed, fiercely passionate creatures of impulse, there is no need for "rape" once they have "made the plunge" and lost their virginity.

In *The Autobiography of a Flea,* we read that "the pretty Bella, now roused into a fury of excitement and half mad with the titillation she had already undergone, *seconded by all the means in her power the audacious attempts of her young lover.*" (p. 22; emphasis supplied.)

In *Fay and Her Boy Friend,* the heroine yields her virginity willingly and knowingly to the man, and even though she at first has to suffer great pain, later freely admits that "after [awhile] the pain deadened and the most heavenly sensation succeeded it." (pp. 23-24.)

The young harem girl in the third of the *Lustful Stories,* entitled "The Slave Market," literally begs to be deflowered.

He said to Anita, "My child, do as I told you," and the little virgin, hot with passion, clasping her hands before me, her bosom heaving with emotion, pleaded that I should permit Jack to take her to him and be the first to give her that rich and joyous experience that she had often seen others enjoy.

"O, I want it so. I want him to be the first. I am burning with desire that none but him shall satisfy. . . ."

And in the midst of losing her virginity, the girl exclaims:

"Oh, sir," she said between sobs and gasps, "don't mind my tears and sobs, they are nothing to the ecstasy I feel. . . ." [pp. 115-116.]

In still another specimen book, *The New Ladies' Tickler,* the girl, about to lose her virginity, says:

. . . So far from recoiling, I gave him every

assistance in my power. I was quite aware . . .
that there would be considerable difficulty . . . I
felt consequently that I was likely to have to submit to a considerable amount of pain. . . . But I
had quite made up my mind to endure this, and so
far from lamenting it, I was only glad that I should
thus be enabled to show that I would willingly undergo any amount of suffering to prove how much
was I devoted to him.

There was some pain, certainly . . . but this was
instantly succeeded by such a charming sensation
of deliciously voluptuous fullness, and irritating excitement, that I had not the least hesitation in
seconding his efforts. . . . But here, alas, I was
doomed to suffer all the woes which a poor maid
must undergo in her first initiation into the mysteries of pleasure, and to pay the sad penalty which
is exacted from us, before we can be admitted to
enjoy the greatest bliss which nature has conferred
upon us. [pp. 71-76.]

In this instance, as also in the previous one, and in
almost every pornographic story which we examined,
the *defloration is accomplished with the aid of others*.
Here, Lady Lovesport and her boyfriend appear on the
scene, and with stimulating flagellations induce the young
man to continue intercourse with the just-deflowered girl,
as he is about to give it up under her pleadings. But
even under these conditions, there is no violent protest
from the girl, and, when the birch is applied to her also,
she is quite reconciled to the whole procedure.

The *participation* of others in these defloration scenes
is so characteristic of "obscene" books that one could
well list it as a separate criterion of identification. It
combines, in itself, various psychological elements; for
instance, the sadistic pleasure involved or the voyeuristic
element in watching.

The element of rape-like defloration in the setting of
a mass orgy is practically absent in nonpornographic
fiction. It is quite unique to "obscene" books.

This does not surprise one upon some reflection. The sadistic element in sexual relations is deeply repressed by most people in the Western world and its attraction denied. Still, sadism is part of our mammalian ancestry and, as a primitive, uncivilized urge is present in all of us. Dr. Theodor Reik has pointed out that for primitive man, before the dawn of civilization, sex meant little more than gratification of his crude and brutal sex needs. For the cave man, romantic love and tender feelings for his partner were non-existent. When the urge struck him, he simply went about looking for a female, overpowered her, and engaged in coitus, whether the woman wanted to or not. (Theodor Reik, *Psychology of Sexual Relations.*)

In the course of time, woman very likely "civilized" man and taught him the first lessons in tenderness, affection, and consideration: the grabbing hold became a sensuous caress, and bites became kisses, or at least "love-bites," as milleniums rolled by. It is only due to this gradual transformation that sexual satisfaction ceased to be restricted to one person—the male—and little by little lost its one-sided, sadistic, cruel character. But, as all clinicians know, it is always latently present and ready to break through when opportunity presents itself.

Sadistic defloration of virgins combines the over-evaluation of virginity in Western culture with the primitive pleasure of inflicting pain. Besides that, "obscene" books add strong voyeuristic and orgiastic elements to these defloration scenes by introducing other participants who take part in the action as aides and spectators. Thus, defloration scenes offer a unique opportunity for authors of "obscene" books to simultaneously touch upon a variety of tabooed subjects. And, as any sexual taboo is known to be especially stimulating to the imagination when violated, the defloration theme lends itself particularly well to the purpose of "obscene" literature, that is, to act for many people as a psychological aphrodisiac.

INCEST

As is shown elsewhere in this book, the *overt* incest theme is as rare in modern literature as it was popular in antiquity. In contemporary literature it appears, with very few exceptions (as in Thomas Mann's novel, *The Holy Sinners*, and his short story, *Blood of the Wolsungs*), only in *veiled* or *allegorical* form. "Obscene" books, however, can hardly do without open, frank, and undisguised incestuous relations. And these relations between the closest of kin, say between brother and sister, father and daughter, or mother and son, are consummated without any, or only minor qualms, guilt, and emotional conflict.

We have already seen in our specimen book *The Lascivious Hypocrite,* that the mother has incestuous relations, not only with her son, but also enjoys homosexuality with her two daughters, and all three children have incestuous relations with each other.

The psychological mechanism operating in this instance is again the presence of the social taboo which acts as a mental stimulant. Psychoanalytic experience has shown that latent incestuous leanings are present in most people in our culture. As these incestuous feelings are discouraged from early childhood, the culture succeeds in inhibiting their overt expression. Our moral training even succeeds in driving incestuous desires out of most people's conscious awareness. However, man's fascination with incestuous relationships prevails in spite of all the forces of repression, a fact to which not only clinical practice, but literature in general and "obscene" books in particular, give eloquent testimony.

In "obscene" literature, the most common form of incest is that between brother and sister. Of our ten specimen books, one, *The Memoirs of a Russian Princess*) is almost exclusively devoted to brother-sister incest. A second book (*The Strange Cult*) deals at great

249

length and over many pages with this theme. And a third volume (*The Confessions of Lady Beatrice*) is not far behind the second in that respect.

Most of the material is unquotable because of the vocabulary. However, we shall try to give the reader at least a flavor of the way in which "obscene" books handle the subject.

In *The Strange Cult,* we read:

> . . . To Alex, Flo was just another maiden. Too many had received his favors to cause him any great excitement. Besides, the banquet was but started. Another maiden, his own sister, was waiting to share in the pleasure!

After a night of debauchery between brother, sister, and another girl (Flo), brother and sister are left alone and continue enjoying each other sexually to the full:

> . . . Finally,—it must have been almost noon— Flo dressed and left.
>
> Later that afternoon, Alice received a telegram. She handed it to Alex. Reading it, he turned to Alice.
>
> "That means that we're going to be alone again tonight. Mother's remaining away another night . . . !"
>
> Alice, who was wearing a dainty little summer frock, gazed wistfully up into his eyes; she toyed with the buttons at the waist.
>
> "But isn't it dangerous . . . with the maid about . . .?"
>
> Her eyes bright, she turned and dashed away. A moment later she returned. "She's leaving," she cried, "she'll be gone in a minute!" Together they heard the front door slam. "I'm going to have a bath," she smiled, turning in the doorway. "When you're ready, come to my room . . . !" [the whole scene covers eight(!) pages. pp. 91-98.]

The same book contains an interesting passage about incestuous Lesbian activities between two sisters:

Midway in these thoughts, Felice, wearing the briefest possible kind of a night dress, came into her room and, without further ado, pulled down the coverlet and slid into her sister's arms. After a lingering kiss, during which they explored each other's mouths with their well-trained tongues, Felice said: "When are you going to take me into the club, Inez, dear?"

Inez, who was in a decidedly erotic mood as a result of her previous thoughts, teased her sister.

"You're only fooling, Felice," she cooed, hugging the other to her. "You have no real desire to join . . . you know what it means. . . ."

"You're just trying to put me off," Felice cried. "For some reason you don't want me to join your old club!"

"You're mistaken, dear," Inez cooed, hugging the other. "The girls have talked about you and you're expected to join, only . . ."

"I know," Felice interrupted. "It's because they think I won't (vernacular for cunnilingus) a girl, but I will!" Here she slipped one hand between Inez' thighs and toyed with the moist [vernacular for the female genital]. . . ." [pp. 25-26.]

In *The Memoirs of a Russian Princess,* the central theme is Princess Varva's passionate affair with her half-brother, the page Alaska. True, she had begun sexual relations with the young manservant before discovering that he was her half-brother, but she is in no wise inclined to give up the relationship after having learned of his identity.

Princess Varva does not disclose the secret of their incestuous relationship to the boy and cries, even at the height of passion, in French, so that he would not understand, "Mon amour! mon roi! mon frère! donne! donne! [My love! my king! my brother! come! come! p. 109.]

The same book contains an intercourse scene between

Princess Varva's maidservant Proscovia and her brother, Ivan. The princess, who has just used the husky *moujik* for her own sexual gratification, proceeds to force the girl into coitus with her brother, saying:

> "Come, Proscovia . . . no shyness and no modesty. Ivan is yet unsatisfied, a pretty girl like you will not do him any harm. See what a state he is in!"
>
> Between them, they hustled her on the couch. She was too frightened of the Princess to offer any serious resistance. In another second the brutal moujik, who seemed to think the affair an excellent joke, had turned her skirts up over her breasts and left exposed her young and well formed limbs. The princess aided him, encouraging him by her voice and example. [There follows a sentence indicating the man's aroused state.] . . . Thus the group of three struggled together, surging sometimes to one side and sometimes to the other, as the fierce Ivan strove to effect his purpose. At length a favorable opportunity presenting itself, he drove forward and, with a cry of triumph, succeeded in forcing the person of his sister. [pp. 36-37.]

In *The Confessions of Lady Beatrice,* Chapter IV is entitled "Incest in the Dark." She (posthumously!) confesses to her husband she had often had leanings toward his brother, but had suppressed these inclinations. Instead, she explains that she frequently substituted the brother-in-law in her imagination during intercourse with her husband.

Having fought such a valiant battle with regard to her brother-in-law, Lady Beatrice succumbs in the end to her passionate love for her own brother, Philip, who, we are told, came to visit her and her girl friend, Clementine, "after leaving school." Her brother is said to have been "such a fine young fellow for his age, nearly seventeen," and it seems only natural that Clementine should also fall in love with the handsome young fellow.

Lady Beatrice, seeing her girl friend's interest in Philip, is not at all possessive, but suggests to Clementine that they shall both share in the pleasure of enjoying her brother. "Well, dearest," I said to her one night, "it is very wrong, but I must have him, and you shall be in on the fun [There follows further pornographic detail] but all in the dark, you understand." (pp. 36-37.)

THE PERMISSIVE-SEDUCTIVE PARENT FIGURE

In keeping with the wish-fulfilling fantasy character of "obscene" stories, they frequently include the kind of *superpermissive parent figures* who not only *condone*, but even *participate* in the sexual activities of the child, or who actually *seduce* and *initiate* the child into various sexual practices.

Psychologically, this principle is extremely sound for the purpose of "obscene" literature. In the first place, it fits into the oedipal attraction of the child for the parent, or of the parent for the child. It has, therefore, the subconscious attraction of the extremely taboo, as is true of all the former criteria, and incest in particular.

Besides, the hyperpermissive parent figure corresponds to the child's fantasy of the "good" mother or father who would unequivocally accept his sexual and scatological interests, who does not scold when the child wets the bed, does not object when it plays with its feces, and who does not criticize or stop the child when it masturbates or engages in sexual play with other children.

In our specimen book *The Lascivious Hypocrite*, these aspects of the permissive parent figure stand out very clearly. We recall that the "lascivious hypocrite," Saint Geraud himself, is, in a way, a rather more than "permissive" father figure: first, toward the niece, whom he rapes in her narcotic sleep; second, with regard to the Second Superioress of the convent, to whom he is not only in a superior position, but whom he "fathers," promotes, and protects—so long as she fulfills all his sexual demands; third, toward the "buxom widow," to whom he is likewise a "fatherly" friend and protector; and fourth, in relation to the widow's children, for whom he is a direct "father" figure, both as the lover of their mother and as their own "benefactor."

The "buxom widow" herself, in this specimen book, is the daughter of such a "permissive" mother who not only initiated her daughter into all kinds of sexual activities, but who also set her up in her own profession, which happened to be that of prostitution. It appears, therefore, only "natural" that the daughter in turn uses and abuses her own children sexually in the same way, as we have seen especially in the last chapter of *The Lascivious Hypocrite.*

In another of our specimen books, *The Strange Cult,* we also find an extremely permissive mother who allows her son and two daughters the utmost sexual liberty and who leads a rather "fast" life herself, even though she does not participate in the erotic activities of her children. In one of the scenes in the book, she comes upon her daughters just as the younger, Felice, is about to perform cunnilingus on her older sister, Inez:

> At that moment Mrs. — entered the room.
> "Here, here," she smilingly cooed, coming to the bed and gazing down upon her two offspring. "What's going on here?"
> "You're just in time, mother," Inez laughed. "Felice has an idea she wants to learn Frenching, and you're just in time to save me from a frightful doing-up . . . the greedy little pig!"

The mother's reaction to this is, to say the least, rather unconventional. Far from being shocked and reprimanding her daughters at such "indecent" speech and behavior, she sounds more "permissive" than even the most sophisticated modern mother one could imagine:

"I should think," she says [to the younger daughter], "that with such a handsome fellow as Jim, you wouldn't want to waste your time on girls, dear."

Felice was, to say the least, overjoyed. Hearing her own mother speak so freely filled her with delight. She, like thousands of other young girls, entertained the silly thought that her mother didn't know what was going on about her. But Felice was not a fool; she knew pretty much everything that was going on in that household, and, becoming daring, she said:

"You're a nice one to talk, mother." [*The Strange Cult*, pp. 27-28.]

In the following passage, the daughter reminds her mother of the latter's own "sins," accusing her of doing the same thing with one of her lovers. The mother does not deny this, but merely retorts that such deviant sex practices are only for "those who have passed the first stage of life and have to practice it as a stimulant." However, her daughter will have none of this and mildly chides her mother for being hypocritical. There is no argument, the mother simply saying:

"Never you mind about that, dear, . . . you forget about me and come into my room. I want to speak with you. . . ."
"Isn't she a wonderful mother?" Felice asked her sister, after her mother had left. [*Ibid.* pp. 27-28; emphasis supplied.]

In *The Autobiography of a Flea,* we find a very similar situation to that in *The Lascivious Hypocrite.* Here, also, the clerical figures of the church "fathers" are not merely permissive toward their young female charges, but outright exploitative. The same applies, of course, to Bella's uncle and Julia's father, who easily succumb to their incestuous attraction toward the two girls.

The Autobiography of a Flea contains, however, still another long passage in which a peasant and his son jointly ravish the heroine Bella and in which it transpires that this father had been in the habit of masturbating his son. [pp. 188-196.]

In *The Confessions of Lady Beatrice,* the much older mistress can be said to stand somewhat in the relation of a "mother figure" to her young page-boy, whom she allows to have sexual relations with her. We have also seen how she plays that same role in her relationship with the much younger brother, Philip, whom she and her girl friend Clementine take to bed together.

The book *Nelly*—or, *Confessions of a Doctor* has as its dominant theme the sexual exploits of a roguish physician with a young woman, Nelly, whom her mother had initially brought to his office for a medical examination. Upon receiving the diagnosis from him that her unwed daughter is pregnant, the mother does not scold the daughter when she throws herself into the mother's arms in tears, imploring forgiveness. The mother simply says, with utter equanimity and almost absent-mindedly, "My child, I heartily forgive you." (p. 34.)

Nelly's father is deceased, so the good doctor arranges (in the role of a substitute father) for Nelly to marry the boy who had impregnated her. It seems, therefore, only fair that he should be a guest of honor at Nelly's wedding party. He is invited to stay with the young couple and the mother overnight, an opportunity which he and Nelly intend putting to good use by encouraging the bridegroom to drink himself into a stupor. However, before the doctor and bride deceive the young husband in the same bed in which he is sleeping off his inebriation, the doctor has to stand "some very unequivocal ogling from the lady mother. . . ." (p. 53.)

Next morning, the merry widow follows up her eloquent look at the doctor by coming into his room to wake him up. The two are in the midst of foreplay when they are interrupted by the bridegroom. The mother-in-law mocks him for not having been able to perform on

his wedding night, and doctor and widow part, hoping
for more privacy and better success on their next meeting.

In the wake of the wedding, Nelly goes through her
confinement. When the doctor calls on her ten days
after that event, he finds her in fine fettle, noting that
"the amorous playfulness of her disposition had returned." But Nelly says, "with an arch smile," she has
to tell him a secret:

> "What is it, Nelly?" I replied. Casting down her
> eyes and assuming the prude for a minute she said
> now, "I rather think, sir, from the way in which
> my mother talks of you, that she has either had
> some carnal knowledge of you or that she wishes
> for it." "Surely, Nelly," said I, "you are not jealous
> of your mother?" "Oh! By no means, sir," she re-
> plied, at once assuming the amazon. "Only if you
> would promise to give me the first [vernacular for
> coitus] after my lying in, as you gave me the last
> before it. I do not care about anything else."

The doctor adds, "I, of course, agreed to this very
reasonable and agreeable proposal." (p. 63.)

Later in the book, the doctor and the widow have
intercourse in her house. Having done so, the widow
"next went to Nelly and told her I know not of what
. . . but which could not deceive that girl's knowing
disposition, who must have been well acquainted with
what was going on in reality." Apparently, the permissiveness in "obscene" books works both ways, and the
children repay their parents with the same "magnanim-
ity" with which they themselves have been treated by
their elders. "Nelly afterwards told me," the story goes
on, "she could not then have enjoyed my company, and
she was therefore unwilling to spoil her mother's sport."
(pp. 65-66; emphasis supplied.)

As a matter of fact, Nelly is not only willing to share
her lover with the mother, but she is also not averse to
playing the secret onlooker during her mother's amorous

encounters with him. Says Nelly to the doctor, "I saw it all, but never mind, I did not think mother had so much spunk." (p. 68.)

Without going into detail and demonstrating the presence of "furiously permissive" parent figures in other "obscene" specimen books, we trust that we have illustrated this point sufficiently. It is, however, worth repeating that such permissive parent figures, who are at the same time unbothered by consciences of their own, are an essential element of "obscene" stories. Their main function is that of relieving superego guilt in the reader (and probably in the writer as well). For if the parent figure, who in psychoanalytic terms represents the conscience, is himself a scoundrel, there is no need for guilt reactions, remorse, and self-accusations. And since sexual activities in our culture are so heavily burdened with guilt, there is a great need to diminish the weight of this burden before the reader is able to enjoy "obscene" stories without getting into trouble with his own censor.

In that respect again, "obscene" books are built around valid psychological principles in the absence of which the books could not have the appeal that they undoubtedly possess for a great many people.

PROFANING THE SACRED

Among the most obvious characteristics of "obscene" books is the tendency of their writers to intermingle the sacred and the profane. Here again, the authors of "obscene" books have intuitively built upon solid psychological ground. It is a clinically well-known fact, attested by many psychoanalytical case histories, that there is a special attraction in mixing that which is supposedly the most "holy" and that which is supposedly the most debased. Even the derivation of the word "sacred," coming from the Latin *sacer*, bears this out. In its original usage, the word could signify either sacred or profane—its meaning was completely interchangeable.

The special value which this strange mixture of opposites has for "obscene" books lies undoubtedly in the heightening of erotic tension which it produces. By using profanity in the presence of the sacred, we are, so to speak, thumbing our nose at our own conscience and at the collective consciences—or superego—of society itself.

Nowhere could we find this principle better illustrated than in the following remarks of Lady Beatrice after having slept with her brother: "There was something so *deliciously wicked* in enjoying one's brother," confesses this woman, "in fact, my vivid imagination made me think how the devil must enjoy the sight of a sister seducing her brother as I had done. *Thoughts of hell and the devil only added fury to my voluptuous emotions.*" (*The Confessions of Lady Beatrice,* p. 41; emphasis supplied.)

At the end of the same book, we find a similar reference to the particular titillation provided by the presence of the two opposites. Lady Beatrice winds up her confessions thus:

. . . I have been [old English vernacular for the passive enjoyment of coitus] by a male friend in Church, to prevent me from going to sleep; oft on a garden seat, or on the grass. In St. Paul's, as I went with a gentleman up into the Ball of the Cross, and then we did the same another day, going up the Monument. *All such places add a peculiar zest to adultery.* [Emphasis supplied.]

Many "obscene" books, like *The Lascivious Hypocrite* or *The Autobiography of a Flea,* have among their central figures persons connected with the clergy and religion, such as nuns, priests, and monks. These "holy" individuals are then depicted as engaging in highly tabooed sexual activities which are considered "mortal sins" by religious standards. In so doing, the objection-

able character of the "crimes" is magnified and the sins
compounded.

To quote an example of "profanity" in conjunction
with the sacred, we refer to a passage in *The Oxford
Professor* in which the Professor is secretly followed to
the church by his friends and spied upon while having
intercourse:

> "Somebody's being [vernacular for intercourse],"
> whispered the salesman, unmindful of the incon-
> gruity of his remark to the reverent tone he used to
> express it; "someplace right under us almost, too."
>
> "It's coming from the choir loft," the druggist
> answered after a moment of listening. "And doesn't
> that sound to you like Professor Marin's voice?"
>
> "Does he do it in the church, too?" the barber
> asked in a shocked undertone. "Come on, let's get
> out of here."
>
> But the salesman demurred.
>
> "This is our chance to get some firsthand infor-
> mation on that technique he's always talking
> about," he said, urging the others through the heavy
> drapes and onto the balcony-like projection. "May-
> be we can get a few pointers, Joe." [pp. 12-13.]

In the above sample, we have not only the fact that
the church is being "desecrated" by the Professor performing coitus within its hallowed walls, but, in addition,
the salesman incongruously uses a reverent tone of voice
to express the observation that their friend, the Professor, is having intercourse with somebody in the church.

The basic principle in all this is that, for many people
in our culture, sex is still inextricably linked to sin. Now,
if sex is sinful, then sexual acts, committed in sacred
surroundings, or with the participation of representatives
of religion, would constitute the ultimate in blasphemy.
In this way it becomes possible for sexual acts to take
on a special meaning as expressions of one's need to
rebel, not only against social and religious institutions,
but ultimately against those cultural inhibitions which

have become part and parcel of one's own character structure. Since most of us are at least to some extent affected by these cultural frustrations, it is not difficult to see why the blasphemous element in "obscene" books holds such a strong attraction for so many people, and especially for those who find their sexual needs in conflict with the moral and religious values of society, from which they have not been able to fully emancipate themselves.

"DIRTY" WORDS IN "DIRTY" BOOKS

The use of taboo words in "obscene" books is closely related to the frequent mixture of the sacred and the profane which we discussed in the preceding section. Its chief attraction lies in the open defiance of the "superego," or conscience, the flagrant violation of the social conventions of polite discourse, the flaunting of one's independence, the throwing off of social responsibility, and the assertion of the instinctual primitive side of life against all the restraining and inhibiting forces of the environment.

Prostitutes the world over have always known the magic of "obscene" words and have used this knowledge to their advantage. In fact, some men cannot be aroused unless the woman uses very profane language. Since not many wives or "good" women in our culture are willing to accommodate the man in this respect, these men seek out prostitutes, some of whom specialize in this type of service. We know of cases where the man would phone a call girl or prostitute and ask her for nothing more than to "talk dirty" to him, often at fees surpassing those for sexual relations. In these cases, the prostitute engages her customer in vulgar sex talk and thus arouses him either in preparation for intercourse, or for auto-erotic purposes.

René Guyon has made some extremely relevant comments regarding the stimulating quality of "dirty" words

in general, and of this kind of sex talk in particular
He says:

> Lastly, the sexual sense is agreeably stimulated
> by the use of a special vocabulary of its own, a
> vocabulary that is at once technical and precise,
> and yet highly emotionalized in virtue of its very
> boldness and directness. Observation shows, in-
> deed, that many women are specially attracted to
> men who in intimate relations manifest a certain
> brazen effrontery in their words, gestures, and
> caresses. Courtesans, accomplished in their art, are
> well aware of this; they know that many men, who
> feel themselves cramped and hampered in public
> by the official puritanism of the societies in which
> they live, joyfully take their revenge by trampling
> this puritanism underfoot in private. But such an
> attitude is not confined to prostitutes or their
> clients. The so-called "obscene" letters, that are
> sometimes read in our law courts, throw a vivid and
> unexpected light (unexpected at any rate by those
> psychologists who have not taken the trouble to
> study the subject) on the important part played in
> the intimacies of sexual life by "smutty" expres-
> sions, depicting in a vivid, crude, and plastic way,
> the organs, the postures, and the functions of sex
> in their most lurid details. Paul Morand [in *Ouvert
> la Nuit*] refers to it as follows: ". . . I love him
> too. He understands so well how to use that lovely
> secret language of the senses; he makes those
> shameful words, so often vile and filthy, serve the
> most precious and delightful purpose."

One may occasionally also find this kind of sex talk
in erotically realistic fiction, but it is more characteristic
of "obscene" books. The reason for this lies, again, in
the fact that "obscene" books intend to arouse the reader
by the use of "dirty" language, just as in the above-
mentioned cases the prostitutes use this technique to
stimulate their customers.

Another characteristic feature of "obscene" books

is the *quantity* of taboo words used, which generally exceeds that of non-"obscene" fiction by several hundred percent.

In contrast to works of erotic realism, "obscene" books do not, as a rule, resort to swear words, probably because the necessity to express angry hostility seldom occurs in such books, whereas in realistic literature swearing is used to serve the same purpose that it does in actual life—the release of emotional tension and hostility. This, however, is not the aim of "obscene" books.

It is obvious that we cannot give a single example of sex talk as used in "obscene" books; we must, therefore, content ourselves with having given the general principles.

SUPERSEXED MALES

In keeping with the unrealistic nature of "obscene" books, one of their outstanding characteristics is the emphasis which they place upon the exaggerated size of the male organ, the largeness of the testicles, and the copiousness of the amounts of seminal fluid ejaculated. It follows that all of these factors add up to the picture of a man whose potency is almost limitless, and whose sex drive is constantly at record strength.

In all these respects, "obscene" writings are reminiscent of the phallic worship which antedates our religious system by several milleniums and which constituted, in pre-Christian times, the basic element of earlier religious cults the world over. In these cults, the male and female genitals, or their pictorial representations, were objects of worship to a people who saw in them not the "instruments of sin," but the symbols of the procreative, life-giving powers of nature. With the advent and ultimate victory of the Judeo-Christian religious systems, these nature cults fell into disgrace, were outlawed by the state and church, and their worshipers were persecuted, and often exterminated, by fire and sword. Yet, here and there, remnants of the ancient sex- and nature-worship and its symbolism have survived in one form or another—not infrequently by the device of changing the official meaning of the symbol. This technique resulted in "obscene" phallic pillars becoming decent church steeples, while ovals and circles, representing the female genitals, have been fashioned into Gothic rosettes and church windows, the shape and decoration of which leave no doubt, in some instances, as to their original meaning as sexual symbols. (See O. A. Wall, *Sex and Sex Worship*.)

It almost seems as though ancient pagan sex worship and sex symbolism have found an odd refuge in "obscene" or pornographic writings, though few, if any, of the authors or readers of "obscene" books could be credited with the same "purity of heart" with which their pagan ancestors apparently worshiped the deities of fertility.

To give some examples about this matter from our specimen book, first concerning the size of the man's genitals:

"Oh, Freddie . . . It's much . . . too big!" [*The Strange Cult*, p. 65.]

But what was Bella's astonishment to discover the gigantic proportions of the Priest who now presented himself. Already his dress was in disorder, and before him stood stiffly erected a member before which even the vigorous Ambrose was forced to cede. [*The Autobiography of a Flea*, p. 71.]

Two huge and hairy (vernacular for testicles) hung closely below, and completed the picture . . . . [*Ibid.*, p. 72.]

Bella fingered the gigantic penis . . . her hands could not go around his member. . . . It stood like a bar of iron in her soft hands. [*Ibid.*, pp. 72-73.]

In *The Lascivious Hypocrite* we also find many references to "the superb member," "its bursting head," the women who "admired its proportions," and so forth.

Likewise, in *The Confessions of Lady Beatrice,* there are passages where the woman sings the praises of her lover's large penis, which is, she says, "in all its hardness pressing against my belly. . . ." [p. 10.]

Other specimen books do not lag behind in this respect; and, more often than not, it is the women who comment glowingly about the man's organ:

> "So big," she murmured, urging me on as, not wanting to force her, I paused to allow her tensed muscles to relax, "so very, very big!" [*The Oxford Professor,* pp. 50-51.]

> But here I was to see exposed before m the 𝑛 ure of a full-grown man, and of an extremely handsome and well-made man too, and from what had taken place, I could not doubt that his peculiar manly attribute would be presented to me in the most imposing state of amorous excitement, nor was I disappointed. The protruding condition of his shirt, when my aunt pulled off his trousers as he sat on the sofa, somewhat prepared me for what was to appear, but when she drew his shirt over his head, and exposed his glowing priapus in the most splendid state of erection, I was thunderstruck. I gazed upon it with astonishment and admiration, and could hardly believe the evidence of my eyes, when the charming spectacle burst upon my sight. [*The New Lady's Tickler,* pp. 58-59.]

The Memoirs of a Russian Princess abounds in detailed references to the huge phalli of the Russian peasants, the *moujiks,* whom the Princess uses to satiate her passion; for example: "his enormous [vernacular for male organ] in violent erection" [p. 52]; "his enormous limb stretched upwards" [p. 74]; "a member, tense as a bar of iron" [p. 76]; "his huge limb" [p. 141].

We shall now have to examine the second aspect of the phallic criterion, that is, the peculiar emphasis which "obscene" books place on the large amounts of semen ejected by the hyperpotent heroes of these stories. For instance, in a single passage from *The Strange Cult,* we read how the man exhibits his huge sex organ, masturbates in front of the girl and finishes by ejaculating large quantities of seminal fluid over the girl's nude body.

All of the other specimen books follow the same pattern, therefore additional quotations would merely be repetitious without adding to our understanding of the phenomenon. All we can say at this point is that the mention of large quantities of semen being forcefully ejaculated seems to act as a powerful erotic stimulant upon the imagination of many readers, and that the repeated description of this type of situation is an essential ingredient not only of the ten specimen books, but of the hundreds of other "obscene" books examined by us, which by sheer summation, provide a fairly representative sample of classic and current pornographic or "obscene" literature.

The last point which we have to discuss under this heading is the exaggeration of male potency, quite aside from references to the size of the genitals or the quantity of semen. Two examples will suffice to illustrate this:

> "First," he said, leading her to and up the three or four steps to the deck, "we're going to have a swim; then we're coming back, and on that nice little bed down there, I'm going to give you a wonderful [vernacular for coitus]. After that, if you're real nice, of course, I'm going to teach you [vernacular for fellatio]. Then I'm going to [vernacular for cunnilingus] till you [vernacular for orgasm], and after that we'll [vernacular for coitus] some more!" [*The Strange Cult,* p. 64.]

"Obscene" books often go far beyond the biologically feasible or likely, such as the following "autobiographical braggery:

> With some I performed only once or twice, with others half a dozen times in the night and with my

darling Nora, did not sleep at all, but gave her cause to writhe in holy joy no less than eleven times. [*Lustful Stories,* p. 84.]

Before leaving this point, which is so very typical for "obscene" books, we shall have to mention two instances from our ten specimen books in which the overemphasis on the male genitals actually reaches the proportions of *phallus worship*. It is truly amazing how closely the parallels between the ancient fertility rites and these scenes in two of our "obscene" books are drawn. In Hellas and Rome, images of the fructifying gods Pan and Priapus were erected to insure increase in crops, flocks, and family. As O. A. Wall points out in his scholarly but now almost unobtainable work, *Sex and Sex Worship*: "Such figures were usually pillars, but often with a head, or a figure of a phallus in front. . . . A figure of a sitting Priapus, with an erect penis, was kept in the temples, to which prospective brides were taken by the priestesses who explained to them the sexual function of the man's parts. The brides usually sat on the lap of the naked god, with his organ introduced into their vaginas, thus rupturing their hymens as an offering to the deity."

We now find an almost identical account in one of our specimen books, in a chapter entitled "The Golden Member," which reads:

On this occasion she disclosed to me her household god, as she termed it. It was an exact replica of my penis, gold mounted on a velvet stand of convenient height, convenient for what, I will tell you!

The occasion of my seeing it for the first time was as follows: After dark, I was taken by Alice to a secret chamber. . . . The [adjoining] place was brilliantly lighted as always and while we looked through the curtains from [our] dark room, the golden member stood in the middle of the room opposite us, and at a signal, the tapestries at the other end of the room were parted sufficiently to admit a file of girls; I counted twenty-seven nude girls, ranging from piquantly pretty to radiantly beautiful.

. . . To the soft strains of hidden music they marched led by Bernice, straight for the Golden Member on its low pedestal. As Bernice reached the upstanding [vernacular for phallus], she . . . sank down [a description of how the girl immolates herself]. The procession halted, every naked girl raised high her arms and there came the sweetly intoned chorus, "Give me, Cupid, the pleasure of such a love arrow in life."

Then Bernice straightened up, took a step beyond the altar, and the second nude beauty replaced her on the golden member. The chorus was repeated, this ceremony being continued until all twenty-seven had immolated themselves. Meanwhile the origin of the golden [vernacular for phallus], felt all the sensations due the metal one. The service over, the procession disappeared behind the tapestry and we entered the hall. [*Lustful Stories*, pp. 82-83.]

It is obvious that we are here dealing primarily with a male wish-fulfillment fantasy, in which the male's vanity ("narcissism") becomes all the more obvious because of the idol being "an exact replica" of the hero's own penis. However, the story retains nevertheless most of the characteristic elements of genuine phallus worship, very similar to that practiced in antiquity.

Aside from cultural speculations as to whether ancient sex rites and pagan ways of thinking may have survived between the covers of "obscene" books, the psychological facts of the matter are, as the reader will recall, that "obscene" writings represent wish-fulfillment fantasies on the part of their (predominantly male) authors. It is therefore not astounding to find the size of the male genitals overemphasized and the man's potency being— hopefully—raised to the nth power.

Clinicians are aware of the universal concern of men over the size of the penis. Typical of man's realistic concern about potency is the kind of discussion which took place between Frank Harris and Maupassant, as quoted in the chapter on Frank Harris. Women, especially modern American women, know of similarly troubled thoughts with regard to the size of their breasts. However, the history of civilization, as well as clinical practice, has shown that women are and have always been among the most ardent worshipers of Priapus, at least in the patriarchal type of society where possession of the penis is associated with status, power, and prestige.

In any case, the overemphasis on male potency and male sex anatomy in "obscene" books is clearly understandable on the basis of man's pride in the erect penis, his wish for unlimited enjoyment of sexual relations, and his underlying anxiety with regard to his sexual powers.

NYMPHOMANIAC FEMALES

In keeping with the wish-fulfilling nature of "obscene" writings, the female characters in these stories are just as men would like women to be: highly passionate, sensuous, and sexually insatiable creatures who like nothing better than almost continuous intercourse.

Conspicuous by its absence in "obscene" writings is any trace of genuine modesty, restraint, or anxiety on the part of the women, which are certainly outstanding characteristics of most females in our culture. For instance it strikes one immediately that none of the women in any of our ten specimen books seem to have the least concern about pregnancy in spite of all their promiscuous behavior. The only apparent exception to this rule the girl in *Nelly*, or *The Confessions of a Doctor*, who initially sheds tears upon discovering her pregnant condition, can be discounted, because the book leaves no doubt that this is not to be taken seriously but was only contrived to provide an opportunity for the author to introduce the two main characters, Nelly and the Doctor, in a "functional" relationship.

"Obscene" books stress the female discharge almost

equally as much as the man's seminal fluid; this is, of course, to be expected, for if the women are supposed to be as responsive as "obscene" books would make us believe, there would be no better proof of this than reference to the physiological manifestations of their erotic excitement. We shall once again turn to our specimen books to illustrate the point:

In *The Autobiography of a Flea,* we find numerous references to the girl's lascivious nature in a single passage. In this particular erotic scene, the young Bella is shown as "insatiable in her passion"; we read of her "frenzied excitement," her "maddening spasms of completed lust," her "passionate rapture" and "ecstatic agony," resulting in "a copious emission," (pp. 24-25.)

In other places of the same book, we read the following about the female response:

> A low moan of salacious gratification escaped the parted lips of Bella. . . . [p. 26.]
>
> "How delicious," murmured Bella. . . . And down came a shower from [her] storehouse . . . while her head fell back and her mouth opened. . . . [p. 65.]
>
> Bella's lewdest feelings were roused. . . . [p. 71.]
>
> The child had caught a sort of lewd madness. . . . [p. 73.]

One of the specimen books, *The Confessions of Lady Beatrice,* is entirely devoted to a description of female passions, as are many other "obscene" works. Right in the first pages of the book, Lady Beatrice asks her husband to try to publish her confessions after her death, "for the benefit of all young ladies who may be troubled with a warm temperament as I have been. . . ." (p. 6.)

We have already seen that in *The Lascivious Hypocrite* the "buxom widow," her daughters, her lady friend, the Second Lady Superioress, and other females in the story were depicted as being equally interested in sexual activities as the male hero, Saint Geraud himself.

We find in "obscene" books that the vagina is often

considered as animated and described as "greedy," "hungry," "thirsty," "clasping," or "sucking," all of which are more appropriately human attributes. At the same time, the vagina is sometimes described with a certain sense of awe, bordering on the uncanny, which would be entirely in keeping with the archaic, superstitious attitudes with which, to a certain degree, modern man still approaches matters concerning sex and procreation.

One of our "obscene" specimen books (*Nelly, or the Confessions of a Doctor*, pp. 74-75) refers to the vagina as "the awful gate of life," and sees it as if soliciting something to fill it.

If we have spoken of the way in which "obscene" books characterize women as "nymphomaniacs" we are not using the term here in its strict clinical meaning. What we wish to convey is the idea that, just as "obscene" books describe men in a satyriasis-like condition of permanent sexual excitement, the women likewise do not seem to fit any cultural norms in our society and are represented as predatory females ever on the prowl for a new sexual partner or a new sexual experience. In this respect, females fulfill the fantasy and wish-fulfilling character of "obscene" literature and are very dissimilar to the female characters generally found in non-obscene literature.

NEGROES AND ASIATICS AS SEX SYMBOLS

In keeping with the popular prejudice that the Negro and Asiatic races are extraordinarily virile, sensuous, and given to all kinds of perversions, "obscene" books frequently feature one or more such persons to provide an added "exotic" element to their stories.

In another connection, we have already mentioned the Negro chauffeur who figures so prominently in the first part of our specimen book, *The Strange Cult*. We now have to consider his role with regard to his presumed racial characteristics. This particular book is especially illustrative of how "obscene" books use these characters to heighten the erotic tension of the stories. to quote:

> Pete stared at Inez. . . . Like his young mistress his sexual ability knew no limit. This giant Negro could satisfy the carnal desires of any woman. . . . "Kiss me," she demanded, and, when he failed to respond, she drew his face close and kissed his gash-like mouth. Like most darkies, Pete's body threw off that violently-stale cocoanut-oil odor . . . but it aroused Inez. [pp. 10-11.]
>
> Like the giant he was, he proved it then and there. Without a pause between ejaculations he [vernacular for sexual intercourse] her like a mad stallion. . . . Pete, like the black hero in the story book, was a lover par excellence! [p. 23.]

In *The Oxford Professor,* an entire chapter is devoted to the description of the most exotic sexual activities in the luxurious Parisian home of a mysterious Javanese girl by the name of "Jacinthe." The author introduces her as follows:

> She was one of the race of Javanese, those graceful vampires who drain the [vernacular for testicles] and purse of an Occidental in three weeks, leaving him as dry as a squeezed lemon, and she could not have been more than sixteen. [p. 133.]

After a long series of various erotic activities during the course of the evening, including coitus in the girl's specially constructed indoor swimming pool, the story reaches the following climactic pitch which, again, we can only reproduce in part, but which will, we think, give the reader the flavor of the scene:

> Jacinthe's fingers tangled in my hair and she played briefly with the lobe of my ear. She locked her legs about my neck and held me crushingly

close. . . . "Dai-erima," she murmured in her native tongue, and even though I did not at that time know the language, her meaning was clear. . . . Then, with a sudden flaming rush like that with which the sun bursts over the hills of her native land, the girl was flung into a paroxysm of wild, delirious passion. [p. 166.]

In the *Lustful Stories,* one entire chapter ("The Slave Market") is devoted to the wild orgies taking place in a Turkish harem, and here also the racial element is played up to the full.

The same book contains a passage about the great erotic desirability of mulatto girls, which follows more or less the same pattern as the previous examples:

My next adventure of note took place at a watering resort which I shall not name. There were stopping there at the same hotel an American widow, her daughter, and their maid, a half-breed negress of decided beauty who appeared to be about sixteen. [p. 84.]

Martha was the most wildly passionate girl I had ever met up to this time. Combined with the savagery of her black origin was the sensitive nerve organization of the Caucasian. [p. 86.]

I may as well confess it now, of all the world, half-breed negresses more white than black, are the very best [lovers]. . . . [p. 89.]

Many other "obscene" books which we have examined do show this feature, and one often also finds it in graphic representations of a pornographic (or "obscene") nature. In *The Memoirs of a Russian Princess,* the rough and tough peasants, or *moujiks,* take the place of the Negroes or Asiatics in other "obscene" books, and are there used by the author to the same effect. We have also seen this device used in *The Autobiography of a Flea,* where a farmer and his son are described as particularly depraved in their brutal and unrefined sexuality.

The basic idea in all these instances is that the members of so-called "inferior" races, or even of lower social groups, are thought of as being closer to the animalistic and instinctual in man. For this reason, members of the "low-caste" minorities provide excellent symbols of untamed passion in the context of "obscene" writings, while they are seldom, if ever, used in this manner by the authors of nonpornographic fiction.

HOMOSEXUALITY

There are strong homosexual elements, if not direct references to homosexual acts and their pornographic description, in almost all examples of "hard core obscenity." As to our ten specimen books, we saw that in *The Lascivious Hypocrite* an entire chapter ("Adonis") was devoted to the hero's homosexual affair with a young man.

There are other homosexual and Lesbian references throughout the text, as, for instance, when two women are described as masturbating in front of a mirror, in the orgiastic activities of the widow and her children where homosexuality and incest become fused, in the Lesbian activities of the nuns in the convent, and elsewhere in the book.

In *The New Ladies' Tickler* (specimen no. 6), all of the flagellation scenes have strong homosexual overtones, but beyond that, two entire chapters, or letters (the book is a collection of supposedly authentic letters), deal exclusively with the homosexual activities (mutual masturbation) between a younger and an older boy.

In our specimen book no. 7 (*Lustful Stories*), the rites surrounding the "Golden Member" are certainly of a Lesbian nature, in spite of the fact that the story is presented in a heterosexual context. This way of introducing homosexual material into otherwise heterosexual affairs by telling a story within a story is rather typical for "obscene" books.

In *The Strange Cult,* we find considerable emphasis on Lesbian activities. The club to which the older sister belongs is strictly devoted to Lesbian love, and even the relationship between the two sisters is definitely of a homosexual nature.

The Oxford Professor has an entire chapter on the relationship between two young women which becomes threatened by the introduction of a man who is "shipwrecked" and forced to spend the night on the private little island which the two Lesbians inhabit.

In our "obscene" specimen book, the two Lesbians first perform cunnilingus on each other as they are accustomed to doing, then one of them goes downstairs to sleep with the stranger, who "proves" to her that man's love (or rather technique) is superior to that of woman, until the other Lesbian gets suspicious and moves in to break up the affair, but is finally persuaded to desist from doing so and joins the party.

The Memoirs of a Russian Princess are remarkable in that they include a scene in which the Princess' favorite (the page, Alaska, who, as we have previously shown, was also her half-brother) turns transvestite in order to watch another man have intercourse with her and then be himself sodomized by the same man.

However, homosexuality and flagellation are unique in that entire "obscene" books have been written with the focus *mainly* on each of these subjects; for instance, our specimen book *The New Ladies' Tickler,* which nevertheless also succeeds in fulfilling most of the other criteria of "obscene" books.

Many "obscene" books place their plot in a Lesbian setting, but the vast majority of these books are written by males for male consumption, like Nicolas Chorier's all-time seventeenth century classic, *The Dialogues of Luisa Sigea, La Puta Errante,* and a number of others. Often the story is told in the form of dialogues between women, as, for instance, in the following exchange from *The Second Dialogue of Tribadicon:*

Tullia. Dear maid, hug me, me who am mad in love with thee. Allow my eyes and handlings a free scope, everywhere it is possible. Caviceo [the husband] will lose nothing thereby, nor thou either. Unhappy me! How vain are my efforts, accordingly as I advance! How madly I love thee!

Ottavia. Appease thy love and yield to that passion of thy soul. That which is thy desire, is mine also.

Tullia. Therefore, bestow this garden of thine upon me, that I may be its mistress: withal it would be useless to me, as I have no key to open its gate, nor hammer to strike it in, nor foot to enter it.

Ottavia. To be sure I present thee with it, being myself wholly thine. Do I own any right which is not also thine? Thou art falling upon me: what does it mean?

Tullia. Pray do not draw back; open thy thighs.

Ottavia. So I have. Thou hast me now all to thyself: thou art pressing thy mouth against mine, thy bosom against mine, and thy womb against my womb: would I could entwine round thee, as thou entwinest me.

• • • • •

Tullia. Cheer up, my goddess, I have been to thee a husband, my spouse! My wife!

Ottavia. Would to God thou wert my husband! What a loving wife thou wouldst have! What a fond husband I should own! [pp. 15-23.]

As very few "obscene" books are written by and for women, we cannot expect the situation to be any different with regard to Lesbian stories. We find many supposedly Lesbian scenes all through the bulk of "obscene" literature and, as pointed out, some books are mainly devoted to Lesbianism. However, they clearly serve the purpose mainly of arousing the male reader, who reacts to them as a heterosexual situation, and not for any hypothetical Lesbians who may happen to read them.

This is, undoubtedly, also the reason why we do not find many references to male homosexuality in "obscene" books, barring exceptions like the transvestite scene in *The Memoirs of a Russian Princess* and the "Adonis" scene from *The Lascivious Hypocrite*. The reason is that, generally speaking, homosexuality is not erotically stimulating to the average (heterosexual male) reader. On the contrary, it may be anxiety-arousing by mobilizing latent, rejected homosexual tendencies.

While "obscene" texts for and by Lesbians are extremely rare, we have been able to study several "obscene" manuscripts written by and for the enjoyment of male homosexuals. Manuscripts of this type are also not common, nor are they generally "professional" as in the case of heterosexual pornography ("hard core obscenity"). Homosexual pornography is usually of the amateurish variety, often consisting of only a few pages, and even if of greater length one encounters it generally in typewritten or mimeographed form rather than printed and bound.

"Obscene" books with strictly homosexual content otherwise follow the formula of heterosexual pornography, though they are by necessity more limited in subject matter. It also appears that the American examples of homosexual "obscenity" which have come to our attention have a decided sado-masochistic flavor. Repeatedly, one finds in them situations in which one or more aggressively dominant males lord it over one or more passive-submissive males whom they subject to various sexual practices, often with the purpose of humiliating the weaker partner.

One of the longer "obscene" stories (ca. 35 pages in all), entitled *Seven in a Barn,* tells of a poker game in which the stakes are that the loser must submit to whatever sexual activities the winner wishes to impose. To give the reader an impression of this type of relatively rare "hard core obscenity," we shall quote portions from this manuscript:

"Well, Bill, I suppose you have won." Bill remained very calm and said: "Yes, I have. Please, John, take away the cardtable and put the mattress in the middle of the floor. You others sit on the floor, beside me. I myself shall keep this chair. You know what the next step is, don't you, John?" —"I do," John answered, who had made up his mind he was going to play the game fairly. "I must announce my surrender."—"Indeed," Bill said, "and in what position?"—"Kneeling down on my bare knees, without my trousers."—"Very well, you may proceed."—In a few moments, the trousers were taken off and the football-player appeared with nothing on but his shirt and shorts. . . . A wave of excitement went through the crowd and all the eyes concentrated on the promising spot between the legs, showing a lovely curve, but still covered. They knew that pretty soon he would be ordered to remove his barrier, and then. . . . Six erections were the result and the excitement grew when the twenty-one-year-old boy knelt before the eighteen-year-old leader, who quietly leaned back in his chair.

These stories show not only the usual exhibitionistic-voyeuristic elements to which we are accustomed in heterosexual pornography, but the emphasis, manifested in the rest of the above specimen, on the size of the genitals, the amount of semen ejaculated, the hyperpotency of the individuals involved, the variation from one sexual activity to another, and the final culmination in the mass orgy which is also characteristic of the closing pages of heterosexual pornography.

Even from the above paraphrase, the reader may be able to visualize that the same principles which we outlined for heterosexual pornography ("hard core obscenity") are equally applicable to "obscene" writings with homosexual content.

FLAGELLATION

No discussion of the main criteria of "obscene" literature would be complete without considering the special role of flagellation. At certain times in Western civilization flagellation has been an important aspect of sexual behavior, most pronounced in those eras when religious sexual repression was strongest. During certain periods, such as in the Middle Ages in Europe, it became almost epidemic, resulting, on occasion, in public mass flagellation.

The sado-masochistic character of medieval sexuality finds expression in the countless caricatures of that period showing nuns being whipped by other nuns or by priests, or priests castigating nuns and pretty female confessors. In this case, religion provided the most convenient and morally most acceptable outlet for this type of sexual deviation; in fact, it was often "proof" of religious fervor.

We have a splendid example of this from the already-mentioned *Dialogues of Luisa Sigea,* by Nicolas Chorier. In the "Fifth Dialogue" of that book, Ottavia tells her girl friend, Tullia, in the course of a long and detailed description of many pages, of how her mother took her to a certain priest in order for both of them to receive flagellation for the "sins of the flesh." We here quote a small portion of the text; the mother has already been whipped at length, but, says Ottavia:

Ottàvia. She did not even dare open her mouth; she let a sigh escape her once: "Ah father!" said she. But he grew angry at this word.—"You shall not go unpunished out of my hands," he cried. He ordered her to double up her body with her head and breast inclined upon the ground. She obeyed; in this position her buttocks came into open contact with the lash, and during a whole hour, he scourged them incessantly.—"Now that sufficient joy has

been infused into thy, soul, rise," said Teodoro. She
got up, let her shift fall down about her heels and,
after having put on her gown, took me, smiling,
into her arms.—"It is now thy turn, daughter. Dost
thou think thou hast courage enough for that
sport?" she asked. "For it is sport and not suffering."

. . . . .

"Take the scourge, daughter; whip this low arena
of voluptuousness, which thou has there in thy
person." My mother, on putting her hand to mine,
showed me how I should strike indiscriminately
and with all my might that spot offered and exposed to the conjugal outrage.

. . . . .

"Come here, Teodoro," said my mother; "honor
my daughter with your office." Whilst my mother
was squeezing my bound hands between hers and
fondly kissing me, Teodoro was lashing and tear-
ing me to pieces."

Another period of widespread flagellation was the
mid-Victorian era, particularly in England, though it
always had its aficionados also on the continent. During
that time, hundreds of so-called "massage salons,"
houses of prostitution, and private clubs in London and
elsewhere were catering exclusively to this specialty,
many of these establishments being equipped with complete torture chambers and huge arsenals of whips,
spikes, lashes, wire brushes, and all the rest of the trade
paraphernalia.

Most of the classic flagellation erotica in the English
language date from that period, and our specimen book,
The New Ladies' Tickler, is no exception. However, it
is one of the best written in its genre, avoiding the san-
guine excesses of this deviation which can have a rather
anti-erotic effect on those who are not of the "set."

We shall see that these specialized books conform in
their general outline to our specific criteria, the established pattern of other "obscene" writings.

In our specimen book, *The New Lady's Tickler,* we find the benevolent, overly permissive mother-figure in the person of Lady Lovesport, who is an ardent flagellant. She is bringing up her young cousin Emily, who reports in a letter to her girl friend Lucy how she was reared by her aunt in the tradition of the rod:

My earliest years passed very pleasantly. My aunt was always kind to me, and though I was kept strictly to my lessons, still, as long as I was attentive and diligent, every indulgence was shown to me. But if, on any occasion, I failed in doing what was required of me, my poor bottom was pretty sure to smart for it. My aunt always undertook the duty of correcting me herself, and when punishment was to be inflicted, I was taken to a small room adjoining her bedroom, where I was placed across her knees, my petticoats were taken up, and a birch rod applied smartly to my naked posteriors.

On these occasions I generally struggled a good deal. I soon fancied that by tossing myself about, and pretending to suffer more than I really did, my aunt's heart was softened, and consequently the stripes inflicted upon me were of a less severe nature than when I lay like a log on her knees, and showed no symptoms of feeling the pain. However this may be, it usually happened that between my struggles and her endeavours to retain me on her knee, her clothes would also be tossed up, and before the conclusion of my punishment, her thighs were generally as bare as my own, and I lay with my naked belly and thighs pressed against her naked person. On these occasions I could not but admire the softness and beauty of the charms which were thus exposed to me, and to wonder at the profusion of beautiful curly hair, which adorned the secret spot often presented to my sight, so different from the bare unfledged gap, which was beginning to attract my own curiosity.

One immediately recognizes the homosexuality toned

exhibitionism in this passage, the erotic effect of which is here heightened by adding the flagellation element.

The following scene, in which the aunt is supposedly "punishing" another girl, brings out the voyeuristic-exhibitionistic nature of the reportage, which is so characteristic of "obscene" writings, even more clearly:

I was very certain that my aunt's purpose was to punish the girl, and I could not help somehow connecting this punishment with the arrival of Mr. Everard. I felt a strong desire to ascertain whether I was right in this conjecture. The idea took such a strong hold upon my mind, that I determined to be a spectatress of the punishment, and knowing a back way to a closet which would give me a full view of all my aunt's doings in her own room, you may guess I soon dropped the work I had to do, and hurried to my place of espionage, finding myself not a moment too soon, for she had already got the trembling Maria divested of everything but her chemise, and I could see that her [vernacular for breasts] were sufficiently grown to swell out, and show their charming rotundity in the most enticing manner possible. As soon as she was thus stripped, my aunt made her place her arms behind her, and tied them with a handkerchief behind her back. She then took another handkerchief and fastened it firmly over her eyes, so as to blindfold her completely.

In this condition she led her to a couch, which, fortunately, was in full view from my hiding place, and made her lie down upon it, at the same time lifting up her chemise, and fastening it around her waist, so as to leave all her person below that perfectly naked. Indeed, from the loose manner in which that garment hung around her, my aunt easily contrived to lay bare the whole of the upper part of her person likewise, the chemise merely forming a sort of girdle round her waist, where it was retained by the manner in which her arms were bound.

When all this was arranged, my aunt made a signal to some one in the bedroom, and, to my great surprise, though, I must say, I had rather anticipated something of the sort, I saw Mr. Everard steal gently from the one room to the other, and place himself at the back of the couch, leaning his arms upon it, and gazing intently, though, of course, in perfect silence, upon the lovely form thus exposed, naked, before his eyes. He had taken off his coat and waistcoat, and his boots, but otherwise he was completely dressed.

No sooner had he taken his place than my aunt began to apply the rod to the exquisite posteriors which were thus presented to her in such an inviting position for the birch. She was not very severe at first, and Maria lay pretty still, though her shrinking, quivering flesh showed that she felt keenly the stinging touches. As the charming buttocks began to be reddened by this exhilarating exercise, my aunt seemed to get excited and heated with her work, and plied the rod more sharply and vigorously.

In proportion as she felt the pain increase, Maria began to exhibit symptoms of the intensity of her feelings, she turned and twisted about, and writhed her body in every manner of strange contortion, sometimes raising up her buttocks by resting on her knees, so as to exhibit her lovely belly, sometimes trying to avoid the sharp stripes by turning herself round to my side, thereby giving me a full view of the front part of her person, with the lovely characteristic which distinguishes our sex. [There follows a description of the labia actively opening and closing; this is physiologically impossible but is nevertheless a frequent feature of "obscene" books, apparently because the idea of the female at the height of excitement is erotically highly stimulating to the male.]

When this took place my aunt was pretty sure, by a sharp application of the rod, to make her turn round again, but when, on the other hand, she moved herself so as to expose the same delightful sight to the evidently charmed gaze of Mr. Everard, she rather suspended her blows, or merely applied them so lightly as to induce Maria to remain for a time in the same attitude.

The rest of the scene concerns itself with the flagellation gathering momentum, which comes to a climax when Mr. Everard, after having watched the whole proceedings, performs cunnilungus on Lady Lovesport while she continues to flagellate the young girl.

Emily then tells how she was deflowered by her boy friend, "the audacious Harry," while the aunt and her lover first secretly watched the procedure, and later assisted in the defloration by Lady Lovesport's use of the birch on Harry's posteriors just as the young man is about to give up his attempts:

> It had occurred to Lady Lovesport to try the effect of the powerful stimulus which she so successfully applied to his posteriors, just in the nick of time, and which so effectively produced all the good effect that she desired.

It follows that "one good turn deserves another." The young couple return the favor and assist Emily's aunt and her lover by using the rod on them as they proceed to have intercourse.

We could cite countless similar instances from the vast "obscene" flagellation literature which exists in every major language, but, for the most part, doing so would be only duplication. Flagellantism obviously has a strong appeal for many people. It is frequently involved with shoe, underwear, and an assortment of other fetishisms. It is therefore not surprising that it should have played such a prominent role in erotic and "obscene" literature.

With this we have completed our analysis of "hard core" obscenity. Admittedly, there are other, minor characteristics of "obscene" literature. They are sometimes fascinating and psychologically highly significant, e.g., the recurrent mention of erotically stimulating odors of the body hair and of the sexual secretions; the frequent emphasis on pubic and axillary hair; or the frequency of animal contact, particularly between women and animals. But if we have neglected some of the "fine points" in this place, it was done because it is feared that they would tend to confuse rather than clarify the issue.

To sum up, "obscene" books not only have a definite structure and organization, they also contain a number of specific criteria which are based on psychological mechanisms serving the purpose of stimulating erotic fantasies and sexual arousal. In the preceding chapters we have demonstrated how these criteria function in the context of various "obscene" books. These major criteria, as we have seen, consisted of:

> Seduction
> Defloration
> Incest
> The Permissive-Seductive Parent Figure
> Profaning the Sacred
> "Dirty" Words in Dirty Books
> Supersexed Males
> Nymphomaniac Females
> Negroes and Asiatics as Sex Symbols
> Homosexuality
> Flagellation

We have also indicated that these are not the only criteria of "obscene" books, but represent the most outstanding, the most common and the most easily recognizable factors.

We cannot overemphasize that *none of these criteria singly, in isolation, constitute any evidence that a given book or writing is "obscene."* As is the case in psychological tests which are designed to give clinical information about an individual, the criteria which are isolated and described must be seen in relationship to the whole.

Thus, in "obscene" books, individual criteria must be evaluated in relationship to each other in the context of the whole piece of writing under examination, or as a *configuration* and *cluster* of factors. The significance of this will become clear when we now return to two famous cases of erotic realism which have been mistakenly classified as "obscene borderline cases." With the background of our examination of bona fide "hard core obscenity," the basic and unmistakable difference between these two types of literature, namely, erotic realism and hard core pornography, will become clearly evident.

PART IV

TWO FAMOUS MISTAKEN "BORDERLINE" CASES

Having studied a representative cross-section of "obscene" books against the background of a variety of books exemplifying erotic realism, we are now in a position to take up two famous literary test cases which have been mistaken for pornography and have, at one time or other, been declared "obscene" by the courts.

Of the two books, the first, *Memoirs of Hecate County*, is still in limbo, banned in the State of New York while on sale in forty-nine States. The other book, *Lady Chatterley's Lover*, has recently been declared not obscene by the United States District Court, Southern District of New York.

In the following pages we shall study these two works in the light of the previous discussion concerning the nature of erotic realism and the psychology of pornography.

MEMOIRS OF HECATE COUNTY
BY EDMUND WILSON

First published in 1942, this remarkable accomplishment in erotic realism has been confused by the courts as "obscene." Consequently, the *Memoirs of Hecate*

County, like the autobiography of Frank Harris and most of Henry Miller's books, is one of the most sought-after items in the speakeasies of the book trade.

The erotic part of the book (about one-third of the total text) concerns mainly the hero's simultaneous attraction to a proletarian girl of Eastern European stock by the name of Anna, and an upper-middle class American housewife named Imogen.

Anna works at the Tango Casino on New York's 14th Street and lives with her mother and stepfather in a household saturated with vice and squalor. However, Anna remains naïve, virtuous, and almost virginal in the midst of all this immorality. Her childlike naturalness is not even sullied by a brief marriage to a sadistic hoodlum of whom she lives in fear, but with an admixture of pity.

After the first date with the writer of the story, the hero closes his diary with an entry describing his impression of Anna as being "passionate for so frail and quiet a girl," an impression based on the blind, childlike concentration she displays in kissing him.

On their second date, a week later, Anna tells the man, again in childlike fashion, that she had had a dream about him in which they were "doing it" on the sofa at her home when her sister came in and remarked that they must have needed it pretty badly.

Another week, and her lover persuades Anna to take down her slip. She tells him even her husband had never seen her naked. Throughout all these scenes, Anna is constantly demonstrating the dual sense of acceptance of the sex drive combined with guilt which is characteristic of her economic level. The gradual breakdown of her guilt-based inhibitions begins when the man takes out one of her little breasts, admires it, and is about to expose the other, whereupon she stops him coquettishly. One breast she will permit, but not two! However, the diary remarks that she is very responsive to the rhythms and tides of love-play, and sensitive to any stimulation.

Anna also discloses on this occasion that she had got into the habit, in sleeping with Dan (her husband) of holding his penis in her hand—as a gesture of affection and respect.

Another time she tells her lover of how, after her husband came out of jail, where he had been for eighteen months, they must have had intercourse for 24 hours. But she confesses that the bed creaked so loudly that they had to put the mattress on the floor because, as she explains, her mother was in the next room and Anna did not want her to hear.

When Anna finally gets fed up with working at the Tango Casino and quits, it is because of the crudities with which the job forces her into contact. She complains to her lover that some of the customers there are perverts, whom the girls call "greaseballs." In his diary, her lover reports her as saying that they came there to get an orgasm by pressing against their partners. She relates with embarrassment that one of the girls had come into the ladies' room in a mess, with semen all over her dress.

These, and many other passages in the book, are characteristic of Edmund Wilson's uncompromising erotic realism, revealing the growth and development of a character expressed, as so frequently happens in reality, through the growth of a human being's sexuality. Many of these scenes are strongly anti-erotic in nature, as honest and perhaps as "shocking" as life itself. Nor does the hero spare himself or his own naïveté. Once, when Anna is sick, he tells of how he visits her at her home and realizes for the first time the meaning of poverty: the miserably crowded rooms; the all-pervasive smell of grease, cooking and unaired bedding; Anna herself, horrified and ashamed, lying in tumbled, filthy sheets. There are still more anti-erotic scenes when the lover visits the hospital where Anna later lies for weeks between life and death.

The same is true of the love story about the hero and Imogen. Here again we find erotic realism, but since the woman has to wear a brace on her back, this kind of erotic realism is a far cry from the uncomplicated sex appeal of "obscene" books.

A mixture of fear and perverted sexual excitement is felt by the man as he is forced to help the woman get into her brace after one of their few experiences of sexual intercourse. In that scene, we also get for the first time an inkling that the harness may be more of a fetish in the woman's perverted sex life than a bona fide orthopedic necessity. In the scene, which is rich in psychological and sexological detail, the hero describes the harness, remarking parenthetically that it is like something one would expect to find at Abercrombie and Fitch, a piece of athletic equipment consisting of steel uprights, leather thongs and rubber pads. He describes himself first as perplexed by the multiplicity of straps, and then abashed when Imogen removes her slip and reveals the collar round her neck, from which two straps descend to hold a band of steel across her chest and two pads under her arms. But her lover is amazed that the whole effect is more like a décolleté which sets off the woman's breasts "in a perverse and provocative way."

Imogen insists that he tighten the straps as firmly as he can, even though he shrinks from seeing the harness sink into her flesh. She apologizes for his having to see all this. Mistaking her flushed cheeks for shame and embarrassment, the hero gently kisses her to reassure her of his love, and discovers to his surprise that she responds with the most passionate kiss she has ever offered. He considers making love to her, just as she is, to prove his indifference to the harness, but refrains partly because of his primitive fear of the contraption, and partly because he is afraid it might simply prove impractical and embarrass her even further. However, he continues to kiss and praise her until Imogen grows impatient, suspecting him of pity, and finds an excuse to break off his love-making.

The hero comes upon a book later on, *The Hysterical Element in Orthopedic Surgery,* and finds in this medical text all the symptoms that fit Imogen's case. He describes his feelings of revulsion, finding the whole situation "unutterably gruesome," even supposing that Imogen is unaware that she is not physically ill.

Recalling his scene with her, he quotes from the book:

> They wear their pads and straps so tight as to produce excoriations, insisting that they do not give them comfort otherwise.

He now realizes he must try to free himself from his prolonged fixation on Imogen, an attachment based on false premises which could lead ultimately to disaster.

Clearly Imogen could be a real person, with a real and distressful perversion, and clearly the author did not intend to convey anything but an honest emotional and intellectual reaction to this reality.

It is difficult to understand how a book of this kind could ever have been considered "obscene." In that respect, *Memoirs of Hecate County* is an outstanding example of how utterly impossible it is to arrive at a sound appraisal as to the nature of erotic literature without a background of comparison and a scientific standard of measurement.

LADY CHATTERLEY'S LOVER, BY D. H. LAWRENCE

From a purist point of view, there is no better example of erotic realism than this novel by a prudish but intellectually honest writer. Contrary to what some critics appear to believe, D. H. Lawrence did not intend to produce an erotic gland-teaser to help him out of his financial difficulties when he wrote *Lady Chatterley's Lover*. If this had been his object, the book would have to be considered a gigantic flop. A single page from any of our ten "obscene" specimen books could accomplish that purpose many times better than the entire romance between Lady Chatterley and her rustic lover.

Nevertheless, although legally cleared as not "obscene" by a United States District Court, some booksellers and wholesalers, fearful of local criminal or civil action, have refused to distribute this classic. To those very few who will not handle the book for reasons of personal conviction, we say again this is their privilege. We do not believe that any citizen in a democracy should be coerced into acting contrary to that individual's personal beliefs in the area of selling, or of purchasing, erotic realism. We ask only for full understanding of the choice to be made.

D. H. Lawrence once wrote to a friend with reference to this book: "You mustn't think I advocate perpetual sex. Far from it. . . . But I want, with *Lady Chatterley's Lover,* to make an adjustment in consciousness to the *basic physical realities.*" That is what makes this book not only erotic realism, but erotic realism *with a cause*.

Very similar to Mark Twain's "1601," Lawrence's novel represents the author's faith in the inherently *therapeutic* value of facing any reality, including gross four-letter Anglo-Saxonisms.

When Mellors, the gamekeeper, uses verbal "obscenity" in his conversation with Constance Chatterley, it is not entirely accidental. The hidden motivation is "to root out and purify," as Harry T. Moore says in his review of the first unexpurgated American edition of the book, "feelings long hidden by shame."

The male contestants in the story are themselves symbols of this struggle between the natural impulses of man and the intellectual entrammelments of a civilization based on human exploitation and the collective sadism called war which leave humanity as emasculated and perverted as Lady Chatterley's husband Clifford. Mellors, the gamekeeper, is—in contrast to this—the symbol of the "simple," natural life, and its devoted preserver.

Constance Chatterley's choice is, therefore, not just between two men, one of whom is impotent anyway, but between two ways of life: Clifford's over-intellectualized, economically secure, respectable, even aristocratic, but unfeeling, de-sexualized, existence, which feeds on self-pity and mental cruelty on the one hand, and on the other, Mellor's virile, natural primitivism, which brings him and anyone near him into immediate conflict with the established social order.

The choice between such frightening alternatives on either side is not an easy one. Lady Chatterley finds the decision difficult to make. D. H. Lawrence describes her conflict in a psychologically credible and consistent manner, and this part, which, to our mind, is the core or "dominant theme" of the book, is at least as realistic as the erotic passages of the story.

From a psychological point of view, the development of Lady Chatterley's feelings about sexuality has all the merits of a penetrating clinical case study, to which the author's poetic language only adds, rather than subtracts.

We are told how both Constance (the later Lady Chatterley) and her sister Hilda "tentatively" experimented in their youth with love and sex when they were involved with the free-youth movement of that period. "The young men with whom they talked so passionately," says Lawrence, "and sang so lustily and camped under the trees in such freedom wanted, of course, the love connection. The girls were doubtful, but then the thing was so much talked about, it was supposed to be so important. And the men were so humble and craving. Why couldn't a girl be queenly, and give the gift of herself?"

So they had given the gift of themselves, each to the youth with whom she had the most subtle and intimate arguments. The arguments, the discussions were the great thing: the love-making and connection were only a sort of primitive reversion and a bit of an anticlimax. One was less in love with the boy afterwards, and a little inclined to hate him, as if he had trespassed on one's privacy and inner freedom. For, of course, being a girl, one's whole dignity and meaning in life consisted in the achievement of an absolute, a perfect, a pure and noble freedom. What else did a girl's life mean? To shake off the old and sordid connections and subjections.

And however one might sentimentalise it, this sex business was one of the most ancient, sordid connections and subjections. Poets who glorified it were mostly men. Women had always known there was something better, something higher. And now they knew it more definitely than ever. The beautiful pure freedom of a woman was infinitely more wonderful than any sexual love. The only unfortunate thing was that man lagged so far behind women in the matter. They insisted on the sex thing like dogs.

Passages such as these show, indeed, a deep intuitive understanding of feminine psychology at that stage and in the cultural environment in which it is presented.

Lawrence was one of the few writers who could capture the depth of both male and female psychology, particularly with regard to the erotic.

The contrast between the feeble love-making of the hypersensitive, somewhat artificial, and, if you will, "neurotic" Michaelis, who is the partner in Lady Constance's first extramarital affair, and the passionate, intense, rapturous "encompassing" of Mellors is a study in the psychology of male sexuality in itself.

The height of the writer's empathy with a woman's feelings is undoubtedly reached in the description in which Constance finally overcomes her last inner resistance toward her lover and the simple, natural life that he represents.

The scene opens with an intercourse experience between Lady Constance and Mellors which ends unsatisfactorily for the woman. She feels she will never be able to love this man who has suddenly become a stranger. During the act, she seems to be "looking on from the top of her head [at] this bouncing of the buttocks, and the wilting of the poor, insignificant, moist little penis"— all this ridiculous motion which is supposed to be love.

She tells Mellors that she is unable to love him, and he, wisely, encourages her not to worry about it now, but to take the good with the bad, admitting that this time it was rather bad. The woman's revulsion turns almost into hatred as the man continues to talk in broad, mid-England idiom, and finally stands in the room, "buttoning down those absurd corduroy breeches, straight in front of her."

But the turning point comes as Mellors, sensing her hatred, draws away, "to rise silently and leave her." Connie clings to him as in terror:

"Don't! Don't go! Don't leave me! Hold me! Hold me fast!" she whispered in blind frenzy, not even knowing what she said, and clinging to him with uncanny force. It was from herself she wanted to be saved, from her own inward anger and resistance. Yet, how powerful was that inward resistance that possessed her!

He took her in his arms again and drew her to him, and suddenly she became small in his arms, small and nestling. It was gone, the resistance was gone, and she began to melt in a marvellous peace. And as she melted small and wonderful in his arms, she became infinitely desirable to him, all his blood vessels seemed to scald with intense yet tender desire, for her, for her softness, for the penetrating beauty of her in his arms, passing into his blood. And softly, with that marvellous swoonlike caress of his hand in pure soft desire, softly he stroked the silky slope of her loins, down, down between her soft warm buttocks, coming nearer and nearer to the very quick of her. And she felt him like a flame of desire, yet tender, and she felt herself melting in the flame. She let herself go. She felt his penis risen against her with silent amazing force and assertion, and she let herself go to him. She yielded with a quiver that was like death, she went all open to him. And oh, if he were not tender to her now, how cruel, for she was all open to him and helpless!

She quivered again at the potent inexorable entry inside her, so strange and terrible. It might come with the thrust of a sword in her softly-opened body, and that would be death. She clung in a sudden anguish of terror. But it came with a strange slow thrust of peace, the dark thrust of peace and a ponderous, primordial tenderness, such as made the world in the beginning. And her terror subsided in her breast, her breast dared to be gone in peace, she held nothing. She dared to let go everything, all herself, and be gone in the flood.

And it seemed she was like the sea, nothing but dark waves rising and heaving, heaving with a great swell, so that slowly her whole darkness was in motion, and she was ocean rolling its dark, dumb mass. Oh, and far down inside her the deeps parted and rolled asunder, from the centre of soft plunging, as the plunger went deeper and deeper, touching lower, and she was deeper and deeper and deeper disclosed, and heavier the billows of her rolled away to some shore, uncovering her, and closer and closer plunged the palpable unknown, and further and further rolled the waves of herself away from herself, leaving her, till suddenly, in a soft, shuddering convulsion, the quick of all her plasm was touched, she knew herself touched, the consummation was upon her, and she was gone. She was gone, she was not, and she was born: a woman.

Ah, too lovely, too lovely! In the ebbing she realized all the loveliness. Now all her body clung with tender love to the unknown man, and blindly to the wilting penis, as it so tenderly, frailly, unknowingly withdrew, after the fierce thrust of its potency. As it drew out and left her body, the secret, sensitive thing, she gave an unconscious cry of pure loss, and she tried to put it back. It had been so perfect! And she loved it so!

And only now she became aware of the small, bud-like reticence and tenderness of the penis, and a little cry of wonder and poignancy escaped her again, her woman's heart crying out over the tender frailty of that which had been the power.

"It was so lovely!" she moaned. "It was so lovely!" But he said nothing, only softly kissed her, ly-

ing still above her. And she moaned with a sort of
bliss, as a sacrifice, and a new-born thing. [pp.
207-9.]

The above passage from *Lady Chatterley's Lover* is
unsurpassed in the beautiful and entirely correct interpretation of what occurs—psychologically—when a female in her association with a real man truly becomes
a woman. We see the complete change of attitude in
Lady Chatterley, now plain Connie, toward the body
(her own as well as her lover's), the physiological side
of sexual relations, and especially the woman's reaction
to the man's penis.

In the negative phase, Lady Chatterley's sex hostility
expressed itself in her belittling of the male organ. After
the great conversion, a sexually satisfied "Connie" regrets the withdrawal of the man's penis, and instead of
revulsion and ridicule for the physical part of love-
making, she can only think of it all as something which
could not last long enough: "It was so lovely!"

Dr. Reik and the authors have pointed out in their
recording *The Psychology of Sexual Relations,* (Helicon, New Rochelle, N. Y.) that a woman only wishes
the man's penis to remain in her after intercourse if she
has been sexually satisfied. It is to her as if the penis
were already the beginning of the baby which she wants
from the man she loves. This aspect is completely borne
out by the novel because the wish for a child was one of
the motivating factors which drove Connie to her husband's gamekeeper in the first place, and, as it turns out,
her relations with Mellors does result in her pregnancy.

As to the use of what could (but should not) be called
vulgar language in the book, its therapeutic role and effect are a complete parallel to the use of bad language
in certain clinical situations, as an automatic release
mechanism for people under stress, as was discussed in
a previous chapter ("Dirty" Words in Clean Books).

For Lady Chatterley, her acceptance of Mellors' peasant dialect and tolerance of four-letter words coincides
with her sexual awakening. Not only does she learn to

tolerate words like "fuck," "cunt," "cock," but she can use them in conversation with her lover, not as a mud-slinging contest, but to express feelings which run deeper than the more refined equivalents are able to convey.

In that sense, the gamekeeper's initial use of four-letter words is therapeutic for his ladylove, because he thus loosens her up and gives her implicit permission to use the same words. More than that, the primitive language of the emotions opens the way for this woman, who has become a victim of overcivilization, to return to the basic realities of life; in other words, to get in tune with life itself.

And once again one wonders, in analyzing books such as *Lady Chatterley's Lover* and *Memoirs of Hecate County*, how these works could have ever been confused with "hard core obscenity." True, they contain a number of four-letter words, serving a definite purpose in their context; true, also, that they include a number of complete intercourse scenes which are certainly integral parts in the whole composition of these books. But aside from these features of erotic realism, there is nothing in these, or in many other books which have suffered a similar fate by the hand of arbitrary censorship, which would bring them even near the classification of "hard core obscenity," as defined.

SUMMATION OF "TWO BORDERLINE CASES"

The main parallels and differences between these two famous modern examples of erotic realism lie in the following facts: the erotic realism in *Lady Chatterley's Lover* at times transcends the limitations of realism in the strictest sense by reaching the height of universal symbolism in the ideas expressed and the almost arche-typical nature of the novel's main characters. One can, for instance, say that Lady Chatterley symbolizes all the frustrated and sexually unfulfilled women in the world who are seeking that inner freedom and happiness which our civilization has denied them. In the same manner, her husband can be considered typical of the emasculated intellectual male who finds gratification in any number of substitutes, be they the writing of devitalized novels, the building of business empires, maneuvering in politics, or just becoming obsessed with fishing, golf, or sports cars. The gamekeeper, Mellors, represents in contrast the "primitive" by his own free choice, and not by limitations of intellect or personality.

In *Memoirs of Hecate County*, one of the main female characters, Imogen, can be said to take the place of Lady Chatterley and to represent the frustrated upper-middle-class American woman, except that in the degree to which her sex life is twisted into a rare perversion she can no longer be considered typical. Her more shadowy husband, on the other hand, can perhaps qualify as the much written about American suburbanite male who takes the commuter train to the office and who returns in the evening unaware of his wife's emotional state, her affairs with other men, or whatever else is going on in his home.

The "low-caste" girl Anna could similarly be seen as representative of working-class, poverty-plagued, immigrant girls. But in fact, she is so much the real girl Anna, an individual, and so little of any universal kind of female symbol in Edmund Wilson's novel, that here we become more aware of the differences between these two masterpieces of erotic realism.

One can compare the two novels from still another point of view, using Kinseyan categories of sex attitudes on different socio-economic levels as the criterion. In *Lady Chatterley's Lover*, upper-level sex attitudes are expressed in the beginning of the novel by Lady Chatterley, her husband, and her first lover Michaelis, a man of her own social set. Lower-level sex attitudes come through with almost shocking effect in the case of Mellors' estranged wife, while Mellors himself seems to stand outside of class attitudes with regard to his highly individualized and deliberately chosen personal sexuality with which Lady Chatterley later identifies.

The differences and similarities between these two books complement each other like two well-mated lovers. For that reason, we find it difficult to see these two great works of erotic realism in isolation from one another. While the ideas and characters in *Lady Chatterley's Lover* are of more universal scope than those in *Memoirs of Hecate County,* the reader—especially the American reader—finds it more difficult to identify with those in the former, and the personalities in that story remain somewhat less real to him as individuals than Imogen, Anna, or the conflict-torn, intellectual urbanite-writer who tells of his affairs with these two women. It is therefore all the more important that both works be freely available to the English reading public on both sides of the Atlantic.

The two books are important also in that they give us rare insights into the psychology of love-feeling and love-making, of which the behavioral sciences still know relatively little. From a mental hygiene point of view, both books are invaluable. In *Lady Chatterley's Lover,* the emphasis on the "rightness" and liberating power of the natural sexual impulse are a relief from the slippery double meanings which characterize so much of our social life, and which permeate most of our current "erotic" bestsellers. The clinician and humanist can only welcome the perfect fusion of the elemental sex drive with the tender and affectionate feelings which the two lovers in Lawrence's novel achieve as the prize of their soul-searching struggle. This pervasive tenderness of feeling is all the more important from a mental hygiene point of view in a time when sexuality has, for large groups of people, lost all connection with such love-feelings.

As for *Memoirs of Hecate County,* its mental hygiene assets lie mainly in its frankness and honesty which do not shy away from the most intimate details of sexual relations, without ever degrading or embellishing them. Its therapeutic advantage lies in the realistic portrayal of life, including the sex life, of groups of people like Anna and her family, of whom the average reader knows little. The more we know of life in all its forms, not excluding its grey and even black sides, the better equipped we are to face its inevitable realities. For that reason, even the realistic portrayal of a sexual perversion, as in the case of Imogen and her harness, has its own intrinsic mental hygiene value. The principle here involved is that we fear far more that which we do not know, and around which we have spun exaggerated fantasies of dread and horror, than the dangers and ugliness in life for which we are mentally prepared through acquaintance with them in erotic realism.

This reasoning leads us to laud the public acceptance and legal sanction of Nabakov's *Lolita* in this country—not as the "comedy" it is reputed to be and which it certainly is *not*—but as the realistic tragedy of a man, compulsively driven to pre-pubertal girls by psychological forces beyond his conscious control from within, and harassed by exploitative and intolerant forces from the social environment without; the hope being that to the thousands of its readers, *Lolita* may bring better understanding and lead to a more enlightened attitude toward this not too uncommon sexual deviation.

Nabakov's novel also correctly conveys the idea that in spite of the man's fixation on young girls, it was really Lolita herself who teased and seduced him into the affair, and that it was not her adult lover who corrupted the morals of this minor. This is a significant aspect of Nabakov's story, because sexological research bears out the fact—contrary to public opinion—that Lolita's case is more often the rule than the exception.

From all these various points of view, erotic realism in literature constitutes an effective mental-health prophylactic against faulty attitudes surrounding sexuality, and against ungrounded or grossly exaggerated fears, while bringing the reader into emotional and intellectual contact with those aspects of life which are commonly undiscussed, hushed-up, or denied because of a false sense of shame. On the other hand, erotic realism satisfies the natural and desirable interest in sex, without turning it into morbid channels, confusing and linking it with violence, or keeping it antiseptically detached from the physical sensations which should accompany it, and by connecting the sexual impulse with those love-feelings which are its highest perfection.

THE STRANGE CASE OF *FANNY HILL*

The genesis of *Fanny Hill* or *Memoirs of a Woman of Pleasure,* occurred, according to the author John Cleland, as follows: in a letter to the court, dated 13th November, 1749, he says that he was visited by "a young gentleman of the greatest hopes that ever I knew (brother to a nobleman now Ambassador at a Foreign Court), above eighteen years ago." The young gentleman brought to Cleland "the Plan for the first Part" of a book that was to become the most popular work of erotica in the English language—all its subsequent bannings and burnings notwithstanding.

Many years later, Cleland explains in the same letter, while he was in debtor's prison—where he had landed after some financial misfortunes, following a quarrel with his superior in the East India Company in Bombay—he "altered, added to, transposed, and in short new-cast" the young gentleman's manuscript, until it became the unconquerable *Fanny Hill* as we know her today.

Actually, the book's sub-title should not have been *Memoirs of a Woman of Pleasure,* but *The Rewards of Virtue,* in contrast to de Sade's *Justine,* or *The Misfortunes of Virtue.* For, if de Sade's book has as its theme the uselessness and dangers of a *virtuous* life, Cleland's novel extols the blessings of the pure in heart. In other words, for all its sexually stimulating erotic realism, *Fanny Hill* is an utterly *moral* book, an impression which is heightened still further by flowery language that was the literary style of the time.

The story, put in the form of two lengthy letters by Fanny to a lady friend, is quickly enough told: an innocent young girl from the country, lured by the bright lights of the big city, soon finds herself in desperate financial straits, goes to a sort of employment agency which turns out to be the recruiting center of a bordello madam, becomes a member of her staff and without ever coming to the actual exercise of her new profession in that house, nevertheless meets the "love of her life" one morning when walking through the drawing room where he is sleeping off the effects of a drunken brawl the night before.

The story might have ended here, with the two—Fanny and her Charles (for that turns out to be his name)—living together happily forever after in domestic tranquillity, had cruel fate not ordained otherwise. For no sooner has Fanny had time to be installed by her lover in an apartment of her own and to get pregnant, when he is whisked away by his father "to the South Seas," the sudden revelation of which well-nigh breaks Fanny's heart and causes, perhaps as a sort of luck in misery, a timely miscarriage.

To support herself, Fanny now has to get back into business, but this time in earnest. However, because she is good hearted and has always had the best of intentions, fate, which has just been so harsh with her, rewards her by letting her fall on her feet: she is introduced to a wealthy man about town who becomes her new protector, to whom she remains faithful, though she secretly keeps pining for Charles, until she discovers her keeper in a compromising situation with her own chambermaid. Thereupon she cuckolds him with *his* young servant, a lad just come from the country, until she is in turn found out, given short notice to leave, and is once again on her own.

But, though Fanny must needs pay for her mistake, fate still keeps its protecting hand over the repentant sinner: it allows her to find a bordello which, in complete contrast to the first one she had landed in, is run by the gentlest and most tactful of madams as a small home industry for the little coterie of English swells who are its steady clients; a kind of model bawdy house, where good sex is served in an atmosphere of utter *Gemütlichkeit* and decency.

It is in this warm, home-like atmosphere of genteel vice that Fanny is to have her most exciting erotic adventures which, by the same token, also furnish the material for the "hottest" parts of the book. In this manner, all goes well for a while, until the nice, elderly madam loses, for one reason or another, the rest of her small stable, leaving her in the end with nobody except Fanny. The good lady, feeling the weight of her years and the twinge of the gout, decides to close down the establishment.

Fanny is now once more on her own, but this time with sufficient means to set herself up nicely in a small house to await in patience the next lucky turn of fortune. In this expectancy she is not long to be disappointed. Walking in the fields one day, she comes upon an ageing gentleman who is just having some sort of fit. Naturally, she rushes to his aid, and the old gentleman, in recognition of her heart of gold first puts her in his keeping, then obligingly dies, leaving her a large property.

Fanny, now a lady of means (though "not yet nineteen") and entirely her own mistress, begins inquiries about her first and only true lover Charles. She learns by rumors that things have not gone well at all in his business overseas and that he may be actually on his way home to England. (She later finds that he had written her several letters "which had all miscarried").

Now Fanny's hopes are high of being reunited with him, and her fondest hopes are to be realized even sooner than anyone might have expected: traveling to her birthplace, which, now that she has made good, she has the pious wish of re-visiting, she puts up for the night at an inn. In the midst of a storm, two travelers appear late in the evening, one of whom turns out to be Charles, who has just been shipwrecked off the coast of Ireland and has thus lost the last of his possessions.

It doesn't matter—Fanny has plenty for both of them —but she isn't going to tell him that, at least not until she has swooned a couple of times in his loving arms, treated him to a sumptuous supper by candle-light, and indulged in a last description of love-making—this time with the man who is to become her legal husband and lord from henceforth. Thus ends the story. The only possible moral to be drawn from it is expressed by the virtuous Fanny: "The paths of vice are sometimes strewed with roses, but then they are for ever infamous for many a thorn, for many a cankerwort: those of virtue are strewed with roses purely, and those eternally unfading ones."

So far so good, and if that were all there was to the story, one wonders why the censors should have raised such a hue and cry about it. And surely, neither the censors, nor, for that matter, anyone else, would have cared much for Cleland's story of morals, had it not been that he included in it a number of detailed descriptions of sexual activities involving the heroine and her erstwhile companions in sin. In fact, so realistic are Cleland's sexual passages that, in some quarters, they have been mistaken for "pornography."

As the reader is aware, we have made the distinction between hard core pornography as pure *fantasy* material, designed primarily for *erotic stimulation,* and erotic realism, as exemplified by such books as D. H. Lawrence's *Lady Chatterley's Lover* or the writings of Henry Miller, in which other considerations predominate over the sexual contents.

In addition, we have pointed out that hard core pornography does not usually have much of a story line, and in so far as it does, this only serves as a flimsy frame on which to hang a series of erotic incidents. Hard core pornography also either neglects altogether or underplays characterization of the persons in the story, description of surroundings, philosophical or political discussion, and so forth. This is done to provide for *maximum erotic concentration* in the story. Furthermore, and most notably, hard core pornography is characterized by a calculated, *progressive build-up of erotic tension.* This is, as we have seen, achieved by a number of literary devices or tricks of the trade, based on the principle of appealing to that which is considered sexually *taboo.* Ranking high among these devices is the liberal use of *four-letter words,* which, through suppression, have become erotically supercharged. The same holds for descriptions of *physiological detail,* frankly *sadistic defloration* scenes, and for inclusion of sexually *taboo personages* in the story, such as parent figures, children, priests, nuns, clergymen, etc., or *taboo places*. Following the same principle, appeal is made to the *instinctual* or animal side of sex by the inclusion of persons thought to be *racially or socially inferior* and acting in an animalistic manner, or by the inclusion of *animals* themselves in conjunction with humans.

If we now apply this test to *Fanny Hill,* we find that the book, while conforming to parts of our definition of pornography, does not conform to others. It was obviously written (and its author as much as said so himself) as an erotic book, meant to be sexually stimulating. On the other hand, it does not bear many of the characteristic marks of hard core pornography: it does not make an appeal through four-letter words; does not include racially or socially inferior persons, acting in animalistic ways (with the exception of one brief scene with the simpleton, a passage which, if taken by itself, comes closest to hard core pornography); it does not include the desecretion of sacred or taboo places or personages (in fact, it painfully avoids just that, as we shall see with regard to its one and only sadistic passage); it does not include descriptions of rape or violent defloration; it does not include physiological fantasy; it is not pornographically structured; and it devotes much less attention than is customary in hard core pornography to descriptions of physiological detail. Besides, where such physiological detail is given, it is, as we shall see, done in a tactful and aesthetically unobjectionable manner, shying away from the unrealistic and usually extremely coarse *exaggerations* so typical of the common run of pornography.

But *Fanny Hill* distinguishes itself even more by what it *does* include of subject matter that is usually absent or only superficially and perfunctorily touched on by hard core pornography: first of all, the *story* is far from incidental, nor is its almost grotesquely underscored *moralistic philosophy* which characterizes the book from beginning to end. Secondly, there is the romantic emphasis on *love*—conspicuous by its absence in hard core pornography (though, admittedly, absent too in some of the newer, "tougher" books of erotic realism). And, finally, Cleland includes much decidedly anti-erotic, though completely realistic detail, such as the heroine's grief and sickness at the time of her separation from her lover; her miscarriage; and later on the description of unattractive physical detail, from pendant breasts in women to impotence in the male.

What is even more in contrast to hard core pornography is the format or the internal structure of the plot of *Fanny Hill*: far from presenting us with a progression of increasingly erotic passages, culminating in more and more unusual sexual activities (generally including the participation of children, animals, etc., in the context of debauchery and mass orgies), the erotic "heat" in *Fanny Hill* begins at a pretty high glow, reaches its peak by the time we are barely half way through the book, then declines steadily towards the end, to die down to a last flicker when Fanny is reunited with her Charles. No real pornographer worth his mettle would be caught making such a fatal mistake.

Why, then, has *Fanny Hill* in the two hundred years of her printed career been so frequently mistaken by the courts for hard core pornography? The unequivocal answer is that offense has been taken to its erotically realistic passages, in a failure to realize that it is precisely this *realism* which in the first and last instance distinguishes this strange book from the fantastic distortions of reality characteristic of hard core pornography.

To demonstrate and prove this point beyond any possible doubt, let us examine some of the typical erotic passages in *Fanny Hill* that have given rise to the allegation of its pornographic nature. In so doing, we shall compare these passages with similar ones in *My Secret Life,* the most authentic erotic autobiography in existence, from the same English cultural milieu and from a period (though a full century later) still accurately reflecting the sexual *mores, attitudes,* and *institutions* prevalent at the time of *Fanny Hill.* Examining these instances chronologically, in the sequence in which they appear in *Fanny Hill,* let us begin with the scene in which Fanny is being introduced to Lesbian contact by a girl named Phoebe, one of the girls in the first bawdy house to which Fanny was lured and who was assigned to share room and bed with her. The passage in question reads as follows in *Fanny Hill*:

No sooner than was this precious substitute of my mistress's laid down, but she . . . turned to me, embraced and kiss'd me with great eagerness. This was new, this was odd; but imputing it to nothing but pure kindness, which, for aught I knew, it might be the London way to express in that manner, I was determin'd not to be behind-hand with her, and returned her the kiss and embrace, with all the fervour that perfect innocence knew.

Encouraged by this, her hands became extremely free, and wander'd over my whole body, with touches, squeezes, pressures, that rather warm'd and surpriz'd me with their novelty, than they either shock'd or alarm'd me.

For my part, I was transported, confused, and out of myself; feelings so new were too much for me. My heated and alarm'd senses were in a tumult that robbed me of all liberty of thought; tears of pleasure gush'd from my eyes, and somewhat assuaged the fire that rag'd all over me. . . . Even my glowing blushes expressed more desire than modesty, whilst the candle, left (to be sure not undesignedly) burning, threw a full light on my whole body.

"No!" says Phoebe, "You must not, my sweet girl, think to hide all these treasures from me. My sight must be feasted as well as my touch . . . I must devour with my eyes this springing BOSOM . . . Suffer me to kiss it . . . I have not seen it enough . . . let me kiss it once more . . . What firm, smooth, white flesh is here! . . . How delicately

shaped! . . . Then this delicious down! Oh! let me
view the small, dear, tender cleft! . . . This is too
much, I cannot bear it! . . . I must . . . I must . . ."
Here she took my hand, and in a transport carried
it where you will easily guess. But what a difference in the state of the same thing! . . . A spreading
thicket of bushy curls marked the full-grown, complete woman. Then the cavity to which she guided
my hand easily received it; and as soon as she felt
it within her, she moved herself to and fro, with
so rapid a friction that I presently withdrew it, wet
and clammy, when instantly Phoebe grew more
composed, after two or three sighs, and heart-
fetched Oh's! and giving me a kiss that seemed
to exhale her soul through her lips, she replaced
the bed clothes over us."

As we have seen, there is a total absence of any kind
of physical exaggeration in this passage which, if it occurred in hard core pornography would have laid much
greater emphasis on the physiological sex response, and,
typically, would have made a great deal more of the
female discharge which is here barely mentioned with
the one matter-of-fact (and, one may add, almost anti-
erotic) statement that it felt "wet and clammy."

We shall compare this passage now with one in Volume VIII of *My Secret Life*. There, we are told of the
relationship between a prostitute by the name of Sarah,
one of the English Casanova's long-time mistresses, and
a younger girl by the name of Liz, with whom Sarah
was having a Lesbian relationship in which Walter often
and enthusiastically played the third partner:

Sarah who, I am sure, had then lost her man,
and was more and more impecunious, used to come
home early, often ill tempered and low spirited.
Unasked she then would get into bed with us. She
was kind in an extraordinary degree to Lizzie,
would kiss her while lying on the side of her, and
put her fingers on the little one's quim.

Previously, I had somehow formed the opinion

that Sarah liked feeling up young girls, but thought nothing much about it. One day, she was slightly screwed (drunk) and got into bed, and catching Liz, lifted her on her belly, began to kiss her passionately, twisted her limbs over her, and wriggling her belly up to her so that their quims were close together, imitated the motions of man with woman.

I thought of this a good deal, and it increased my desire for knowledge. This form of sexual voluptuousness amongst women now haunted me. I questioned Liz about Sarah's behaviour in bed with her, for she always now slept with her, and no man was ever there, and threatened Liz not to see her any more, if she did not tell me the truth. She disclosed that Sarah liked to pull her on top of her, and pressing clitoris to clitoris, rubbed them together, till Sarah at least had the full enjoyment of that voluptuous friction: It was tribadism, the amusement of girls at boarding schools and perhaps harems (*and often, as I know since, of some harlots*).

We see then, that already in this first instance, the parallels between *Fanny Hill* and *My Secret Life* are rather striking. In fact, the Lesbian activities described are almost identical in the two cases, except, of course, for the presence of the man in the Lesbian situation which is absent in *Fanny Hill*. (One could, however, cite numerous passages from Lesbian literature, written by women—autobiographical, as well as fiction—which would substantiate even further the essential realism and credibility of the relevant passage in *Fanny Hill*.)

Another passage from *Fanny Hill*, which has frequently been disputed as to its credibility, concerns the famous "peeping" scene in which Fanny watches from a closet while a couple in the adjoining room have intercourse, a sight which proves so exciting to her that she has to relieve herself through masturbation:

One day about twelve at noon, being thoroughly recover'd of my fever, I happen'd to be in Mrs.

Brown's dark closet, where I had not been half
an hour, resting upon the maid's settle-bed, before I
heard a rustling in the bed-chamber, separated
from the closet by only two sash-doors, before the
glasses of which were drawn two yellow damask
curtains, but not so closely as to exclude the full
view of the room from any person in the closet.

I instantly crept softly, and posted myself so,
that seeing every thing minutely, I could not myself
be seen. . . .

Fanny then sees the well-matured madam of the first
house in company with a much younger man, a "Horse-
grenadier, moulded in the *Hercules* style."

The preliminaries for intercourse are described, and
here we find two particularly anti-erotic passages, referring to the lagging charms of "Mrs. Brown." Says
Fanny:

. . . he gave her some hearty smacks, and thrusting
his hands into her breasts, disengag'd them from
her stays, in scorn of whose confinement they broke
loose, and swagged down, navel-low at least. A
more enormous pair did my eyes never behold,
nor of a worse colour; flagging-soft, and most lovingly contiguous:—yet such as they were, this
neck-beef eater . . . after toying with them thus
some time, as if they had been worth it, he laid
her down pretty briskly. . . .

As he stood on one side, for a minute or so,
unbuttoning his waist coat and breeches, her fat,
brawny thighs hung down, and the whole greasy
landscape lay fairly open to my view; a wide open-
mouth'd gap, overshaded with a grizzly bush,
seemed held out like a beggar's wallet for its pro-
vision.

As we see, these passages are, by their revolting,
mercilessly realistic emphasis on anti-erotic detail, entirely comparable to similar descriptions in Henry Miller
and constitute, as we have likewise pointed out, a fea-

ture which is understandably rare in genuine hard core
pornography.

The passage goes on in a more pleasing way and, in
the end, the watching Fanny is stimulated to auto-erotic
gratification:

Long, however, the young spark did not remain
before . . . he threw himself upon her, and his back
being now towards me, I could only take his being
ingulph'd for granted, by the directions he mov'd
in, and the impossibility of missing so staring a
mark; and now the bed shook, the curtains rattled
so, that I could scarce hear the sighs and murmurs,
the heaves and pantings, that accompanied the action, from the beginning to the end; the sound and
sight of which thrill'd to the very soul of me, and
made every vein of my body circulate liquid fires:
the emotion grew so violent that it almost inter-
cepted my respiration.

Prepared then, and disposed as I was by the discourse of my companions, and Phoebe's minute detail of everything, no wonder that such a sight gave
the last dying blow to my native innocence.

Whilst they were in the heat of the action, guided
by nature only, I stold my hand up my petticoats,
and with fingers all on fire, seized, and yet more
inflamed that center of all my senses: my heart
palpitated, as if it would force its way through my
bosom; I breath'd with pain; I twisted my thighs,
squeezed, and compressed the lips of that virgin
slit, and following mechanically the example of
Phoebe's manual operation on it, as far as I could
find admission, brought on at last the critical
extasy, the melting flow, into which nature, spent
with excess of pleasure, dissolves and dies away.

It has been argued that the above quoted passage
is supposedly unrealistic in that women are generally
not thought to respond so strongly to the witnessing of
sexual scenes of this kind. However, as we have pointed
out elsewhere (see Kronhausen, *The Sexually Re-*

sponsive Woman, Grove Press, New York, 1964),
many women indeed do show a definite, positive sex
response to such visual or acoustic stimuli, similar to
that of the average male, and often demanding immediate sexual release.

In *My Secret Life* we find several such instances of
women becoming highly stimulated by observing the
sexual activities of others. We shall confine ourselves,
however, to a single comparison from Volume VII, in
which the author speaks of his voyeuristic seances in a
small London brothel, such as described in *Fanny Hill,*
at which occasions he was accompanied by the same
Sarah whom we have already encountered in connection
with the Lesbian passage:

> During all this time (when I was at the peep-
> hole), I kept telling Sarah in a whisper what I saw.
> She got as impatient as I and wanted to see as
> much. It often was, 'Let me have a look.' 'I shan't.'
> 'What is she doing?' 'She is doing so and so.' Then I
> would let her peep, and she would tell *me.* I sat on
> the sofa whilst she was standing and looking,
> grasped her behind, and pulled her towards me,
> giving utterance to all sorts of bawdy extravagances
> in whispers. 'It's exciting,' said she; 'I have not
> seen such a thing since the night you had the fine,
> tall, fair woman—and it makes me randy as be
> damned,' (her favorite expression).
>
> It is odd, it occurs to me, that all she wanted to
> see was what the woman was doing; what I principally wanted to see was what the man was doing.
> At all times that I was at the peep-hole, the same
> feelings were predominant in both of us. But the
> most amusing thing to me was that Sarah wanted
> to see so much.

In her exclusive interest in watching the women and
not the men, we have a clear indication of Sarah's latent
(and perhaps, not even so latent) Lesbian interests
which, as we have seen, come out so unmistakably later
on. (In our English Casanova, however, his curiosity

about the sexual activities of other men does not have quite the same homosexual connotation, but indicates his attempts to abreact a genital trauma and inferiority feelings about his own sex organs.)

We shall leave the matter with one final observation: It appears from the erotic art of the time that in the 18th and 19th century voyeurism of *both* sexes was probably more widespread than it is today. In the light of these factors, the closet-scene in *Fanny Hill* must therefore be considered completely in accordance with historical evidence. In fact, in the context of contemporary 18th and 19th century sex mores in this respect the episode strikes one as rather mild.

Skipping the rest of Fanny's experiences at the first house of prostitution (which include another voyeuristic scene and the story of how Fanny *almost* lost her maidenhead to an old letcher to whom the wicked Mrs. Brown had been trying to sell it), we arrive at the time when she has found her Charles and is now in his personal keeping.

It is at this point that we encounter a curious passage, referring to the classic 'Pygmalion' theme which was later to be so masterfully elaborated by George Bernard Shaw.

In our cessations from active pleasure [Fanny writes], Charles fram'd himself one, in *instructing me,* as far as his own lights reach'd, in a great many points of life that I was, in consequence of my no-education, perfectly ignorant of: nor did I suffer one word to fall in vain from the mouth of my lovely teacher: I hung on every syllable he utter'd, and receiv'd as oracles, all he said. . . .

We shall pass over Fanny's coming into the keeping of "Mr. H." who betrayed her with her maid and who was then, as we have indicated, himself cuckolded by her in turn with his young valet (the description of the latter episode being erotically quite strong and particularly well written).

Thus we come to the point where Fanny joins the other three girls of sweet "Mrs. Cole's" establishment.

> Here, at the first sight of things, I found everything breath'd an air of decency, modesty and order.
> In the outer parlour, or rather shop, sat three young women, very demurely employ'd on millinery work, which was the cover of a traffic in more precious commodities . . .

Here again, we find an interesting verification in *My Secret Life* (Vol. 1), where the English Casanova tells us of one of his youthful adventures in company with his cousin Fred. In this instance, the impoverished girls, working on lace, doubled as prostitutes, and not, as in Fanny's case, the prostitutes doubling as milliners:

> One day we rode to the market-town, and putting up our horses, strolled about. Fred said, "Let's both go and have a poke." "Where are the girls?" said I. "Oh! I know, lend me some money." "I only have ten shillings." "That is more than we shall want."
> We went down a lane past the Town-Hall, by white-washed little cottages, at which girls were sitting or standing at the doors, making a sort of lace. "Do you see a girl you like?" Fred asked. "Why, they are lace makers." "Yes," he replied, "but some of them let you have them for all that; look, there's the one I had with the last half-crown you lent me."
> Two girls were standing together; they nodded. "Let's try them," said Fred. We went into the cottage; it was a new experience to me. He took one girl, leaving me the other. I felt so nervous, never having been with a gay woman before.

We see, then, that it was entirely realistic, in *Fanny Hill,* for Cleland to choose a millinery shop for the front of his small bordello. In fact, he obviously had only to take the description of this milieu directly from life, as there must have been at that time scores of such houses with one business front or another. In another part of

My Secret Life (Vol. II) Walter tells of a tobacco and cigar shop serving exactly this dual purpose:

> One night three of us [Walter, his cousin Fred, and another man] went to a cigar shop, kept by two women. It was not an unusual thing for two women to have a cigar shop with a big sofa in the back parlour, one keeping shop, whilst the other attended to more delicate business in the back.
>
> On talking to them, we came to terms with the girls, without really intending it. Fred began joking with them, and it ended with us going into the back parlour and having some wine with them. One asked my cousin, if he did not want to lie down and rest himself. He said, "Yes," but that he wanted warmth to his belly when he rested. "You may have my belly to warm you," said she. "What here?" "Oh, they can wait," said the girl, "and your quiet friend can find his tongue with my sister [the other girl]. . . .
>
> Whilst the strumming was going on in the parlour, people bought cigars and tobacco—for it was really sold there. Little did they guess the fun going on behind that red curtain of the shop parlour. . . .

Focusing on those passages which best demonstrate the historical and psychological realism of Cleland's famous novel, we come to the amusing story of Fanny's second virginity, or how she managed—with the help of old, experienced Mrs. Cole—to humbug an ageing and jaded rake-hell who offered a high price for her maidenhead which, of course, she had willingly surrendered to dear Charles several years before.

> As soon as he was in bed, he threw off the bedclothes, which I suffered him to force from my hold, and I now lay as expos'd as he could wish, not only to his attacks, but his visitation of the sheets; where in the various agitations of the body, through my endeavours to defend myself, he could easily assure himself there was no preparation; though,

to do him justice, he seem't a less strict examinant
than I had apprehended from so experienc'd a prac-
titioner.

After much struggling with Fanny and a premature
ejaculation, the man is finally willing to give up the
battle at least for the time being, and get some sleep, a
lucky circumstance which Fanny uses to complete the
deception of the gullible male:

Tired, however, at length, with such athletic
drudgery, my champion began now to give out, and
to gladly embrace the refreshment of some rest.
Kissing me then with much affection, and recom-
mending me to my repose, he presently fell fast
asleep: which, as soon as I had well satisfy'd myself of, I with much composure of body, so as not
to wake him by any motion, with much ease and
safety too, played of Mrs. Cole's device for perfect-
ing the signs of my virginity.

In each of the head *bed-posts,* just above where
the bedsteads are inserted into them, there was *a
small drawer,* so artfully adapted to the mouldings
of the timber-work, that it might have escap'd even
the most curious search: which drawers were easily
open'd or shut by the touch of a spring, and were
fitted each with a shallow glass tumbler, full of a
prepared fluid blood, in which lay soak'd, for ready
use, a sponge that required no more than gently
reaching the hand to it, taking it out and properly
squeezing between the thighs, when it yielded a
great deal more of the red liquid than would save
a girl's honour; after which, replacing it, and touching the spring, all possibility of discovery, or even
of suspicion, was taken away; and all this was not
the work of the fourth part of a minute, and on
which ever side one lay, the thing was equally easy
and practicable, by the double care taken to have
each bed-post provided alike. True it is, that had
he waked and caught me in the act, it would at least
have covered me with shame and confusion; but

then, that he did not, was, with the precautions I
took, a risk of a thousand to one in my favour.

Comparing these passages with the relevant references to virginity and its surreptitious restoration in the
pages of *My Secret Life,* we find that Cleland's description is once again entirely in keeping with the customs
and practices surrounding virginity at that time. More
than once, the English Casanova fumed and fretted in
fear of being humbugged in a manner similar to Fanny's
client, but unlike him, he always made absolutely sure
that there was little chance of any girl getting away with
such deception. He does, however, describe an instance
in which one of his many mistresses managed to hood-
wink her husband on her wedding night:

> We laughed about her marriage night. She'd
> consulted Lydia, and named a day when her poorli-
> ness could be just over, thinking his poking would
> bring it on again. She'd noticed that at that period,
> if she masturbated herself, it returned slightly. And
> so it did indeed on her marriage night. She de-
> scribed to me with delight how she writhed, jerked
> her bum back, and cried out, "Oh, you are hurting
> me so!" as he got into her. We laughed heartily at
> it. Poor man, had he but known!

Of course, such situations would be much rarer in
most western countries today. With the greater emanci-
pation of women, virginity, fortunately, is not the highly
overprized commodity that it used to be in the days
when the woman was more or less considered the man's
chattel and part of his movable property.

Next in sequence in our reality analysis of Cleland's
erotic novel is the flagellation scene in which Fanny first
whips a young gentleman, who experiences orgasm in
that manner, after which she is treated by him in the
same way, but without, at first, experiencing anything
but pain. Later, however, she explains, the weals on
her backside began to tingle with a sensuous heat that
demanded immediate satisfaction through intercourse,

which her youthful client could, nevertheless, not provide for her, until re-aroused by further birching. She comments, however, when it is all over, that she would never permit a repetition of this kind of service, never at any time would she "renew with him, or resort again to the violent expedient of lashing." And she adds some further acid remarks about this form of sexual stimulation.

As for ourselves, we agree with the English critic Marghanita Laski who testified in London in favor of the book. On the whole, she declared, it had "cheered her up" and sexually excited her—which she took as an entirely wholesome and enjoyable effect of the book— but she thought Cleland could have well done without the flagellation scene.

On the other hand, we must point out that the scene is entirely realistic and paralleled by a lengthy flagellation sequence in *My Secret Life* which Walter witnessed (though, like Fanny, he had no taste for sado-masochism), and which we shall here only mention in passing. We also wish to point out that Cleland explained in the letter to the Court, mentioned earlier, that the scene was taken entirely from true life experience of which he had reliable knowledge (though, apparently not of his own direct experience). Moreover, in that letter, Cleland calls the Court's attention to the fact that the story had in reality concerned a "Divine of The Church of England," for whom, out of "tenderness" of feeling, he had substituted a "Lay-character," so as to avoid the appearance of "profaneness."

Be that as it may, the details of the flagellation passage in *Fanny Hill* ring, alas, true enough, and it is an undeniable fact that this particular, and, from our point of view, regrettable deviation was highly popular in England. It was, no doubt, encouraged by the common punishment of children by whipping, birching, and similar methods of discipline. Fortunately, corporal punishment is now less common. However some members of Parliament, prison administrators, and churchmen even to this day advocate whipping for adult offenders, a phenomenon which goes to show how deeply engrained these attitudes are in the English culture. It is therefore not surprising that at the time of the English Casanova, more than one generation after *Fanny Hill,* flagellation was still very common, as he found out from inquiries among his prostitute acquaintances, some of whom produced a positive arsenal of flagellantistic instruments for his inspection to convince him that they had customers who, indeed, demanded this sort of treatment.

The flagellation sequence in *Fanny Hill,* is followed, as those who are acquainted with the book will recall, by the mention of another gentleman, "whose peculiar humour was a delight in combing fine tresses of hair," a fetishistic deviation which—at the time of long tresses —was fairly common, but which, with the change in women's hair styles has today almost become extinct.

"Another peculiar taste" of this gentleman, consisted in presenting Fanny with "a dozen pairs of the whitest kid gloves at a time," which played a role in his sex activities. Here again, we find a parallel reference in *My Secret Life,* in which a French prostitute, operating in London at Walter's time, kept a number of these gloves in her room and initiated him into their various sexual uses.

In closing we would like to say of these passages in *Fanny Hill* that if they have to occur at all in erotic literature, the way in which they are here presented is the least obnoxious and might even serve some useful purpose. For in *Fanny Hill,* in distinction to what is so often the case in hard core pornography, these deviations or perversions are never glorified, glamorized, or recommended as superior forms of sexual pleasure. On the contrary, Cleland depicts their devotees as poor, misguided, pitiable individuals, whose twisted sexual tastes hold little to recommend them to those who find ample gratification in simpler and more direct sexual outlets.

Moreover, one may well argue that the inclusion of such episodes in an erotic novel of this kind, depicting, as it does, the life of a "woman of pleasure," even adds to the truthfulness and reality of the story: for, after all, these and many other forms of sexual deviation do exist, and there are few professional prostitutes indeed who have not at one time or other come into contact with some of them. It is, we think, even permissible to think that if *children* are to read erotic fiction, it is better that they be made familiar with the existence of these sexual aberrations in a dispassionate and rather factual manner, as it is done in *Fanny Hill* (where the presentation is almost clinically objective in this respect), than to remain ignorant of these matters altogether and possibly later be traumatized by sudden, and totally unexpected contact with them.

With these considerations, we have arrived at the end of our analysis of the strange case of *Fanny Hill*. But we are still faced with the problem of how to classify this useful little book: for there is no doubt that the overall effect of *Fanny Hill* is to act as a psychological aphrodisiac. And yet, we most emphatically wish to repeat that we do not consider Cleland's erotic novel an example of hard core pornography.

The reason for this seeming paradox lies in the fact that the aphrodisiacal effect of a book or piece of art, even if its erotic effect constitutes its predominant appeal, is in itself not sufficient evidence for considering it as hard core pornography. To qualify as such, it must deviate far from the reality of sexual matters as they are, and furthermore, incorporate (in the case of literature) a number of specific methods of appeal based on a certain way of distorting erotic reality. It is by these specific reality distortions that we distinguish the sexual or erotic from the "prurient" (in the sense that the appeal is not to the normal, healthy sex drive of the average individual, but to certain morbid, unhealthy, and anti-social forms of sexuality). But even these reality distortions must be for their own ("dirt for dirt's") sake —not, as in the case of de Sade, to express a certain philosophical point of view, and not, as with Jean Genet and others, to create an over-riding artistic impression which may, or may not, be erotic in nature.

We shall return to these problems later on in our discussion of the psychological effects of erotic literature. Here, we merely want to point out that books like *Fanny Hill* clearly show the need for the creation of another category of erotic art and literature. This type of artistic expression, while appealing primarily to sexual interests and desires, either does not deviate significantly from the realities of sexual relations as they are (and is therefore to be considered as still within the main stream of erotic realism) or, where consisting of a mixture of reality and fantasy material, (or even entirely of erotic fantasies which may appeal to "normal" or deviant sexual interests) does not achieve this effect by the techniques which we have described as typical for the common run of hard core pornography.

This category of erotic literature shows within itself a wide range of subject matter and various degrees of deviation from or adherence to reality or fantasy, as well as every shade and degree of adherence to or deviation from "normalcy" in the nature of its erotic content. However, it can, for matters of taste, quality, content, and underlying attitudes, in no wise be equated with what is commonly understood by the term hard core pornography. It is this group of erotic art and literature which we shall, for want of a better term, simply call *"quality erotica."*

Of this fascinating type of erotic literature, John Cleland's *Fanny Hill* is the outstanding example in the English language. There has, until recently, been little to put at its side in Western civilization, except for a number of quality erotica in the French language, beginning with the 17th and 18th centuries, and continuing—in spite of much official suppression—up to the present.

Far from wanting to suppress *Fanny Hill*, we regard Cleland's celebrated book as a laudable exception to the generally vulgar run of hard core pornography in the English language. We have no doubt that future generations, less panicked and confused by sexual matters than we, will have only an indulgent smile for all the noise and furor that a book of lusty sexual adventure was still able to create at a time when man's creative genius and ambition in science and technology was already reaching to the stars, and the innermost secrets of life were beginning to be laid bare before the eyes of his enquiring, restless mind.

Meanwhile, we hope that the legal publication of *Fanny Hill* will encourage contemporary writers of fiction to produce a new type of healthy and cheerful erotica that will make old-fashioned hard core pornography as obsolete as the artificial taboos and fears that created it.

THE PSYCHOLOGICAL EFFECTS OF EROTIC LITERATURE

We come now to that little understood and hazy area of "effects" on which most people nevertheless base their opinions in regard to the reading of erotic literature, and from which stem their feelings either for or against censorship. Due to the fact that there has been such total confusion between erotic realism and "hard core obscenity," most people, perforce, have confused the effects of reading the former with the effects of reading the latter. We shall discuss the differences here in some detail, and moreover with particular regard to young people for, realistically speaking, this is the area of effects which is of genuine concern to most individuals, average or otherwise, even though the law, of necessity, confines itself to effects on the "average" person.

In preceding chapters we have already referred to the psychological effects of reading erotic realism at some length, and we have demonstrated that, from many points of view, these effects are highly desirable for the average person. We believe the reading of erotic realism is, if anything, even more desirable for young people, and we shall discuss this at greater length later in this chapter.

For the moment however, let us examine, insofar as it is possible, the effects of reading "hard core obscenity," and if we can do nothing else, at least dispel the many wrong assumptions that exist in this area.

First we would point out that for academic psychologists to speak dogmatically about the psychological effects of reading "obscene" books would, in the present state of our knowledge, be as unbecoming as venturing guesses about the nature of the Oedipus complex in outer space. The truth of the matter is that there are not sufficient conclusive research data available to answer the question directly and with the same assurance as one could, for example, state that unhealthy family life is one of the contributing causes of juvenile delinquency.

It is amazing, nevertheless, how many people have felt called upon to voice the most authoritative opinions about the effects of "obscene" writings, including law-enforcement officers, educators, clergymen, housewives, women's clubs, men's fraternal organizations—in short, all those who are least qualified to give an authoritative opinion on a subject of such confusing dimensions and such width of scope, but who, because of their own deep emotional involvement, have felt no hesitation in expounding "ex cathedra" and with omniscient finality on the matter. Among them there have even been a few members of the behavioral sciences, though we can say to the credit of professional groups such as psychologists, psychiatrists and sociologists, who would be best qualified to give such opinions, that very few have ventured to do so. Nevertheless, we must here concern ourselves with this aspect of "effects," since it alone is the main motivational basis for the consideration of any censorship at all. But it behooves us to walk cautiously, and speak softly, though not without personal conviction, about the possible emotional and behavioral consequences of "obscene" books.

To us, the most hopeful approach to the problem of effects is to start out with the almost tautological assertion that "obscene" books are designed to be *psychological aphrodisiacs*. On this assumption rests the validity of our twelve major criteria of "obscene" books (counting "structure" as one of these), and without agreement on this point, further discussion of the problem would seem meaningless.

It is, however, perfectly permissible from a research point of view to begin with an elemental hypothesis of this order. If others disagree with our hypothesis, they are free to set up another hypothesis of their own preference and to develop criteria of "obscenity" in accordance with it.

Once we have passed this initial hurdle, things become a little clearer. The problem now changes into the question as to whether or not "obscene" books accomplish their main purpose of erotic stimulation; for whom, and with what behavioral consequences?

It seems to us undeniable that the vast majority of "obscene" books fulfill their first and primary function of stimulating most readers erotically. This, at least, has been the subjective experience of the authors during their survey of literally hundreds of "obscene" books in several major languages. Fortunately, or unfortunately, depending on one's point of view, the aphrodisiacal effect of "obscene" books seems to follow the law of diminishing returns after a certain saturation point is reached. However, even at the end of this study, which necessitated the authors' overexposure to "obscenity" in large quantities, neither the male, nor the distaff member of the research team could report on having achieved 100 percent immunity to this type of literature.

As to the small sample of people whom the authors interviewed with regard to the effect of "obscene" reading matter, testimony was almost unanimous that they had been sexually stimulated by their reading. A very small number of individuals, however, both males and females, showed very little reaction to the "obscene" books which they read. These people felt "bored" by the material, finding it almost completely uninteresting, and a few individuals were revolted and antagonized by it.

Our sample was, at this stage, far too small to be statistically useful. The only thing one could conclude from it was that, as one might have expected, most of the people interviewed by us did respond positively to the massive and consistent erotic stimulation of "obscene" books.

In this consistency and progressive intensity with which "obscene" books stimulate erotic imagery in the reader lies one of the essential differences between the psychological effects of erotic realism and "obscenity." An erotically realistic passage in, say, Frank Harris' autobiography, or the *Memoirs of Hecate County,* or *Lady Chatterley's Lover,* may momentarily have an erotically stimulating effect. However, this effect is not long sustained, nor adequately reinforced by a progression of more and more sexually provoking scenes, as is the case in genuinely "obscene" books.

The reason for this difference must lie in the fact that erotic realism attempts to portray life as it is, or as it appears to the author, whereas "obscene" books are products of sheer fantasy. Life seldom presents us with a succession of erotic experiences, one more stimulating and exciting than the other. Erotic realism is therefore not "competitive" with "obscene" books, which are not bound by the realities of existence, but can make possible the impossible by indulging the reader's fantasy from cover to cover with the most provocative erotic imagery whose only limitation is the resourcefulness of the author's imagination.

Another "advantage" of "obscene" books as against erotic realism is that realism sometimes includes highly anti-erotic subject matter. The erotic mood may be quickly dispelled by anxieties over possible pregnancy, venereal disease, illness in general, death, economic distress, and similar concerns, evoked by the reading.

All of this is strictly avoided in "obscene" books. In only one of our ten "obscene" specimen books do we find a reference to venereal disease (no. 2, *Fay and Her Boy Friend*), and then it is presented in the form of a joke.

In the same book, the woman voices, in passing, her fear of getting pregnant, but the remark is merely parenthetical and without serious consideration. In the specimen book *Nelly* (no. 4), pregnancy is a dominant feature, but, as previously pointed out, it is not taken seriously, in spite of the fact that it is here not just a fear, but a reality.

None of the other "obscene" specimen books concern themselves in the least with such mundane and disconcerting issues of life. Nowhere do we find among them references to contraceptives, prophylactic devices, pregnancy, abortion, venereal disease, and so forth. "Obscene" books resemble in this respect *fairy tales* in which everything turns out according to one's fondest fancy and every erotic wish can be lived out without punishment or any unpleasant effects whatsoever.

As already indicated, we feel that *"hardcore obscenity" does stimulate, in the vast majority of people, what the law calls "lascivious thoughts" and "lustful desires."* It is meant to do so, and if erotic stimulation is not the *only* aim of "obscene" books, it certainly is the *main* object of it.

We also affirm that works of erotic realism, such as *Lady Chatterley's Lover,* may have similar psychological effects as to those passages which are descriptive of sexual activities, or even with regard to realistic portrayals of physical beauty. But in that respect, erotic realism is no different from any other psychological stimulus of an erotic nature, e.g., perfume, certain types of music, sexually provoking advertising, fashions in dress, the use of cosmetics to enhance attractiveness, or any other of the many psychological aphrodisiacs with which our culture is so familiar, and on which it is dependent. The main difference between all these stimuli and "hardcore obscenity" lies in the fact that "obscene" books sustain and build up erotic tension over a longer period of time and do so more effectively than any of the other sources of erotic stimulation mentioned.

Nevertheless, while it is perfectly true that the aim and the effect of an "obscene" book is to act as an erotic stimulus, the ultimate test of whether something is "obscene" or not cannot be conclusively deduced from its effects; it can only be determined on the basis of a content analysis of the book itself.

The major difficulty of the subjective test for obscenity lies in the fact that, as already pointed out, erotically realistic literature (or art) may also cause a momentary psychological and physiological sex response; herein lies much of the problem of censorship, for even this perfectly normal and healthy response is abhorrent to some segments of our society, who consciously, or unconsciously, then confuse erotic realism with obscenity, and condemn both.

It seems to us that the basic argument for censorship ultimately rests on the personal prejudice of those in favor of it because, *in their view,* the activities to which the reading of "obscene" books (in the confused sense) may lead are inherently and potentially dangerous to the individual and society. We will, therefore, have to carefully analyze the problem with regard to the social desirability or undesirability of the possible behavioral effects of "obscene" books, as against the possible behavioral effects of erotic realism.

The fear on the part of those who most strongly condemn "obscene" literature and discourage its reading, professedly is that it leads to delinquency and criminal acts, especially those involving violence, for instance, rape, sexual assault, the molestation and abuse of children by adult sex deviates, and a variety of similar offenses.

Everyday, the newspapers carry some release from pro-censorship quarters, blithely linking "obscene" literature with the perpetration of the most ghastly crimes, making everything erotically provocative responsible for every social evil from juvenile delinquency and the disintegration of the American family, to the increasing rate of mental breakdown, and communism. These wild assertions are usually couched in the highly emotional phraseology of "scandal sheets," which is beyond reasonable argument, and which, again, make no distinction whatever as to what they mean by "obscene."

Let us, however, not fall into the same trap. The basis of one's attitude toward "effects" lies in one's attitude toward sexuality. If sex in and by itself is considered shameful, undesirable, dangerous, unethical, or damaging to the individual and to society, then the effect of "obscene" *as well as* of erotically realistic books and art is definitely to be viewed with the utmost suspicion and alarm, *along with,* presumably, all other sexual stimulants of any kind.

But from a mental health point of view, it is established that such negative sex attitudes are not only regrettable, but can, indeed, be dangerous. As previously stated, all the clinical evidence indicates that guilt-based sexual inhibitions, restrictions, and repressions result in perversions of the sexual impulse, general intellectual dulling, sado-masochistic inclinations, unreasonable (paranoid) suspiciousness, and a long list of neurotic and psychotic defense reactions with unmistakable sexual content or overtones.

Our own position with regard to the legitimacy of sexual acts is in complete accord with that of René Guyon, who, more than any other contemporary thinker aside from Freud, affirmed man's right to use his body and his sexual organs in complete freedom, "as long as this occurs without violence, constraint, or fraud against another person."

If, therefore, erotic literature or art tend to lead to sexual acts, we would consider this a natural phenomenon that much more likely than not would enhance mental health and human happiness, provided that it met the conditions of not being forcefully or fraudulently imposed on another person.

If the pro-censorship leaguers believe that an erotic stimulus may lead to physical violence, this strangely paradoxical belief demands some further explanation. It would be totally absurd, were it not for the unspoken corollary that the normal sexual outlets of the individual are to be blocked and frustrated to the extent that he (or she) will then have to turn to sadism, rape, and murder as a substitute for the natural sexual activities which the reading may have stimulated. For the welfare of society then, no less than for individual mental health, it is incomprehensible why one would not want to accept the normal sex drive rather than to try and remove all temptation toward it, even if that were possible.

But antisexualists cannot contemplate with equanimity the free acceptance of man's sexual role, nor any literature which tends to inform, educate or increase interest in that role. The best proof of this is that literature of an erotic nature is the constant and foremost target of self-appointed censors who connect this type of reading to crime and acted-out violence, but who virtually ignore the vast body of books dealing with violence in the most gruesome detail, and even comic-strip versions of private and war-like mass-murder, "adapted for all ages." Unfortunately, many well-meaning people who have no bias against sex per se also mistakenly connect erotica with violent crime, misled by exploitative headlines and the confusion that has existed between erotic realism and obscenity.

The *philosophical* problem behind the present censorship debate is that those who advocate censorship of erotic materials (in the wider sense) are either overtly —as in the case of Christian orthodoxy—or tacitly subscribers to the Pauline doctrine of Carnal Sin, whether they realize this connection or not. They cannot regard the natural manifestations of the sexual drive as something quite "beyond good and evil." Instead, they are conditioned to feel—by the strength of their inner convictions, instilled by religious and other educational processes of one kind or another—that sex is inherently evil, dirty, and dangerous, or at least potentially so, if not carefully checked and circumscribed by a number of social prohibitions.

It is this ideological element which gives the censorship controversy, which ought to remain intellectual and matter-of-fact, "a startling turn of fanaticism which recalls the religious battles of former times; but doubtless this is natural enough, since perforce it (the concept of Carnal Sin) is a superstition of a religious nature which is here accepted by some and rejected by others." (René Guyon.)

A number of psychologists and psychiatrists have come out strongly against censorship of erotic literature. One of the studies bearing on the problem was that of Dr. Marie Jahoda and the staff of the Research Center for Human Relations at New York University. The results, published about six years ago in a mimeographed brochure entitled, *The Impact of Literature: A Psychological Discussion of Some Assumptions in the Censor-*

ship Debate, seem to indicate that reading matter in general is credited with causing behavior or attitude changes to a much larger extent than it actually deserves.

Attitudes, sexual and otherwise, are established early in life, and once incorporated are not easily altered. If this were not so, we could hand the patients who come to us for help with their emotional problems a reading list of books on mental hygiene instead of taking them into long and expensive treatment.

This does not contradict in any way our earlier assertion that books of erotic content, and especially "hard core obscenity," stimulate erotic fantasies which may lead to sexual behavior. Sexual behavior in all its "normal" and non-hostile "deviant" varieties is basically instinctual, though its modes of expression are largely "learned." On the other hand, sexual criminality and delinquency are the social symptoms of sick individuals in a sick society which has made the satisfaction of some of the basic biological and emotional human needs problematic, and often unattainable. The results of these cultural frustrations manifest themselves in perversions of the natural drives, in neurotic and psychotic symptoms, and—*as a socially conditioned variety of the latter* —in delinquent or criminal behavior.

Let us illustrate the point with an example from our clinical practice. Several years ago, one of the authors was treating a young man who, though in his late twenties had never succeeded in consummating a sexual relation with a girl. Every time he tried to do so, he suffered from a premature ejaculation.

The young man, who had been infantilized or "babied" by his parents to a ridiculous extent and had lived what one might aptly call a "sheltered" life, was filled with the most blood-curdling and vengeful fantasies, directed mostly against women. Some of his ideas actually bordered on the delusional, as when he fancied himself to be a werewolf or vampire and felt that his upper-front incisors were growing into fangs.

This patient's masturbation fantasies consisted mainly of scenes of human sacrifice; of monsters making off with helpless female victims; of himself, as a vampire, attacking a woman, sinking his claws into her, ripping her body open, and getting drunk on her blood. He said he had a great desire to act out these fantasies and was, at times, much concerned that "something" would force him to do so against his better judgment regarding the unavoidable legal consequences—if not the ethics of the acts themselves.

And yet, this same young man was capable of holding a fairly responsible job, of doing voluntary community work in his spare time, and of generally keeping in remarkably good touch with reality, aside from his morbid preoccupations which had their bases in the frustrations imposed upon him largely by his family.

In his case, sadistic imagery and desires had almost entirely supplanted the natural erotic impulses; in fact, his sadism increased with every failure in his repeated attempts at heterosexual relations, and decreased only in the measure that he was able to establish a very tentative homosexual relationship with another young man.

During the treatment of this patient, the therapist had a number of very interesting subjective reactions which, we think, are extremely relevant to the problem of the effect of erotic literature on human behavior. Several times the patient brought the therapist certain horror magazines to look at which were his sole delight and excited him tremendously. But he was distressed and much surprised when he discovered that the therapist could not find anything either amusing or erotically stimulating in these pulps.

The therapist then reversed the "experiment" which his patient had unwittingly initiated and asked him about his reactions to a number of girlie-type magazines. As might be expected, the young man did not show the least interest in the nudes and seminudes in the most alluring poses, except for one sequence of pictures which he had found in a girlie magazine a long time before showing a fully dressed female whose facial expressions seemed to indicate that she was being tortured and was experiencing great pain. This, the patient readily admitted, was the only type of picture which excited him sexually and which he preferred to use for stimulation in achieving the release of successful masturbation.

Now, if this young man had lost his ego controls entirely and had gone out and sadistically killed some person, the police would have found in his apartment large quantities of horror magazines, a record collection of the world's best martial music, among them snappy and blood-thirsty Nazi storm-troop songs, a complete series of Hitler's speeches, besides an assortment of guns, switchblade knives, rope, handcuffs, a riding whip, ammunition, a Nazi uniform, and similar items.

One can well imagine some of the newspaper reports which might have appeared in the wake of such a hypothetical crime. The police might have put on exhibit the boy's fantastic collection of arms and horror magazines, among them a few of the "lewd" type which he had acquired in the hope of finding some "different" or "unusual" pictures of torture in them, and the police and the sensational newspapers could have had another infallible "proof" that the magazines, which the scandal-sheets would undoubtedly have described as a "vast collection of pornography," had driven this patient to committing a horrid murder.

We believe that it is clinically very dangerous to block by critical or prohibitory attitudes and actions the few remaining fantasy outlets of sexually disturbed individuals. Our patient was greatly relieved when he found that his therapist did not condemn or ridicule his morbid preoccupations, as his family had done, even though he realized that the therapist did not consider them a sign of emotional well-being.

The patient's symptoms were always exacerbated whenever he tried to suppress his interest in the mixture of sex and horror which had an especially strong appeal for him. Once, he made a valiant effort to "reform" by destroying his entire collection of pictures and weapons, but became so restless and disturbed that the therapist feared really serious consequences. It was therefore a relief for patient and therapist alike when the patient announced in one of his next sessions that he had decided it was no use fighting his "evil nature" and that he had made a start of a new collection. Immediately, he became quieter and able to function more effectively in other areas of his life, which were relatively unaffected by his "sexual" problem.

But not so long ago we had a real murder case in this country which corresponded in many psychological details to the more benign case which we have cited. When Nebraska's Starkweather killed some dozen persons, it was played up in some quarters that he was an avid comic-book fan. Much less was made of other factors which an alert reporter elicited from Starkweather's father and which clinically have a much closer connection to the boy's criminal behavior. Among these disclosures was the fact that his father had lived in constant fear of the son, with whom he had never had a warm and friendly relationship.

In other words, the young killer evidently did not have the kind of wholesome, harmonious, acceptive and informative family life which is essential for a child's personality growth and healthy psychological development. To the contrary, one can easily detect in even these sparse accounts of Starkweather's family background that it shows hatred and vengeful fantasies on the part of the son, directed mostly against the father, but extending blindly to anything alive in his environment; in short, the well-known generalized, overflowing hostility or latent rage of a deeply disturbed individual.

It is, however, much easier and socially much more comfortable to blame a person's reading for a hideous crime than to explore and expose the poisoned family dynamics which are much more closely related to his criminal or otherwise disturbed behavior. Sometimes the suggestive questions asked the delinquent in this connection by the police, reporters, and other investigators, are eagerly picked up by him and used as a welcome excuse for his actions. These are psychologically interesting cases in which the law, the public, and the

PSYCHOLOGICAL EFFECTS OF EROTIC LITERATURE 337

criminal enter an unconscious conspiracy together and agree on a more convenient scapegoat which absolves society as well as its victim from the painful possibility of delving more deeply into the social and personal causes for the crime.

The body of clinical and psychological experience to date strongly points to much deeper causative factors in violent crime than reading. For example, Dr. Robert Lindner, well-known psychoanalyst and writer (*The Fifty-Minute Hour, Rebel Without a Cause*), specialized in the treatment of offenders with regard to the problem under discussion, and had this to say:

> I am utterly opposed to censorship of the written word, regardless of the source of such censorship or the type of material it is directed against. As a psychoanalyst who has had more than a decade of experience with the emotionally disturbed, and especially with delinquents, I am convinced of the absurdity of the idea that any form of reading matter, including the so-called comics and "other objectionable books," can either provoke delinquent or criminal behavior or instruct toward such ends. . . . I am convinced that were all so-called objectionable books and like material to disappear from the face of the earth tomorrow this would in no way affect the statistics of crime, delinquency, amoral and anti-social behavior, or personal illness and distress. The same frustrating and denying society would still exist, and both children and adults would express themselves mutinously against it. These problems will be solved only when we have the courage to face the fundamental social issues and personal perplexities that cause such behavior.

Indeed, it is our view that instead of the comics, "lewd" magazines, or even hard core pornography causing sex murders and other criminal acts, it is far more likely that these "unholy" instruments may be more often than not a *safety valve* for the sexual deviate and potential sex offender. This is not only our own view, but that of many other experienced clinicians, especially among those who have worked with more severely disturbed patients and delinquents. Representative of this type of clinical thinking is the conclusion of Dr. Benjamin Karpman, chief psychotherapist of St. Elizabeth Hospital in Washington, who says, "Contrary to popular misconception, people who read salacious literature are less likely to become sexual offenders than those who do not, for the reason that such reading often neutralizes what aberrant sexual interests they may have."

There is much corroborative evidence to back up Dr. Karpman's argument in favor of the therapeutic effect of expressing antisocial impulses (sexual or otherwise) through the operation of fantasy instead of by direct action. The whole concept of "catharsis" or "ab-reaction" of such tendencies in a therapeutic setting—in the case of children, with various play materials, destructible dolls, darts, toy guns, etc., or in the case of adults, with symbolic representations of strong emotional reactions, free indulgence in otherwise unacceptable fantasies, swearing and cursing, expression through art media or in psycho-drama—are standard accepted clinical practice.

Our experience in the projective testing of schizophrenics completely coincides with that of other clinicians with regard to the hostility content in the fantasy stories the patients tell in response to the pictures of the Thematic Apperception Test. This problem has its eminently practical side in decisions about the hospital discharge of mental patients who express, in tests such as the TAT, the Rorschach inkblot test, Sentence Completion Tests, etc., hostile and violent fantasies, often with a decidedly sexual flavor.

The inexperienced clinician in these situations is frequently tempted to assume that patients with aggressive fantasies are greater discharge risks than those who only express benign and lovely ideas. Contrary to this assumption, clinical experience has led to the conclusion that those patients whose projective test records show a conspicuous absence of hostile and aggressive, suicidal, or sexual fantasies, are more apt to act out their anti-social impulses than those who are able to express them verbally.

We have before us a striking parallel to this from the world of "hard core obscenity." Among the cases of fetishism which came to the attention of the late Wilhelm Stekel was one of a thirty-six-year-old German police-man, W. G. He was the author of a piece of "hard core obscenity" which Stekel called *The Bible of the Fetish-ist,* and which showed, in connection with the patient's corset fetishism, a marked sadistic bent of fantasy. (Dr. Wilhelm Stekel, *Sexual Aberrations.*)

One day this man handed Stekel a very elegantly bound, well-thumbed volume and asked him to study it, adding that he would return in about two weeks' time to talk to the therapist and pick up the book.

As Stekel describes it, the handwritten book con-sisted of several poems reflecting the patient's fetishistic preoccupation, a few confessions, a lengthy "obscene" fantasy of the flagellation type, and finally, a whole series of pictures, most of them clippings from newspapers and magazines. Most of these pictures the man had changed by drawing "obscene" figures into them, and by adding genitals or extravagant breasts, held in by tight corsets.

In this pornographic "bible," the policeman-patient tells how the women who have provoked his passions, quite regardless of their age, class, profession, or educa-tion, become, in his mind, his "victims" and "vassals."

He further describes how he excites himself by imagining his fantasy women being kissed, embraced, touched, and finally tortured. The patient enlarges on these fantasies and weaves them into an elaborate porno-graphic story, very similar to the "professional" speci-mens we have been analyzing.

Did this man become a famous lust murderer? One certainly might have expected so. Scenes of violent rape and sexual assault dominated his entire fantasy life: yet this man, for all his gory sexual fantasies, was so hopelessly and helplessly impotent that, like our own patient, he was never able to consummate a single act of sexual intercourse, even after his marriage. He never molested anybody and was a problem only to himself. He suffered from a severe religious conflict, and—as Stekel points out—his basic orientation was ascetic and masochistically submissive; in other words, quite the opposite from the surface appearance of his stories.

There is still further evidence in favor of the point of view here taken that the reading of erotic material, including even "hard core obscenity," is not nearly as likely to lead to antisocial acts as is often taken for granted, leaving aside the question of whether—as we suggest—such reading (and writing) may actually serve a therapeutic function.

Let us first examine the problem with regard to younger children, which is a facet that, very naturally, concerns all kinds of people. What, if any, would be the effect of their reading erotic material (in the wider sense)?

G. V. Ramsey in 1943 published a list, gathered from a group of 291 younger boys whom he had interviewed with regard to the nonsexual and sexual sources of erotic stimulation of which they were aware. Using the data, as completed and tabulated by Kinsey, *et al., Sexual Behavior in the Human Male,* we find the following, chiefly *physical,* stimuli among the nonsexual sources of erotic response in pre-adolescent boys:

Sitting in class	Fast bicycle riding
Friction with clothing	Fast car driving
Taking a shower	Skiing
Punishment	Airplane rides
Accidents	A sudden change in environment
Electric shock	
Fast elevator rides	Sitting in church
Carnival rides, Ferris wheel	Motion of car or bus
	A skidding car
Fast sled riding	Sitting in warm sand

Urinating
Boxing and wrestling
High dives

Riding horseback
Swimming

Other nonsexual sources of erotic response of a chiefly *emotional* nature, include:

Being scared
Fear of a house intruder
Near accidents
Being late to school
Reciting before a class
Asked to go to the front in class
Tests at school
Seeing a policeman
Cops chasing him
Getting home late
Receiving grade card
Harsh words
Fear of punishment
Being yelled at
Being alone at night
Fear of a big boy
Playing musical solo
Losing balance on heights
Looking over edge of building
Falling from garage, etc.
Long flight of stairs
Big fires
Setting a field afire

Hearing revolver shot
Anger
Watching exciting games
Playing in exciting games
Marching soldiers
War motion pictures
Other movies
Band music
Hearing "Extra! Paper!" called
Adventure stories
National anthem
Watching a stunting airplane
Finding money
Seeing name in print
Detective stories
Running away from home
Entering an empty house
Nocturnal dreams of fighting, accidents, wild animals, falling from high places, giants, being chased, or frightened

The list finally also includes some specifically *sexual* stimuli which are able to evoke an erotic response in these youngsters, though they constituted only 13 out of the total 77 sources of erotic response listed by the boys. The specifically sexual stimuli were:

Seeing females	Physical contact with females
Thinking about females	
Sex jokes	Love stories in books
Sex pictures	Seeing genitalia of other males
Pictures of females	
Females in moving pictures	Burlesque shows
	Seeing animals in coitus
Seeing self nude in mirror	Dancing with females

Of these sexual situations to which the boys responded, only one refers directly to "love stories in books" (which could be anything from "true romances" to "hard core obscenity"), but evidently even the younger boys do react erotically to stories involving sexual matters in the wider sense. Furthermore, among these younger boys, it is, as Kinsey remarked, "difficult to say what is an erotic response and what is a simple physical, or a generalized emotional situation." Kinsey states that "originally the pre-adolescent boy erects indiscriminately to the whole array of emotional situations, whether they be sexual or nonsexual." But nowhere in this study is there any indication that the boys reacted with delinquent behavior to any of the stimuli mentioned.

Kinsey adds some further comments which have considerable bearing on the whole question of the effect of erotic literature:

By his late teens the male has been so conditioned that he rarely responds to anything except a direct physical stimulation of genitalia, or to psychic situations that are specifically sexual. In the still older male even physical stimulation is rarely effective unless accompanied by such a psychologic atmosphere. The picture is that of the psychosexual emerging from a much more generalized and basic physiologic capacity which becomes sexual, as an adult knows it, through experience and conditioning. [p. 165.]

In other words, pre-adolescent boys may be "sexually aroused" by a variety of stimuli which are not necessarily sexual at all, as well as by a number of specifically sexual stimuli, of which reading is only one. As boys become men, however, the nonsexual stimuli no longer have the same effect, and the sexual stimulation has to be very direct, preferably a combination of specifically erotic physical and psychological stimuli.

We now have to consider those studies which were expressly undertaken to ascertain the causes of juvenile delinquency in order to see whether erotic books seem to have any influence on this type of behavior.

Let us begin with the classical study of the Drs. Sheldon and Eleanor Glueck, who intensively examined 1,000 delinquent boys from the Boston area. They found basically five highly significant factors contributing to delinquency: 1. culture conflict; 2. unwholesome family environment; 3. educational deficiencies; 4. socially undesirable use of leisure time (e.g., gambling, drinking, drug addiction, and sex misbehavior); and 5. psychological defects. Nowhere did the Gluecks mention erotic or any other kind of reading materials as a contributing factor in the causation of delinquency.

In the same vein, a prominent children's court judge, George S. Smyth, of New York, informed an inquiring state commission that of 878 causative factors which troubled children, reading was not even on the list, but that difficulty in reading was! (D. Fellman, *The Censorship of Books*.)

In a report by a committee of Brown University psychologists (Drs. Nissim Levy, Lewis Lipsitt, and Judy F. Rosenblith), commenting on a series of statements linking delinquent behavior to salacious reading, our attention is called to several other studies bearing on this question: one is a comprehensive study of 90 cases of delinquency reported recently by Mitchell in the *Australian Journal of Psychology*. The study lists such complex conditions as personal tension, defective discipline, insecurity, lack of home guidance, and emotional instability as the prime contributors to delinquency. One notes immediately that all these factors refer to deep-seated emotional problems and disturbances in interpersonal relations, in comparison to which the reading of comics or even "hard core obscenity" appears a rather trifling surface concern.

Another report, based on data in the United States, resulting from round-table conferences of professional workers chaired by Dr. Benjamin Karpman at the occasion of two annual meetings of the American Orthopsychiatric Association, concluded that there are three types of delinquency: 1. that due to organic brain damage; 2. that due to faulty dynamics in the relations of the family unit; and 3. that based primarily on social dislocation. Once again, there is no mention of "undesirable" reading materials of an erotic or any other nature.

The Brown University report also refers to a study of the chief stimuli of the "lascivious thoughts" and "sexual impulses" of college women. In that study it was found that dancing, music, and, to some extent, even reading, seemed to have aroused "lascivious thoughts." By far the largest number of those questioned answered, on the other hand, very simply that their chief erotic stimulus had been—of all things!—*man*: that is, contact with other individuals, particularly of the opposite sex.

While in complete agreement with the concluding statement of the Brown University group of psychologists that *"there is no reliable evidence that reading or other fantasy activities lead to antisocial behavior,"* we would go further and suggest that *erotic books may fulfill several eminently useful and therapeutic functions.*

We have already elaborated on the principle of catharsis through vicarious participation by reading. It always strikes us as strange that this ancient idea should be considered by some to be so novel and highly controversial. As far as we know, the concept is at least as old as Aristotle, who recommended that Athenians go and watch the tragedies in the theater to avoid succumbing to antisocial impulses. We believe that this may apply equally to the antisocial sex impulses which are often given free rein in so-called "hard core obscenity," and occasionally also in erotic realism.

Given the limitations and inadequacies of present sex education in our society, *erotic realism in literature can serve a most useful function* in sex education. In fact, we believe that there can hardly be any argument on this point among sensible people.

It has been argued by some that adequate sex information is now available from many sources, and that there is consequently no need for children (or adults) to learn from books such as *Lady Chatterley's Lover, Memoirs of Hecate County,* or any other examples of erotic realism.

It is perfectly true that some wonderful sex educational materials—books, pamphlets, scale models of sex anatomy, movies, etc.—have been prepared and are available to parents and teachers, at least in the larger metropolitan centers, and it is fortunate that more and more schools are now offering, usually from the seventh grade on, a limited program of sex education. However, it would perhaps be more fitting to call these programs by other names (as they, indeed, sometimes are called), for instance, courses in "family life," "preparation for marriage," or the "get-along-with-your-neighbors" type of "human relations" curriculum.

One could think of still other and better-fitting titles for what is currently offered in most of our public schools as sex education (if anything is offered at all); for instance, "birth education," "venereal-disease education," "maternity education," "menstrual education," or "sex-anatomy education." Those acquainted with the educational system will immediately recognize the kind of "topics," or "units" which these titles fit, and realize that this is essentially the kind of knowledge which the schools, or at least some of the schools, have agreed to impart to the young.

Most of it, good as it is as far as it goes, unfortunately comes much too late and remains too little. Due to pressure from certain groups, or to legal limitations, it is usually fragmentary: it often does not include contraceptive education; nor does public sex education, as a rule, extend to the physiology of the sexual act itself, let alone to techniques of intercourse; nor does it include information about homosexuality and other sexual deviations.

There is still another deficiency in what is commonly offered as sex education, namely, the split between the sexological facts and what Harry Stack Sullivan called the "lust mechanism." We could, perhaps, accept the idea that a selected group of sex facts be presented to the child as separate from the emotional and pleasurable aspects of sex, in short, as something which pretends to have nothing to do with the "lust mechanism," but, in that case, we would expect that the home should fill in the missing link. The parent should make it possible for the child to connect the rudimentary sex anatomy which it has studied *with the emotional aspects of sexuality,* and not merely with its procreative side. Only then can the anatomical facts make any real sense to the child, and only by such a connection with what confronts the child in terms of all the emotional aspects of sexuality can a young person meaningfully and therapeutically integrate his factual knowledge about sex.

We suggest that by omitting the pleasurable and other emotional aspects of sexuality from sex education, a vacuum has been created between that which the child has learned and what he or she experiences *as the most urgent part of the sexual question: namely, what to do about the lustful emotions,* which assert themselves with ever-increasing strength as the individual reaches puberty and full biological maturity, and which, from lack of free discussion or information, give rise to deep feelings of guilt and fear.

In this situation, the ideal supplement to what the average enlightened home or school offers in the form of sex education would be books of erotic realism, such as Lawrence's *Lady Chatterley's Lover,* Wilson's *Memoirs of Hecate County,* or autobiographical works like *The Life and Loves of Frank Harris.* These books would connect that which the young person has learned in the way of sex anatomy and physiology with the lust mechanism and the appropriate emotional states which accompany sexuality under a variety of conditions.

We have no doubt that this will be the type of complete sex education which good homes and schools will offer in the not-so-distant future. It will be part of a total educational process which in all parts of the relevant curriculum—for instance, Biology, English, History, Physical Education, etc.—is purposely designed to prepare boys and girls for the most vital functions and most significant roles in their lives, both personal and as members of a democratic culture.

Sexual freedom can be the privilege only of a free society. Like dynamic psychology, it does not flourish in a climate of political tyranny and economic restriction. The more actual democracy a society allows, the more sexual freedom is granted to its members. The more authoritarian the political organization of a society, and the more discriminatory its economic structure, the less sexual freedom can it afford to grant to the mass of the population.

We have some illustrative examples for this relationship between sex and authoritarian politics from the recent and current political scene. In Russia, during the democratic phase of the Twenties shortly following the revolution, the Peoples' Councils passed the most liberal sex legislation of modern times, abolishing, for instance, their antiquated marriage and divorce laws, and legalizing medical abortions and homosexuality. This democratic phase ended with the change to Stalinist-type dictatorship. From then on, all the previous gains of sex reform were lost; abortion and homosexuality once more became punishable crimes, divorce and marriage laws were reshaped according to the traditional pattern, and sexuality in the Russian youth movement was strongly discouraged as a sign of "bourgeois (democratic) decadence."

The same development can presently be seen in the traditional land of sexual freedom—France. There, authoritarian politics under the leadership of General de Gaulle have imposed strict censorship of erotic publications. The de Gaulle government has actually tried to silence the famous Olympia Press, which, among other things, originally published several of Henry Miller's books, launched Nabokov's *Lolita,* Donleavy's *Ginger Man,* and some of Beckett's works.

All these instances demonstrate how a democratic society is inclined to believe that its citizens are sufficiently intelligent and mature to decide for themselves what they might want to read. Authoritarian government, on the other hand, assumes that the citizenry is incapable of self-government and of watching out for their own morals. It therefore imposes governmental or religious restrictions from without, telling its subjects just exactly what is good or bad for them to read, to look at, or to do.

In the future, we hope to supplement our investigations into the nature and effects of erotic literature by controlled experiments, designed to further remove the various problems here outlined from the area of personal prejudice and opinion on both sides. In fact, the authors would have been able to present more conclusive data along these lines at this time were it not for the same resistance toward this type of research which is preventing psychology as a science from entering wholeheartedly into the investigation of other aspects of sexual behavior.

At the present time, about all that the public and the professions can tolerate is basic sex research of a primarily statistical nature, such as the famous Kinsey and similar studies. As matters stand, it is almost impossible to make funds available and assure sufficient professional and public cooperation to conduct the type of research which would be necessary to shed more light on such questions as 1. the differential sex response of males and females with regard to "hard core obscenity"; 2. the differential sex response of various age, occupational, and economic groups to "obscene" literature; 3. the effects which "obscene" literature has had or not had on known sex offenders; and 4. the effects of reading and writing "obscene" stories as a possible means of "catharsis" on the part of (a) "normal" individuals, and (b) hospitalized mental patients of various diagnostic categories.

Further experimentalism is also needed in the area of the effect of reading on *existing attitudes*, and whether a causal relationship can be established between reading and behavior.

Now, to return to the role of "hard core obscenity" in our society. Let us repeat that the "obscene" books which we have studied clearly reflect the cultural neuroses of Western society. A certain small percentage of this material may actually be written by deeply disturbed individuals, such as we have seen in the case of Dr. Stekel's pornographer-policeman. We have also seen that "obscene" books are generally not only devoid of reality, but that they purposely distort reality in order to better suit the over-all purpose of this type of literature as psychological aphrodisiacs. In this connection, the absence of concern over possible pregnancy, disease, and social repercussions has been pointed out. Attention has also been drawn to the positive distortions as well as to their frequent fetishistic features.

It seems that every epoch and society has the pornography which it deserves. If much of what meets the eye on the American or Western world (including the European) market of "hard core obscenity" is artistically worthless and often aesthetically offensive, we may have to look for the causes of this in our censorial, sex-suppressive attitudes. We can hardly expect contemporary writers of the stature of a Maupassant or Goethe who, among other major writers, have secretly contributed works which would fall in the category of "hard core obscenity" (as defined), to devote themselves to the production of high-class erotica if the society in which they operate and on which they depend to a certain extent for security and livelihood would merely ostracize them for so doing.

In the Orient, for example in old Japan, important

artists and writers have contributed large numbers of erotic woodcuts, paintings, and other art objects, as well as prose and poetry, obviously designed to fulfill the function of psychological aphrodisiacs. In these cultures, which were relatively unaffected by antisexual prejudices as compared to our own culture, the need for psychological aphrodisiacs was clearly recognized and the science and art of the period strove to perfect them in the interests of an appreciative society.

In America, public sentiment has been particularly opposed to erotic literature of any kind, including erotic realism. In fact we have discouraged our best writers and artists from dealing with erotic subject matter in any mature fashion. On the other hand, the American public has been more lenient toward erotic literature by foreign authors. Needless to say, we most heartily welcome the popularity of such books as *Lady Chatterley's Lover,* which was written by an English author, or Nabakov's *Lolita,* written by a native Russian living in the United States.

However, one cannot help but feel deep regret for the treatment accorded one of the few works of erotic realism by an American writer, Edmund Wilson's *Memoirs of Hecate County.* It is true that erotic realism in literature frequently deals with rather "shocking" aspects of sexuality: perversions and deviations of the natural sex drive, cruelty, and a variety of pathological emotions. But this does not detract either from the literary or the clinical value of such books.

Attempts to shelter children from the pleasant and the unpleasant realities of life are of questionable therapeutic value; the chances are that this will produce the opposite of the desired effect. As an example of what can happen with such "sheltered" children, we have lying before us a newspaper account of a tragedy, containing the letter of a father whose little girl had been sexually approached and murdered by a fifteen-year-old "model boy." The young killer was said to have been an exemplary student at his parochial high school; a quiet, polite, if somewhat indrawn, child; the pride of his parents, his church, and his teachers.

With great insight into the dynamics of this horrible event, the grieving father notes correctly that "there is something truly terrifying about the model child." He points out that the tragedy which befell him and his family could not have taken place if there were a better understanding and acknowledgment in our society of what he calls "the full range of feeling and emotion which is our common human heritage, and which, for convenience's sake, we are so fond of denying."

In the letter, this unusual father pleads for understanding of the boy who the day before had killed "the most precious thing" in his life. In an almost superhuman effort to redeem the otherwise senseless slaying of his infant daughter, the dead girl's father admits that, had he been at the scene of the crime, he would have wanted to take the boy's life in blind rage. Now, however, at the dawn of a new day, he merely wants his daughter's untimely death to bring new life to many others.

Speaking with the lucidity which only his profound grief could give him, the father contrasts his daughter's happiness and radiant freedom with the sullen politeness and constriction of her killer, who must have envied this little girl for everything that she possessed and which he most wanted and could never attain. Here was a radiant, life-accepting, spontaneous little human being, her basic human needs fulfilled and satisfied, while his remained thwarted and forever frustrated by an environment which denied him the privilege of being what he was. Nobody seemed to realize that this child, like any healthy boy, could not *only* obey, get top marks in school, smile, bow, and remain silent when his elders spoke, but also wanted, and needed, at times to hit, scratch, scream, fight—in short, to be an all-around teenage nuisance.

The father of the murdered girl asks society not simply to punish the boy for what he has done and which cannot be undone, but to try to account for his pent-up hostility. He asks us to inquire what cause this young fellow had to be so angry at society, or to feel so guilty about being what he is, that his emotions exploded in this wanton act of violence and human destruction.

In his letter, the dead girl's father suggests that there "simply are no villains," but that "some of these human beings have had their basic drives so profoundly inhibited—often by being overwhelming goodies for much longer than health and sanity will permit—that the problem of their control poses a most serious problem for society."

Referring to the way in which the boy disposed of the dead girl's body, the father says that "for the sake of a most immature passion for self-esteem—perhaps immature in the development of our race rather than in the development of an individual human—we are wont to label everything which we prefer to stuff in a closet (even as was done to my child), as 'inhuman.'" And he closes, asking society: "Let no feelings of caveman vengeance influence us. Let us rather help him who did so human a thing."

We have dwelled on this tragedy—one in many hundreds and thousands every year—perhaps longer than the nature of this book seems to warrant. However, we cannot help but feel that what took place between one "model" boy and one healthy little girl in a hidden basement has a decided bearing on what this book wishes to convey.

The dead girl's father warns, "Beware citizens. The human animal cannot be cheated forever. It will have love or kill."

Yes, the human animal will have love. But even before it can accept and give something so far progressed on the scale of racial and individual evolution as that complicated emotion called love, the human animal must have its physical and instinctual needs accepted and taken care of. Frustrated human animals are poor risks for the tricky experiment of civilization.

Let us not compound this frustration by closing, especially to our young people, those sources of additional sex information which are available in the form of erotic realism, and which incorporate and include the emotional realities that are the highest expression of man's sexuality.

We suggest instead that we educate the young that there is nothing to be ashamed of about our corporeality and its desires except shame itself. As Mark Twain put it:

> Man has been called the laughing animal . . . but the monkey laughs, and he has been called the animal that weeps—but several of the others do that. Man is merely and exclusively the Immodest Animal, for he is the only one with a soiled mind, the only one under the dominion of a false shame.

PART V

THE EROTICA OF TOMORROW

In our "Critique of Legal Theory and Practice concerning "obscenity," as well as in our discussion of *Fanny Hill,* we have stated the need for a new classification of erotic writings to include that large group of literature which does not fit the narrow category of hard core pornography on the one hand, nor the broader group of erotic realism and erotic humor on the other. We have also proposed that for this larger category of erotic literature (and art—for the same principle naturally applies to pictorial representations, the plastic arts, and the film) one might want to adopt the label of *quality erotica.* This sort of modified designation suggests itself because the simple term "erotica" encompasses hard core pornography in both common and scientific usage.

It is understood that under this category of *quality erotica* one would include the types of literature already discussed, namely *erotic realism, erotic autobiography, erotic humor* (and *satire,* which, as we have seen, is really a special kind of erotic humor, used as a vehicle for social criticism). To these classifications we would now add *philosophical erotica,* and *erotic surrealism* as other sub-divisions in the major category of quality erotica. We expect still further types to develop in the future as erotic subject matter becomes more and more an integral part of modern art and literature.

We are aware of the fact that any classification of this sort must of necessity be somewhat arbitrary, and that no real work of art or creation of the mind can be forced into categorical strait-jackets that would make it either one thing or the other. Erotic realism, for instance, frequently contains—as we have seen in the case of Henry Miller, and as we shall see in the case of other writers as well—much philosophy and social criticism; likewise, erotic writings of an even more pronounced philosophical bend than those of Miller, such as, say, the works of de Sade or Genet, may contain highly effective erotic elements, just as erotic autobiography is certainly related to erotic realism. But, broadly speaking, and for purposes of quick differentiation, we think that this category of quality erotica will, for all practical purposes, prove the most workable.

The first thing that strikes one about these various sub-divisions of erotica is that they encompass a very wide range of subject matter. In fact, one might say that they include the whole field of literature. It is also noteworthy that erotic surrealism is a rather recent literary development. We might add that by far the largest segment of good erotic literature in the English language is of our own times, and that what we are witnessing today is obviously only the mere beginning of a new literary tradition, with the bulk of erotic literature and the most important works in this field undoubtedly yet to come.

In view of these facts, it would seem that erotic literature, in Western civilization, is only now coming into its own, and that compared to the literary and artistic renaissance that is taking place today in this field, even the hightide of French erotica in the eighteenth century will appear as relatively insignificant. In other words, erotic literature (and, we are sure, erotic art) is only now, with the greater social tolerance of sexual matters, beginning to find its rightful place in our cultural life. (That such a development is already well on the way, at least in continental Europe, is demonstrated by an official, government sponsored art exhibition on the theme of "L'Amour" presented in Paris in the winter 1963-1964. This exhibition of works by noted painters, graphic artists, and sculptors on the various expressions of "Love," in the widest sense of the term, included frank representations of human intercourse: indeed an encouraging sign of increasing public maturity and a sharp contrast to the otherwise narrow-minded and bigoted exercise of censorship by the French courts and police.)

We are now ready to examine more closely some representative examples of the kind of quality erotica which one may expect to play an increasingly significant role in Western literature in the future. It is, of course, impossible to do full justice to a piece of writing by quoting portions of it out of context. Nevertheless, the samples presented should suffice to convey at least an impression of the nature and style of this type of erotic literature, and give both those interested in the legal aspects of the problem, as well as those approaching the matter more from a general interest in literature, a chance to acquaint themselves with these still difficult to obtain types of writing.

EROTIC SURREALISM

As already indicated, erotic surrealism has flourished and is still flourishing in France as part of the larger surrealist movement in art and literature in that country. It is also, from a psychological point of view, perhaps the most rewarding type of erotica, since the erotic fantasies which it expresses are frequently indicative of the pathogenic effects of the traditional anti-sexualism in our culture against which this movement constitutes, among other things, a violent form of rebellion.

Among the writers of erotic surrealism, the most important figure was undoubtedly George Bataille. Under various pseudonyms (he was by profession a librarian, employed by the French civil service), he wrote a number of surrealistic stories of highly erotic content. Of these, perhaps the best known work that has survived (for many years most of his books have been out of print), is the *Histoire de l'Oeuil,* literally translated, "The Story of the Eye," but rendered as "A Tale of Satisfied Desire" in the English translation of the Olympia Press.

To this story, published in both the French and English versions under the pseudonym of Pierre Angelique, Bataille wrote an "Introduction" under his own name. In this Introduction, the author intimates that the psychological background material to the story, though not the events themselves, were furnished by his own lifelong preoccupation with certain erotic images and symbolism. These erotic images, in turn, were—as he explains—derived from some of his unhappy childhood experiences, especially those connected with his father's progressive syphilitic illness which rendered him, in the end, not only helpless, blind, and incontinent, but also mentally deranged and frankly hallucinatory.

Bataille gives us furthermore to understand that among his strongest childhood impressions, connected with his father's illness, were those of *urine* (associated with the latter's incontinence) and of the *eye* (related to the father's blindness). It is therefore not surprising that urine, the eye, and its equivalent, the egg, should become the symbolic key images of his story.

In the book itself, a teen-age girl by the name of Simone and the narrator, speaking in the first person, have a kind of weird affair involving these symbols; into this affair at times other individuals are drawn, almost in the way of props, to accentuate the erotically supercharged relationship between the two main characters.

Without going any further into the structure of the story, we shall quote a passage which is representative of the tenor of the book. As we shall see, the passage has no relation whatever to reality, while abounding in surrealistic images and symbolism. The sequence describes a wild bicycle ride during torrential downpours, and involves Simone and her lover:

A little later (having found our bicycles), we

were able to afford each other the irritating, theo-retically filthy, spectacle of a nude but shod body mounted upon a machine. We pedaled rapidly, without laughter or words, in the common isolation of immodesty, of fatigue, of absurdity.

The wind had slackened a little, a part of the sky held stars; the idea occurred to me that death being the only issue for my erection, Simone and I once killed, for the universe of our personal vision would be substituted by the chaste stars, which were coolly realizing what seemed to me the state in which my debauches would terminate, a geometric incandescence (the coinciding of, among other things, life and death, being and nothingness), a perfectly fulgurating incandescence.

But these images remained attached to the con-tradictions of a protracted state of exhaustion and of an absurd stiffness of the virile member. It was difficult for Simone to see this stiffness because of the darkness and also because my left leg would rise and hide it with each turn. It seemed to me, however, that her eyes were turning in the night towards this point where my body was broken. Then she had not, any more than had I, finished with the storm called alive by her nakedness. I could hear her hoarse moaning; her naked body's joy literally tore her asunder and she was hurled upon the side of the road, amidst a noise of steel dragging upon gravel.

The other surrealistic piece of contemporary erotica with which we shall acquaint the reader is the famous *Story of O* (*L'Histoire d'O*). The French woman writer Pauline Réage is alleged to be the author, but the book has been variously attributed to several other authors, including Jean Paulhan who wrote an introductory essay for the work.

The book, like those of Bataille, is a work of consid-erable literary merit and follows (even more than the writings of Bataille) in the tradition of de Sade, though it is not as disturbing as de Sade's *Justine,* or as the erotic novels of Apollinaire (*The Debauched Hospodar* and *Memoirs of a Young Rakehell*, published jointly as "Two Novels by Guillaume Apollinaire" by Olympia Press, Paris). In another respect, however, *The Story of O* resembles rather closely Bataille's *Tale of Satisfied Desire* in that it stresses the "bondage" theme between the sadistically-dominant male and the masochistic-submissive female characters of the story. However, as we shall presently see, *The Story of O* has several other aspects, among them a strong interest in clothes-fetishism and a fascinating by-play on the theme of sexual jealousy and love which is perhaps psychologically its most powerful feature and alone worth the rest of the tiresome sado-masochistic content without which, apparently, French erotic literature simply cannot do.

The sequence presented here involves a surrealistic taxi ride in Paris, which sets the stage for the "bondage" theme, running through the whole book. It also gives us an indication of the type of eroticism (already encountered in Bataille) that derives its special dynamism from the idea of not only bending the woman to the male's will and whim, but also of destroying female "modesty," of which the undergarments the girl has to remove during the ride are the symbols. These ideas are presented in a context of such voluptuous sensuality that it is easy to overlook them: the following passage is taken from *The Story of O: The Lovers of Roissy,* by Pauline Réage, translated by Sabine Destre, which originally appeared in *Evergreen Review,* (Vol. 7, No. 31 Copyright © 1963 by Evergreen Review, Inc.):

> One day her lover takes O for a walk in a section of the city where they never go—the Montsouris Park, the Monceau Park. After taking a stroll in the park and sitting together on the edge of the grass, they notice a car which, because of its meter, resembles a taxi. And yet the car is at an intersection where the park turns a corner, at a spot where there is never any taxi stand.
> "Get in," he says.

She gets in. It is autumn, and coming up to dusk. She is dressed as she always is: high heels, a suit with a pleated skirt, a silk blouse, and no hat. But she is wearing long gloves which come up over the sleeves of her jacket, and in her leather pocketbook she has her identification papers, her compact, and her lipstick.

The taxi moves off slowly, without the man having said a word to the driver. But he pulls down the shades on the windows on both sides of the car, and on the back window. She has taken off her gloves, thinking he wants to kiss her or that he wants her to caress him. But instead he says:

"Your bag's in your way; let me have it."

She gives it to him. He puts it out of her reach and adds:

"You also have on too many clothes. Unfasten your stockings and roll them down to above your knees. Here are some garters."

By now the taxi has picked up speed, and she has some trouble managing it; she's also afraid the driver might turn around. Finally, though, the stockings are rolled down, and she's embarrassed to feel her legs naked and unfettered beneath her silk slip. Besides, the loose garter-belt suspenders are sliding back and forth.

"Unfasten your garter belt," he says, "and take off your panties."

That's simple enough, all she has to do is slip her hands behind her back and raise herself slightly. He takes the garter belt and panties from her, opens her bag, and puts them in, then says:

"You shouldn't sit on your slip and skirt. Pull them up behind you and sit right on the seat."

The seat is made of some sort of imitation leather which is slippery and cold: it's quite an extraordinary sensation to feel it sticking to your thighs. Then he says:

"Now put your gloves back on."

The taxi is still moving along at a good clip, and she doesn't dare ask why René just sits there without moving or saying another word, nor can she guess what all this means to him—having her there motionless, silent, so stripped and available, so thoroughly gloved, in a black car going God knows where. He hasn't told her what to do or what not to do, but she's afraid either to cross her legs or squeeze them together. She sits with gloved hands braced on either side of her seat.

"Here we are," he says suddenly. The taxi stops in front of a relatively modest mansion which can be seen nestled between the courtyard and the garden, the type of small private dwelling one finds along the Faubourg Saint-Germain. The street lamps are some distance away, and it is still fairly dark inside the car. Outside it is raining.

"Don't move," René says. "Sit perfectly still."

His hand reaches toward the collar of her blouse, unties the bow, then unbuttons the blouse. She leans slightly forward, thinking he wants to fondle her breasts. No. He is merely groping for the shoulder straps of her brassiere, which he snips with a small penknife. Then he takes it off. Now, beneath her blouse, which he has buttoned back up, her breasts are naked and unencumbered, as is the rest of her body from waist to knee.

"Listen," he says. "Now you're ready. This is where I leave you. You're to get out and go ring the doorbell. Follow whoever opens the door for you, and do whatever you're told. If you hesitate about going in, they'll come and take you in. If you don't obey immediately, they'll force you to. Your bag? No, you have no further need for your bag. You're merely the girl I'm furnishing. Yes, of course I'll be there. Now run along."

Other episodes from *The Story of O* take place in a de Sadian type of castle in which a number of women are held prisoner and subjected to a forced training course in sensuality and submission. It is here that we encounter the most interesting theme of breaking the woman from her sexual jealousy toward the lover, thus making her enter into another sphere of eroticism from which sexual possessiveness would otherwise have barred her. The preoccupation with clothes as psychological sex stimuli remains a prominent feature in *The Story of O* from the first to the last.

With these examples from two outstanding works of French surrealist erotica, we hope to have given the reader at least a glimpse into this important type of literature to which there is practically no parallel in the English and Teutonic languages. It is, however, predictable that over the next few years, some of these works will appear in translations and that, together with an ever increasing familiarity with surrealist art on the part of the sophisticated public outside of France, other countries will develop their own brand of surrealism. If and when that happens, such new surrealism will, hopefully, incorporate more of the positive features of its parent movement, while leaving aside those aspects that are merely indicative of a lack of liberation from values and ideas which are no longer of current concern. It may not, perhaps, be altogether "surrealistic" to expect that even in France this artistic and literary movement will undergo a much needed renaissance, regain its lost vitality, and become more fully relevant to the problems of today.

EROTICA WITH EMPHASIS ON PHILOSOPHY OR SOCIAL CRITICISM

We are now ready to examine that type of erotica which is primarily concerned with philosophical questions or problems of social criticism. Doubtful as it may seem to those not familiar with this type of literature, the concern with these problems—contrary to what we know with regard to hard core pornography—is absolutely genuine and not simply a subterfuge to conceal a primarily erotic or pornographic interest. If de Sade's material is gruesome in the extreme (indeed, revolting is not too strong a word), it must be remembered that none of his literary excesses equalled the actual excesses which were perpetrated in his time—and in ours. By embracing evil, he pointed the theme of man's inhumanity to man.

The first quotation is taken from de Sade's *Justine* or *The Misfortunes of Virtue,* and concerns a scene at the castle of a sadistic character by the name of Roland whom the unfortunate Justine had previously rescued after he had been ambushed by a band of robbers and left seriously injured by the side of the road—in base "gratitude" for which he has lured her to his sinister hide-out where he amuses himself by torturing his mistress Suzanne and now also Justine:

"Oh dear! in mammaeistical matters," said Roland, "you've got to yield to Suzanne; never had you such fine teats, wait, we'll have a look at this noble furniture," and with those words he pressed the poor girl's breasts till his fingers punctured holes in them. At this point it was no longer I who was exciting him, for Suzanne had replaced me; scarcely had she fallen into his clutches when his dart, springing from its quiver, began to menace everything surrounding it. "Suzanne," said Roland, "behold an appalling triumph . . . 'tis your death decreed, Suzaane; I feared as much," added that ferocious man as he nipped and clawed her breasts. As for mine, he only sucked and chewed them. At length, he placed Suzanne on her knees at the edge of the sofa, he made her bend her head and in this attitude he enjoyed her according to the frightful manner natural to him; awakened by new pains, Suzanne struggles and Roland, who simply wishes to skirmish, is content with a brisk passage of arms, and come to take refuge in me at the same shrine at which he has sacrificed in my companion whom he does not cease to vex and molest the while. "There's a whore who excites me cruelly," he says to me, "I don't know what to do with her." "Oh Monsieur," says I, "have pity upon her; her sufferings could not be more intense." "Oh, but you're wrong!" the villain replies, "one night . . . ah! if only I had with me that celebrated Emperor Kié, one of the greatest scoundrels ever to have sat on the Chinese throne,[1] with Kié we'd really be able to perform wonders. Both he and his wife, they say, immolated victims daily and would have them live twenty-four hours in death's cruellest agonies, and in such a state of suffering that they were constantly on the verge of expiring but never quite able to die, for those monsters administered that kind of aid which made them flutter between relief and torture and only brought them back to life for one minute in order to kill them the next. . . . I Therese, I am too gentle, I know nothing of those arts, I'm a mere apprentice." Roland retires without completing the sacrifice and hurts me almost as much by this precipitous withdrawal as he had upon inserting himself. He throws himself into Suzanne's arms, and, joining sarcasm to outrage; "Amiable creature," he apostrophizes, "with what delight I remember the first instants of our union; never had woman given me such thrilling pleasures, never had I loved one as I did you . . . let us embrace, Suzanne, for methinks we're to part, perhaps the season of our separation will be long." "Monster!" my companion retorts, thrusting him away with horror, "begone; to the torments you inflict upon me join not the despair of hearing your terrible remarks; sate your rage, tigerish one, but at least respect my sufferings." Roland laid hands on her, stretched her upon the couch, her legs widespread, and the workshop of generation ideally within range. "Temple of my ancient pleasures," the in-

---

[1] Kié, the Emperor of China, had a wife as cruel and debauched as he; bloodshed was as naught to them, and for their exclusive pleasure they spilled rivers of it every day; within their palace they had a secret chamber where victims were put to death before their eyes and while they enjoyed themselves. Théo, one of this Prince's successors, had, like him, a very bloodthirsty wife; they invented a brass column and this great cylinder they would heat red-hot; unlucky persons were bound to it while the royal couple looked on: "The Princess," writes the historian from whom we have borrowed these lines, "was infinitely entertained by these melancholy victims' contortions and screams; she was not content unless her husband gave her this spectacle frequently." (Hist. des Conj. VOL. VII p. 43.)

famous creature intoned, "you who procured me delights so sweet when I plucked your first roses, I must indeed address to you my farewells . . ." The villain! he drove his fingernails into it and, rummaging about inside for a few minutes while screams burst from Suzanne's mouth, he did not withdraw them until they were covered with blood. Glutted and wearied by these horrors, and feeling, indeed, he could restrain himself no longer, "Come, Therese, come," he said, "let's conclude all this with a little scene of funambulation; it'll be cut-the-card dear girl;" that was the name he gave that deadly legerdemain of which I gave you a description when I mentioned Roland's cavern for the first time. I mount the three-legged stool, the evil fellow fits the halter of my neck, he takes his place opposite me; although in a frightful state, Suzanne excites him manually; an instant passes, then he snaps the stool from beneath me, but equipped with the sickle, I sever the cord immediately and fall uninjured to the ground. "Nicely done, very neat," says Roland, "your turn, Suzanne, there it is, and I'll spare you, if you manage as cleverly."

Suzanne takes my place. Oh Madame, allow me to obfuscate that dreadful scene's details . . . The poor thing did not recover from it.

As the reader will have noticed, de Sade in this scene describes tortures similar to those actually inflicted on people by various governments, in this case those of a former Emperor of China and his equally sadistic wife, to both of whom his detailed footnote specifically refers. The point which de Sade is trying to make here is that no personal crime, no matter how heinous, vile, and depraved, can surpass or rival those atrocities committed daily, both in war and in peace, by governments themselves.

Unfortunately, the argument has altogether too much basis in historical and current fact to be dismissed lightly. The atrocities committed by the Nazis, by the Soviet authorities during the Stalinist period, or by the

French soldiery during the Algerian war, all bear eloquent witness to the correctness of de Sade's thesis up to this point. The sickening scene in the quoted passage by de Sade in which Roland cruelly lacerates with his bare hand the vagina of his mistress for instance, is outstripped in horror by the account of an Algerian girl having her vagina torn open with a broken bottle by the French militia. Likewise, de Sade would have found ample material for his stories in incident after incident of police brutality in France during the height of the Algerian "crisis," when the guardians of the law clubbed and beat scores of Algerian residents in the capital to death, or simply threw them into the icy waters of the Seine from which their corpses were being fished almost daily during that period. Similarly, de Sade would have found ample corroboration for his point of view from the torture by whipping and burning, and the "legal" killings of Negroes, perpetrated or tolerated by local authorities under one pretext or another, or similar persecutions of other races by the white colonial powers. Most recently, de Sade could even have found background material in the inhumanities of black governments against the members of their own race who happen to be in opposition to them and which, in the future, may turn into persecution of the white man by the black.

A grisly parallel to the strangulation incident quoted above is the recent legal execution of a political prisoner, carried out through strangulation or garroting *by hand,* in one of the supposedly civilized countries of Europe where this incredible form of punishment is still an officially sanctioned mode of execution, (though the horrors of execution by the electric chair or poisoning through the inhalation of deadly cyanide fumes are hardly less "de Sadian" in character).

In other words, as long as governments resort to one form of violence or other to enforce their wishes or even the law, de Sade's argument is irrefutable. It is only when he turns it into a rationalization to justify *personal* crime that pornography replaces the solid ground of logic and reason.

In our quotations from Genet, we shall restrict ourselves to his semi-autobiographical *The Thief's Journal** (translation by Bernard Frechtman, Olympia Press, Paris). In that book, Genet tells of his status as an illegitimate child, abandoned as a baby by both of his parents to be raised, first by foster parents, and subsequently (after his first theft from them) by the authorities of various correctional institutions which became house, home, and parent substitutes to him.

Later, he gives an account of some of his times of imprisonment (mostly for theft and dope smuggling or peddling), his relations with some of his criminal friends, including his homosexual experiences with them (as with a French police detective and with British soldiers at Gibraltar), and his wanderings as a beggar and tramp from one end of Europe to the other.

In the following quoted passage, we pick him up on one of these beggar's odysseys along the South coast of Spain (which was then still as unspoiled by mass-tourism as it was impoverished by centuries of indifference and neglect):

> . . . Andalusia was lovely, hot and barren. I went all through it. At that age, fatigue was unknown to me. I carried with me such a burden of sorrow that I was sure my whole life would be spent in wandering. Vagrancy was no longer a detail which would embellish my life, but a reality. I no longer know what I thought, but I remember that I offered all my woes to God. In my solitude, remote from men, I came quite close to being all love, all devotion.

Already in this opening paragraph, we notice the essentially *religious* bent of his mind, a fact which Jean-Paul Sartre realized sooner than anyone else, and to which he devoted his 600-odd page book *Saint Genet*. It must, of course, be understood that what Genet—

---

* Copyright © 1954, Frechtman and Olympia Press: to be published by Grove Press, Inc.

(and Sartre)—mean by a sense of religion has nothing whatever to do with the conventional idea of religion, for Genet can be counted on to be as violently anti-clerical as he is anti-society. However, his religious amoralism becomes more understandable if one recalls that the Latin root *sacer* from which the English is derived, originally used to express both things sacred *and* their opposite. Thus, Genet, by diametrically reversing all moral values and embracing evil while repudiating good, seeks to find God in the only places where he feels bourgeois society has not been able to drive Him out—that is, in the dark corners of crime, vice, and shame.

Walking the shores of Spain, begging, and stealing like some unholy Francis of Assisi, Genet blasphemously but innocently worships God in the rising sun, and later takes upon himself the burden for the deliverance of smugglers—indeed, for the criminals and outlaws of the whole world—allowing a Spanish coast guard to pederize him in a shack by the sea:

> San Fernando is on the sea. I decided to get to Cadiz, which is built right on the water, though connected to the mainland by a very long jetty. It was evening when I started. Before me were the high salt pyramids of the San Fernando marshes, and farther off, in the sea, silhouetted by the setting sun, a city of domes and minarets. At the outermost point of western soil, I suddenly had before me the synthesis of the Orient. For the first time in my life I neglected a human being for a thing. I forgot Stilitano.
>
> In order to keep alive, I would go to the port early in the morning, to the pescatoria, where the fishermen always throw from their boats a few fish caught the night before. All beggars are familiar with this practice. Instead of going, as in Malaga, to cook them on the fire of the other tramps, I went back alone, to the middle of the rocks overlooking Porto Reale. The sun would be rising when my fish were cooked. I almost always ate them without bread or salt. Standing up, or lying among

the rocks, or sitting on them, at the easternmost point of the island, facing the mainland, I was the first man lit up and warmed by the first ray, which was itself the first manifestation of life. I had gathered the fish on the wharves in the darkness. It was still dark when I reached my rocks. The coming of the sun overwhelmed me. I worshipped it. A kind of sly intimacy developed between us. I honored it, though without, to be sure, any complicated ritual; it would not have occurred to me to ape the primitives, but I know that this star became my god. It was within my body that it rose, continued its curve and completed it. If I saw it in the sky of the astronomers, I did so because it was the bold projection there of the one I preserved within myself. Perhaps I even confused it in some obscure way with the vanished Stilitano, [a notorious criminal, pimp, and lover of his].

Every two or three miles along the coast of Spain the coast-guards have put up little sheds overlooking the sea. One night someone entered the shed where I had lain down to sleep. When I walked miserably along in the rain and wind, the tiniest crag, the most meager shelter became habitable. I would sometimes adorn it with an artful comfort drawn from what was peculiar to it: a box in the theater, the chapel of a cemetery, a cave, an abandoned quarry, a freight-car and so on. Obsessed by the idea of a home, I would embellish, in thought, and in keeping with its own architecture, the one I had just chosen. While everything was being denied me, I would wish I were made for the fluting of the fake columns that ornament facades, for the caryatids, the balconies, the stone, for the heavy bourgeois assurance which these things express.

"I shall have to love and cherish them," I would tell myself. "I shall have to belong to them so that they may belong to me and that the order which they support may be mine."

Alas, I was not yet meant for them. Everything set me apart from them and prevented this love. I lacked a taste for earthly happiness. Now, when

I am rich but weary, I ask Lucien to take my place.

All doubled up, wrapped in my coat so as to keep out the ocean dampness, I forgot my body and its fatigue by imagining details which would make the cane and reed hut a perfect dwelling, built expressly for the man I became in a few seconds, so that my soul might be in perfect harmony with the site—sea, sky, rocks and heaths—and the fragility of the structure. A man stumbled against me. He swore. I was no longer afraid at night. Quite the contrary. It was a coast-guard of about thirty. Armed with his rifle, he was on the lookout for the fishermen and sailors who engaged in smuggling between Morocco and Spain. He wanted to put me out; then, turning his flashlight on my face and seeing that I was young, he told me to stay. I shared his supper (bread, olives and a few herrings) and I drank some wine. We talked for a while and then he began to caress me. He told me that he was Andalusian. I don't remember whether he was good-looking. The water could be seen through the opening. We heard oars striking the water and voices speaking, but were unable to see any boat. He knew he ought to leave, but my caresses grew more artful. He couldn't tear himself away; the smugglers must have landed peacefully.

In submitting to the whims of the coast-guard I was obeying a dominating order which it was impossible not to serve, namely, the Police. For a moment I was no longer a hungry, ragged vagabond whom dogs and children chased away, nor was I the bold thief flouting the cops, but rather the favorite mistress who, beneath a starry sky, soothes the conqueror. When I realized that it was up to me whether or not the smugglers landed safely, I felt responsible not only for them but for all outlaws. I was being watched elsewhere and I could not back out. Pride sustained me. After all, since I held back the guard by feigning love, I shall hold him back more surely, I said to myself, if my love is more potent, and, unable to do better, I loved him with all my might. I granted him the loveliest of

my nights. Not so that he might be happy but that
I might take upon myself—and deliver him from—
his own ignominy.

De Sade and Genet, perhaps more than any other
writers, combine within their works the most cogent
philosophical arguments and the most patent rationalizations; the highest moral standards, and the lowest im-
moralities; and in Genet's case, besides these, the
paradox of the most chaste and the most carnal sentiments.

As far as Genet is concerned, it seems obvious that in
spite of all his obscenities he is a purist at heart, and in
his moral demands, in spite of his flagrant blasphemies,
"more" popish than the Pope." In an extraordinarily interesting interview with *Playboy* (April 1964), he
said, with reference to the erotic aspects of some of his
writings, "I now think that if my books arouse readers
sexually, they're badly written, because the poetic emotion should be so strong that no reader is moved sexually. In so far as my books are pornographic, I don't
reject them. I simply say that I lacked grace."

His words are well worth pondering: They express
both a deep truth and a dangerous over-simplification.
The truth of his statement lies, we would think, in the
fact that in a *pure work of art*, such as a poem or a
painting, the aesthetic qualities should be such as to
submerge *any* emotional or ideological appeal (not just
the erotic one) in the greater involvement in the purity
and perfection of its form, (a point of view, which has,
in the fine arts, led from representational to abstract art
where the concern is solely with forms, texture, color,
space, and motion, but no longer with any kind of idea-
tional content as such). To that extent, Genet—who,
incidentally, is moving more and more into the direction
of "pure" art and away from ideological content—is entirely correct.

Where he is wrong (in our view) is that not all literature and art is "pure," in the sense of art for art's sake,
without concern for the communication of ideas or emo-

tions. For the moment that literature or the arts concern themselves with the communication of ideological or emotional content (and his own earlier writings certainly do just that), it is precisely the effectiveness of such communication that distinguishes good from bad art, and, particularly, good from bad writing. And it does not seem logical that an appeal to *erotic* feeling should be any less "artistic" than, say, an appeal to the emotion of pity, awe, derision, sympathy, or any other feeling. We would, however, concede that in geninue erotic art or literature—as contrasted with pornography—the "raw" sexual ideas and images are aesthetically transformed or elaborated beyond the mere physical realities, and are presented within an ideological or emotional context which transcends any interest in the simple reproduction of physical reality. It would, however, be a mistake to assume that such erotic works of art or writing are, for that reason, of necessity less stimulating sexually than, for instance, a straight-forward pornographic photograph or a plain literal description of sexual activities— in fact, quite the opposite can be the case!

With regard to de Sade's and Genet's writings, it also becomes plain how socially dangerous the suppression of erotic literature can be. For, more often than one might expect, erotic writings do contain worthwhile ideas and points of view, the communication of which is prevented by the suppression of these writings. One may even say that some writers (and artists), and this is particularly true for de Sade, expressly employed the description of sexual activities as a means of social protest, knowing full well how unacceptable precisely these ideas are to bourgeois morality. In view of the continuing intensity of feeling on these matters, it is therefore more than likely that we will see a great deal more of erotic shock-art and literature until a more rational approach to sexuality and human relations renders such protest unnecessary and obsolete.

AUTOBIOGRAPHICAL EROTICA

Autobiographical erotica can be roughly divided into two main categories: *straight-forward autobiography* or reportage (such as Samuel Pepsy's diary, *My Secret Life* by the unknown English Casanova, or even the *Memoirs* of Casanova de Seingalt which are already somewhat fictionalized) and *autobiographical fiction,* of which Henry Miller's writings are the outstanding example.

Among Miller's writings, some are again more autobiographical than others, and some more erotic than the rest. But it appears that those of his works which are the most autobiographical are also the ones with the strongest erotic content (e.g., the *Nexus, Plexus, Sexus* series and his *Quiet Days at Clichy*). There is good reason for this: in an interview with the British trade magazine *Books and Bookmen* (April 1963), Miller explained, in reply to a question as to why there was so much sex in his books: "That's hard to answer. You know, I think I have written as much of what my hostile critics call 'flapdoodle'—that is, metaphysical nonsense —as I have about sex. Only they choose to look at the sex. No, I can't answer that question, except to say that it's played a great part in my life. *I've led a good rich sexual life, and I don't see why it should be left out.*" (Italics ours).

We do not here want to go further into a detailed analysis of Miller's erotic writings, save to point out again that the feature by which they distinguish themselves, to our mind, from those of other writers, is their brutally honest and often unsparing self-revelatory character. It is in this quality of *self-revelation* that we see in Miller a parallel to the religious spirit in Genet's early writings: both are admittedly purging their souls by this sort of public confession, thereby throwing themselves, as it were, on the judgment of their fellow men, but also putting on *them* the burden for throwing the first stone.

In Miller, moreover, the quality of self-revelation goes hand in hand with a more general revelation of human nature in all its weakness, and often in all its untarnished sordidness, especially in the area of sex. And yet, Miller never for one moment engages in this sort of merciless reportage of human vulgarity without putting himself right into the unflattering picture. Nor is his documentary style ever accompanied by a spirit of accusation or moral condemnation; rather, it seems to be meant as a plea for human understanding and sympathy, even with the all-too humanly obscene in his characters' attitudes and behavior.

EROTIC REALISM

Many, and very likely the most important, works of erotica may in the future be produced by women. We have an example of this sort of writing in the unpublished manuscript of a well-known American authoress. The story, entitled *Life in Provincetown,* deals frankly with a series of sexual relations between various people in the locality in which it is set (a sort of *Peyton Place,* but focusing much more directly on the erotic aspects of these relationships than on the sociology of a hypocritical, sex-obsessed suburbia).

In the passage which we are about to quote, a Portuguese sailor, living in a room next to that of an unattached girl, has overheard her making love to a succession of men. He has been highly stimulated by these nocturnal scenes, and has been participating in them in fantasy, putting himself in the place of the other men, almost to the point of hallucination. However, what deeply disturbs him about this girl's love-making is the fact that invariably, at the height of passion, she begins to laugh hysterically and derisively, as if to humiliate her casual lovers at the very acme of their supposed sexual conquest of her.

It is the taunt of this defying laughter which the sailor, who has otherwise no contact with the girl, sets out to meet and conquer, as if he represented all challenged male virility and she all frigid femaleness. So personally has this stranger taken the implied affront to his masculinity, that he is determined, if need be, to kill her in his embrace rather than have her emasculate him in the same manner as he has heard her finish his luckless predecessors.

The Portuguese entered her studio, looking very tall and very dark, filling the room with his vivid and potent presence. The woman's mouth could be seen in the darkness. He lit a candle, and in its flickering light she smiled at him . . . it was all he could do not to throw himself upon her. Her mouth was so inviting, so swollen . . . as if for kissing.

He sat near her bed and they talked. But as they talked she fell asleep, and the Portuguese was able to look at her. Her dark hair was all over the pillow, a dark pillow all around her. Even in the candle light her mouth shone red, and it was half open like a flame.

The Portuguese approached her and gave her a kiss. She awakened and put her arms around him. He kissed her again. The mouth melted under his strong lips. It was warm and soft and cushioned, as no mouth he had ever tasted.

It yielded to his kiss, opened. The tips of two tongues met. Her breasts were so hard he felt them against his chest as he kissed her.

What he felt was that he wanted to do something to her that no other man had done, he did not want her to laugh as she had laughed for the others, he wanted to experience something new, and he did not know what it would be.

The minute she laughed she would be the woman all men could possess, and he did not want this. He continued to kiss her and think about it. Something she had not felt yet, laughed at, with pleasure. What new pleasure could he give her?

The story of the boy haunted him. He wanted to frighten her. Above all he wanted her not to laugh, as she had laughed for the other men. The way she abandoned her mouth made him hate her . . .

the way she closed her eyes. She closed her eyes and opened her mouth as if any man, any mouth or penis could please her at the moment.

She was in a trance. Soon she would begin to laugh hoarsely and suggestively if he touched her. First he gripped her backside fiercely, with his two hands, and brought her up against him and she felt his virility. It was of such strength and power that as she felt it first against her hair, before it penetrated her, she gasped at the electric touch of it.

He buried his mouth deeper into hers, feeling every nook under her lips, under tongue, feeling her tongue licking at him, flung back at his tongue each time, like a palpitation and vibration between them.

He did not caress her. He pushed himself straight inside of her, firmly, powerfully and then lay still. She had never been so well filled, every nook of her flesh filled by this strong virility, and it seemed to her that once inside of her it stretched a little more, pushed the walls of her soft flesh, installed itself leisurely, for good.

That was what she loved, the way he nestled inside of her, so completely as if to stay. She could enjoy him leisurely too. She loved this. The feel of the hard sex inside of her, not moving, nestled there, and only vibrating when she contracted to feel it more.

Imperceptibly at times he withdrew, just slightly, as if to make room for the contractions which pressed him, and lured him back into the depths of her.

She did not laugh. She was strangely silent. The quietness with which he entered her, without caresses, and the quietness with which he lay inside her, as if to feel every motion and ripple of her flesh around his sex. The quietness and hardness of his penis filling her completely, so that when the womb began to breathe, as it were, inhaling and exhaling there in the dark, to envelop him, encompass him and then open like a mouth and close again, she felt a quiet long drawn out pleasure which made her silent.

He was enjoying reaching into the depths of her and not moving, not giving her an active pleasure. They lay entangled, his naked body the whole length of her, and she flung back, legs apart, and eyes closed, and their mouths together.

Then the pleasure was too much for her, she wanted to move, to push against him, to feel him deeper, to cling and rub against him, but he prevented her from doing so, with such a strength of his powerful sailor muscles that she was paralyzed. Without moving inside of her, his bigness and hardness stirred her.

She continued to lick and press and caress him with her womb, trying to engulf him more, trying to move more inside of herself since he did not let her move her body.

Her body he kept pinned and paralyzed. Then as she contracted and moved, she felt her pleasure increasing, and she was nearing her paroxysm, and out of her closed mouth there struggled to escape some guttural sound, from the depths of her belly, that would have been laughter of pleasure if he had permitted it, but he suddenly flung his two hands around her neck and whispered fiercely: "If you laugh I will strangle you!"

A strange fear came into her eyes, the sounds of pleasure died instantly, but she could not stop the mounting, invading pleasure, like some molton magical lava beginning to pour through her veins, inflaming her flesh, and he kept his hands around her throat, and she thought that her pleasure was all that mattered, she felt suddenly like the boy that she must have her ultimate pleasure for she could not control it, the violence with which it ran through her veins and sought to explode in her.

In her fear, she was immobilized, yet she continued to contract in her womb and he felt this, and it gave her pleasure to see that pleasure was getting hold of his body too and that he might be forced to release his grip on her throat, but he did not release it, he tightened it, and she experienced a real and absolute fear then, that in his pleasure he might strangle her, for his pleasure was mixed with hatred, hatred to think she could so easily be made to feel this joy, responding to it like a perfect animal, not to him alone but to all ... to any man with a mouth to kiss and an erect penis ...

In spite of the fear and with the fear there came a surcharged, tense joy in her, running through all her veins, tickling the soles of her feet, running up along the inside of her legs, touching off the backside and warming it, touching the tips of the breasts as if he were caressing her, nothing but this wine of desire coursing now all inside of her and the pain of his hands on her neck could not stop it, it increased.

If she had laughed obscenely with her pleasure he would have tightened his hands, perhaps strangled her. But instead of laughing, as her pleasure was so excruciating and as he did not move and therefore did not bring it to an end, but prolonged the excruciating suspense, a strange long whining sound came from her as if she were in pain, a deep animal whine which he loved and which then threw him with new fervor on her and loosened his hands and then he moved, he moved in all directions, like a tourniquet, round and round not stopping, as if he would plough her completely and absolutely, leaving no corner untouched, and she moaned, she did not laugh, she moaned in the grip of such a deep joy that she wept. ...

The quoted passage is indicative of the difference in experience and description of the sexual act as reflected in the erotica written by women, compared to those of men. We shall examine this difference at greater length elsewhere (*The Sexually Responsive Woman,* Grove Press, New York, 1964); it is sufficient here to point out that, both in the communication of the physical sex experience, as well as in its emotional context, erotica written by women are an especially rich source of information on many little understood aspects of the female sex response. It is also self-evident from the single example given that erotica contributed by women show a profuse sensuality, in many respects surpassing that generally communicated by male writers, and with the additional advantage that such works lack the male writer's tendency toward coarseness of expression.

EROTIC WIT AND HUMOR

As previously stated, we expect erotic wit and humor to represent a major branch among the erotica of tomorrow, and that American writers will contribute a large share to this amusing and fascinating type of literature. This is all the more to be expected since there exists in America, a widespread popular appreciation of this type of work, as well as a tradition of robust erotic humor, of which Mark Twain's "1601" and his meditations on "The Science of Onanism", and some of Benjamin Franklin's writings are a clear indication.

The first example which we would like to cite is a story entitled *Paula the Piquose,* by a talented American ex-patriate writer and painter, living in Paris. It is taken from a collection of similar stories under the collective title *The Fetish Crowd,* published by Olympia Press under the pseudonym Akbar del Piombo, evidently chosen to make fun of the fantastic and often exotic pseudonyms assumed by the authors of hard core pornography.

This entire collection is one great and brilliant spoof on pornography, and at the same time a satire of our sex-ridden society. It is generally so well written and witty that it was difficult to decide on a representative sample. We have finally decided on the passage given below, not because it is funnier or better done than any of the others, but simply because it constitutes a parody on sex education which is, in many respects, a direct parallel to English biologist and writer Alex Comfort's

hilariously funny *Come Out To Play*. We quote now
from *Paula the Piquose*:

The last thing one would have expected on an
occasion of this sort was a public lecture. Yet, in-
congruous as it seems, in the adjacent room that is
exactly what was taking place. Intrigued by the
novelty of the thing, I entered and took my place
at the end of the hall. There were in all about twenty or so in the audience, and mostly women. . . . At
the head of the room was a large screen and from
time to time the images shifted, coming from a tiny
projection machine in the rear. The lecturer was a
young female, wearing, appropriately, horn-rimmed
glasses and wielding a long stick which she used to
point out on the diagrams the elements she wanted
to elaborate in her speech.

". . . and the most important of all are the testicles. In the average ejaculation, there are from
sixty to one hundred million sperm cells. This virile
apparatus is contained in a sack hung outside the
body which is called the scrotum."

On the screen there flashed a giant-size version
of the "male organ" cut in a cross-section view
which showed the canals leading to the hanging
shaft duly labeled and numbered.

"Furthermore," she went on, "from six to ten
billion of these sperm cells are produced in one
day alone. The implication is obvious as you can all
see, that the average man is capable, physically, of
from sixty to one hundred ejaculations a day!"

She looked at her audience with a glow of
triumph and challenge. A chorus of sighs went up
from the female contingent . . . The figure was indeed staggering.

"Unfortunately," and she sighed herself, "few
men are aware of their real potential, and give but
a ludicrous proportion of this generous endow-
ment. But, we shall not linger on this matter, and
proceed to the female organ."

The screen now revealed a gigantic illustration
of the female gland. From the cervix at the head

of the uterus, one followed the canal downward into the vagina and thence to the labia surmounted by an intriguing little organ called the clitoris.

"The clitoris is the very sexual center of the female and is capable of erection much like the penis. However, it is an uncomfortable fact that the female orifice is located where it is, that is, hygenically speaking. It is so placed as to be between two orifices of excretion, and this means that the genital area must be kept under continual surveillance."

She gave a few hints about the proper washing and care of the vagina and then hurried on to the more exciting part of her lesson, actual copulation.

"We in the Occident have a rather limited knowledge and practice in the fine art of sexual intercourse . . .

"In the Orient, custom and ancient knowledge have handed down a variety and number of positions which far surpass our limited and hurried habits. We generally content ourselves with the classic coupling in which the woman lies on her back with her legs widespread."

The (vagina) vanished from the screen and was replaced by a provocative view of a pair of outstretched legs leading to the promontory of assault. This was followed immediately by a side view of the same position, seen in cross-section.

"We shall see exactly what happens when the penis enters the vagina in this 'normal' position."

The screen went black as the operator shut off the slide-projector to turn on a motion picture machine alongside.

Almost the same scene was reproduced but this time with the more convincing illusion of movement. A one hundred times life-size male organ appeared in full erection. Everyone moved forward in their seats, and cries of awe went up at the impressive vision. Next appeared the projective hairs of the waiting (vagina). The penis moved slowly forward, restraining its straining muscles and nerves in abeyance, showing a great discipline on the part of its owner. The (vagina) lay there in readiness, one almost felt in bated breath, anxious, trembling with anticipation . . .

Slowly, irrevocably, like some strange primeval monster, it moved across the screen. The scrotum hung down with its arsenal of sperm ready to send up its sixty to one hundred million sperm-cell load . . . No one spoke nor coughed; a peculiar, tense, hush fell over the audience and even the lecturer herself fell silent, lost in the contemplation of the hypnotic scene. [There follows a straightforward description of the male organ entering the vagina.]

"What you have just witnesed may be properly called the 'simple' or 'direct' entry. It was accomplished with 'brio,' for the performers are by no means amateurs. However simple it may have seemed, I dare any of you to accomplish this entry with an equal ease of performance."

In the darkness her eyeglasses reflected back at her listeners, in scorn, like the eyes of an owl. Her attitude was beginning to grate me. What the hell, she sounds like she's the only one in the world who knows how . . . [There follows a description of the activity on the screen]. If she thought she was the only one who knew about the "brio" of the performers, I was going to show her a trick or two which I didn't learn in any classroom.

The darkness of the room and the intense absorption of her audience afforded me perfect cover to steal quietly round to where she was standing. I came up directly behind her and stood still to make sure I hadn't been observed. But she herself was gazing up in fascination at the comings and goings of the great organs on the screen. I prepared myself for the daring coup . . . Her skirt was short and was no problem to lift. What was difficult was to lift it so that she would not feel it. In this I was again aided by her close attention to the movie. All that stood between me and her was a thin pair of lace panties.

Just when I was about to grab her she started again to talk. My heart beat fast for I was sure I would be discovered. But by an incredible convergence of circumstances, she altered her position, while speaking, unconsciously spreading her legs apart, no doubt in a subconscious reaction to the stimuli of her own discourse.

"You can see how the movement is controlled, regular and not at all jerky. It is just this kind of movement which gives the utmost sensations."

You don't say, I thought to myself with a satanic smile. I held the skirt up with one hand, and with the other took an edge of the panties, right by a fringe of lace, and as quietly as a mouse, moved it to one side ... I caught her right in the middle of a sentence ... and the rest of her phrase whined out like a caterwaul. In an ordinary lecture an audience would have been startled out of its wits at such an unexpected break, but here no one noticed it, and if they did, it no doubt fit in beautifully with the erotic trance in which they were.

We do not intend to quote from any further examples of erotic wit and humor. The form does not lend itself readily to quotation by excerpt, half a joke being worse than useless in attempting to make a point. Fortunately an excellent example of satirical erotic fantasy has now been published in America and can be read in its entirety. We refer, of course, to *Candy*, by Terry Southerland, (Putnam, New York) an outrageous spoof on the sexual hypocrisies that plague the Western world. Candy, a wide-eyed, protected, innocent, generously all-giving sophomore, becomes involved in one episode after another of impossibly ridiculous vulgarity wherein her virtue is assaulted in bizarre fashion by a procession of characters whose tastes are, to say the least, peculiar. Throughout, however, Candy maintains her air of shining naïveté, unblemished by the seamiest of realities and apparently unaware that anything untoward is taking place even while she girlishly cooperates in the wildest sexual adventures.

Candy is a projection, expressed in the extreme terms which are a function of satire, of the ambivalent feelings which demand that the adult population behave sexually in ways totally at variance with their professed attitudes. By battering at hypocrisy it serves an enormously useful function; by forcing the confrontation of myth with reality, it performs a service well beyond its lightly worn cloak of humor.

Our short survey of erotica of the future can obviously lay no claim to completeness or finality. There is, for instance, the long neglected area of the erotic theater, popular in the eighteenth century among the upper classes of France, of which we have in the English language two outstanding examples: the Restoration play *Sodom,* probably by the notorious Earl of Rochester, long-time favorite of King Charles II; and the nineteenth century farce, *Harlequin, Prince Cherrytop,* of uncertain authorship. Very little has since been written in this vein, unless we include Genet's superbly done and highly philosophical play, *The Balcony.* But it is possible that there may some day be a revival of erotica in the theatre, or that it may find its continuation in the so-called "musicals," which undoubtedly enjoy their vast popularity because of their frank erotic appeal.

As far as we are concerned, we welcome what we believe to be a present trend toward quality erotica of all types. It seems fairly obvious that they fufill a useful and needful function in the arts and literature, and there is every reason to assume that they will, in the long run, raise the general standard of erotica. In other words, we believe that good erotica will have a tendency to drive out bad erotica. But this can take place only if the relaxation of censorship encourages writers and artists of real talent and aesthetic sense to produce such quality erotica, instead of leaving the field to third-grade hack writers.

At the same time, we would like to repeat our warning with regard to the dictation of taste by means of the law. For, while greater freedom will undoubtedly result in the production of better erotica, there is no reason to assume that everybody will suddenly appreciate only the best in erotic art and literature (just as not everybody appreciates the best in wines, food, fashions, home furnishings, industrial design or other areas involving "taste"). But to advocate the banning of some erotica because it is not a literary or artistic triumph is to assume to oneself the role of arbiter in taste—an intellectual snobbery which is presumptuous. There is no reason why that educated and enlightened segment of society which approves and enjoys *Lady Chatterley's Lover,* for instance, should be privileged beyond any other part of the population. In a free society, we feel, all tastes should enjoy equal protection before the law.

Nor is it the case, as we have previously pointed out, that the least artistic, that is, the least well written books, or the most poorly executed pictures (nor yet the most "realistic" writings and pictures) are necessarily those with the strongest erotic appeal to everybody. Here again, quality—that is, artistic or literary merit—must not be made the basis of legal decisions with regard to censorship. Instead, we suggest that as long as *any* form of literary and artistic censorship still exists, the hard core pornography test alone be applied, and all considerations of taste and quality be left to non-coercive means of public education. If that is done, we have no doubt that in the long run, a free, competitive market in erotica will result in the same general raising of the artistic standards as similarly free competition in other fields has tended to raise the quality of the products concerned. More legislation, on the other hand, and a reversal to stricter controls and censorship can, in our opinion, only result in the continued suppression of quality erotica, while the illegal traffic in the worst forms of hard core pornography continues unabated.

In view of these facts, there seems to us, therefore, no reasonable alternative: sooner or later society must take the plunge and abandon *all* forms of literary and artistic censorship for adults. When this occurs there will follow, we predict, a gradual *decline* in the public interest in erotica, and especially in hard core pornography. For it is axiomatic that the artificial taboo on the frank expressions of sexual interests tends to create an equally artificial demand for precisely that which is forbidden. On the other hand, all experience and reason point to the conclusion that the abolition of sexual censorship for adults, together with a general relaxation of sexual taboos, will diminish rather than increase the inordinate or "prurient" interest in sex which the law wishes to curb and which is, needless to say, also the hidden dynamism in the production and consumption of hard core pornograhy.

A POSTSCRIPT TO "THE PSYCHOLOGICAL EFFECTS OF EROTIC LITERATURE"

It is five years since the original edition of this book was first published. Since then, there has been no significant new research from any quarter into the psychological effects of erotic literature and pictorial representations. However, what additional scientific opinion has been voiced on the subject only supports our own impression that there is little, if any, positive correlation between the reading of erotic material (or the viewing of pictorial material) and overt anti-social acts. Thus, for instance, we read from a statement by Edwin J. Lucas, director of the Society for the Prevention of Crime: "I am unaware of the existence of any scientifically established causal relationship between the reading of books and delinquency. It is my feeling that efforts to link the two are an extension of the archaic impulse by which, through the ages, witchcraft, evil spirits, and other superstitious beliefs have in turn been blamed for anti-social behavior."

Mr. Keating, chairman of the Citizens for Decent Literature Committee, is reported to have said that they get a lot of mail indicating that people have picked up nudist magazines and found them filled with the semen from boys who have masturbated on the pictures. Granting that this were true, it is still not anti-social behavior; it is not hostile, it hurts no one, least of all the boys who have used auto-erotic outlets as a harmless way of releasing sexual energy.

It hardly needs stating that, in the efforts of the censors, scientific considerations and objective reasoning play no part whatsoever. Their arguments are never based on an appeal to reason but rather on conditioned prejudice and unquestioningly accepted values, while their aggressive and intolerant tactics make it necessary to protect the constitutional freedoms, as well as the personal safety and liberty of those segments of the community holding differing views.

In fact, it would be well to study not only the effects of erotica, but also the psychology of the censor, in order to arrive at a better understanding of the issues at stake. For although any reasonable evidence we have to date indicates that there is no correlation between the study of erotica and overt anti-social behavior, it would appear that there is a connection between the study of erotica and the psychopathology of censorship. In this connection, Dr. Benjamin Karpman, Chief Psychotherapist of St. Elizabeth's Hospital in Washington, D. C., has said (concerning the morbid, "prurient," interest of some individuals in pornographic materials): "This interest in obscenity—pornophilia—may take another direction . . . It may be covered up by a reaction formation. The interest may be denied by bitter opposition to all forms of obscenity, the same as a condemnation and attack against homosexuals can cover up latent or unconscious interest in it; that is, it may cover up latent homosexuality. Crusading against obscenity has an unconscious interest at its base."

Or, as Mr. John Chandos writes in his excellent study *To Deprave and Corrupt*: "They [a certain section of newly respectable middle-class] developed a veritable obsession with sin, especially sexual sin, and since the only way they could with propriety maintain constant contact with the forbidden pleasure was by censoring its presence in others, they nosed out sex with an industry as indefatigable as it was ingenious . . ."

It seems clear that the mind of the censor is particularly susceptible to the influence of erotic material and easily upset by it. Is is by no means as clear what the effects of erotica might be on the rest of the population. But in this regard, we believe we can at least make the following observation: we suggest that erotica are not obnoxious to the "average", "normal" person, that the courts are quite correct in their view that perfectly nice, normal and mature people could and indeed frequently do appreciate a wide variety of deliberately erotic material at many different social levels, and not excluding hard core pornography.

Focusing for reasons of precision on hard core pornography, we would say that it has a wide appeal, not in sipte of, but precisely because of its frequent and admitted vulgarity. In order to understand this seemingly paradoxical situation, one must keep in mind certain facts about the nature of this type of material upon which we have already touched in our discussion of the *cathartic* quality of the more vulgar types of erotica. To this we would now like to add a definition of pornography as offered by Maurice Girodias, head of embattled Olympia Press in Paris: "What is known as pornography is a simple and elementary reaction against an age-old habit of mental suppression, of deliberately conditioned ignorance of 'the facts of life.' True, pornography is a very crude and excessive form of protest—but the very intensity of the protest proves that it is not gratuitous, and that there is a deep and general need for free expression which is still far from being gratified. In other words, contrary to current belief, pornography is simply a consequence of censorship. Suppress censorship and pornography will disappear."

In fact, Mr. Girodias is saying in his own way very much the same thing we have said in our discussion of the psychological effects of erotic literature; namely, that one of its functions seems to be that of acting as a relatively harmless way of defying (at least in fantasy) the unreasonable and unrealistic sexual taboos of society. It goes without saying that these taboos frequently concern not only certain sexual activities, but also the vernacular verbal symbols or common expressions for these activities and for the sexual organs themselves.

Hard core pornography therefore, offers to the "average," "normal" person one of the few mechanisms of release from these taboos, and allows him to participate in fantasy in equally forbidden sexual activities from which in reality he would probably shrink. If the need for such defiance of overly strict cultural taboos is then said to be "infantile" and "immature," such judgment, though perhaps quite valid in the absolute sense, must be tempered by the recognition that these manifestations of "immaturity" are provoked by immature or pathological aspects of the culture itself.

BIBLIOGRAPHY

1. *Ananga-Ranga,* (Burton, R. F., transl.) The secret places of the human body. Known as the Ananga-Ranga, or the Hindu art of love. Priv. print. 1935. (orig. 12th cent. A.D.?).

2. Anon., *The Autobiography of a Flea.* London & New York: The Erotica Biblion Society, 1901.

3. Anon., *The Confessions of Lady Beatrice. Showing how she kept the XIth Commandment "Thou shalt not be found out."* London & New York: The Erotica Biblion Society, n.d.

4. Anon., *Fay and Her Boy Friend.* n.d.

5. Anon., *The Lascivious Hypocrite,* or, *The Triumphs of Vice.* A free translation of *Le Tartuffe Libertin.* "Done at Cythera: By the Keeper of the Temple." (MDCCXC ?)

6. Anon., *Lustful Stories.* London & New York: The Erotica Biblion Society, 1901.

7. Anon., *Memoirs of a Russian Princess, Gleaned from her Secret Diary—Compiled, noted and arranged by Katoumbah Pasha* (pseudon.). Paris: Erotik Biblion Societé, n.d.

8. Anon. (Dr. Mortimer R., pseudon), *Nelly,* or *Confessions of a Doctor.* Paris & London: n.d.

9. Anon., *The New Ladies' Tickler,* or *The Adventures of Lady Lovesport and The Audacious Harry.* Paris & London: n.d.

10. Anon., *The Oxford Professor. In which L. Erectus Mentulus, Ph.D., late of Oxford College, is taken further in the narration of his adventures and misadventures, erotic, alcoholic, and otherwise; not to mention a choice accompaniment of drolleries, notes and excursi of one sort or another, metaphysical & also miscellaneously edifying and entertaining.* "Done By The Hand Of The Author Into a Manuscript at Natchitoches, Louisiana." n.d.

11. Anon. (Clement, G., pseudon.), *The Strange Cult*. Priv. Print., n.d.

12. *Antiquarian Bookman,* December 1, 1958.

13. Aretino, P. (Conrad, H., transl.), *Die Gespräche des göttlichen Pietro Aretino*. 2v. Leipzig: Inselverlag, 1903 (orig. 1535-1536?).

14. Arieti, S., *Interpretation of Schizophrenia*. New York: R. Brunner, Inc., 1955.

15. Ashbee, H. W. (Pisanus Fraxi, pseudon.), *Index Librorum Prohibitorum: Being Notes, Bio- Biblio- Icono-graphical and Critical on Curious and Uncommon Books*. London: priv. print., 1877.

16. Beauvoir, S. de (Parshley, H. M., transl.), *The Second Sex*. New York: Alfred A. Knopf, 1953.

17. Bettelheim, B., *Love Is Not Enough, The Treatment of Emotionally Disturbed Children*. Glencoe, Ill.: The Free Press, 1950.

18. *Bilder-Lexikon* (Schidrowitz, L., ed.), *1. Kulturgeschichte. 2. Literatur und Kunst. 3. Sexualwissenschaft. 4. Ergänzungsband*. Wien & Leipzig: Verlag für Sexualforschung, 1928, 1929, 1930, 1931.

19. Binswanger, L., *Drei Formen Missglückten Daseins. Verstiegenheit, Verschrobenheit, Maniriertheit*. Tübingen: M. Niemeyer, 1956.

20. Bleuler, E., *Dementia Praecox,* or *The Group of Schizophrenias*. New York: International Universities Press, 1952.

21. Bloch, I., *Das Sexualleben unserer Zeit in seinen Beziehungen zur modernen Kultur*. Berlin: Louis Marcus Verlagsbuchhandlung, 1909.

22. Bloch, I., *Sex Life in England*. New York: The Panurge Press, 2v. in 1., 1934.

23. Brameld, T., *Philosophies of Education in Cultural Perspective*. New York: The Dryden Press, 1955.

24. Brantôme, P. de B. de. (Allinson, A. R., transl.), *Lives of Fair and Gallant Ladies*. Paris: Charles Carrington, 2v., 1901, 1902 (orig. 16th Cent., ed. 1, 1666).

25. Brody, E. B. and Redlich, F. C., eds., *Psychotherapy with Schizophrenics. Monograph Series on Schizophrenia No. 3*. New York: International Universities Press, Inc., 1952.

26. Bourke, J. G., *Scatologic Rites of All Nations. A Dissertation upon the Employment of Excrementitious Remedial Agents in Religion, Therapeutics, Divination, Witchcraft, Love-Philters, etc., in all Parts of the Globe. Based Upon Original Notes and Personal Observation, and Upon Compilation From Over One Thousand Authorities*. New York: American Anthropological Society, 1934.

27. Calitri, C., *Strike Heaven On The Face*. New York: Crown Publishers, Inc., 1958.

28. Calverton, V. F. and Schmalhausen, S. D., eds., *Sex in Civilization*. New York: Macaulay, 1929.

29. Chesser, E., *Love Without Fear. How to achieve sex happiness in marriage*. New York: Roy, 1947.

30. Chideckel, M., *Female Sex Perversion; The Sexually Aberrated Woman as She Is*. New York: Eugenics Publishing Co., 1935.

31. Chorier, N., *The Dialogues of Luisa Sigea. (Aloisiae Sigeae Satyra Sotadica de arcanis Amoris et Veneris.)* (Transl. from the Latin Ms., dating ca. 1660, transl. anon.) Paris: Isidore Liseux, 3v., 1890.

32. Cory, D. W., *Homosexuality. A Cross-Cultural Approach*. New York: Julian Press, 1956.

33. Crawley, E. (Besterman, T., ed.), *The Mystic Rose. A Study of Primitive Marriage and of Primitive Thought in its bearing on Marriage*. New York: Boni & Liveright, 2v., 1927, ed. 2.

34. Day, D., *The Evolution of Love*. New York: The Dial Press, 1954.

35. Dubois-Desaulle, G. (A.F.N., transl. and ed.), *Bestiality. An Historical, Medical, Legal and Literary Study*. New York: Panurge Press, priv. print., 1933.

36. Ellis, A., *The American Sexual Tragedy*. New York: Twayne Publishers, 1954.

37. Ellis, A., *The Folklore of Sex*. New York: Charles Boni, 1951.

38. Ellis, H., *Studies in the Psychology of Sex*. New York: Random House, 6v. in 2, 1936.

39. Erikson, E. H., *Young Man Luther, A Study in Psychoanalysis and History*. New York: A. W. Norton & Co., 1958.

40. Federn, P. (Weiss, E., ed.), *Ego Psychology and the Psychoses*. New York: Basic Books, 1952.

41. Fellman, D., *The Censorship of Books. An address delivered at the annual meeting of the Association of American University Presses, Lincoln, Nebraska, May, 1957*. Madison, Wisc.: The University of Wisconsin Press, 1957.

42. Ferenczi, S. (Jones, E., transl.), *Sex in Psychoanalysis*. New York: Basic Books, 1950.

43. Fishbein, M. and Burgess, E. W., eds., *Successful Marriage*. Garden City, New York: Doubleday & Co., 1947.

44. Fleishman, S., Rosenwein, S. and Murrish, W. B. In the Supreme Court of the United States, October Term, 1956. No. 61, David S. Alberts, Appellant, vs. State of California, Respondent. Brief for the Appellant.

45. Flügel, J. C., *Man, Morals and Society. A Psycho-analytical Study*. London: G. Duckworth & Co., Ltd., 1945.

46. Flügel, J. C., *Studies in Feeling and Desire*. London: G. Duckworth & Co., Ltd., 1955.

47. Forel, O., *Einklang der Geschlechter, Sexuelle Fragen in unserer Zeit*. Zürich: Rascher Verlan, 1955.

48. Forel, A. H. (Marshall, C. F., transl.), *The Sexual Question. A Scientific, Psychological, Hygienic and Sociological Study*. Brooklyn, N. Y.: Physicians and Surgeons Book Co., 1922. (es German ed. 2. 1906.)

49. Foster, J. H., *Sex Variant Women in Literature. A Historical and Quantitative Study*. New York: Vantage Press, 1956.

50. Freud, S. (Brill, A. A., transl.), *Three Contributions to the Sexual Theory*. New York: Journal of Nervous & Mental Disease Publishing Co., 1910.

51. Freud, S., *Wit and its Relation to the Unconscious*. New York: Moffat, Yard & Co., 1917.

52. Fuchs, E., *1. Geschichte der erotischen Kunst. Das Zeitgeschichtliche Problem*. München: Albert Langen, n.d. (1908?)

53. Fuchs, E., *2. Geschichte der erotischen Kunst. Das individuelle Problem*. München: Albert Langen, n.d. (1923?)

54. Fuchs, E., *Illustrierte Sittengeschichte vom Mittelalter bis zur Gegenwart. 1. Renaissance. 2. Die Galante Zeit. 3. Das bürgerliche Zeitalter*. München: Albert Langen, 3v.: v. 1, 1909, v. 2, 1910, v. 3, 1912.

55. Fuchs, E., *Illustrierte Sittengeschichte vom Mittelalter bis zur Gegenwart, Ergänzungsband 1. Renaissance. Ergänzungsband 2. Die galante Zeit. 3. Das bürgerliche Zeitalter.* München: Albert Langen, 3v.: v.1, 1909, v.2, 1911, v.3, 1912.

56. Gandhi, M. K. (Desai, M., transl.), *An Autobiography of The Story of My Experiments With Truth.* Ahmedabad: Navajivan Publishing House, 1948.

57. Gichner, L. E., *Erotic Aspects of Hindu Sculpture.* U.S.A.: priv. print., 1949.

58. Gichner, L. E., *Erotic Aspects of Japanese Culture.* U.S.A.: priv. print., 1953.

59. Gichner, L. E., *Erotic Aspects of Chinese Culture.* U.S.A.: priv. print., 1957.

60. Ginzburg, R., (Reik, Th., Intro. Nathan, J., Pref.), *An Unhurried View of Erotica.* New York: The Helmsman Press, 1958.

61. Grant, V. W., *The Psychology of Sexual Emotion. The Basis of Selective Attraction.* New York, London, Toronto: Longmans, Green & Co., 1957.

62. Greenwald, H., *The Call Girl: A Psychoanalytic Study.* New York: Ballantine Books, Inc., 1958.

63. Guyon, R., (Flugel, J. C. and Ingeborg, transl. Haire, N., Intro. and notes), *The Ethics of Sexual Acts.* Garden City, N. Y.: Blue Ribbon Books, 1941.

64. Hall, R., (Ellis, H., comment.), *The Well of Loneliness.* New York: Covici, Friede, 1928.

65. Harris, F., *My Life and Loves.* v.1. Paris: Priv. print., 1922; v.2., v.3., The Obelisk Press, 1945; v.4., 1958; v.5., The Olympia Press, 1958.

66. Hirschfeld, M., *Sex in Human Relationships*. London: John Lane, 1935.

67. Hirschfeld, M., *Sexual Pathology. A Study of Derangements of the Sexual Instincts*. New York: Emerson Books, 1940. rev. ed.

68. Hirschfeld, M., *Sexual Anomalies. The Origins, Nature, and Treatment of Sexual Disorders*. New York: Emerson Books, 1948. rev. ed.

69. Hirschfeld, M. and Linsert, R., *Liebesmittel. Eine Darstellung der geschlechtlichen Reizmittel (Aphrodisiaca)*. Berlin: Man Verlag, 1930.

70. Jahoda, Marie, *The Impact of Literature: A Psychological Discussion of Some Assumptions in the Censorship Debate*. Research Center for Human Relations, New York University, N. Y., 1954.

71. Kinsey, A. C., Pomeroy, W. B. and Martin, C. E., *Sexual Behavior in the Human Male*. Philadelphia & London: W. B. Saunders Co., 1948.

72. Kinsey, A. C., Pomeroy, W. B., Martin, C. E. and Gebhard, P. H., *Sexual Behavior in the Human Female*. Philadelphia & London: W. B. Saunders Co., 1953.

73. Klein, Melanie, (Jones, E., Intro.) *Contributions to Psychoanalysis, 1921-1945*. London: The Hogarth Press, 1950.

74. Klein, Melanie, Heimann, P. and Money-Kyrle, R. E., ed. *New Directions in Psychoanalysis. The Significance of Infant Conflict in the Pattern of Adult Behavior*. London: Tavistock Publications, Ltd., 1955.

75. Knight, R. P., *A Discourse on the Worship of Priapus*. The Dilettanti Society, priv. print., for members only, n.d.

76. Knight, R. P. and Wright, T., *Sexual Symbolism. A History of Phallic Worship*. New York: Julian Press, 1957.

77. Kronhausen, E. and Phyllis, *Family Milieu Therapy, the Non-Institutional Treatment of Severe Emotional Disturbances.* Psychoanalysis, Vol. 5, No. 3, Fall, 1957.

78. Kronhausen, E. and Phyllis, *The Therapeutic Family—the Family's Role in Emotional Disturbance and Rehabilitation.* Marriage and Family Living, February, 1959.

79. Kronhausen, E. and Phyllis, *The Therapeutic Family—A Family Life approach to the Rehabilitation of the Emotionally Disturbed.* IInd International Congress for Psychiatry, Congress Report, Vol. III, pp. 75-79.

80. Kronhausen, E. and Phyllis, *The Smell of Love.* Esquire, August, 1958.

81. Kronhausen, E. and Phyllis, *Sweden—Modern Sex Pioneer.* Candida, Vol. 1, No. 3, 1959.

82. Kronhausen, E. and Phyllis, *Sex and Modern Youth.* Candida, Vol. 1, No. 3, 1959.

83. Lawrence, D. H., *Lady Chatterley's Lover.* Priv. print., 1928.

84. Lewinsohn, R. (Mayce, A., transl.), *A History of Sexual Customs.* New York: Harper & Bros., 1958.

85. Lindner, R., *Must You Conform?* New York & Toronto: Rinehart & Co., Inc., 1956.

86. Lindner, R., *Rebel Without A Cause.* New York: Grune & Stratton, Inc., 1944.

87. Lindner, R., *The Fifty Minute Hour.* New York & Toronto: Rinehart & Co., Inc., 1955.

88. Lipton, L., *The Holy Barbarians.* New York: Julian Messner, Inc., 1959.

89. London, L. S. and Caprio, F. S., *Sexual Deviations.* Washington, D. C.: Linacre Press, 1950.

90. Lorand, S. and Balint, M. eds., *Perversion—Psychodynamics and Therapy*. New York: Random House, 1956.

91. Machen, A., (transl.), *The Memoirs of Giacomo Casanova Di Seingalt*. London: Priv. print., The Casanova Society, 1922.

92. McKeon, R., Merton, R. K. and Gellhorn, W., *The Freedom to Read—Perspective and Program*. New York: R. R. Bowker Co. for: The National Book Committee, 1957.

93. McPartland, J., *Sex In Our Changing World*. New York: Rinehart & Co., 1947.

94. Malinowski, B., *The Sexual Life of Savages in Northwestern Melanesia*. New York: Halcyon House, 1929.

95. Mantegazza, P., (Alexander, H. transl., Robinson, V., ed.), *Physiology of Love*. New York: Eugenics Publishing Co., 1939.

96. Mantegazza, P., (Bruse, J., transl.), *Sexual Relations of Mankind*. New York: priv. print. Anthropological Press, 1932.

97. Maxey, W. de Ortega, *Man Is a Sexual Being*. Fresno, Cal.: Fabian Books Publications, 1958.

98. Mead, Margaret, *From the South Seas. Studies of Adolescence and Sex in Primitive Societies*. New York: William Morrow & Co., 1939.

99. Miller, H., (Nin, A. Pref.), *Tropic of Cancer*. Paris: The Obelisk Press, 1958.

100. Miller, H., *The World of Sex*. Paris: The Olympia Press, 1957.

101. Moravia, A., *Two Adolescents. The Stories of Agostino and Luca*. New York: Farrar, Straus and Co., 1950.

102. Murtagh, J. M. and Harris, Sara, *Cast the First Stone*. New York: McGraw-Hill Book Co., 1957.

103. Parsons, T. and Bales, R. F., *Family, Socialization and Interaction Process.* Glencoe, Ill.: The Free Press, 1955.

104. Pepys, S. (Wheatley, H. B., ed.),*The Diary of Samuel Pepys, M.A., F.R.S., Clerk of the Acts and Secretary to the Admiralty, Transcribed by the Rev. Mynors Bright, M.A. from Shorthand Manuscript in the Pepysian Library Magdalene College, Cambridge.* 2v., New York: Random House, n.d.

105. Pilpel, H. F. and Zavin, T., *Your Marriage and the Law.* New York & Toronto: Rinehart & Co., 1952.

106. Poggio, B., (Brandes, P. de, transl.), *Les Facèties de Pogge, Florentin.* Paris: Librarie Garnier Frères, 1919.

107. Rank, O., *Das Inzest-Motiv in Dichtung und Sage.* Leipzig: Franz Deuticke, 1912.

108. Rank, O., *The Trauma of Birth.* New York: Robert Brunner, 1952.

109. Redl, F. and Wineman, D., *Children Who Hate.* Glencoe, Ill.: The Free Press, 1951.

110. Reich, W., (Wolfe, T. P., transl.), *The Sexual Revolution. Toward A Self-Governing Character Structure.* New York: Orgone Institute Press, 1951.

111. Reik, T., *Psychology of Sex Relations.* New York & Toronto: Rinehart & Co., Inc., 1945.

112. Reik, T., Kronhausen, Phyllis and Kronhausen, E., *The Psychology of Sexual Relations. On Love-Making and Love-Feeling.* New Rochelle, N. Y.: a spoken recording by Helicon, 1958.

113. Robie, W. F., *The Art of Love.* New York: Eugenics Publishing Co., Inc., 1933.

114. Rosen, J. N., *Direct Analysis. Selected Papers.* New York: Grune and Stratton, 1953.

115. Rougemont, D. de-., (Belgion, M., transl.), *Love in the Western World*. Albert Saifer, 1940.

116. Russell, B., *Marriage and Morals*. New York: Horace Liveright, 1929.

117. Schilder, P., *Psychoanalysis, Man and Society*. New York: W. W. Norton & Co., 1951.

118. Scott, G. R., *Far Eastern Sex Life. An Anthropological, Ethnological and Sociological Study of the Love Relations, Marriage Rites and Home Life of the Oriental Peoples*. London: Gerald G. Swan, 1949.

119. Sechehaye, M., *La Realisation Symbolique*. Berne: Hans Huber, 1947.

120. Sechehaye, M., *A New Psychotherapy in Schizophrenia. Relief of Frustrations by Symbolic Realization*. New York & London: Grune and Stratton, 1956.

121. Smith, T. R., ed., *Poetica Erotica. A Collection of Rare and Curious Amatory Verse*. New York: Crown Publisher, 1927.

122. Sorokin, P. A., *The American Sex Revolution*. Boston: Porter Sargent, 1956.

123. Stekel, W., (Van Teslaar, J. S., transl.), *Sex and Dreams. The Language of Dreams*. Boston: Richard G. Badger, 1922.

124. Stekel, W., (Brink, L., transl.), *Sadism and Masochism*. New York: Liveright Publishing Corp., 2v., 1922.

125. Stekel, W., (Parker, S., transl.), *Sexual Aberrations*. New York: Liveright Publishing Corp., 2v. in 1, 1952.

126. Stekel, W., (Van Teslaar, J. S., transl.), *Auto-Eroticism. A Psychiatric Study of Onanism and Neurosis*. New York: Liveright Publishing Corp., 1950.

127. Stone, H. M. and Stone, A. S., *A Marriage Manual*. New York: Simon & Schuster, Inc., 1937.

128. Sullivan, H. S., (Perry, H. S. and Gawell, M. S., eds., Cohen, M. B., Intro.), *The Interpersonal Theory of Psychiatry*. New York: W. W. Norton & Co., Inc., 1953.

129. Szondi, L., *Schicksalsanalyse*. Basel: Benno Schwabe & Co., 1948.

130. Twain, Mark (Clemens, S. L.), (Meine, Franklin J., ed., Winkler, A. H., illus.), *Conversation as it was by the social fireside in the time of the Tudors*. Chicago: Mark Twain Society, priv. print., 1939.

131. Twain, Mark (Clemens, S. L.), *Some thoughts on the science of Onanism. Being an address delivered . . . before the members of the Stomach Club . . . Paris . . . 1879*. Priv. print., 1952 (1879).

132. Van Teslaar, J. S., *Sex and the Senses*. Boston: Richard G. Badger, 1922.

133. Vatsyayana, (Burton, R. F. and Arbuthnot, F. F., transl.) *The Kama Sutra of Vatsyayana*. Translated from the Sanskrit by the Hindoo Kama Shastra Society. Benares & New York: printed for the Society of Friends of India, priv. circulat. (Guy d'Isère), 1883-1925.

134. Wall, O. A., *Sex and Sex Worship*. St. Louis: C. V. Mosby Co., 1919.

135. Weinberg, K., *Incest Behavior*. New York, Citadel Press, 1955.

136. Whyte, W. F., *Street Corner Society. The Social Structure of an Italian Slum*. Chicago: The University of Chicago Press, 1949.

137. Wilson, E., *Memoirs of Hecate County*. Garden City: Doubleday & Co., Inc., 1946.

138. Windsor, E., *The Hindu Art of Love*. New York: The Panurge Press, 1932.

139. Wylie, P., *Generation of Vipers*. New York & Toronto: Farrar & Rinehart, Inc., 1942.

INDEX

abortion, 329

abstinence of Gandhi, 74

Aday paperback book case in U.S. District Court, 18

Adventures of Huckleberry Finn (Mark Twain), 43

advertising, sexually stimulating, 329

Ajanta cave-temple in India, 27

All Quiet on the Western Front (Erich Maria Remarque), 149

American Law Institute, 167, 168, 172, 176, 177, 197, 199, 200

American Orthopsychiatric Association, 344

anal eroticism and intercourse, 186-187

Ananga Ranga, 27

Ane Pleasant Garden, 39-41

animals, contacts with, 189-191, 237; pairs in copulation, exhibitions of, 67

Antony and Cleopatra (Shakespeare), xiii

aphrodisiac qualities of pornography, 217, 326-329

Appollinaire, Guillaume, 209, 359

"Aretines," 60

Aretino, P., xv, 26, 41-42, 57, 59-60, 89, 99

Asiatics portrayed as sex symbols, 187

Augustine, St., 79

Australian Journal of Psychology (Mitchell), 343

autobiographical erotic realism, 73-79

autobiography, erotic, 110, 373, 374f.

autobiographies, sex in, 73-79

Autobiography of a Flea, The (anonymous), 211, 240, 246, 250, 256, 259, 264, 270, 273

auto-eroticism, 313, 386

"babying" of children, 333

Balcony, The (Jean Genet), 384

Bataille, George, 356-358

bawdy house, 113-114

"beast with two backs," 185

Beckett, Samuel, 348

BIOGRAPHIES

Eberhard W. Kronhausen, Ed.D
Born 1915, Berlin, Germany.

Attended University of Minnesota 1945-1951 B.S. University of Minn., 1947. M.A. in Psychology, Univ. of Minn., 1951. Columbia Univ. Teachers College, 1954-1956. Ed.D. in Marriage and Family Life Education, 1956. Psychologist with Group for Community Guidance Centers, New York, 1954-1958. Private psychoanalytic practice, New York, 1954-1958 Co-director, Research project "The Therapeutic Family," supported in part by research grant M-1136 (r), National Institute of Mental Health, U.S. Public Health Service, 1956-1957 Presented research findings on family milieu therapy with severely disturbed patients at the 2nd International Congress for Psychiatry, Zurich, Switzerland, 1957.
Member of: The American Psychological Association. New York State Psychological Association, Division of Clinical Psychology: The American Academy of Psychotherapists: (associate) member of the Council of Psychoanalytic Psychotherapists.

Phyllis C. Kronhausen, Ed.D.
Born 1929, Minnesota.

Attended University of Minnesota, 1947-1951 B.B.A (With High Distinction), University of Minn., 1951. Assistant to the American Vice Consul, U.S. Consulate General, Bombay, India, 1951-1953. Attended Teachers College, Columbia Univ., 1954-1958. Ed.D. in Marriage and Family Life Education, 1958. Co-director, Research project, "The Therapeutic Family," supported in part by research grant M-1136 (r), National Institute of Mental Health, U.S. Public Health Service, 1956-1957. First psychologist to appear as expert witness in an obscenity case in the State of California, U.S. District Court of Appeal, U S. vs. Aday, 1958. Presented research findings on family milieu therapy with severely disturbed patients at the 2nd International Congress for Psychiatry, Zurich, Switzerland, 1957
Member of· The American Psychological Association. and (associate) member of the Council of Psychoanalytic Psychotherapists